THE EGALITARIAN SPIRIT OF CHRISTIANITY

THE EGALITARIAN SPIRIT OF CHRISTIANITY

THE SACRED ROOTS OF AMERICAN AND BRITISH GOVERNMENT

STEPHEN STREHLE

TRANSACTION PUBLISHERS
NEW BRUNSWICK (U.S.A.) AND LONDON (U.K.)

This book is printed on acid-free paper that meets the American National Standard for Permanence of Paper for Printed Library Materials.

Library of Congress Catalog Number: 2008019915
ISBN: 978-1-4128-0816-3
Printed in the United States of America

Library of Congress Cataloging-in-Publication

Strehle, Stephen, 1952-
The egalitarian spirit of Christianity : the sacred roots of American and British government / Stephen Strehle.
p. cm.
ISBN 978-1-4128-0816-3 (alk. paper)
1. Christianity and politics—United States—History. 2. United States—Politics and government. 3. Christianity and politics—Great Britain—History. 4. Great Britain—Politics and government. I. Title.

BR516.S875 2008
261.70973—dc22 2008019915

To my three sons,
the pride and joy of my life,
Josh, Stephen, and Matthew.

Contents

Abbreviations

AM	Foxe. Actes and Monuments. London: Iohn Dag, 1563.
ASG	Buchanan. The Art and Science of Government. MacNeill (trans.). Glasgow: William MacLellan, 1964.
CC	Corpus Chistianorum. Turnholt: Brepols, 1953-.
CC	Calvin's Commentaries. Edinburgh: Calvin Translation Society, 1843-1855.
CO	Opera Calvini. Brunsvigae: C. A. Schwetschke et Filium, 1863-1900.
CR	Corpus Reformatorum. Halle, Brunsvigae, and Berlin, 1834-.
DDM	Bèze. Du Droit des Magistrats. Genève: Librairie Droz, 1970.
DJR	Buchanan. De Jure Regni apud Scotos, Dialogos. Edinburg: Apud Iohannem Rossem, 1579.
DLT	A Defence against Tyrants. J. Brutus (trans.). London: G. Bell and Sons, LTD., 1924.
EL	Montesquieu. De l'Esprit des lois. Paris: Garnier, ca. 1961.
F	The Works of Jefferson. P. L. Ford (ed.). New York: G. P. Putnam's Sons, 1904-1905.
FVE	Foxe. The First Volumes of Ecclesiastical history contayning the Actes and Monumentes. London: Iohn Daye, 1570.
L	The Writings of Thomas Jefferson. A. A. Lipscomb and A. E. Berg (Washington, D. C.: The Thomas Jefferson Memorial Society, 1905.
LW	Luther's Works. St. Louis: Concordia Publishing House, 1958-.
PG	Patrologiae cursus completus, Series Graeca. J.-P. Migne, 1857-1886.
PJA	The Politics of John Althusius. F. S. Carney (trans.). Boston: Beacon Press, 1964.

PL Patrologia cursus completus, Series Latina. J.-P. Migne, 1844-1864.

PMD Althusius. Politica Methodice Digesta. Cambridge, MA: Harvard University Press, 1932.

PS Edwards. Polypoikilos Sophia. London, 1699.

RM Bèze. Right of Magistrates, in Constitutionalism and Resistance, J. H. Franklin (trans. and ed.). New York: Pegasus, 1969.

SL The Spirit of the Laws. Cambridge: Cambridge University Press,1997.

WA D. Martin Luthers Werke. Weimar: Herman Böhlau, 1883-.

Z Huldreich Zwinglis Sämtliche Werke. Berlin: C. A. Schwetschke and Sohn, 1905-.

Introduction

Religion no longer serves a preeminent role in the every day consciousness of modern Western society. Most of its people view life as a practical set of problems, which look to secular and rational resources for answers, independent of ultimate metaphysical concerns.[1] If religion finds some significance in life, its influence remains hidden from view, deep down within the subconscious of its subjects, finding an outward manifestation only at the bottom and edges of society as a private means of self-fulfillment.[2] In 1947 the Supreme Court established this view of life in *Everson v. Board of Education* by erecting a "wall" of separation between church and state that was "high and impregnable" and made this doctrine the fundamental principle for directing government policy in regard to religion. The decision represented the culmination of secular forces evolving in society since the times of the Enlightenment.

Today this secular view of life represents the basic mentality of the culture and the government in general; yet there is much to contradict it. The last half of the twentieth century witnessed a surge of grassroots movements from all sides of the political/religious spectrum, including the Civil Rights movement of the 1960s and the Moral Majority of the 1980s, which provided an effective challenge to a simple division between the two realms. The majority of the American people seemed to tolerate this kind of religious activism in the public square and displayed overwhelming support for the continued use of traditional practices, symbols, and formulas associated with the civil religion. A few of the traditional practices were tested in the courts and eliminated from the public forum, but an absolute wall separating religion from the state was breached along the way as an all-too-simplistic solution to a more complicated relationship. The wall was no longer thought as "high and impregnable." Specific cases entangled the Court in a conundrum of semantic games, labeling certain practices as religious and others as secular without much justification and using the most elliptical form of arguments at times to repair the wall. In *Lemon v. Kurtzman* (1971) the Court seemed to recognize the inconsistency of its own decrees and admitted that the wall looked more like a "line" or a "blurred, indistinct, and variable barrier."[3] Even if the doctrine of separation remained a normative principle, the problem of dividing the two realms involved the Court in the difficult process of defining the nature of religion in a clear and coherent manner, and so distinguishing it from the secular world of civil government. Too often labels were assigned through the a priori biases of whatever the jurists wished to promote in society, rather than a coherent philosophical search for a Platonic form or definition, if a world of definitions was even possible to find in the first place. This problem proceeded beyond the question of assigning a simple label to groups like the "church" of Scientology or the Declaration of Independence and asked deeper questions about the very nature of the Republic. Are the laws of this country and the Court based upon religious principles or not? Can moral/political ideals subsist without a Platonic notion of the Good or a belief in God? Did America or Mother England develop its notions of liberty, democracy, and federal government apart from any contribution from the religious community? Are these notions secular—pure and simple?

This study is designed to provide a partial answer to these deeper questions. The goal is to shed some light on the subject by conducting an archaeological search for the sacred roots of modern political ideas, looking for significant religious influence during the early stages of development. Among the topics of study are found a number of the most cherished political ideals, including equality and democracy, liberty and natural rights, progress and capitalism, federalism and mixed government. The project is large and ambitious and has some pretense in trying to probe deeper, fuller, and broader than other historical treatments in the field, but there is no illusion about forging an exhaustive study that includes all possible forces—inside or outside the religious community. There is no intention to dismiss the vital contribution of other possible sources of inspiration from the world of religion or undermine the well-established place of "secular" sources like the sons of the Enlightenment, who wielded the emerging political ideas together into a permanent system of governance. The study finds fulfillment in demonstrating that certain ideas associated with the religious community were entangled within the overall process and left an indelible mark upon significant aspects of the emerging political landscape.

Too often religious influences are missed by scholars reared within a secular understanding of the world and unable to recognize or admit the importance of these ideas in the process. Their secular view of life tends to exalt secular accounts of the past as providing a linear progression toward the future. Their focus typically centers upon the sons of the Enlightenment because these "Founding Fathers" emphasized rational argumentation, dismissed the importance of revealed religion, and provided secular sounding presentations in developing the principles of government. But these scholars fail to probe deeper into the antecedent cultural influences of that era. Too often American and British scholars limit their study to later English literature and misinterpret what is plainly before them because of this. Too often they fail to discover the deeper sources from which democratic, federal, and egalitarian ideals first arose on the continent of Europe—much in contrast to their English ancestors, who were not so provincial in their understanding of the world and its ideas.

> English thought, it is often said, was parochial. In religious matters, the English were narrow-mindedly Scripturalists; on secular questions they were equally hidebound, but looked for guidance to the common law rather than the Bible. This view has little to recommend it. Perhaps the most frequently cited source in the whole of early seventeenth-century English literature were Calvin, Beza, Aquinas, and Bellarmine—none of whom was English. Books were written in Latin, the international language of learning, circulated widely. Gentlemen visited the Continent in increasing numbers.[4]

To understand their ideas one must travel to the continent with them and learn to appreciate a much larger tradition—a tradition that grows out of the Reformation and inspires their religious/political concepts, even if it inspires them to create their own unique formulations and use other sources as well.

This study finds its basic purpose by proceeding back in time to the Reformation, searching for the religious roots of modern political ideology, and demonstrating the importance of religion in the formative years. The study makes no attempt to advance any set of political/religious ideas presented in the research as if beneficial to the maturation of a society. It makes no concerted effort to defend or promote the American way of life, the Puritan religion, democracy, capitalism, or any other political/religious agenda—left or right wing. It provides no specific guidance on how the church and state should be related in the present era beyond questioning an absolute distinction between the two realms based on historical analysis. One could use the material to evaluate or question current beliefs and practices through their origin, following the critical, genealogical method of Michel Foucault—a method that finds powerful testimony in a number of disciplines and seems sensible in the present case.[5] Or, one could reject the "genetic fallacy" in that method and try to establish current political ideas on non-religious grounds, leaving their entanglement to a bygone era. But if one chooses to move away from the religious moorings and create a secular state, free from religious practice and teachings, there is no justification for turning to the past and imposing a secular, post-Enlightenment view of the world on earlier times. There might be a number of secular antecedents that contributed to the total development of the modern world, but one cannot exorcise the religious spirit from the past as if it existed in a separate reality and inspired none of the elements around it. Religion stood at the very center of culture during the formative years of the present political system and bestowed its blessings (and curses) upon it.

To facilitate the study of the text an annotated outline is provided. The reader might find the summary a valuable guide before considering the more detailed account in each individual chapter.

Chapter 1—The Priesthood of the Believers: The Growth of Congregationalism

Robert Browne and the Congregationalists spread the gospel of liberty, democracy, and federal government throughout England and New England beginning in the 1580s. They believed that each believer possessed an unmediated relationship to God and preferred to live without priestly authority under the Lordship of Christ. They saw each church as an autonomous, voluntary association, forged through its own covenant (*foedus*) and based upon a democratic understanding of polity. This doctrine played a crucial role in the development of the modern world as the Congregationalists used it to reconstitute their whole society in its image. Their doctrine found early inspiration from a number of sources: one, the emphasis upon the authority of Scripture and its polity; two, Martin Luther's challenge to papal authority at Leipzig (July, 1519) and his belief in the priesthood of the believers; three, the rejection of an episcopal (hierarchical) form of government by Thomas Cartwright and the Cambridge Puritans; four, the open espousal of liberty, autonomy, and democracy among the Huguenots, especially as mediated through the work of Jean Morély and Peter Ramus; five, the emphasis of the Reformed Church upon the doctrine of covenant as set forth by Ulrich Zwingli and Heinrich Bullinger, which became a means of interpreting all of Scripture and all of life. These elements and others provided the impetus toward the development of democracy and federal government among the Congregationalists and the world to come.

Chapter 2—Power to the People: The Origin of Democratic and Federal Government

The Puritan Revolution brought the cause of democratic and federal government to the forefront in English society. The radical change in church polity prompted a call for similar changes within the structure of the civil government according to the testimony of all sides of the debate—William Walwyn, Richard Baxter, and Clarendon. Radical groups like the Levellers arose out of the new ecclesiastical movement and demanded freedom of conscience and democratic reform in society at large. These groups wanted to translate their Christian faith into all aspects of life and rejected any compromise with "Machiavilian policy" that would sentence collective and political life to the utter depravity of this world. They saw no reason why the redemptive purposes of Christ should limit its scope to the confines of the local church. They wanted to reform everything—the churches, the schools, the wards, and the state. Eventually their point of view gained ascendancy through the power of Cromwell's New Model Army, which was dominated by Independent churches and like-minded members of the "Reformed." The radical program was reversed in part by the Restoration in 1660, but the people and the political landscape were changed forever. Within a few decades, the Glorious Revolution began the irreversible march toward a free and democratic state, once the people were prepared through their churches.

These Congregationalist principles came to America in the early seventeenth century with the Puritan forefathers. Theologians like John Cotton, Thomas Hooker, Cotton Mather, and John Wise all deconstructed the federal, democratic principles of their churches and applied them to the society at large. The founders of the Massachusetts Bay Colony forged a government based on democratic and federal principles that spread throughout the colonies and incited revolt against Mother England. Their federal theology provided the matrix out of which the many covenant-based documents emerged in the eighteenth century—the Articles of Confederation, the Federalist Papers, the Declaration of Independence, the Constitution of the United States, and the many state constitutions.

Chapter 3—Countervailing Government: The Separation, Balance, and Limitation of the Powers that Be

The Long Parliament met in the 1640s and began to promote a limited form of government through the work of Stephen Marshall, Henry Parker, and Philip Hunton. The people were accorded the right to depose whatever leader abused their trust, and the government was limited by a system of checks and balances to prevent one branch from ruling beyond its measure. At the end of the decade, Cromwell and his army provided a radical expression of the new political arrangement by executing Charles I.

This new system of government represented a natural development within the Reformation as the need to justify the revolt against papal authority became the self-same need to revolt against kings and emperors who wanted to impose Catholicism upon Protestant lands. The transition took place early on when Luther was faced with the destruction of his Reformation if he continued to follow the old policy of simple obeisance to a Catholic emperor. He found it necessary to reject his earlier stance against armed resistance during the peasants' revolt and accept a more expedient policy—a policy that sanctioned the use of force against Charles V and his designs to bring Protestant countries back into the fold of Catholicism. Luther's position was cited by Protestants in the Schmalkald League and innumerable conflicts thereafter, including the Thirty Years' War.

Calvinists found special inspiration in the Lutheran revolt and produced the most radical doctrine of rebellion and countervailing government during the sixteenth century. They were unwilling to accept any compromise with the Catholic cultus—unlike Luther and the German Protestants—and rejected any participation in its "idolatrous" practices, even for those living under Catholic rule. John Knox, Charles Goodman, and the Scottish refugees in Geneva advocated a full-scale revolution of the people against Mary Tudor in the 1550s, following the Reformed emphasis upon the OT covenant and its commission to slay idolaters. After the massacre on St. Bartholomew's Day (1572), the French Calvinists became more radical in their concept of rebellion and began to use the covenant as a fundamental justification for taking measures against the king and limiting his rule. Their work laid the foundation for limited government in the coming era and inspired the writings of more celebrated authors like James Harrington, Algernon Sydney, and John Locke.

Chapter 4—Three Pillars: The Development of Common Law, Natural Rights, and Mixed Government

The new concept of government was supported by several doctrines from the world of theology. These doctrines were conjoined in the vast majority of treatments from the sixteenth, seventeenth, and eighteenth centuries to justify the notion of countervailing government.

The first doctrine was the English concept of common law, which began its ascendancy during the time of Henry II in the twelfth century and received its most definitive treatment in the writings of Edward Coke, Samuel Rutherford, and William Blackstone a few centuries later. The common law represented a belief that the unwritten customs and wise decisions of judicial precedent, descending from "time out of mind," served the people as an authoritative body of tradition. This common law assumed the aura of eternal wisdom and divine righteousness in the land, exacting submission from all authority, including the king, and withstanding any legislative fiat that tried to establish its own separate estate through the mere will to power.

The second doctrine was a fundamental part of the common law, known as natural rights theory. It had antecedents in the Graeco-Roman world, where Aristotle, Cicero, and many others spoke of a universal law (*ius*) in nature binding all humankind to its demands. This theory was expanded by the Decretalists in the Middle Ages to include the God-given rights (*iura*) that all people possess against the powers that would enslave them. William Ockham was the most notable advocate of the theory in the late medieval period as he rejected the "plenitude of power" within the papacy and underscored the inalienable "rights, liberties, and possessions" of the people. The temporal powers of the pope were diminished at the end of the Middle Ages, and the divine right of kings followed in the subsequent era, which witnessed Huguenots and Puritans asserting their natural rights against all temporal authority.

The third doctrine found inspiration in the ancient world and its concept of mixed government, but received a major impetus from the struggles of Charles I and Parliament during the Puritan Revolution. Puritans helped disseminate the teaching by providing a theological justification in the Augustinian concept of original sin and its dark view of the human condition—a view that is shared by Montesquieu, Adams, Madison, and all the great patriarchs of the separation and balance of powers. The Puritans thought of the human race as fallen in Adam and inheriting an innate depravity, or hubris, causing people to overstep their God-given bounds. This view of the human condition served as a fundamental rationale for placing restraints upon rulers to check and balance their will to power.

Countervailing government also received a decided impetus from the doctrine of covenant theology, which receives a separate treatment at the end of chapter one and some mention throughout the next two chapters. Zwingli and Bullinger first developed the doctrine to justify the ongoing practice of infant baptism in the Zurich Church during the 1520s.

They found a precedent for baptizing children within the OT practice of circumcision but needed to assume that the message and rituals of both testaments (or covenants) were one and the same, regardless of their outward differences, in order to support the analogy. This meant that the entire message of the Bible found its deeper essence within a doctrine of covenant (*foedus*), which represented the one and eternal will of God to all humankind. The doctrine was disseminated to all Reformed Europe through Bullinger's *De Testamento seu Foedere unico et aeterno* (1534), which emphasized the bilateral nature of the covenant and the mutual responsibilities of the parties to each other. At Cambridge the one and eternal covenant became a means of redefining all our relationships in the church and state during the latter part of the sixteenth century. The church became a covenant community, in which the people could elect and depose their ministers. The state became a federal government, based upon a social contract, where the "powers that be" are subject to the rights of the people. The one message of Scripture became the one message of life, holding all parties accountable to fulfill their federal duties, including the ministers and magistrates. Even though the secular world ascribes the development of this doctrine to others (Lock, Rousseau, Montesquieu, Jefferson, and Adams) there is no doubt that the notion of a social contract and limited government permeated society long before the tenure of these and other "Founding Fathers" through the work of a special religious community and its distinctive theology. It is this community that served as the basic impetus behind the fuller development of the covenant in the eighteenth century within the society as a whole.

Chapter 5—The Protestant Work Ethic: The Origin of Capitalism and the Use of Money

Max Weber, the most renowned sociologist of this past century, believed that the Reformation provided the spiritual matrix out of which modern day capitalism was born. He found this spirit embodied in a most telling way within the Puritan communities of Britain and America and considered Benjamin Franklin as the very incarnation of Puritan/capitalistic piety. While his presentation has a number of flaws, his basic thesis is correct. Puritanism made a valuable contribution to the development of capitalism through its emphasis upon austerity, hard work, pragmatism, communal responsibility, and millenarian eschatology. Like all good capitalists, Puritans believed in the future betterment of their society. They viewed themselves as the center of a historical process that hoped to make the world a better place for their children and usher in the kingdom of God. They rejected a monastic or contemplative life as useless to the building of the community (*corpus Christianum*). They rejected those who squandered their riches upon an idle or extravagant life-style, eating French pastries or going on foxhunts. Instead of wasting the day on idle meditation or frivolous bemusements, their people were encouraged to invest their time and capital in the community with the hope of building a city on a hill, a light to the nations, and preparing the way for the kingdom of God. Their vision was far removed from the Jansenists concept of capitalism, which viewed self-interest (*l'amour-propre*) as possessing a societal benefit, so much associated with the greed and materialism of its present form. The Puritan divines tried to motivate the people by appealing to an altruistic impulse to invest in the community and build a better tomorrow for future generations, accomplishing much the same goal through a different inward intent.

The most serious flaw in Weber's thesis is his failure to understand the importance of the covenant and the practical syllogism in analyzing the Puritan concept of obtaining assurance. He is correct in his basic understanding of the relationship between assurance and hard work, but he overemphasizes the dark mysteries of predestination as the cause of their anxieties and impetus toward worldly asceticism. He underestimates the practical orientation of the Puritans as they tried to fulfill the conditions of the covenant and discover their assurance through the means provided by the practical syllogism. Weber's miscue is exemplified by his own favorite example, Richard Baxter. Contrary to Weber's account, Baxter rejected the Antinomians of his day and their emphasis upon predestination and the all-sufficiency of divine grace in obtaining assurance. Baxter expressed a special concern throughout his work for those who used the doctrine of predestination to preach "cheap grace" and preferred to incur the charge of "synergism" by emphasizing the conditional force of the covenant. He exhorted his people to look upon the covenant and find assurance through its condition of perseverance and hard work, not *sola gratia*.

Chapter 6—Manifest Destiny: The March toward the Future

There is no idea that proved more powerful in shaping the hopes and dreams of Western civilization than its belief in progress. The Puritans reflected the spirit of capitalism not merely through hard work or worldly asceticism—the hallmark of Weber's treatment—but also through their willingness to surrender present day security, take risks, and create something new and better in the future. They believed that change was good, the future was good, and they possessed a manifest destiny before God to bring all good things to pass. The Reformation brought the hope to the Puritan community that the church and the world could change for the better, that the destruction of the Antichrist was imminent, that a godly kingdom would dawn in the near future and take the place of evil forces here on earth. The Puritans developed millenarian expectations, which dreamed of a "Great Instauration" or renewal of the entire world, and saw life advancing toward a universal state of perfection in science, religion, and culture at the present time, with Britain and America leading the way. This expectation dominated Puritan circles from the middle of the seventeenth century and included noteworthy names like Joseph Mede, Thomas Goodwin, Samuel Sewall, Cotton Mather, Jonathan Edwards, and so many others. Their favorite verse was Dan. 12:4, which speaks of the latter days and predicts that "many shall run to and fro, and knowledge shall increase."

This emphasis is best illustrated through the thesis of Robert Merton, which finds the spirit of Puritanism at the foundation of modern science. Merton observes that the Royal Society of London was dominated by Puritanism and its philosophy during the early days. It seems that Puritanism served an important role in arousing its scientific interest, given the disproportionate number of Puritans involved in the society and the discipline. While the precise reason remains obscure, it is probable that the practical, concrete, and utilitarian philosophy of the Puritans worked together with their belief in the advancement of knowledge and played a significant role in developing the modern scientific mentality.

Chapter 7—The Noble Lie: The Growth of Toleration, Pluralism, and Separation

The modern era is marked by an emphasis upon religious liberty. The cries for freedom were heard in the medieval period, but it was not until the Protestant Reformation that all the discontent came to a head. The majority of the main line reformers believed that the temporal powers of the church had corrupted its ways in the Middle Ages and called for the church to leave the corrupting influence of the state for its own sake. Many dissident groups championed a radical separation of the church from the state and promoted general toleration of all religious groups in society. The advocates of toleration justified their position by discounting the value of the OT dispensation and accentuating the fullness of divine revelation in Christ. This approach is followed by many sectarian groups (Anabaptists, Baptists, Levellers, and Arminians) and many of the early champions of toleration (Castellio, Erasmus, Williams, and Locke). It is even followed by those who rejected the basic dogma of the church—all still admiring the simple, moral teaching of the carpenter from Nazareth (Diderot, Voltaire, and Jefferson).

Roger Williams and the Baptists became so enamored with promoting toleration that they created a "noble lie" about the relationship between church and state. They advocated the complete separation of the church and state, maintaining that the two realms did not inform each other whatsoever. They were motivated by a heart-felt desire to defend the purity of the church and promote genuine toleration between religious groups in society, but in trying to preclude religion from the state they proceeded to deny the actual, *a posteriori* influence that various religious groups exerted on the government in history, and so created a "noble lie" or a view of history that was not strictly true. They even denied their own place in forging the modern corporate world and created an arresting contradiction in the very statement of their own position, which defended church/state separation through religious argumentation! Their promotion of pluralism became the hallmark of American society, but their view of a more extensive wall, separating all religious influence upon the government and its policies, remains controversial to this day, dividing the American people and the Court.

Notes

1. H. Cox, *The Secular City: Secularization and Urbanization in Theological Perspective* (New York: Macmillan, 1966) 1, 2, 80; M. Weber, *Economy and Sociology: an outline of interpretive sociology* (Berkeley: University of California Press, 1978) 1.25, 26; "The Social Psychology of the World Religions," in *From Max Weber: essays in sociology*, H. H. Gerth and C. W. Mills (ed. and trans.) (London: Routledge, 1991) 293; J. Habermas, *The Theory of Communicative Action*, T. McCarthy (trans.) (Boston: Beacon Press, 1984) 1.168, 171, 254; 2.302, 312.
2. J. Moltmann, *The Theology of Hope: On the Ground and the Implications of a Christian Eschatology* (New York: Harper & Row, 1967) 314-16. Modern Textbooks often represent the world of religion through groups like the Amish, who serve as objects of curiosity at the margins of the civilized world. Special credit belongs to the sons of the Enlightenment for developing the modern system of civil government. If there are antecedents to the eighteenth century, they are found in the classical world of Athens or the revival of those ideals during the Italian Renaissance, which subsist outside the influence of religion. R. Whittemore, *Makers of the American Mind* (Freeport, NY: Books for Libraries, 1971) 49, 50; A. Bloom, *Confronting the Constitution* (Washington, D.C.: The AEI Press, 1990) 1; R. Bryan, *History, Pseudo-History, Anti-History: How Public School Textbooks Treat Religion* (Washington, D.C.: Leran, Inc. The Education Foundation, 1984) 3, 10; P. Vitz, *Censorship: Evidence of Bias in Our Religion and American Children's Textbooks* (Ann Arbor, Mich.: Servant Books, 1986) 14-16, 39-41, 58, 59, 75-78; W. A. Nord, *Education: Rethinking a National Dilemma* (Chapel Hill and London:

University of North Carolina Press, 1995) 69, 139ff., 190, 197. Vitz, a professor of psychology at New York University, examined "ninety widely used elementary social studies texts, high school history texts, and elementary readers" to arrive at his conclusions. Nord analyzed forty-two high school textbooks, written from 1989-92 and used by his state of North Carolina, in the areas of history, economics, and science. All these texts are published by major publishers and represent standard works used nationwide. For similar results, see T. L. Smith, "High School History Adopted for Use in the State of Alabama: The Distortion and Exclusion of Religious Data," *Religion and Public Education* 15 (Spring 1988); P. Gagnon, *Democracy's Untold Story: What the World History Textbooks Neglect* (Washington, D.C.: Education for Democracy Project, 1987); T. Podesta, "The Uphill Battle for Quality textbooks," *Religion and Public Education* 13 (Summer 1986): 60-62.

3. *Lemon v. Kurtzman*, 403 US 614. Cf. *Everson v. Board of Education*, 330 US 8-11, 16, 31. Over a decade later Chief Justice William Rehnquist expressed the frustration of some conservative members on the Court:

> [A] State may lend to parochial school children geography textbooks that contain maps of the United States for use in geography class. A state may lend textbooks on American colonial history, but it may not lend a film on George Washington, or a film projector to show a history class. A state may lend classroom workbooks, but may not lend workbooks in which parochial school children write, thus rendering them nonreuseable. A State may pay for bus transportation to religious schools but may not pay for bus transportation from the parochial school to the zoo or natural history museum for a field trip. A State may pay for diagnostic services conducted in the parochial school but therapeutic services must be given in a different building; speech and hearing 'services' conducted by the State inside the sectarian school are forbidden, but the State may conduct speech and hearing diagnostic testing inside the sectarian school. Exceptional parochial school students may receive counseling, but it must take place outside the parochial school, such as in a trailer parked down the street. A State may give cash to a parochial school to pay for the administration of state-written tests and state-ordered reporting services. Religious instruction may not be given in a public school, but the public school may release students during the day for religious classes elsewhere, and may enforce attendance at those classes with its truancy laws. . . . It is impossible to build sound constitutional doctrine upon a mistaken understanding of constitutional history, but unfortunately the Establishment Clause has been expressly freighted with Jefferson's misleading metaphor for nearly 40 years. Thomas Jefferson was of course in France at the time the constitutional amendments known as the Bill of Rights were passed by Congress and ratified by the States. His letter to the Danbury Baptist Association was a short note of courtesy, written 14 years after the Amendments were passed by Congress. He would seem to any detached observer as a less than ideal source of contemporary history as to the meaning of the Religion Clauses of the First Amendment. . . . Notwithstanding the absence of a historical basis for this theory of rigid separation, the wall idea might well have served as a useful albeit misguided analytical concept, had it led this Court to

unified and principled results in Establishment cases. The opposite, unfortunately, has been true; in the 38 years since Everson our Establishment Clause cases have been neither principled nor unified. Our recent opinions, many of them hopelessly divided pluralities, have with embarrassing candor conceded that the "wall of separation" is merely a "blurred, indistinct, and variable barrier," which "is not wholly accurate" and can only be dimly perceived. . . . The "wall of separation between church and State" is a metaphor based on bad history, a metaphor which has proved useless as a guide for judging, It should be frankly and explicitly abandoned" (*Wallace v. Jaffree*, 472 US 92, 106, 107, 110, 111).

4. J. P. Sommerville, *Royalists & Patriots: Politics and Ideology in England 1603-1640* (London and New York: Longman, 1999) 77.
5. M. Foucault, "Omnes et Singultim: Toward a Criticism of 'Political Reason'," in *The Tanner Lectures on Human Values*, S. McMurrin (ed.) (St. Lake and Cambridge, 1981) 254; "Afterword: the Subject and Power," in *Michel Foucault: Beyond Structuralism and Hermeneutics*, H. Dreyfus and P. Rabinow (ed.) (Chicago: University Press, 1982) 216; R. Viser, *Michel Foucault : Genealogy as Critique*, C. Turner (trans.) (London and New York: Verso, 1995) 101; G. Gutting, *Foucault: A Very Short Introduction* (Oxford: Oxford University Press, 2005) 49.

1

The Priesthood of the Believers: The Growth of Congregationalism

The Protestant Reformation prompted a radical change within the church and society, far beyond the limited purview of the sixteenth century. Its intention was fixated upon the redemption of the church, but its gospel went on to liberate all of society with a message of freedom and empowerment in the centuries to come. The people were given a word, spoken and written in their own language. They were urged to examine that word and judge for themselves what was necessary to believe, apart from the mediation of higher powers or outside authorities. The message was intended to liberate them from the mediation of priests but was extended in a more general way and became a means of liberation in the culture at large. To confess the priesthood of believers was to advocate the rights of citizens. To reject the Vicar of Christ was to deny the divine right of kings.

The Reformation brought this new direction to society through the efforts of the Puritans in England. The Puritans were not so successful in their immediate plans to reform the Church of England, but they did serve as a major instrument in laying the foundation of liberty in the culture at large through the many Congregationalist churches that were planted throughout the country. These churches embodied the Puritans' dissatisfaction with the pace of the reformation in the Anglican Church. They wanted the Church of England to renounce all papal practices and become "fully reformed." They disliked most of all the hierarchical structure of the church and wanted to form a much different polity, representing the antithesis of the universal, totalitarian visions of Rome. This reaction led to the opposite extreme in church government—the creation of independent congregations, who drafted their own covenant, ruled their own affairs, elected their own ministers, and disciplined their own members. These churches might have come to fruition as early as the

1560s when certain Puritans started their own congregation in London.[1] However, the most noteworthy of them all was planted by Robert Browne in Norwich around 1580 with the help of his friend, Robert Harrison.[2] Browne and this church became a lightning rod of controversy, attracting debate and discussion of the issue throughout England.

Congregationalism

Robert Browne was born around 1550 in Tolethorp, Rutlandshire to a good family with some standing in the community. He studied at Corpus Christi College in Cambridge during the 1570s, where Thomas Cartwright had engendered much commotion over his criticisms of the Church of England. Browne became a radical critic of the church at this time and preached at Cambridge for a few years during the latter part of his education without a license, refusing ordination and attacking the authority of bishops.[3] Around 1580 he went to Norwich at the behest of Harrison and together planted the first Congregational church of note, challenging the authority of the Anglican Church. The Bishop of Norwich was not amused, and persecution precipitated an exodus to Middelburg, Holland in January of 1582. Browne published three books that year, which embodied the essence of congregational polity and included a caustic analysis of the Anglican Church and civil magistrates: *A Treatise of reformation without tarying for anie, A Treatise upon the 23. of Matthewe*, and *A Book which sheweth the life and manners of all true Christians*.[4] His notoriety spread through the publication and distribution of these tracts. They caused such a stir in England that those who were caught distributing them were thrown into prison and sometimes executed. Nevertheless, after a couple of years in exile, which witnessed some turmoil and division within the church, Browne decided to split with Harrison and return to Britain.[5] He and a few followers moved to Edinburgh, and then back to England, where persecution continued to hound them. Browne eventually submitted to the authority of the church, after a life of hardship, including bouts in prison, threats of execution, and years of excommunication. He died a broken and obscure man several decades later in Northhampton, never realizing the force he brought and unleashed upon the world to come.[6]

His tracts provide testimony to an ideology that rejects outside authority and bases its conclusions upon the exegesis of Scripture. His analysis is filled with verses and passages from the sacred text, showing the same devotion toward the Scripture that inspired the early Reformers, along with a like-minded contempt for scholastic sources.[7] He condemns whatever detracts from the simple reading of Scripture, including the use of "rhetorike" as needless ornamentation and the recitation of liturgy as vain repetition (Matt. 6:7).[8] Above all, he dislikes the use of "philosophie" and its many accouterments—Aristotle, logic, and syllogisms. He cites the admonitions of Paul against the "wisdom of the world" and singles out Theodore Beza and his use of Aristotelian categories for special reproach, as one who compromises the integrity of the message. Instead, he prefers to employ the simple logical categories of Peter Ramus, the opponent of Aristotle and Beza, as a less intrusive means of unfolding the message of Scripture.[9] *A Booke which sheweth the life and manner of all true Christians* renders clear and continuous testimony to Ramian logic with its propensity to divide categories into two subsets, the hallmark of that system.[10] He finds no tension between his devotion to Ramian logic and his conviction concerning the sole authority of the Scripture (*sola scriptura*). His devotion to the Word of God can bear no rivals.

Browne believes that nothing should replace or rival the authority of God. Christ is the only authority in the life of the believer. No other authority—scholastic, civil, or religious—is allowed to challenge the Lordship of Christ and the freedom of his subjects to serve him and serve him only.[11] Every Christian is given "liberty and power" as a "king and priest unto god" to bind and loose sin.[12] Every Christian receives a special calling from God to serve the Lord and fulfill his will in the mundane tasks of daily life. No one can replace the anointing of the Spirit or usurp the rights of believers with an "outward calling" based on outside authority.[13]

Browne takes this doctrine and develops a view of the church, which stresses local authority and democratic rule within the fellowship. He combines the priesthood of the believers with the Reformed doctrine of covenant and says that each church must make a "covenant with the Lord to be under his government."[14]

> The Church planted or gathered, is a companie or number of Christians or beleeuers, which by a willing couenant made with their God, are vnder the gouernment of god and Christ, and kepe his lawes in one holie communion: because Christ hath redeemed them vnto holines & happines for euer, from which they were fallen by the sinne of Adam. The Church gouernment, is the Lordshipp of Christ in the communion of his offices: wherby his people obey to his will, and haue mutual vse of their graces and callings, to further their godlines and welfare.[15]

Each church subsists as a voluntary association, gathered by the consent of the people and responsible to the Lordship of Christ. There is no authority outside the local community and its duty to keep the unique and special covenant it forges with God. The fulfillment of the covenant depends upon the faithfulness of the people in meeting the "condiciones" of the divine law and living under its stipulations.[16] The ministers cannot supersede this arrangement so as to replace the rule of Christ in the life of the believers. They rule under the authority of God and are subject to the consent of the church. The people have the right to examine the gifts and piety of the ministers, elect them under certain conditions, and then call, ordain, and submit to their authority once the process is completed.[17] Of course, the process can reverse itself when the ministers neglect their obligations and the church decides to depose them. No one, not even an Apostle, is above the authority that God has invested in the church.[18] The covenant with God supersedes all other possibilities and arrangements in governing its affairs.

The social implications of the new doctrine were vast and far-reaching. Browne directs his attention to the special needs of the church and tends to limit the application of the covenant within its walls, but the power of the idea cannot be bound. Even Browne cannot resist the temptation to draw certain implications and interpret other relations in its terms. Masters are said to rule over their servants by way of covenant, in which a wage and housing are rewarded for service rendered. Teachers are said to make a covenant with students to provide guidance in education and receive their stipend in due turn.[19] A bride and groom exchange wedding vows, in which they make a covenant to hold communion as long as death or divorce does not break the bond.[20] The covenant is applied to relations outside the church and begins to transform all of life into its image.

Browne also connects his concept of a church covenant with the way a civil government should relate to its subjects. The covenant (*foedus*) becomes a means of reestablishing the government into a federal and democratic institution. "For the Church governours there must be an agreement of the church. For civil Magistrates, there must be an agreement of the people or Common welth."[21] Civil magistrates are subject to the same stipulations as those who rule the church. They are subject to the acceptance, consent, and call of the people.[22] The parties remain in "this communion so longe, as it tendeth not to the confusion or destruction of either of them."[23] This notion of a federal government does not play an important role in Browne's work or mission, but the decades to come will witness a decided move in this direction as the doctrine develops.

Browne conceives of his mission in terms of reforming the church, not changing the government into a more Christian image. The other mission resides with his followers—the Levellers, the Pilgrims, and the

New Model Army—all those who arose out of the Independent churches in the seventeenth century. Browne is more concerned with creating a space for the church to reform itself and eliminating the interference and negative influence from the government in the process. If anything, he would like to separate civil and ecclesiastical offices as much as possible, not create a like-minded compact between them. He believes that magistrates possess no ecclesiastical authority whatsoever. They are not "prophetes, priestes, or spiritual kings." They have no authority to compel religion, ordain ministers, or plant churches.[24] Their authority is limited to "the common wealth in all outwarde iustice, to maintaine the right, welfare, and honor thereof, with outward power, bodily punishment, and civil forcing of men."[25] Far from infusing the government with Christian ideas, Browne is accused of espousing the Anabaptist concept of church/state separation, which would cause Christians to flee the government altogether.[26] Of course, he denies the charge and claims that his teachings are derived from the exegesis of Scripture, not a sectarian group, but the effect of his words is much the same. He certainly believes that the church is best served in the present conflict by severing its ties with the government. His analysis displays a continuous reliance upon sacred passages and verses, but his motivation stems from a frustration with the pace of reformation. He believes that pastors need to take the bull by the horns and no longer "tarie for the magistrates authoritie."[27] The magistrates and Parliament have failed to bring about the necessary reforms.

The call for separation is essential to the purity of the fellowship. It includes a call to separate from the state government and the corrupting influence of temporal powers, but its special concern is designed to protect the true church from mingling with the "false church" and so extinguishing its light. Browne wants a "visible" church, cleansed of sin and evil influence, providing a testimony to what God has wrought within it, and serving as a beacon of light to the world at large.[28] In this design he anticipates the call of later Puritans, who wish to limit the membership of the church to "visible" saints and set up their own light or holy experiment in England and America as a "City on a Hill." Browne's concept is most concerned with the corrupting influence of papal practices in the Church of England and the need to separate from evil religious practices. He considers the call for toleration a device of the "Antichrist" to compromise with evil. The government instituted by Christ cannot receive the mark of the Beast and submit to the administration of "Popish offices." It cannot serve "Christ and Belial." It cannot serve "two contrarie Masters."[29] Once again, he is accused of siding with the

Anabaptists or even worse, reviving the ancient heresy of the Donatists, which he denounces in the strongest terms. He disclaims any hope of cleansing the church from evil and creating a perfect fellowship in the manner of these sectarian groups,[30] but his concept of discipline is more severe than most of his colleagues or those who generally sympathized with his movement. He scolds Thomas Cartwright for making discipline a minor aspect of the church and for regarding the Church of England as the church of God no matter how corrupt or vile it becomes.[31] He fights continually with Harrison and other members of the fellowship over the matter of discipline and finally shuns his own church over this and other points at issue. Apparently, he wants a more strict or limited count of members in the fellowship, proving his zeal for the principles of the movement and making discipline an end in itself.[32]

In spite of the differences, the movement continued to exhibit many of the same basic proclivities as Browne. Harrison's writings display an ideology that is basically the same as his more famous colleague. They studied together at Cambridge, lived together in Norwich, and served the same church, so one would expect a similar philosophy of ministry. Their acrimonious breakup was based upon the proclivity within the doctrine of separation to cause division, but it did not represent a serious or fundamental difference between their positions. Indeed, one sees within Harrison's work the same basic themes—condemnation of Catholicism, rejection of compromise, call for separation, and a decided emphasis upon the autonomy of the local church. Harrison starts out his work with the same issue as Browne—the corrupting influence of Rome and the "popishe government" of the Church of England.[33] He points out the same basic problems with this influence, even though his measures go beyond Browne when he invites the magistrates to tear down the altars of the Antichrist and remnants of its hierarchy with the sword if necessary.[34] After a while he grows weary with the pace of reformation and can tarry no longer, so he joins Browne in calling the people to separate from the false church and follow Christ without compromise.[35] Harrison, Browne, and all ministers can defer no longer to a civil government and church hierarchy, which is slow to act, but must undertake the mission of reforming the church as their own, God-given responsibility.[36] This reformation must begin with the corrupt hierarchy of the church, which has withstood all attempts to change its ways. The greatest offense of the papal church is its polity.[37] Where Christ does not reign and the government is false, the church does not exist.

> Where Christ doth rule & raigne there he is King, but where rule and regimt is taken out of his handes, he is dispossessed of the right of his inheritance, wch is his Kingdome; but or mynisters confes that we haue not the true Church gounmt, that is as much as to say, Christ his regimt & scepter, therfore thei haue not his Kingdome, & therfore not his Church.[38]

The true church is marked by freedom. Harrison continually speaks of the "libertie & authoritie" that Christ has given to the church.[39] God's ministers and his people are called to serve Christ, not kings or bishops,[40] and Harrison spells out the same rights that Browne assigns to the fellowship as a means of living in direct communion with God. He rejects the calling of ministers by other bishops as an invalid call to the ministry.[41] He exhorts the people to tear down the hierarchy, set up free elections, and ordain or depose their own ministers as the case may be.[42]

The Reformation

Browne and Harrison represent the radical fringe of a movement, which seeks to overturn the *Weltanschauung* of ancient and medieval times. The political structure of the Catholic Church developed out of the Graeco-Roman world and its hierarchical view of life. The early church developed its understanding of polity at a time when life itself was interpreted and structured in terms of levels of authority. Plotinus (205-270) speaks of the world as deriving its being and relation to what is ultimate through intermediate stages of the Intellect and Soul. Nature contemplates the Soul, the Soul contemplates the Intellect, and the Intellect contemplates the One, which is related to all but only through intermediate sources.[43]

The church fell under the influence of the Hellenistic worldview as it became more and more a part of mainstream society. As it approached the Middle Ages, that view of the world began to dominate much of what the church believed and represented. For example, Dionysius the Areopagite came to accept much of the Neo-Platonic philosophy of Plotinus and Proclus in the fifth century.[44] He speaks of a heavenly and earthly hierarchy, which serves to mediate the believer's relation to God. The hierarchy receives the light from on high, reflects it like a mirror, and passes it on down the scale.[45] The angelic hosts are ranked in a hierarchy of three triads, much like Proclus, Porphyry, and other Platonists.[46] The first triad passes its light to the second, the second to the third, and these angels pass the light of revelation unto us as simple messenger boys of the angelic hierarchy.[47] The earthly hierarchy answers to the same pecking order with deacons obeying priests, priests bishops, and bishops the

Apostles.[48] Of course, the laity are found at the bottom and receive grace through the sacramental blessings of those above them.[49]

Gregory the Great (ca. 540-604), the first pope of the church, followed the view of Dionysius, along with much of the Middle Ages, which used both men as a constant source of inspiration and authority.[50] Gregory develops a nine-fold hierarchy much like Dionysius, ranging from the Seraphim, who are highly exalted and know all things possible, to the lower angels, who provide messages of minor significance for those on earth.[51] This process he continues on earth by arranging the church into a similar hierarchical structure. He puts himself at the top of the pyramid, helping to found the theology of his own office, and is recognized by the church universal as its head.[52] He assigns to himself and the priestly office the power to bind and loose sin, grant absolution, re-sacrifice Christ on the altar, and manufacture the presence of Christ in the eucharist.[53] The laity are required to adhere and cleave to the priestly office, which mediates their relation to God by dispensing the means of grace. There is no salvation outside the church and no truth outside its words.[54] The laity must listen to the words of the church, "not to judge but to follow them."[55]

In the sixteenth century, the Reformation brought a challenge and alternative to this paradigm for much of the church. In July of 1519, Martin Luther presented at Leipzig in his debate with John Eck a challenge to the papacy and its medieval concept of power. There were challenges to Rome in certain quarters throughout the Middle Ages, but none would prove so consequential for the church and the world to come as Luther's Reformation. His words at Leipzig emboldened other Reformers to revolt against the church[56] and refashioned much of European society into a whole new image. The next year, Luther would inscribe his teaching in a Treatise, *To the Christian Nobility of the German Nation*, where he provides for that generation and those to come a systematic presentation of his problems with the "Romanists" and challenges their hierarchy with a new-fangled doctrine—the priesthood of the believers. This doctrine is strongly emphasized by Browne, the Congregationalists, and all those who moved toward democracy in early Protestant churches.

The treatise begins with an assault upon the "three walls," which the papacy has erected to protect its will to power. The first protects the pope and his spiritual power in an attempt to usurp the temporal powers of rulers, the second protects the pope's authority to interpret Scripture above the rest of the faithful, and the third protects the right of the papacy to convene councils and determine dogma.[57] Through the three walls

Luther hopes to depict a papacy that will not bow before king, council, or Scripture. He depicts a papacy that is filled with the hubris of Satan, coveting the power of the Almighty and basking in pompous spectacles like kissing the pope's feet or carrying his "ass" on a throne.[58] "How does such satanic pride compare with Christ, who went on foot as did all his disciples? Where has there ever been a worldly monarch who went about in such worldly pomp and glory?"[59] But even with all this vitriol, Luther does not wish to eliminate the office *in toto*—at least not at this point in his career. Even if he refers to the rule of the pope as Satanic and wonders whether the church could live without it, his main concern is limited to reforming the current state of the papacy into a more sublime image.[60] He is not the enemy of the papal office. The enemies of the pope are those who fail to reprove him and prefer instead to gain his favor by flattering him with titles like the "Vicar of the Christ" or bestowing upon him infallible authority as if "the pope cannot err in matters of faith, no matter how righteous or wicked he may be."[61] In fact, the pope needs the reproof of the faithful in light of the current crisis. The greed of Rome has turned the gospel of Jesus Christ, which offers grace and mercy to sinners without charge, into a money-making enterprise through the sale of indulgences, dispensations, benefices, and bishoprics, all to enhance its coffers.[62] "There is buying, selling, bartering, charging, trading, drunkenness, lying, deceiving, robbing, stealing, luxury, harlotry, knavery, and every sort of contempt of God."[63] It is time for the fire and brimstone of heaven to rain and "sink Rome in the abyss, as [God] did to Sodom and Gomorrah of old."[64]

It is in this context that Luther preaches for the first time his doctrine concerning the priesthood of the believers. He looks to 1 Pet. 2:9 and maintains that all who partake of Christ are priests and kings to God.[65] All Christians share in the "same baptism, faith, and Spirit." All share the same spiritual status, whether they be "people, bishops, priests, . . . princes, lords, artisans, [or] farmers. . . . There is no true, basic distinction between laymen and priests, princes and bishops."[66] The magistrate is just as spiritual as the pope. He should exercise his temporal powers on his own, even convene ecclesiastical councils without interference from Rome.[67] The laity are just as spiritual as the clergy and entitled to fulfill their "proper work without restriction" from those who exalt themselves as superior.[68] Luther goes so far in this direction as to reject the sacrament of orders and its belief in a special *character indelibilis*, which was bestowed at that time upon the clergy for its ministry and designed to set them apart. All believers can administer the sacraments. The clergy possesses no special power to baptize infants or grant absolution to sinners. The office of priest does not confer a special status or depend upon the calling of bishops, but affords a ministry that is subject to the "consent and election" of the entire community of believers, who stand equally as priests before God.[69] Luther raises the possibility of developing a democratic polity with these words, even though he chooses not to proceed any farther in this direction. The message at this point preaches a new and radical egalitarianism, which others will take and develop in the coming era toward democratic reform.

The movement toward democracy found fertile ground in Cambridge, England toward the end of the sixteenth century.[70] Thomas Cartwright was the leading theologian at the school and challenged the episcopal form of government in the Church of England as incompatible with the ideals of the Reformation. He wanted to replace the hierarchical structure of the church with a presbyterian model, where each local church would choose its own ministers and presbyters apart from the blessings of bishops or the external sanction from the church at large.[71] His lectures on these and other subjects found a devoted following among the students but created much contention and powerful opposition from the party of prelates, headed by John Whitgift, a colleague at the school, and Richard Hooker, who wrote the classic work on the subject, *Of the Laws of Ecclesiastical Polity* (1594), from the Anglican perspective. In the early 1570s, Cartwright was deprived of his professorship and fellowship at Trinity College because of the controversy. He would spend over a decade in exile on the continent among important Reformed communities in Geneva, Antwerp, and Middleburg, and then return to his native land in 1585 only to be cast into prison.

The years of persecution suggest the radical nature of his ideals, but he was not so extreme as other reformers and remained steadfast in his loyalty to the church and state. He certainly was less extreme than Browne, Harrison, and other students from Cambridge who went out to form rival churches and reject the mother church altogether. During his interrogation in 1590, he declared his loyalty to the Crown and maintained that he had done nothing to warrant the proceedings against him. He admitted his part in composing the first draft of *Disciplina ecclesia sacra* (later translated and published by the Long Parliament in 1644) which was subscribed by a number of ministers and brought a storm of controversy, but he did so only to provide an ideal form of governance, not to implement an experiment and cause a schism.[72] He and his group might have inspired more radical followers like Browne and Harrison to go out and plant churches, but his own views were less radical in their opposition to the church and more balanced in their polity. In fact, Cartwright disparaged Browne's *Treatise of reformation without tarrying for anie* because of its excessive measures and sanctimonious tone. The church needed reformation, but it did not need those who would treat it like the whore of Babylon, as if it had no genuine confession or proper assembly.[73] Cartwright preferred a more moderate or cautious approach, which marked much of his rhetoric and style, especially during the last few decades of his life. After 1577 he no longer published any controversial works and died of natural causes in his native land (1603).[74]

Cartwright produced several works, written in association with Walter Travers and others, which provide first-hand testimony to his moderate approach to polity. The works represent an important witness to early Presbyterianism in England as it tries to steer a middle course between the prelates and separatists, who find no basis for reconciliation between them. The middle course agrees with the separatists that the people and the local church should possess more authority in ruling their own affairs in accordance with the priesthood of the believers, but it also agrees with the other side, that the leaders of the church have a primary role in the decision-making process and the people must "tarry" for the magistrate to bring about the necessary reforms. Cartwright, Travers, and his group served as a major source of inspiration for Browne and his early followers, but they refused to go all the way with the separatists, rejecting both poles in the debate as extreme, aberrant, and unnecessary.

The group starts out its analysis of the church much like the separatists, emphasizing the Word of God as the one and only foundation of polity. The church is obligated to follow Christ as the one, true Lord of all believers and his laws as the only standard in governing the fellowship.[75] The kingdom of the Antichrist has corrupted the polity of the early church and raised a papal hierarchy in its place. This kingdom derives its teaching outside the Scripture, finding justification for its practice from canon law, and those who follow the teaching do much the same.[76] The prelates of England follow the same line of thinking when they argue that no pattern of outward order is found in Scripture and defer to the magistrate or some ecclesiastical body to determine what they consider a matter of indifference.[77] But this contention is far from the truth and dishonors the Word of God. There is a "certayne and perpetuall order set downe in the Word of God," ordained from the very beginning.[78] God gave Moses specific and detailed instruction in designing his fellowship, the Book of the Hebrews bearing witness to a most decided will of God in the matter of discipline, order, and service.[79] The Apostles followed this pattern and set down a very specific polity and order in the churches they planted. The Apostolic Church serves as a standard for all fellowships and all times, sealed and set forth in the Holy Scripture as an eternal witness for generations to come.[80]

> The Discipline of Christs Church that is necessary for all times is delivered by Christ, and set downe in the holy Scriptures. Therefore the true and lawfull Discipline is to be fetched from thence, and from thence alone. And that which resteth upon any other foundation ought to be esteemed unlawfull and counterfeit. Of all Particular Churches there is one and the same right order and forme: Therefore also no one may challenge to it selfe any power over others; nor any right which doth not alike agree to others.[81]

The offices that were planted by the Apostles consist of pastors, doctors, elders, and deacons. These make up the ordinary and perpetual offices of the church (as opposed to the extraordinary offices, which consist of Apostles, evangelists, and prophets).[82] The pastors administer the Word and Sacrament, the teachers preserve sound doctrine, the deacons provide relief for the poor, and the elders rule the church, observing the behavior of all its people and insuring that its doctrine, order, and discipline conform to the will of God.[83] These offices represent the ideal polity as set forth in Scripture, but there is no sanction in God's Word to practice separation from the church if it falls short of what is expected. The church can subsist without an ideal form of government as long as it remains faithful for the most part.[84] A restoration of its true polity would prove invaluable, but one should remain patient for the time being and thankful for monarchs, like Elizabeth I, Edward VI, and even Henry VIII, who have restored some semblance of biblical teaching and order after centuries of papal darkness.[85]

A major goal, shared by all Puritans, is to eliminate the hierarchical structure of the church and create more autonomy within the local community. The episcopal system erects "Lord Bishops," who usurp the authority of local assemblies and pretend they represent the entire body of Christ.[86] The presbyterian system prefers to treat all ministers, pastors, and elders as equal in power.[87] It prefers to place all churches on the same footing and make them subject one to another during special gathered assemblies of the fellowships in question.[88] It prefers to respect the spiritual nature of each individual community and provide as much space as possible for that spirit to work, letting the community handle its own affairs. In this system, an officer no longer possesses a general call to serve the church at large, but each one is summoned to a certain place by a special call to serve a local church. No one is called or ordained as an extraneous bishop to enjoy the benefit and privilege of office apart from a special assignment within a local community.[89]

The elders are given the primary responsibility to run the church. This plurality of leadership is intended to inhibit the corrupting influence of unrestrained behavior associated with the rule of one person. Not even the Apostles ruled the early church as isolated individuals.[90] The elders are given the authority to create constitutions, exercise discipline, and elect or depose ministers—although the church is allowed to approve or reject a given nominee.[91] The elders rule as an "Aristocratie" in managing the basic affairs of the church but seldom act on their own without the consent of the people.[92] Those who believe that the church should have the primary role in this and other matters are simply in error. The contention that the whole church possessed a greater role in Acts 6 and 14 when it was first established might be right, but this was a special circumstance during a transitional period in its history and it is better to let those who possess spiritual maturity run the church in the present day and time.[93]

The radicals looked at this position as little more than a compromise with the established order and preferred to proceed in a more consistent manner. Both Luther and Cartwright were concerned about fanatical followers and intemperate ideas, but many of their own ideas contained disturbing implications and clearly inspired those groups who wished to take the seminal ideas of the Reformation into more radical directions. The separatists exalted the priesthood of the believers above and beyond what Luther had envisaged. They thought that it was most essential to serve Christ directly without the mediation of other authorities; develop a polity based upon the Word of God, not human tradition; and decide from their own authority, as kings and priests before God, who is best equipped to serve and participate in the fellowship. They could not envision another authority to rival the Lordship of Christ in the life of the believer. One must serve Christ and serve him only. One must develop doctrine and practice from the Scripture and the Scripture alone. The radicals found in Cartwright and Cambridge an impetus toward these ideas. Cartwright served as a conduit through which Luther's reformational ideas challenged the structure of the Church of England and became an inspiration for those who wished to develop the viewpoint in more extreme directions, both in the church and in the society to come. The radicals identified with his stress upon the priesthood of believers as seen in the Lordship of Christ, authority of Scripture, and autonomy of the local community, even if he did not proceed far enough in their minds toward complete democracy in the church.

Huguenot Church

Sectarian groups also served as a source of inspiration in the movement toward democracy. The Puritans looked to the example of the Protestant churches in France, Scotland, and the Netherlands who regarded the authority of Scripture and freedom of the local assembly as important aspects of a sound polity.[94] The French Church proved a special source of inspiration early on. The Huguenots developed a congregational-type of church government, in which the laity controlled the fellowship and the decisions of the local church were honored—at least during its early days before the Genevan leadership forced the Reformed Churches of France to conform with its demands.[95]

The Puritans probably came into contact with this position through Peter Ramus, a member of the church and advocate of democracy in his later years. Ramian ideas had an extensive impact upon Continental Europe in the sixteenth century,[96] but they enjoyed their most lasting and decided impact in that century and the one to come among the Puritans.[97] His *Dialecticae libri duo* (1556) was circulated throughout England and underwent a number of English editions, eight in the sixteenth century and eleven in the seventeenth century.[98] The indelible mark of the Ramian system is found and observed in its division of categories into two parts, which is seen throughout his works and those who follow him. Ramus would define a subject, then divide it into two halves, then halve the halves until an irreducible entity is obtained. When all things are divided and placed in their proper order, one could teach and communicate the subject at hand in a more effective manner. But it did not matter where one begins. One might wish to work backwards when a specific matter is better known to an audience, proceeding from the specific toward the more general and abstract in presenting the material.[99] This method was adopted by a number of Puritan theologians and intellectuals. The Ramist dichotomies are readily observed, often in the form of charts, in a wide spectrum of their works. They are found most notably in the works of those who opposed the episcopal church—in particular, within the works of the principles already mentioned: Cartwright's *A Treatise of Christian Religion*,[100] Travers' *Ecclesiasticae disciplinae*,[101] and Browne's *A Booke that sheweth the life and manner of all true Christians*.[102] Those on the opposite side are the ones who opposed the Ramian system in general,[103] providing at least some indication that Ramus represented to the polemical parties more than what a simple method of presenting material would indicate.

Pierre de la Ramée was born in 1515 at Cuts in Picardy, the son of an immigrant family of modest means. He was born into a well-ordered society that believed the son of a peasant should remain in the caste of his birth. However, in spite of the obstacles, he managed to rise above the limitations of his background. He became the rector of the Collège of Presles (1545-1572) and was made a royal professor in July of 1551, even though this distinction was awarded to most recipients on the basis of patronage and oligarchic privilege. He would spend much of his career challenging the privileges of the few, the veracity of certain authorities, and the obstinance of the status quo. He wanted an educational system that was made available and affordable to all people.[104] He wanted a society that would honor its citizens based upon merit, without any mixture of favoritism, nepotism, or simony.[105] This conviction led him to despise the *ancient régime* of his day and desire to replace it with something new. It was out of this attitude that he gained notoriety as one who would challenge even the authority of Aristotle. While he did not want to reject the old out of hand and even liked some ancient philosophers like Socrates, who would follow the truth wherever it might lead, he despised the dependence of institutions upon the authority of one man.[106] This contempt is seen from the outset of his career when he formulated the following provocative statement as the subject of his master's thesis: "All that Aristotle has said is false." *Aristotelicae animadversiones* would follow, published in 1543, in which he conducted his first extensive attack upon the Aristotelian system.[107] Of course, the basic motivation was not to destroy the work of this great mind but to free the minds of students so they could think for themselves without dependence or reference to ancient authorities. Many were afraid to question Aristotle. If he was proven wrong, then all that went before is challenged, the entire rational system of the Middle Ages is challenged, and the Catholic Church would lose much of its authority.[108] Even some Protestants were uneasy with the excessive nature of the enterprise. Beza informed Ramus that he and his school were "resolved to follow Aristotle, without deviating even one line."[109] But Ramus was undeterred. He was prepared to discard the entire scholastic tradition in order to create a new form of logic and a new spirit of freedom.[110]

During the last decade of his life, Ramus sided with the Protestant movement in a public way. He displayed tendencies all along toward the movement, but it was not until the end of his career that a specific profession is discerned and displayed for all to see. One telling moment was the Colloquy of Poissy (September, 1561) in which the Cardinal of Lorraine acknowledged the corruption that infected the church down through the centuries and his predilection for the moral excellence of the early church. In a letter, which was written around nine years later, Ramus would praise the cardinal for his remarks and make a special reference to his comments on the "golden age" of the church as inspiring his current theological interests.[111] In his most significant work on theology, *De Religione Christiana Libri IV*, one can discern his new, Protestant orientation with its emphasis upon Scripture and the all-sufficiency of divine grace. Even though the work is not as dogmatic or polemical as others, it shows a decided tendency toward Protestantism, especially as it was interpreted within the Reformed Church of Zurich.[112] Heinrich Bullinger expressed appreciation for his work and developed an amicable relation with him, but it is clear that Beza and Geneva were not so disposed.[113] To welcome Ramus into the fellowship would bring the corrupting influence of his anti-Aristotelian, anti-authoritarian, and anti-Bezan ideas.

Much of the animosity between Beza and Ramus came to a head at La Rochelle in April of 1571 when Beza, the moderator of the Synod, tried to impose his authoritarian rule upon the free churches of France. Ramus championed the autonomy of these churches and gained a reputation among historians as an exponent of democracy, even though his precise position is not so clear. In his most revealing statement, a letter written to Bullinger in September of 1571,[114] he complains about the attempt of Beza and Geneva to impose its heavy-handed polity upon the French churches. Geneva wants to make a "separate senate," consisting of ministers outside the local church, in charge of "doctrine and discipline, election and removal, excommunication and absolution," with the people of the churches providing assent or dissent as a secondary stage of the process. The scheme is designed, in his mind, to make the local assembly inferior and subservient to a church-wide hierarchy. Ramus says that the Reformed Church in his region has a long tradition of freedom, which allots a primary role to the elders, deacons, and people of a local community. He tries to bait Bullinger by mentioning Beza's use of the term *substantia* in regard to the Eucharist and his attempt to impose its usage at the synod, but Beza decides to withdraw this demand in order to placate Bullinger. The issue for both men is polity, and the nature of

Christ's presence in the Eucharist is a matter of secondary importance, which one can mention or not as a tactical move.

Ramus was murdered a year later during the massacre of St. Bartholomew's Day, a horrific chapter in the history of the French church.[115] His death appeared to bring an end to the impact of his life, much to the solace of his enemies and chagrin of those who love freedom. He did not change the hierarchical structure of his society or preserve the fledgling experiment in democracy within his own church. His logical system began to fade at the turn of the century, and philosophers today show little interest in the program. But his impact transcends any conscious, direct, or literal espousal of his precise ideas. Those Puritans who followed his system in outlining their theology knew what they were teaching was an act of rebellion. They knew about the origin of the system and would come to respect the man, whose example encouraged them to rebel against their own *ancient régime*. They saw within him an example of many of the things that they came to believe—the rejection of ancient authority, the distaste for privilege and hierarchy, the freedom of the believer, and the autonomy of the local church. His example encouraged them to do likewise, and through their dedication and determination, the spirit of the man came to have a most decided impact upon the world to come—above and beyond the limited range of his precise philosophical treatment.

The polity of Ramus and that of his colleague, Jean Morély, were known in England and became a part of the consciousness of those involved in the debate. If not through direct sources, the position of the French church became known by other means. It became known through opponents like Beza, whose works were available throughout England, many of which were translated into English in the 1570s. It became known through personal contact with those familiar with the controversy and conversing with their Reformed brethren on the continent. For example, Cartwright and Travers enjoyed a congenial relation with Beza. During Cartwright's exile from England, Beza offered him a chair at the Academy of Geneva, believing that "the sun doth not see a more learned man,"[116] and the respect was mutual. Travers would speak of Beza as "the best interpretour of the newe Testament,"[117] and he along with Cartwright would remain with Beza in Geneva for some time, gaining an intimate, first-hand knowledge of the Morély affair.[118] This knowledge would continue on into the seventeenth century, where those involved with the debate display some sense of its history. Commissioners were familiar with Ramus and Morély at the Westminster Assembly. One of its prominent members, Robert Baillie, requested a copy of Morély's work, and Wilhelmus Apollonius makes a reference to his fanatical democratic ideas.[119] Herbert Thorndike blamed Ramus for bringing the position of Morély and the French church into the universities, inflaming the radicals, and corrupting the Church of England.

> Morellus, in the French Churches, disputed downright that the state of government in the Church ought to be democratic, the people to be sovereign: wherein by Beza's epistles, it appears that he was supported by Ramus: for the man whom Beza calls *ozon arēos*, and describes by other circumlocutions, who put the French Churches to the trouble of divers synods, to suppress this position, as there it appears, can be no other than Ramus. Perhaps Ramus's credit in our Universities was the first means to bring this conceit in religion among us: for about the time that he was most cried up in them, Brown and Barrow published it. Unless it be more probable to fetch it from the troubles of Frankfort. For those that would take upon them to exercise the power of the keys in that estate, because they were a congregation that assembled together for the service of God—which power could not stand, unless recourse might be had to excommunication—did by express consequence challenge the public power of the Church to all congregations; which I have shewed to be otherwise. And the contest there related, between one of the people and one of the pastors, shews that they grounded themselves upon the right of the people. So true it is, that I said afore that the presbyterians have still held the stirrup to those of the congregations, to put themselves out of the saddle.[120]

On the continent, the controversy was centered around the person and work of Jean Morély. He was born around 1524 and spent much of his life on a small piece of land not far from Paris. This area proved a fertile ground for his revolutionary ideas as many were attracted to the movement from that area in the subsequent period, even the most powerful members of society.[121] He reached the zenith of his career when he was invited to serve as the tutor of Henry IV by his Reformed mother, but the disclosure of several subversive letters forced his premature dismissal from the post.[122] The direction of his ideas proved too radical for the leaders of his country and those of his own Reformed Church. Bad blood developed in the church when he was called in 1560 to appear before a pastoral council in Geneva, which included the likes of Calvin and Beza, and received a stiff rebuke for suggesting that they had commended the use of armed resistance on behalf of those persecuted in France (the context being a failed conspiracy against the king). Morély admitted his misunderstanding of their position, but it is questionable whether the council ever forgave him for the transgression. The animosity appeared to continue and came to a head in the next decade as he championed the cause of freedom for the French churches against Geneva and its consistory-based system.[123] In the 1550s, the French churches of Strasbourg, London, Wesel, and Frankfurt displayed their penchant toward democracy by allowing the faithful to participate in the election of ministers and the management of the local community. These experiments did not please the leadership in Geneva, who found it necessary in 1558 and 1560 to summon and chasten some of the ministers—Ardoin de Maillane, Jean de Maillane, Antoine de Lautrac, and Claude de Rohault.[124] But it was Morély who became the center of the storm and incurred the wrath of Geneva when he published the *magnum opus* of the movement, *Traicté de la discipline & police Chrestienne* (1562). This work was published only a few years after the *Gallican Confession of Faith* (1559) had established the need for *superintendants* to devise "what means should be adopted for the government of the whole body."[125] As a result, the work was condemned in a series of councils and synods after its publication. The Third Synod of Orleáns (1562) saw Beza and Chandieu serving on the council, ready to try their adversary and condemn his work accordingly. They followed their wont by erecting their own consistory-based system, anointing themselves as judges, condemning the work for containing "wicked doctrine," and causing "confusion and dissipation" in the church.[126] Calvin would lend his authority to the decision a year later and, after his death, the Genevans made Morély sign a statement retracting his "insolence" even though they knew, and Morély admitted, that his signature was just a sham.[127] The Second Synod of Paris (1565) followed with another condemnation of his work and exhorted him to no longer publish any more heretical opinions, just as he had promised with his own signature.[128] The Synod of Nîmes issued letters of censure against Morély and his "companions" (Ramus, Bergerson, and du Rozier) but, in a rare act of toleration, it provided space for congregations in the Ile of France and other provinces to exercise freedom of opinion in these and other matters.[129]

Morély's treatise contains many of the themes that are found in the polity of Browne and Harrison, including an emphasis upon the Lordship of Christ, the authority of Scripture, and the freedom and equality of all believers. The work starts out much like the Congregationalists pointing to the Lordship of Christ in the life of the believers as the cornerstone of the church.[130] It says that all believers have a direct relationship with Christ and stand before the throne of grace in *liberté* and *égalité*. Their Savior has redeemed and delivered them from slavery to all other masters.[131] Their relation to God is direct in Christ Jesus and has no need of outside mediation.

The knowledge of God is provided to all believers as they read and study the Scripture, the complete and final revelation of God.[132] Morély believes that the Word is the source of all knowledge and devotes his efforts throughout the treatise to the exegesis of it. Patristic sources and historical analysis are brought in to enliven the discussion, but they can never replace what the believer receives directly from the Word.[133] Scripture remains the final source of authority for all things, even in matters of discipline and polity. Morély derives his polity from "the expressed Word of God," whose guidance is specific, certain, and binding for all generations to come.[134] The Bible, as the complete revelation of God, does not leave the choice of government to the caprice of the church or relate its conformation as a matter of indifference to the vicissitudes of changing circumstances.[135] In clear and unequivocal terms, it provides a polity for all times, and this polity gives power to the people throughout its many dispensations. The saints of old possessed this sovereign power in the nation of Israel from the beginning of its foundation. In the days of Moses they elected seventy elders to rule over them and three high priests to lead them in worship.[136] This power remained intact throughout the Old Testament, from Joshua to Ezra, and was abandoned only late in its history during the reign of John Hyrcanus and the Hasmoneans when these enemies of liberty took the right away.[137] In the New Testament the Apostles reestablished the authority of God's people, prescribing a specific polity and allowing the church to participate in the election of its officials (Acts 1 and 6).[138] The Apostles did not impose their authority on the church. The council of Jerusalem did not command other churches to follow its decrees.[139] Even the worst of churches, whom Paul chastened for immorality (1 Cor. 5) and heresy (Gal.1), did not lose their power to elect ministers and conduct discipline.[140] Morély refers to this initial phase as the "golden age" of the church, using the same phrase that so captivated Ramus.[141] He says the age lasted around two hundred years, before the bishops usurped the authority of the church and the hierarchy began to take over.[142]

Morély believes that the hierarchical structure of bishops destroyed the sole rule of Christ, bringing graft, greed, and corruption to his church.[143] Christ warned his disciples against this nefarious system when he told them to become like servants and children and shun any form of governance that would extol worldly ambition and exalt one individual above another (Mk 10).[144] The disciples followed the admonition in the book of Acts and created no special ranking among themselves,[145] but "little by little" the bishops and clerics started to change all this, beginning in the third century.[146] Morély wants the church to return to the polity of Scripture, where all ministers are ordained to an office of equal power and dignity (*d'une egale puissance & d'une mesme dignité*).[147]

Morély proceeds to extend the spirit of egalitarianism to encompass the entire church. All of its members are afforded equal liberty in running and determining its affairs.[148] The church judges doctrine, disciplines sinners, elects ministers, and determines the validity of synods and their decisions. Its members hear the voice of their shepherd (Jn 10) and know how to interpret the Scripture and judge what is fitting.[149] The entire church is equipped with the gift of divine wisdom to discern the spirits, judge matters of doctrine, and exercise discipline.[150] It is the church that stands as the "pillar and support of the truth" (1 Tim. 3:15), not a consistory or special board of representatives.[151] Even the early church and the council of Jerusalem refused to impose Apostolic authority upon others but submitted the decisions of the leaders to the spiritual discernment of the people.[152] This policy changed only later on when the fathers of the Nicene Council decided to excommunicate the Arians by their own authority and created a crisis within the fellowship in the subsequent era. The church needed to act together in discipline with one and the same voice, otherwise the excommunicated could find acceptance in part of the church and so divide the fellowship as they did in this instance.[153] The ministers and pastors should work with the church to fulfill its will, not their own. It is the church as a whole that judges what is fitting and sound and beneficial.[154] It is the church that elects these officials to serve its interests, and it is the church that can depose them in accordance with its own sovereign power before God.[155]

His emphasis upon equality and democracy is so strong that a number of questions arise concerning the extent to which he is willing to proceed and the overall viability of his program. One wonders how far democracy can extend itself and whether some structure or chain of command becomes necessary in the end. At first, he seems to maintain consistency and advocates complete democracy, believing that the Word of God would constrain its people and insure unanimity in some mystical way through the workings of the Holy Spirit.[156] But then he becomes more sober in analysis and begins to talk much in the manner of Ramus through the use of a phrase like "*l'egalite geometique*" and attempt to exalt the wiser and older over others, in order to dispel the charge of promoting complete chaos. At this point his equality is not so arithmetic or even-handed in the way it calculates the will of the people, but measures "*la proportion and le mérite de chacun.*"[157] He sets the minimum age of voting at fifteen[158] and finds it wise to establish a couple of councils within the church, consisting of ministers and elders, who offer advice to the members.[159] While Christ provides no precedence for the practice,

Morély finds the establishment of such a council consonant with his will and necessary for the promotion of good order and sound instruction in the church, otherwise there would be chaos.[160] Outside the local church he finds the need for some synods, colloquies, and councils to wield the church together and offer help in time of need.[161] Even though he speaks of past abuses in these extra-church gatherings, he refuses to denounce them altogether and proceed in the direction of the later separatists, who advocate complete autonomy for the local community. He even cedes to the magistrate and his officials an important role as "feeders and protectors" (*nourissiers & tuteurs*) of the church to help insure unity in the fellowship.[162] The magistrate is commissioned to promote piety among the people, suppress heresy, summon councils of the church, and watch over its doctrine, discipline, and polity to keep it pure.[163] Morély is content to let the magistrate wield power above and beyond the democratic process. He says that hierarchy is "necessary within the political realm, whereas . . . it pleased the Lord to govern the church in a different manner, so that its preservation is entirely up to him."[164] The tension created between the two realms produces a strain within his system, which Morély himself could not mend. He planned on writing a second volume in which he hoped to relate ecclesiastical and civil government in a more satisfactory way, but it was never completed and it is doubtful that he would have extended his democratic program to encompass the government, given the times and circumstances of his life.

Morély was fortunate to survive the massacre on St. Bartholomew's Day. He, along with sixty-two pastors, four to five thousand Huguenots, and "some of his children" fled their native land and found a place of refuge in England. After a few months of uncertainty, Sir Francis Walsingham, the future secretary of state, placed him in Wales to help that region along in its spiritual development. (Walsingham was sympathetic with the cause of Puritans, a defender of Thomas Cartwright, and an acquaintance of Peter Ramus, who paid him a couple of visits in December of 1571.)[165] Morély wrote another treatise, *De Ecclesiae ordine*, during this time although it is unclear whether it was published or anyone read it. He confessed a certain affinity to Puritan reforms in the work, but he considered their excessive measures to border on anarchy and preferred to deal with more responsible leaders within the Anglican Church. It is difficult to assess what impact his efforts exerted upon them or anyone else in England during his time in exile.[166] It is clear that he returned to France a number of years later in 1578 a less significant figure than what he represented in the debate of earlier days, but he certainly did not die a failure.[167] The overall influence of Morély and his church was recognized in the next century by Edward Hyde, the Earl of Clarendon, who wrote the most celebrated history of the Puritan Revolution just after the Restoration in 1660. Clarendon understood the demise of Episcopalian polity during the period as a product of the corrupting influence of "French, Dutch, and Walloon" churches upon certain sectarian groups, especially in the diocese of Norwich, where Browne and his church first took roots. As a royalist, he considered the Huguenots most responsible for the uprising and commended their excommunication from the Church of England.[168] Clarendon understood like many of his contemporaries the power of church fellowships to mold the ideology of a people. The Huguenot Church served as a powerful force during his time in spreading the message of liberty on the grassroots level. The movement that Morély helped shape was a part of the consciousness of those who went forward, whether or not they knew his name or read any of his works. The Puritans experienced the impact of Morély through the many sources that converged together, none of which were copied in a slavish manner and all of which were forged to create their own unique synthesis.[169]

Covenant Theology

Among the more noticeable areas of influence is included the doctrine of covenant—an important feature of the Reformed theology in general. Morély's treatment does not utilize this doctrine in any significant way, but Browne and the Congregationalists make it an integral part of their polity. They understand the local church in terms of a covenant forged with God and each other. They will take this concept of covenant and transform the relations of other segments of society to reflect what is true in the church. It is within the Reformed doctrine of covenant (*foedus*) that the notion of a federal government develops.

Covenant theology goes back to the early days of the Reformation in Zurich.[170] It was developed by Zwingli and Bullinger in their polemical struggles with the Anabaptists over the doctrine of infant baptism. Both sides rejected the notion of baptismal regeneration, refusing to connect the *signum* and the *res significata*,[171] and both preferred to interpret the sacrament as a sign of the new life in Christ, a covenant of our relationship with God, and a pledge to follow the Lord in heart-felt obedience.[172] However, Zwingli wanted to include infants within the sacrament and decided to transfer the pledge of obedience to the parents, making them promise to rear their children in the ways of the Lord.[173] He sought to justify this move by using an age-old analogy between baptism and circumcision.

Parents are told that their children are no less blessed than Abraham's, and they should baptize their children just like he circumcised his own. The sacraments are one and the same, regardless of the differences between their outward form.[174] But if the sacraments are the same, this meant that the message and substance of the underlying covenants are one and the same,[175] and so covenant theology was born. To support the analogy of baptism and circumcision Zwingli was forced to assume the fundamental unity of all the covenants in the Old and New Testament, engulfing the entire message into one simple construct. No diversity was allowed to undermine this deeper essence. The entire message of Scripture was subsumed under the one eternal covenant of Christ.

Bullinger wrote the first systematic disquisition upon the doctrine, *De Testamento seu Foedere Deo unico et aeterno* (1534), which helped to make it a permanent fixture within the Reformed community. His treatment is much like that of his colleague, but there are a couple of differences worth noting. The first concerns the place of the doctrine in theology. Bullinger's treatment provides the doctrine with a life of its own, independent of its application to the specific problem of infant baptism. He finds the unity of the covenant a key to unlocking the entire mysteries of Scripture, providing it a fundamental place in one's overall theological understanding.[176] The Reformed community will adopt this point of view and make the covenant a central part of their system, without finding some tension or any specific problem with its overall understanding of theology. However, the second point will cause them much more difficulty as it appears to clash with the Reformed doctrine of divine grace and human depravity. In it, Bullinger displays one of the tendencies of his theology, which is not so devoted to divine grace as Zwingli and tends to gravitate toward the synergism of Erasmus and the humanists.[177] This tendency causes him to recast the covenant into a relationship of mutual responsibility between God and the people, contingent upon the faithfulness of both parties to fulfill their respective roles. In this respect, the covenant is not a simple act of divine grace working its efficacious power upon an unwitting subject, but involves certain "conditions" from the human side to reach its fulfillment.[178] This and other tendencies make their way into the Reformed doctrine of covenant through Bullinger's monumental work as it spreads throughout the Reformed world in the sixteenth and seventeenth centuries, leaving its indelible mark upon the discussion to come.[179] More than any other work it helps establish the covenant as a central and permanent fixture within that community, even though its influence threatens the overall supremacy of divine grace within the Reformed system.[180]

The doctrine of the covenant made its way to England and took up residence in Cambridge about the time of Browne's tenure at the school. The precise history of its evolution is unknown to historians of the covenant, but there is ample evidence to suggest that Browne first came into contact with the notion in this setting—the most natural setting for his ideas to germinate. Shortly after his tenure, he and others associated with the school put forth their own analysis of the covenant in writing, following the typical Reformed understanding of the day. Dudley Fenner, an associate of Cartwright, published his *Sacra Theologia* (1585) and included a section on the doctrine in which he speaks of the covenant much like Bullinger. He writes, "The action of God is the first part of the covenant, by which he promises to be our God and provide us with eternal life, if we fulfill the necessary stipulated condition."[181] William Perkins, a preacher and teaching fellow at Cambridge, advanced the tradition more than others by providing an extensive treatment of the covenant in his *Golden Chaine* (1590), where he speaks of its bilateral nature and other features in a typical Reformed manner.[182] His treatment is most significant due to the enormity of his stature in Puritan circles and the wide-dissemination of his works, insuring the place and credibility of the doctrine for his constituency. In fact, the doctrine became so significant to the Puritans that the Westminster Confession (1648) was the only Reformed symbol in the era to treat it as a separate article of faith.

The covenant developed beyond its original context to envelop much of life in the seventeenth century as it became a centerpiece of Reformed thinking. The Puritans used it as a means of interpreting all levels of social relationships within its matrix. Already in the sixteenth century, the Cambridge school seems to lead the way in the deconstruction. Its theologians envision the covenant as defining our relationship to God and determining our relationship with each other as a consequence. Fenner can speak of a "double covenant," in which the people and the magistrates hold each other responsible to fulfill their federal duties because of their unique relationship to God by means of covenant. Perkins also can cast the net of covenant over the whole nation and its people, preaching its blessings and curses in the later style of a New England Jeremiad and referring to the unique federal relationship the nation has with God and each other.[183] These developments seem to surprise scholars, even those who display some familiarity with Reformed theology and the covenant, but there is nothing unexpected here. Scholars have failed to understand these developments because they center too much attention upon a specific line of historical causality and fail to grapple with the meaning of the theology they study. To *understand* the covenant is to *understand* its history. These developments only represent a consistent application of what is already in place. It is all a simple deduction from first principles, which view the Scripture as the full and final revelation of God and the covenant as the essence of its message. The covenant develops its ubiquity as these two ideas merge together in a simple syllogism. The covenant is the unifying principle of Scripture, the Scripture contains the final and complete revelation of God, its authority relates to the practical details of our lives, and so the covenant must relate to the details of our relationship to God and humankind. This process is observed in its infancy within the writings of Browne, who translates the covenant into the realm of church polity, civil government, and the prosaic relations of everyday life—master/servant, teacher/student, and husband/wife. The Puritans followed this pattern in the next generation as they translate the relations of this life in terms of the all-sufficiency of Scripture, suffering few matters of indifference to remain in their world, and understand its essential message by means of the covenant.

Outside its application to the government, the best example of the process is seen in the new concept of marriage. Many Puritans began to deconstruct the marital bonds in terms of the covenant, and a dramatic version of the process can be found in the writings of John Milton, the famous poet. Milton was reared in a Puritan home, studied at Cambridge, and aspired to pursue a career in the ministry. He was barred by the prelates from fulfilling his dream, but his acerbic tongue was not silenced and continued to advocate the cause of Puritanism and reform through the power of the printed page. His writings attacked the system of bishops[184] and advocated the typical staple of Puritan beliefs, including the supremacy of Scripture in matters of polity,[185] the equality of ministers throughout the church,[186] and the priesthood of the believers.[187] But what proves most interesting in his writings is the unusual application of the doctrine of covenant. This application provides testimony to the power of the doctrine as it is applied to a subject outside its original setting and changes the customary ways of addressing that subject. The covenant is used in this case to dissolve the bonds of marriage outside the typical reasons found in canon law. Milton was involved in an ill-conceived marriage, which ended after a short period of time, and he spent much of his life trying to reduce the social stigma, writing four tracts dealing with the subject. In his first and foremost treatise, *The Doctrine and Discipline of*

Divorce (1643), he complains about the church interpreting the Scripture much too literally when it tries to limit the grounds of divorce to the sin of adultery.[188] The church fails to understand the fundamental nature of marriage, which he interprets much like Browne in terms of the bilateral covenant. Marriage is a mutual covenant based upon love and peace,[189] and if these conditions are not present, it becomes a duty to end it.[190] But the decision is left up to the couple.[191] There is "no power beyond their own consent to hinder them from unjoyning."[192] This application of the covenant creates a new way of thinking about divorce outside the typical teaching of the church. Many other Puritans would follow the same fundamental understanding of marriage as a covenant and allow for greater freedom in terminating the relationship than was true of the church in the past.[193]

The covenant became an instrument through which all relationships in society were reconfigured. There was no way of limiting a message that served as the key to unlock and comprehend the entire breadth and depth of the biblical text. There was no following the one message of Scripture without interpreting all other relationships of life in its terms. In fact, the Puritans make this very transition most visible when they seize political power in the seventeenth century, insuring the supremacy of the covenant in culture. The covenant becomes a pervasive force during the times of the Puritan Revolution and continues as a permanent fixture in society providing the modern world and its government with a new structure.

The ascendancy of the covenant appears to dumbfound most scholars of the seventeenth century. Christopher Hill, the great scholar of the Puritan Revolution, seems mystified by the origin of the covenant and writes, "The exact process by which the all-pervading contractualism of seventeenth-century thought evolved still await[s] their historian."[194] Some try to find a semblance of influence in the constitutionalism of Venice or the Dutch revolts in the sixteenth and seventeenth centuries. According to this theory, Puritans were aware of these developments and found some inspiration within them, but the exact nature and extent of the influence is difficult to ascertain.[195] Even those who wish to point in this direction must confess the nebulous nature of the evidence and influence and look for other, perhaps deeper sources of inspiration to discover the real story. Other scholars seem frustrated with the results and try to buttress the evidence by adding other "secular" references. Some exalt the "secular" accounts of men like Thomas Hobbes and Jean-Jacques Rousseau, believing that their sheer rational acuity helped liberate them and the modern world from slavery to the religious past.[196] These secular scholars appear to be controlled by a belief in the separation of church and state and allow this view of the relationship between the two realms to color their historical results in an anachronistic manner. Their view of government causes them to discount religious contributions in the past and exalt "secular" ideas and people as the founders of modern federalism, but this prejudice blinds them to the reality of life in the early modern period, which was entangled within the central place of the church throughout culture. While a multitude of factors contributed to the evolution of modern political ideas beyond the influence of specific religious communities, it makes sense to believe that the church played a vital role within the vast causal influence, given its exalted status at the time. Those scholars who wish to find a secular patriarchy are revising history through ideological commitments, looking for a linear fulfillment of ideas within a current paradigm of church/state relations, but this prejudice can blind them to basic historical facts. It can blind them to the simple and undeniable fact that the covenant already pervaded culture before secular patriarchs like Hobbes, Rousseau, and the sons of the Enlightenment were on the scene. It can blind them to the fact that Hobbes and Rousseau exerted no significant influence upon the great experiments of federalism in Britain and America according to the many specialists in the field. The problem with these scholars comes from a lack of knowledge or appreciation of the theology of the Reformation. Many of them are conversant in what transpires in England and America as the covenant reaches fruition in the political order, but possess little or no knowledge of the religious heritage of this and other ideas on the continent, whether wittingly or not.

Notes

1. H. G. Alexander, *Religion in England, 1558-1662* (London: Hodder & Stoughton, 1968) 85, 86; C. Burrge, *The Church Covenant Idea: Its Origin and Its Development* (Philadelphia: American Baptist Publication Society, 1904) 43.
2. G. Maddox, *Religion and the Rise of Democracy* (London and New York: Routledge, 1996) 152; T. William and J. Youngs, *The Congregationalists* (Westport, CT and London: Praeger, 1998) 11.
3. "A True and Short Declaration," in *The Writings of Robert Harrison and Robert Browne*, A. Peel and L. H. Carlson (ed.) (London: George Allen and Unwin Ltd., 1953) 397, 404; W. Haller, *The Rise of Puritanism* (Philadelphia: University of Pennsylvania Press, 1972) 29, 182; William and Youngs, *The Congregationalists*, 11, 12.
4. S. A. Yarbrough, "The English Separatist Influence on the Baptist Tradition of Church-State Issues," *Baptist History* 20, no. 3 (July 1985): 15. Brownism remained in Norfolk after the congregation made its exodus on the Netherlands.

Thomas Wolsey, Henry Barrow, and William Hunt found inspiration in the group and amassed a number of followers despite the continual persecution. The movement also inspired the ministry of John Robinson, a fellow at Corpus Christi, Cambridge and the erstwhile pastor of the Pilgrim Fathers. M. Reynolds, *Godly Reformers and their Opponents in Early Modern England: Religion in Norwich, c.1560-1643* (Woodbridge, Suffolk: The Boydell Press, 2005) 92-101.

5. Browne describes the rancorous relation with Harrison in terms of his colleague constantly bringing false accusations against him. However, it seems that the two had a genuine disagreement over the matter of discipline. Browne wants to count only believing adults in the fellowship, whereas Harrison wants to include children. "A True and Short Declaration," 424ff., 428. All the references to their works are taken from *The Writings of Robert Harrison and Robert Browne*.
6. S. Bredwell, "Raising of the Foundations of Brownisme," in *The Writings of Robert Harrison and Robert Browne*, 134 (III) (507); "An Aunswere to Mr. Flowers," 519. Bredwell tells us that he submitted to the Archbishop of Canterbury on Oct. 7, 1585.
7. E.g., "A Treasure upon the 23. of Matthewe," 203.
8. Ibid., 182; "A True and Short Declaration," 415, 416.
9. Ibid., 173-81.
10. E.g., "A Booke which sheweth the life and manner of all true Christians," 230, 233.
11. "A Treatise upon the 23. of Matthewe," 212, 217.
12. "An Answer to Master Cartwright," 465; "A Booke," 276, 277.
13. "A Booke," 323, 333, 387; "A Treatise," 219, 220.
14. "A True and Short Declaration," 421; "A Treatise upon the 23. of Matthewe," 202.
15. "A Booke," 253.
16. "A Booke," 226, 255.
17. "A Booke," 334-40.
18. "A Booke," 309.
19. "A Booke," 343.
20. "A Booke," 385.
21. "A Booke," 334.
22. "A Booke," 335, 353.
23. "A Booke," 353.
24. "A Treatise upon reformation without tarying for anie," 152-64; "A True and Short Declaration," 413. After he is reconciled to the church, he will speak in favor of a greater role for the magistrate in the church. "An Aunswere to Mr. Flowers Letter," 521, 522.
25. "A Booke," 335.
26. "A Treatise upon the reformation without tarying for anie," 165. Some scholars have speculated over the possibility of Anabaptist influence upon Browne. Dutch Anabaptists came to England during the time of Henry VIII, and there was somewhere between four and five thousand of them in Norwich during the 1570s and 1580s. In Middleburg, there was some interaction between the Separatists and the Anabaptists. Harrison appears to adopt their concept of the sacraments. However, the impetus toward the separatist view of church and state antedates this interaction, even if these and other sectarian groups like the Baptists and Quakers will evolve together with a certain amount of fluidity between them. Browne himself does not follow the Anabaptists on a number of issues—predestination, infant baptism, use of the OT, use of the sword, the taking of oath, etc. Cf. C. N. Knaus,

"Anabaptist Influence on English Separatism as seen in Robert Browne," *The Mennonite Quarterly Review* 34 (Jan. 1960): 6, 14-19.

27. Ibid., 153.
28. Ibid., 201, 202, 212.
29. Ibid., 205-10; "A Booke," 263.
30. "An Answer to Master Cartwright," 459, 460; "A Treatise upon the 23. of Matthewe," 215.
31. Ibid., 438, 439, 462; "An Aunswere to Mr. Flowers Letter," 525, 526.
32. "A True and Short Declaration," 428. It is possible that Harrison is more favorable to Anabaptist theology and Browne more favorable to the Reformed when it comes to the doctrine of the sacraments. Cf. Harrington's "Three Formes of Catechismes, . . ." (139, 140) with Browne's "A Booke" (258, 287). Browne's discussion of the sacraments lacks clarity.
33. "A Little Treatise upone the firste Verse of the 122. Psalm," 88.
34. "A Little Treatise," 74-76, 118-20.
35. "A Treatise of the Church and the Kingdom of Christ," 48, 49, 58.
36. Ibid., 39, 40.
37. Ibid., 38.
38. Ibid., 31.
39. "A Little Treatise," 120.
40. "A Treatise of the Church and the Kingdom of Christ," 32, 33.
41. Ibid., 36, 40, 41.
42. "A Little Treatise," 100, 119, 120.
43. Plotinus, *Enneads*, A. H. Armstrong (trans.) (Cambridge, MA: Harvard University Press, 1967) 3.8 (3.360-401); D. J. O'Meara, *Plotinus: An Introduction to the Enneads* (Oxford: Clarendon Press, 1993) 72, 76.
44. A. Louth, *Denys the Areopagite* (Wilton, CT: Morehouse Publishing, 1989) 10-13.
45. *Pseudo-Dionysius: The Complete Works*, C. Luibheid (trans.) (New York: Paulist Press, 1987) 105, 106, 154.
46. Louth, *Denys the Areopagite*, 37.
47. *The Complete Works*, 158ff.
48. Ibid., 276. Even Jesus did not possess direct, unmediated access to God while on earth but was subject to angelic administration. Ibid., 42, 43.
49. Ibid., 202ff., 236, 237.
50. Ibid., 21, 26ff.; A. Harnack, *History of Dogma*, N. Buchanan (trans.) (Gloucester, Mass.: Peter Smith, 1976) 5.263. Thomas Aquinas quotes Dionysius some 1700 times.
51. Gregorius Magnus, *Homiliae in Evangelia*, 34. 7-10 (CC 141. 305-309); *Moralia in Iob*, 4.55; 32.48 (CC 143.199; 143B.1666, 1667); F. H. Dudden, *Gregory the Great: His Place in History and Thought* (New York: Russell & Russell, 1967) 1.360ff.
52. Gregorius Magnus, *Registrum Epistularum Libri*, 5.37; 9.27 (CC 140.309, 310; 140A.588, 589).
53. Gregorius Magnus, *Dialogorum Libri IV*, 4.58 (PL 77.426, 427).
54. Gregorius Magnus, *Moralia in Iob*, 14.5; 35.13 (CC 143A.7101, 143B.1781, 1781).
55. *Moralia in Iob*, 20.2.2 (CC 134A.1004).
56. For example, Zwingli points to Leipzig as providing inspiration for his and other reformers' break with the church. He compares Luther to David and Hercules. *Huldreich Zwinglis Sämtliche Werke*, in E. Egli and G. Finsler (Hrsg.), *Corpus*

Reformatorum (Berlin: C.A. Schwetschke und Sohn, 1905-) 5.722; M. Brecht, "Zwingli als Schüler Luthers: Zu seiner theologische Entwicklung," *Zeitschrift für Kirchengeschichte* 96, no. 3 (1985) 305, 311; W. P. Stephens, *The Theology of Huldrych Zwingli* (Oxford: Clarendon Press, 1986) 30; J. V. Pollet, *Huldrych Zwingli et le Zwinglianisme* (Paris: J. Vrin, 1988) 22.

57. WA 6.406, 411-13 (LW 44.126, 134-36). WA represents *D. Martin Luthers Werke* (Weimar, 1883-) and LW the corresponding section in *Luther's Works* (Philadelphia, 1955-).
58. WA 6.435, 436 (LW 44.168, 169).
59. WA 6.436 (LW 44.168.169).
60. WA 6.453, 454 (LW 44.194, 195). In the *Freedom of a Christian* (Nov. 1520), he is more conciliatory. He makes it clear the he does not wish to attack Leo, only the Roman see and curia, which are corrupt. WA 7.43, 44 (LW 31.335-37). Later he becomes more harsh in his judgment, and the pope is considered the Antichrist. WA 54.283, 284 (LW 41. 357, 358).
61. WA 6.411 (LW 44.133). See WA 7.47, 48 (LW 31.341, 342).
62. W 6.418ff., 446, 450 (LW 44, 143ff., 184, 189).
63. WA 6.425 (LW 44.153).
64. WA 6.421 (LW 44.148).
65. WA 6.407, 408 (LW 44.128). See WA 12.308; 17/2.6 (LW 30.54).
66. WA 6.407, 408 (LW 44.127-29). Cf. WA 7.56-58 (LW 31.354-56).
67. WA 6.409, 413 (LW 44.131, 136, 137).
68. WA 6.409, 410 (LW 44.130-32).
69. WA 6.408 (LW 44.129). See WA .716, 722 (LW 35.12, 21); 10/3.394ff. George Williams cites another passage from Luther [WA 19.75 (LW 53.63, 64)], which was used by Lambert of Avignon and Melchoir Rink, along with other Anabaptists to justify a free church association, but Luther goes on to say in the same passage that he does not wish to form this type of congregation. G. H. Williams, "'Congregationalist' Luther and the Free Church," *Lutheran Quarterly* 20, no. 3 (Aug. 1967): 286, 287. Luther prided himself in preaching to the masses and rejected scholastic, hair-splitting dogma as unedifying. The Puritans will follow Luther's example in this regard. WA, Tr 3.3573 (LW 54. 235, 236), WA, Tr 4.5047 (LW 54.383); Haller, *The Rise of Puritanism*, 130-35, 140, 141.
70. W. Haller, *Liberty and Reformation in the Puritan Revolution* (New York and London: Columbia University Press, 1967) 11.
71. Haller, *The Rise of Puritanism*, 10, 11. Those sympathetic with Cartwright's polity gathered together in London and composed a pamphlet under the auspices of John Field and Thomas Wilcox in 1572, entitled "An Admonition to the Parliament." The pamphlet was addressed to the Parliament and called for the reformation of the church as its most essential duty. It called for the "uniformity of all Protestant Churches" under a presbyterian model, which would supersede the current polity of the Church of England. It felt that the rule of bishops was subject to corruption, and it demanded a total overhaul of the system. In the new system, ministers would not receive a call from the bishops at large or exist outside the local fellowship, enjoying benefits and privileges. They would serve in a specific church, based upon the election and ordination of that church. "An Admonition to the Parliament," reprinted in *Puritan Manifestoes: A Study of the Origin of the Puritan Revolt*, W. H. Fere and C. E. Douglas (New York: Burt Franklin, 1972) xxx, 8-13, 19.
72. *Cartwrightiana*, A. Peel and L. Carlson (ed.) (London: George Allen and Unwin LTD, 1951) 25-27. During the 1560s and 1570s, Puritans fought to adopt a presbyterian form of government, hoping to place control of the Church of England

within the care of local congregations and ministerial associations, but Parliament blocked their effort. William and Youngs, *The Congregationalists*, 16, 17.

73. *Cartwrightiana*, 48ff., 58ff., 68, 69, 74. He makes these comments in two letters: one to Robert Harrison, which Browne copies and then sends a reply, and the other to his sister-in-law, Anne Stubbe, who has joined the separatist movement.
74. *Cartwrightiana*, 2, 3, 7, 19.
75. [W. Travers], *A directory of Church-government* (London, 1644) [1]; W. Travers, *A Full and Plaine Declaration of Ecclesiastical Discipline* (Reprinted, 1617) 5, 8.
76. W. Travers. *A Defence of the Ecclesiastical Discipline ordained of God to be used in his Church* (1588) 76ff.
77. [Travers], *A directory*, [1].
78. *A Defence*, 14, 15.
79. *A Defence*, 10, 11.
80. *A Defence*, 17.
81. *A directory*, [1].
82. Ibid., 38, 72, 73, 104; *A Defence*, 72.
83. *A Defence*, 72; *A directory*, [2].
84. *A Defence*, 34, 35.
85. *A directory*, [2, 3, 103]. The magistrate has the duty to provide for the "order of Religion," which includes the establishing of sound doctrine, appointing officers, and calling an assembly of elders unto a synod. This duty is not essential to the well-being of the church, which subsists in perfect order without it, as it did before the times of Constantine. *A Directory*, [103]; *A Defence*, 148, 167-69. There is some talk of dividing church and state, just as Levi and Judah, Moses and Aaron held separate offices in OT times. The leadership of the church is told not to meddle in civil affairs. The magistrate is directed toward the physical needs of the state as the primary responsibility of the office. *A directory*, [41-43, 97]; *A Defence*, 90.
86. *A directory*, [99-101].
87. *A directory*, [1].
88. *A directory*, [3]. Synods and conferences play a more vital role in presbyterian polity than they do among the separatists. *A directory*, [18ff.].
89. *A directory*, [5]; *A Full and Plaine Declaration*, 19ff.; *A Defence*, 89, 90.
90. *A directory*, [24ff.].
91. *A directory*, [2, 13]; *A Defence*, 45; *A Full and Plaine Declaration*, 88, 105.
92. *A Full and Plaine Declaration*, 23, 28, 29; *A directory*, [3].
93. Ibid., 28, 29.
94. *A Defence*, 21, 22, 27; "An Admonition to the Parliament," 19.
95. J. Delumeau, *Naissance et affirmation de la Reforme* (Paris: Presses Universitaires de France, 1968) 147; J. V. Skalnik, "Ramus and Reform: The End of the Renaissance and the Origins of the Old Regime" (PhD, diss., University of Virginia, 1990) 203, 204.
96. J. Moltmann, "Zur Bedeutung der Petrus Ramus für Philosophie und Theologie im Calvinismus," *Zeitschrift für Kirchengeschechte* 1968 (68):296, 297.
97. Perry Miller was the first to stress his impact on Puritans in the 1930s. *The New England Mind: The Seventeenth Century* (Cambridge: Harvard University Press, 1963) 1.116ff. This work was first published in 1939. See W. J. Ong, *Ramus and Talon Inventory* (Cambridge, MA: Harvard University Press, 1958) 523, 524; D. McKim, "The Function of Ramism in William Perkin's Theology," *The Sixteenth Century Journal* 16, no. 4 (1986): 503-505.
98. Skalnik, "Ramus and Reform," 97, 102, 195-99.

99. P. Ramus, *De Religione Christina Libri IV* (Frankfurt: Minera GMBH, 1969) 1.3; *The Logike of the Most Excellent Philosopher P. Ramus Martyr*, R. MacIlmaine (trans.), C. M. Dunn (ed.) (Northridge, CA: San Fernando Valley State College, 1969) 1.3; 2.2 (10, 41); P. Lobstein, *Petrus Ramus als Theologe* (Strassburg: C. F. Schmidt, 1878) 12; F. P. Graves, *Peter Ramus and the Educational Reformation of the Sixteenth Century* (New York: The Macmillan Co., 1912) 130,138, 155; Miller, *The New England Mind*, 1.126ff.; Skalnik, "Ramus and Reform," 82, 83. Along with the impact of his dichotomies, one can discern among the Puritans an influence from his interest in praxis and the empirical world. He was called "usuarius" by his opponents as he appealed to the ordinary citizen and considered practice the real end of all method. His method of logic was intended for the real world around us.
100. *Cartwrightiana*, 152.
101. J. G. Rechten, "Antithetical Literary Structures in the Reformation Theology of Walter Travers," *The Sixteenth Century Journal* 8, no. 1 (April 1977): 52, 53, 58, 59.
102. See pp. 22, 23. Walter Org lists Browne as a Ramist. *Ramus and Talon Inventory*, 514.
103. Ong, *Ramus and Talon Inventory*, 521. Christopher Hill finds "most of the great English Puritans . . . followers of Ramus," including Perkins, Chaderton, George Downham, Ames, and Milton. "Downham published his *Commentarius in Rami Dialectiam* at Frankfort in 1610." *Intellectual Origins of the English Revolution* (Oxford: At the Clarendon Press, 1965) 292, 293.
104. Skalnik, "Ramus and Reform," 71, 134, 145, 148.
105. Ibid., 8, 38, 39, 126ff.
106. Graves, *Peter Ramus and the Educational Reformation*, 24, 25. Ramus tries to show that Christianity is compatible with Plato and Graeco-Roman philosophy. Lobstein, *Petrus Ramus*, 11, 16, 76, 77.
107. Ibid., 26, 30.
108. G. Huppert, "Peter Ramus: The Humanist as Philosophe," *Modern Language Quarterly* 51 (1990): 216, 217.
109. "Bèze à Pierre Ramus" (Dec. 1579), in *Correspondance de Théodore de Bèze,* recueillie par H. Aubert, publiée par A. Dufour, B. Nicollier, et C. Chimelli (Genève: Droz: 1983) 11.295 (810).
110. This analysis agrees with Charles Waddington's general assessment. *Ramus: sa vie, ses écrits et ses opinions* (Paris: Libraire de Ch. Meyrueis et ce, 1855).
111. P. Ramus, *Collectaneae praefationes, epistolae, orations* (Hildesheim: G. Olms, 1969) 257-58.
112. It connects the sacraments to military oaths and relates baptism to circumcision much like the theologians in Zurich. It follows Zwingli's memorial Eucharist and displays some of the semi-Pelagian tendencies of Bullinger. *De Religione Christiana,* 265ff., 271, 272, 279 (4.3, 5, 6); Lobstein, *Petrus Ramus als Theologe*, 38, 39, 74, 75; Moltmann, "Zur Bedeutung des Petrus Ramus," 304-06, 317. For the position of Zurich on the relation of covenant/oath, baptism, and circumcision, see my book *Calvinism, Federalism, and Scholasticism: A Study of the Reformed Doctrine of Covenant* (Bern and New York: Peter Lang, 1988) 118ff. For Zwingli's memorial Eucharist and Bullinger's semi-Pelagianism, see my other book *The Catholic Roots of the Protestant Gospel: Encounter between the Middle Ages and the Reformation* (Leiden and New York: E. J. Brill, 1995) 32-35, 53-60, 87-90.
113. Skalink, "Ramus and Reform," 217, 232, 332.
114. The letter is reprinted in Waddington, *Ramus*, 433-35.

115. Speculation surrounds the death of Ramus. Waddington and Graves believe that he was killed by a jealous rival (Jacques Charpentier), but others disagree and seem to think that his death was probably due to his open association with the Huguenots. Waddington, *Ramus*, chap. 9; Graves, *Peter Ramus*, 105-107; W. J. Ong, *Ramus, Method, and the Decay of Dialogue: From the Art of Discourse to the Art of Reason* (Cambridge, MA: Harvard University Press, 1983) 28; Skalink, "Ramus and Reform," 44.
116. *Cartwrightiana*, 2.
117. Travers, *A Defence*, 86.
118. P. Denis et J. Rott, *Jean Morély (ca. 1524-ca. 1594) et l'utopie d'une démocratie dans l'Eglise* (Genève: Droz, 1993) 75, 81, 199ff.
119. R. M. Kingdon, *Geneva and the Consolidation of the French Protestant Movement* (Madison, WI: The University of Wisconsin Press, 1967) 131-34.
120. *The Theological Works of Herbert Thorndike* (Oxford: John Henry Parker, 1894) 1/2. 445, 446. Scholarship contains some division on the exact nature of the influence. Kingdon sees a possible link between Ramus, Morély, and the Congregationalists. Kingdon, *Geneva and the Consolidation,* 129. Denis and Rott reject any connection between Morély and later democracy, and contend that Morély died a failure. They point to several differences between Morély and the Congregationalists. One, Morély believed that the state should interfere with the church. Two, Morély emphasized the importance of the synod and diocese. Three, Morély lacked the spirit of separatism with its emphasis upon an exclusive membership. Denis et Rott, *Jean Morély,* 82, 83, 208. However, none of these reasons seem convincing. It is true that Morély presents a more unified vision of the church, but no group is a monolith, especially during its inception, and the Congregationalists contain different relations to each of the three items listed above, as already seen in Browne and Harrison. Besides, no influence walks of all fours, and most movements are affected by more than one linear cause. This work tries to display some of the more apparent or important influences on the Congregationalists and believes that the stature of Ramus, along with the anti-authoritarian texture of his work and a knowledge of his democratic principles would serve among them as an impetus toward democratic reform, not that the Congregationalists slavishly copied him or anyone else.
121. Denis et Rott, *Jean Morély*, 17, 27, 28; R. Kingdon, "Calvinism and Democracy," in *The Heritage of John Calvin: Heritage Hall Lectures 1960-70*, J. H. Bratt (ed.) (Grand Rapids: William B. Eerdmans, 1973) 181, 182.
122. R. Kingdon, *Geneva and the Consolidation*, 82ff.; Denis et Rott, *Jean Morély*, 62.
123. Denis et Rott, *Jean Morély*, 48, 49.
124. Ibid., 53-56, 155-57, 166, 167.
125. *Confessio Fidei Gallicana*, in P. Schaff, *The Creeds of Christendom* (Grand Rapids, MI: Baker Book House, 1977) art. XXXII (3.378). It makes all pastors equal [art. XXX (3.377)].
126. J. Quick, *Synodicon in Gallia Reformata* (London, 1692) 1.23, 27 (I, 2 and III, 7).
127. Denis et Rott, *Jean Morély*, 59-65.
128. J. Quick, *Synodicon*, 1.56, 57 (II).
129. Ibid., 1.11-13 (VII, 3, 4, 12). In Geneva Calvin established an ecclesiastical order with teaching doctors, preaching pastors, disciplining elders, and deacons in charge of charity. He served as the moderator of the company of pastors, which met once a week and elected pastors when there was a vacancy. The elders met once a week with the company in a body called the Consistory. It handled discipline in the

church, although Calvin had to fight the civil government to keep it from interfering with its power. The basic form of discipline was excommunication or denial of the sacraments. (The church was not allowed to inflict corporeal punishment.) Calvin did attend city council meetings, although he had no official position and hoped to keep the realms of church and state separate. Cf. *Institutio* [in *Opera quae supersunt omnia* (Brunsvigae: C.A. Schwetschke et Filium, 1864)] 4.3.4, 8; 4.1; 9.3, 4. In his *Institutes*, the ideal form of election involves a symbiosis between the people and the clergy and appears less heavy-handed than Beza's concept. *Inst.* 4.3.15; 4.12. See Calvin's commentaries on Deut. 1:14-16 and Mic. 5:5, where he speaks of the common consent of the people establishing civil government. In a letter to Bullinger (Nov. 13, 1572) Beza describes his concept of polity as *aristocratia*. In his system, the church would rubber-stamp the decisions of others. A member of the church would have an eight-day waiting period to bring an objection against the candidate, who was selected by the company of pastors. Kingdon, *Geneva and the Consolidation*, 38, 39, 53, 209, 210, 212. (Kingdon reprints the letter to Bullinger in Appendix II, 209-15.) The synods at Orléans, Paris, Rochelle, and Nîmes fell under the auspices of Geneva and repeated its fundamental designs for the church. They speak of ministers and professors of divinity determining doctrinal controversies, a consistory of ministers and elders insuring the discipline of the church, and a colloquy of ministers choosing the pastors of each church, subject to the objection of the people. Quick, *Synodicon*, 1.23 (I, 2), 58, 59 (III), 96 (VII, 3, 7), 106-08 (III, 17; IV, 18; V, 19).

130. J. Morély, *Traicté de la discipline & police Chrestienne* (Lyon: Ian de Tournes, 1562) preface; *De Ecclesiae ordine*, 1.77ff., 83ff.; Dennis and Rott, *Jean Morély*, 330-32 This latter work is found as no. 4361 in the Department des Manuscripts de la Bibliothèque Nationale de Paris and is summarized for our convenience by Denis and Rott.
131. Ibid., 174, 175, 272. These two words are used continually in the work.
132. Ibid., 325.
133. R. Kingdon, *Geneva and Consolidation*, 59.
134. *Traicté*, preface. Denis wishes to connect Morély with Aristotle and Athens, but there is little evidence of this. Morély is aware of Graeco-Roman democracy and makes a brief mention of it (115, 183). He uses the word democracy a couple of times in connection with his polity, although the term is pejorative at this time and best to avoid. At one point he rejects the term as an inappropriate description of his view, since he advocates living under the rules and laws of Christ and receiving advice from pastors and elders (32, 33). Kingdon, "Calvinism and Democracy," 181, 187. His later work, *De ecclesiae ordine*, 2.1-6, follows an Aristotelian form of mixed government when it speaks of the church's polity consisting of a leader, a few administrators, and the people, although the precise source is difficult to identify. P. Denis, "Penser la démocratie au XVIe siècle: Morély, Aristote et la Réforme," *Bulletin de la société de l' Histoire du Protestantisme Français* 137e anée (jullet-septembre 1991) 373-75; Denis et Rott, *Jean Morély*, 131-33, 333, 334. But the *Traicté* makes scant reference to the Graeco-Roman world and its democracy and only by way of comparison. It is better to understand the treatise as working within its natural setting and unfolding a Protestant understanding of Scripture. The work provides ample testimony to this matrix. The democratic ideals develop naturally from Protestant theology and do not require outside or foreign sources to explain it.
135. *Traicté*, preface. He finds the Bible practical. He finds philosophy filled with worthless speculations, which have little to do with public or private life. It has no "*vtilité*." Ibid., 323, 324.

136. *Traicté*, 31, 129, 182.
137. *Traicté*, 131, 132.
138. *Traicté*, 175, 176.
139. *Traicté*, 72.
140. *Traicté*, 65.
141. *Traicté*, 18, 280.
142. *Traicté*, 25, 65, 66.
143. *Traicté*, 20, 21, 219, 279, 280.
144. *Traicté*, 216, 267.
145. *Traicté*, 269.
146. *Traicté*, 177-79. He takes on Cyprian for believing we must submit to priests, and Jerome for promoting the inequality of pastors (276ff.).
147. *Traicté*, 266ff. (*quatrieme livre*), 275, 279. He even suggests the possibility of term limits to preserve equality (283ff.).
148. *Traicté*, 107.
149. *Traicté*, 78, 213; Denis, *Penser la démocratie*, 382ff.
150. *Traicté*,76-78.
151. *Traicté*, 51-53, 61, 62; Kingdon, *Geneva and Consolidation*, 51-53.
152. *Traicté*, 118, 289, 294.
153. *Traicté*, 160, 213, 314. Cf. *Traicté*, 297, 298. He relates the history of bishops usurping the rights of the church and abusing the practice of excommunication (155ff.).
154. *Traicté*, 60-62, 170.
155. *Traicté*, 116, 209, 210; Kingdon, *Geneva and Consolidation*, 53, 54.
156. *Traicté*, 46, 60ff., 78; Denis, "Penser la démocratie," 381, 382.
157. *Traicté*, 123, 278; "Jean de Lestre à Beze" (March 19, 1572), in *Correspondance de Théodore de Bèze*, recueillie par H. Aubert, publiée par A. Dufour et B. Nicollier (Genève: Droz, 1968) 13.96 (909). Denis and Rott consider Aristotle's *Politics* (1301^{b}29-1302^{a}8) the basic source of inspiration behind this idea, but the precise source is hard to identify. It clearly is a phrase used in the circle of Morély and Ramus. *Jean Morély*, 170, 337, 338. In *De ecclesiae ordine*, 2.68ff., Morély limits the vote to confirmed believers, who make a public confession, and he excludes vile sinners, dishonest merchants, women, and children under fifteen years of age from participation. Denis, "Penser la démocratie," 371, 378.
158. *Traicté*, 119.
159. *Traicté*, 114.
160. *Traicté*, 246-48. These councils are subject to the "continual election" and review of the church, so they will not deteriorate into oligarchies.
161. Kingdon, *Geneva and Consolidation*, 55, 58.
162. *Traicté*, 12.
163. *Traicté*, 3, 4, 8, 16, 20, 25, 41, 96, 101, 102; Denis et Rott, *Jean Morély*, 342, 343 (*De ecclesiae ordine*, 3.71, 72). When it comes to church discipline, the magistrate is considered no more than a member and is subject to ecclesiastical reproof, even excommunication. *Traicté*, 146, 171, 286, 287, 301.
164. *Traicté*, 218.
165. *Journal of Sir Francis Walsingham, From Dec. 1570 to April 1583*, C. T. Martin (ed.) (New York: Johnson Reprint Corp., 1968) 9, 13; Denis et Rott, *Jean Morély*, 73, 74 (*De ecclesiae ordine*, 1.29). We owe a debt of gratitude to Jean Rott and Philippe Denis for their excellent historical research, even though we must depart from some of their conclusions. It was Jean Rott who found the work *De ecclesiae ordine* in Paris, along with certain materials that speak of his later years, unravel-

ing a mystery that long plagued scholars concerning the whereabouts of Morély after the massacre (12-14).

166. Denis et Rott, *Jean Morély*, 77-81, 93 (*De ecclesiae ordine*, 1.33, 34). At this point in his career, he is more willing to live with bishops and dioceses as long as they are subject to elections and abuses are curtailed. He disapproves of separatism and autonomous churches. Ibid., 337-41 (*De ecclesiae ordine*, 2.14ff., 85, 86, 111ff.).
167. Cf. Ibid., 208.
168. Clarendon, *The History of the Rebellion and Civil War in England* (Oxford University Press, 1840) 349, 350.
169. Most Americans today have not read or heard of Robert Browme, John Locke, or Montesquieu, but no one can discard the profound influence these men exerted over the American concept of government. Their impact is conveyed through the many secondary sources that come together, none of which are copied in a slavish manner and all of which are forged together to create their own unique synthesis.
170. Switzerland provided the political context for the covenant to become a theological idea. The three mountain republics—Uri, Schwyz, and Unterwalden—established a confederacy in 1291 by way of covenant (*bundesbrief*) and oath (*coniuratio*). This confederacy became the foundation of the Helvetic Confederation, which came to include Luzern (1332), Zurich (1351), Glarus and Zug (1352), Berg (1353), and more cantons in the centuries to come. It involved a series of covenants, which served to unify laws, codes, policies, treaties, and military operations. The alliance was disrupted at the beginning of the Reformation but resumed later in 1815 during more secular times. D. J. Elazar, *Covenant & Commonwealth: From Christian Separation through the Protestant Reformation* (New Brunswick, NJ: Transaction Publications, 1996) 91-100, 163. The precise origin of the covenant is a mystery.
171. Z 4.218, 222-24.
172. Z 2.120, 478; 3.227, 228, 341. Zwingli depicts baptism as an *usserlich pflichts zeichen* or *pundtszeichen*, by which the candidate pledges service to God. Z 3.759-61. His usage of the term *sacramentum* suggests this meaning. The church since the days of Tertullian used the term to describe baptism, although the earlier usage related more to the Greek concept of *mysterion* and less to a solemn promise or oath. Balthasar Hubmaier, a pastor from Waldshut, presented Zwingli with the first systematic defense of baptism from an Anabaptist point of view. He refers to the sacrament as an *offenliche zeücknuss* of inward faith and an *eüsserlich pflicht* or *verpflichtung* of our submission to the word of Christ and discipline of the church. *Schriften*, in *Quellen und Forschungen zur Reformationsgeschichte*, G. Westin and T. Bergsten (Hrsg.) (Gütersloh: G. Mohn, 1962) 111, 112, 121, 145, 210, 642, 644, 645, 650-52; C. Windhorst, *Täuferisches Taufverständnis* (Leiden: E. J. Brill, 1976) 30, 31, 130, 131, 226. Others connected baptism with the concept of a pledge or covenant at the time, including Erasmus, Luther, and Müntzer. The latter recast his whole ecclesiastical society into a league of the elect. Luther's translation of 1 Pet. 3:21 as a "*Bund eines guten gewissen mit Gott*" proved an inspiration to the Anabaptists in connecting baptism and covenant. WA 2.731-37; L. Zuck, "Anabaptist Revolution through the Covenant in the Sixteenth Century Continental Protestantism" (PhD diss., Yale University, 1954) 221; R. S. Armour, *Anabaptist Baptism: A Representative Study* (Scottsdale, PA: Herald Press, 1966) 118.
173. Z 8.569-71.

174. Z 3.773, 823; 4.219, 588, 632; 6/1.48; 8.271. His *Taufbüchlein* conjoins baptism with circumcision, and his *Antwort über Balthasar Hubmaier* posits a fundamental unity of the covenant throughout Scripture. J. W. Baker, *Heinrich Bullinger and the Covenant: The Other Reformed Tradition* (Athens: Ohio University Press, 1980) 2.
175. Z. 6/1.156-58, 163-69; G. Shrenk, *Gottesreich und Bund im älteren Protestantismus: vornehmlich bei Johannes Cocceius* (Gütersloh: Bertelsmann, 1923); J. W. Cottrell, "Covenant and Baptism in the Theology of Huldreich Zwingli" (PhD diss., Princeton Theological Seminary, 1971).
176. H. Bullinger, *De Testamento seu foedere Dei unico & aeterno* (Tiguri: C. Frosch, 1534) 24^{v}, 25^{v}, 28^{r}; E. G. Korff, *Die Anfänge der foederaltheologie und ihre erste Ausgestaltung in Zürich und Holland* (Bonn: E. Eisele, 1908). Baker finds in Bullinger some emphasis on the covenant as a standard for societal relationships, although he admits that Bullinger does not forge a specific *political* covenant and does not bind the ruler to the people in this way. "Faces of Federalism: From Bullinger to Jefferson," *The Journal of Federalism* (Fall 2000): 27; "Covenant and Community in the Thought of Heinrich Bullinger," in *Covenant Connection: From Federal Theology to Modern Federalism*, D. J. Elazar and J. Kincaid (ed.) (Landham and Oxford: Lexington Books, 2000) 19-25. The Importance of Bullinger is found in his *De Testamento*, which contains no overt political message. The work is important because it spreads the message of covenant and the message contains political ramifications for those who deconstruct it in that way.
177. Strehle, *The Catholic Roots of the Protestant Gospel*, 53-58; CR 8.23ff.; 14.208-10, 483-89.
178. Bullinger, *De Testamento*, 5^{v}, 11^{v}, 16^{r}, 44^{r}; *Sermonum decades quinque* (Tiguri: C. Frosch., 1567) 121b; Baker, *Heinrich Bullinger and the Covenant*, 13, 16, 18, 87, 226. Leonard J. Trinterud suggested the bilateral nature of Bullinger's covenant in a 1951 article and found scholarly support for his belief in the work of Jens Møller, Kenneth Hagen, J. Wayne Baker, and myself. Baker served as the main apostle of the thesis in the book just cited, and I demonstrated the wide-dissemination of Bullinger's concept of covenant among the scholastics of the sixteenth and seventeenth centuries. L. J. Trinterud, "The Origin of Puritanism," *Church History* 20 (1951); K. Hagen, "From Testament to Covenant," *Sixteenth Century Journal* 3 (April 1972); J. G. Møller, "The Beginnings of the Puritan Covenant," *Journal of Ecclesiastical History* 14 (April 1963); Strehle, *Calvinism, Federalism, and Scholasticism*; Elazar, *Covenant & Commonwealth*, 178, 179.
179. Friedrich Lampe begins his brief discussion of the covenant in history with Bullinger and his *De Testamento*. *Geheimnis des Gnaden-Bunds* (Bremen: Nathanael Saurmann, 1715) 1.18-20. The influence of Bullinger is seen throughout its history in a number of areas, but the bilateral nature of the covenant provides the most telltale sign. With a few notable exceptions (e.g., Gaspar Olevian), the Reformed follow Bullinger and speak of he covenant as a *mutua pactio mutuis obligationibus*. Strehle, *The Catholic Roots of the Protestant Gospel*, 59, 60. Besides the bilateral nature one can see his influence upon the subsequent Reformed tradition in its emphasis upon the unity of the biblical message, the beginnings of the covenant in the garden, the importance of the Abrahamic covenant, the relationship between baptism and circumcision, and the affinity between the OT State and NT Church. Strehle, *Calvinism, Federalism, and Scholasticism*, 134ff. According to Baker, an appendix of Bullinger's NT commentary contains *De Testamento* up until the fifth edition in 1558, making the work and its ideas widely available. "Faces of Federalism," 28 (fn. 5), 32 (fn. 24).

180. A good illustration of the problem is the "Half-way Covenant." The Puritans of New England debated whether they should baptize the children of those who had not become "visible saints" or joined the church as adults, even though these parents had received the sacrament in their youth. According to the theology of Bullinger, these parents would no longer be considered members of Christ's body. There is no theological problem with them losing their salvation in the course of time if they spurn the covenant later in life. *De Testamento*, 8^r-9^r. However, the Puritans followed John Calvin's doctrine of predestination and eternal security, which considered the beginning, middle, and end of salvation the work of God, allowing no room for synergism. In this scheme, there was no room for a child to grow up and become a reprobate as an adult if it received the covenant of grace through baptism. The Puritans were left with an arresting contradiction in their theology when the seal of God upon a baptized infant did not manifest its visible fruit in adulthood.

181. D. Fenner, *Sacra Theologia* (T. Dawson, 1585?) 87, 88.; J. G. Møller, "The Beginnings of Puritan Covenant Theology," 58; C. J. Somerville, "Conversion versus the Early Puritan Covenant of Grace," *Journal of Presbyterian History* 44 (1966): 185.

182. *The Workes of that Famous and Worthy Minister of Christ in the Universitie of Cambridge, Mr. William Perkins* (London: Iohn Legatt, 1626) 1.32, 70, 164, 165, 576, 610, 611; 2.74, 75. There are more editions of Perkins' works in England than any other author. A. W. Pollard and G. R. Regrave, *A Short-Title Catalogue of Books Printed in England, Scotland, & Ireland and of English Books Printed Abroad 1475-1640* (London: The Bibliographical Society, 1926) 450-52; Somerville, "Conversion versus the Early Puritan Covenant of Grace," 51.

183. Perkins, *Workes*, 3.415, 420. An anonymous work, *The Reformation of religion by Josiah* (1590) also speaks of a national covenant. Fenner speaks of the laws of the republic in terms of a two-fold covenant. The first part is made between God and the republic where *all* the people, both great and small, swear to follow God under the penalty of death. The second part is forged among the people themselves, in which they swear to rule and act justly under the penalty of removal (death?) from the community (*tollantur è medio*). It is the role of the *Ephori* or an assembly of the people, whether through peaceful means or warfare, to remove a king who undermines the worship of God, oppresses the people, or transgresses the *pacta*. *Sacra Theologica*, 161, 162, 185-87, 243; M. McGiffert, "Covenant, Crown, and Commons in Elizabethan Puritanism," in *The Covenant Connection*, 170, 171, 177-79. Other Continental theologians speak like Fenner of the Ephors of Sparta as providing checks and censors on the king, including Calvin, Hotman, Beza, Mornay, and Althusius, all of whom we will discuss in the third chapter. Mornay provides a similar analysis of the two-fold nature of the covenant in society and sees society itself as a series of *pacta*. Fenner's church polity runs along the lines of Thomas Cartwright and Theodore Beza. *Sacra Theologica*, 243, 244. T. D. Bozeman sees within Cartwright and John Knewstub a nascent movement toward a national covenant, which includes a warning of divine displeasure over its transgression and a call to days of fasting and prayer. The early seventeenth century gives rise to a number of Puritan divines who bind the nation into a covenant with God and call for its renewal (or else). T. D. Bozeman, "Federal Theology and 'National Covenant': An Elizabethan Presbyterian Case Study," Church History 61(1992): 394-407; E. Vallance, Revolutionary England and the National Covenant: State Oaths, Protestantism and the Political Nation, 1553-1682 (Woodbridge, Suffolk: The Boydell Press, 2005) 31-35. Resistance theory

is not widespread until the 1630s/1640s in Britain. J. P. Sommerville, *Royalists & Patriots: Politics and Ideology in England 1603-1640* (London and New York: Longman, 1999) 71-74.

184. "Of Reformation in England," in *The Works of John Milton* (New York: Columbia University Press, 1932) 3/1.11, 24-26, 67; "Of Prelatical Episcopacy," 3/1.83-85, 90, 95, 96; "The Reason of Church-government Urg'd against Prelaty," 3/1.201. All works are cited from the Columbia University edition.
185. Ibid., 30ff.; "Of Prelatical Episcopacy," 3/1.102-104; "The Reason of Church-government,"3/1.183ff.
186. "The Reason of Church-government," 3/1.273. He prefers a presbyterian form of government. Ibid., 253, 254.
187. Ibid., 257ff.
188. "The Doctrine and Discipline of Divorce," 3/2.409-11, 415, 427. He sees the patriarchs of old sending away unbelievers [Abraham (Hagar), David (Michal), Moses (Zippora), Ezra (Gentile wives), et al.]. He finds idolatry a righteous pretext for divorce, more than adultery.
189. Ibid., 400-402.
190. Ibid., 391, 392, 403, 404, 410, 411.
191. Ibid., 489.
192. Ibid., 480.
193. Hugh Peter, Mrs. Attaway, Francis Osborne, and John Locke to name a few. Hill, *The World Turned Upside Down*, 253; J. T. Johnson, "The Covenant Idea and the Puritan View of Marriage," *Journal of the History of Ideas* 32, no. 1 (Jan.-March 1971): 107, 116-118; M. Walzer, *The Revolution of the Saints: A Study in the Origin of Radical Politics* (Cambridge, MA: Harvard University Press, 1965) 196; J. Locke, *Two Treatises on Government*, M. Goldie (ed.) (London: Everyman, 2003) xxvi, 153-55.
194. Hill, *The Intellectual Origins of the English Revolution*, 268.
195. Hill, *Puritanism and Revolution*, 134; *The Intellectual Origins of the English Revolution*, 276, 280-83; H. H. Rowen, *The Low Countries in Early Modern Times: A Documentary History* (New York: Harper and Row, 1971) 44; Elazar, *Covenant & Commonwealth*, 213, 214, 217, 222.
196. Elazar, *Covenant & Commonwealth*, 45-48.

2

Power to the People: The Origin of Democratic and Federal Government

Parliament

The doctrine of covenant permeated all aspects of ecclesiastical, social, and political thought by the time of the Puritan Revolution in the middle of the seventeenth century. Its political application is seen from the very beginning of the revolution as the Long Parliament opens its session on Nov. 17, 1640, with sermons preached by Cornelius Burges and Stephan Marshall, exhorting the Parliament and the people to forge a covenant with God.[1] Both divines are frustrated with the pace of reform and need some device to insure its future success. They commend the efforts of Edward VI and Elizabeth I, but neither of these monarchs were able to rid the land of "Papist Idolatry" and create a pure church without mixture.[2] In order to stop the "ebbings and flowings" and find full deliverance from "Babylon,"[3] it is necessary to forge an "indissoluble covenant" with God, just like the people of old.[4] The Jews entered into an "everlasting covenant" when they were delivered from Babylon (Jer. 50:5, Neh. 9 and 10), binding themselves together through a public and solemn fast, and all England is bound to do likewise as the people of God.[5] It is a sacred duty to join together as a nation by way of covenant.[6] It is the neglect of this duty that brought failure in the past.[7] While God must take the initiative in choosing a people, it remains a sacred obligation to make a "voluntary" and "mutual" covenant, binding the people to accept their responsibilities and pay what is stipulated.[8]

Parliament tried to follow much of the advice of Burges and Marshall about the need and manner for conducting reform. It began its session by issuing fast days on a monthly basis.[9] It forged a solemn league or covenant with Scotland in September of 1643, and most of its members looked to the covenant as a means of encouraging reform, promoting liberty, extirpating the hierarchy of bishops, and constructing a just and responsible society.[10] It wanted to fulfill its noble commission and reform both church and state, but the expectations never came to fruition in any definite, concrete, or lasting way. It always seemed to vacillate between alternatives. For example, the majority of the delegates seemed to favor the presbyterian model, which wanted some sense of religious unity throughout the kingdom and some power within the presbytery or classis over matters such as discipline and ordination—at least more than what the Congregationalists had in mind.[11] The Presbyterians wanted to limit the power of individual congregations to the mere acceptance or rejection of the hierarchy's decision,[12] while the Congregationalists wanted the local elders and laity to run their own churches. But even this distinction between the Presbyterians and Congregationalists was not always so clear in the sixteenth and seventeenth centuries. The Presbyterians seemed to claim *jus divinum* for their polity and wanted to establish a network of responsibility much like the old Episcopalian system, but then they would reverse themselves and sound much like the Congregationalists when speaking of the local church and its elective powers. There was no clear plan or establishment in mind, and no settled form of governance to insure stability. Even scholars trying to sort out the chaos use denominational distinctions as little more than anachronisms for this early stage of Protestantism with so-called "Presbyterians" attending "Independent" churches and vice versa. Any scholastic distinction refers to the fuzzy matter of emphasis upon local authority, consociation, and leadership in ecclesiology, all of which have a place of some merit and varying degrees of mixture in their accounts.[13]

Some members expressed a certain amount of sympathy toward the Congregationalists and their plight. John Goodwin emphasized the advice of Gamaliel in Acts 5, who thought it best to tolerate the "Way" in the absence of clear evidence and see "if the purpose or activity is of human origin."[14] Many Presbyterian ministers were concerned about losing their sheep to other pastors, but Goodwin felt their concern was over-exercised. God's people hear the voice of their Shepherd, and the truth will triumph in the end. It is best to let peace reign between the two fellowships without resorting to violence, else "we might be found fighting against God."[15] The Congregationalists were invited to participate in the Westminster Assembly as delegates and used the opportunity to call for the same spirit of toleration expressed by Goodwin and others. In *An Apologeticall Narration* (1643), they presented their position as consonant with the Reformed churches abroad, where they spent a number of years in exile as faithful servants of the movement.[16] They thought of themselves as moderates, steering "a middle way betwixt that which is falsly charged on us, Brownisme; and that which is the contention of these times, the authoritative Presbyteriall Government."[17] It was their opponents who label them as Brownists, Separatists, and Independents in order to mislead the people and create a negative stereotype of the movement as extreme or radical.[18] These delegates wished to distance themselves from the radical posture and image of their group associated with its earlier days. They wished to sever ties with a severe form of separatism, which would label much of the established church as anti-Christian and create independent churches with no sense of accountability.[19] They provided each church with the freedom to run its own affairs but distanced themselves from radical expressions by subjecting it to the same constraints as other forms of polity. They subjected each church to the reproof of other churches if it miscarried justice, and they proceeded to cite a specific instance where this very policy was enacted, displaying how the movement now functions in accordance with the Reformed understanding of the church today.[20]

The Congregationalists gained more and more power in Parliament after 1643 due to the ascendancy of Oliver Cromwell and his New Model Army.[21] Military events dictated a new strategy, which found Parliament more interested in appeasing the radical army than the Scottish commissioners. Cromwell's army was dominated by these Independents or Non-Comformists, who rejected the call for religious uniformity, demanded an end to the gathering of state-sponsored tithes, and promoted the cause of religious liberty.[22] Cromwell's victory dealt a decided blow to the Presbyterian aspirations for a uniform polity throughout England as he directed the parties to settle their disputes and make peace. Cromwell wanted as much liberty as possible, favoring a society in which all could worship as they please—Presbyterians, Congregationalists, Quakers, Catholics, and Anglicans alike.[23] He believed that the Spirit provided unmediated inspiration to all Christians as priests before God and received the initial impetus for his own revolution from this very source. He aligned himself with the "Independents" as the particular group of his own affections. His army consisted of commoners with like-minded, Congregationalist convictions.[24] According to Richard Baxter, they spoke in idealistic terms concerning liberty of conscience, the abolition of tithes, a civil magistrate who had no ecclesiastical power, and the establishment of democracy throughout the land in both church and state.[25] But Cromwell and his compatriots could never curb the chaos of their revolution and establish its ideals in a specific form of governance. Cromwell was forced to become more conservative than the ideology of his earlier, radical days as a member of Parliament would demand. As the protector, he was caught between the Independents of his army and the need to preserve the unity of a society that was coming unglued and unprepared for a radical break with the past.[26] At the Putney debates he ended up turning his back upon the Levellers, who wished to push the movement into more and more radical, democratic directions. He wanted to restore the free elections of Parliament ("None can desire it more than I"), but he was not a political ideologue. He was not sure the people were ready to assume this responsibility and maybe feared that the outcome of free elections would result in a defeat of reform or a return of the Stuart monarchy.[27] He and his cohorts tried to move with dexterity between factions, but in trying to please all sides they never formulated a permanent structure of governance that could withstand the test of time, and they seemed to resign themselves to reform the old system of king and Parliament.[28] Because of the lack of structure, the revolution did not survive the death of Cromwell in any overt form. The Restoration witnessed the return of the monarchy in Charles II (1660-85) and James II (1685-88). Regicides were drawn, quartered, and hanged, including Cromwell's corpse at Tyburn. The Act of Uniformity (1662) reinstated the old policy of persecuting the Congregationalists and other dissidents, leaving America as the only place they could worship unmolested.[29] However, despite the defeat of Puritanism, the social agenda of the Puritans gained triumph over England and its church in a multitude of ways. The monopoly of the national church, the power of the bishops, the High Commission, and the Star Chamber were broken forever. Industrial monopolies were overthrown, and government interference in the market place ended. The seeds of liberty were planted in the hearts and affections of the people, assuring its place in the society to come, regardless of the specific form its spirit might inhabit. The people had changed, the churches were filled with the message of freedom, and there was no going back to the times of religious and political tyranny. Nonconformity was here to stay.[30] Charles II was invited back to the throne but only under certain conditions. When James II tried to re-impose Catholicism upon the people, both Anglicans and Puritans joined in bringing about the Glorious Revolution of 1689, which placed William and Mary on the throne. In 1689 the Act of Toleration brought the vision of those days to fruition with its accent upon the freedom of worship, and the Act of Settlement placed limitations on the king and helped establish the independence of Parliament. Representative government began to evolve into its present image, slowly but surely, even though it took time and ever remained a work in progress.[31]

Levellers

The Puritan Revolution produced a prophetic movement that understood more than others the ramifications of its doctrines for the coming age. The movement only lasted for a brief, four-year period of time during the late 1640s, but it displayed more than others the wide-ranging power of Puritan ideals and the direction those ideals would take in the coming era. The hard core of the movement were common people—traders, artisans, and apprentices—who populated the Independent churches of the land and developed their teachings within that spiritual matrix.[32] They were devoted to their faith and refused to limit the application of their teaching to the separatists' enclaves. They demanded rights for the entire people of England on a nation-wide scale. They wanted freedom of religion, [33] freedom of conscience, [34] and freedom of the press.[35] They wanted equal representation for all regions and people in Parliament, [36] local and continuous elections,[37] leaders responsible to the consent of the people, [38] and irresponsible members removed.[39] They wanted plain laws,[40] proper defense,[41] speedy trials,[42] just punishments,[43] a jury of their peers,[44] and an end to the capricious acts of the system of courts.[45] They wanted all to stand before the state and its courts as they stood before God—free and equal. They even proposed to redistribute the wealth of the nation and level the disparity between estates, provided the electorate would offer its consent.[46] It is for this reason that their opponents mocked them and dubbed them as "Levellers." Their ideas proved too extreme for the time in which they lived, even for the sensibilities of Cromwell, whose army they helped equip, man, and radicalize through their own personal efforts. They dissipated in the 1650s as a specific group—out of touch with the expectations of moderates and the demands of the Restoration, but the churches out of which their ideas arose remained to fight another day as they became more and more political through their influence.[47]

John Lilburne served as a lightning rod for the movement. He developed a particular genius for inciting publicity and "dramatizing in his own person the most far-reaching implications of the Puritan Revolution."[48] His service included a brief stint in the New Model Army as a lieutenant colonel, where he and his movement had secured a strong foothold.[49] Cromwell gained sympathy for his cause and found him to be an able and useful officer, inviting him at one point to command the army's regiment in Fairfax,[50] but Lilburne's designs proved all-too-radical for Cromwell in the end. When Cromwell's army prevailed, Lilburne criticized his former ally as exercising tyranny over Parliament, comparing him to Jehu of old, the Israelite king who assassinated his wicked predecessor just to continue the evil reign he was commissioned to depose.[51]

The method and message of Lilburne represented a radical departure from the old way of kings, as it centered upon his commitment to the Christian faith and the example of NT saints. He made constant reference to his conversion (ca. 1636) as a most essential element to political action and considered his whole life and actions devoted to the divine principles that were instilled in his soul.[52] While the precise nature of his affiliation is not easy to identify, he seems to gravitate toward Baptist circles early in his career and end up moving toward the Quakers later on.[53] His ideas are developed in concert with the radical wing of the Puritan reform, which emphasized the priority of the New Testament over the Old.[54] He conceived of the Christian life as a religious dissident and saw the NT church as a suffering remnant, living on the fringes of society in a world filled with the darkness of tyranny. He thought of himself as enduring the same type of abuse and slander that Jesus and the Apostles experienced in NT times, and looked to the example of more recent martyrs—Hus, Wyclif, and the Marian martyrs—as a source of inspiration.[55] These examples were set forth in Foxes' *Acts and Monuments* (the so-called *Book of Martyrs*), which Lilburne and much of England read with pious devotion and incarnated within their very lives.[56] Lilburne followed the tradition as he was whipped, pilloried, and imprisoned—all of which served the hand of God as a fulfillment of prophecy and a means of drawing attention to the cause.[57] "The blood of martyrs is the seed of the church." Lilburne believed and followed this dictum in a most literal way. His ultimate goal was to die for the Lord and have his tombstone engraved with the simple words, "A faithful Martyr of Our Liberties."[58]

Alongside Lilburne the movement was served in a good and effective way by the work of William Walwyn. If Lilburne was the lightning rod, Walwyn served in a more genteel manner as the Levellers' most articulate, intelligent, and fair-minded spokesman.[59] Walwyn first met Lilburne in 1645 at Windmill Tavern, the center of Lilburne's political activity, and in spite of "some differences" in matters of religion they developed a healthy respect for each other and an effective political alliance.[60]

Like Lilburne, Walwyn considered Christianity the driving force behind all of his activities. He presented himself as a "born again"

Christian, pointing to a specific time of conversion, and displayed much the same fervor as Lilburne and other adult converts exude toward their newfound religion.[61] His friend, Humphrey Brooke, considered him the most pious person he knew.[62] He was a member of St. James Garlickhythe for fifteen years where he served as a lay leader, but his zeal was more for the Lordship of Christ than any specific, sectarian expression.[63] He preferred to distance himself from direct ties to Anabaptists, Brownists, Independents, or any other specific group and serve the truth of God wherever it might lead him.[64]

His political convictions were a product of his Christian faith. He felt that "true Christians are of all men the most vigilant defenders of the just liberties of the country. . . . [T]rue Christianity abhorres tyranny, oppression, perjury, cruelty, deceipt and all kinde of filthinesse."[65] The admonition is embodied in his own personal maturation. His pamphlets display a dramatic evolution as they proceed from a discussion of free worship in the early 1640s and embrace the rights of all citizens in all aspects of life toward the middle of the decade.[66] Through this maturation Walwyn provides an explicit challenge to the pessimism of "Machiavilian policy," which resigned the realm of politics to the depravity of this world. Walwyn believes that the love of Jesus Christ could serve as a guide for all private and public undertakings with its accent upon toleration and impartiality. No dichotomy needs to exist between private Christian ethics and the brutal world of collective reality.[67]

The Bible serves him as the leading guide for inspiration and authority in developing all of his principles.[68] It provides a unique basis of authority, which is established by the witness of the Holy Spirit, working above and beyond the power of human comprehension.[69] "Reason and philosophy" cannot discover the love of our enemy or the God who died for our sins—things that are too wonderful for us (Ps. 31:1).[70] The Word of God must accost our hearts and minds with the efficacy of its truth and provide the most essential and necessary insights into human existence. The Bible is the fundamental authority for developing all our concepts, even if reason and other sources of inspiration might prove helpful in discerning the meaning of the message. (Walwyn is not so enamored with the authority of Scripture as to inflate its importance beyond due measure and exclude other books and the power of reason from illuminating the message. In fact, he is accused by one of his critics of undermining the authority of Scripture and basic Christian belief through impudent questioning, learned at the altar of human sagacity. This accusation is false and his loyalty to Scripture remains firm, but

Walwyn is not a simple biblicist. He combines his reverence for the text with the deductive powers of reason, which relate its truth to specific areas of concern.)[71]

Religious freedom represents the first and foremost passion of Walwyn's soul. It is presented as the clear message of the Bible, especially as it is unfolded in the writings of the New Testament.[72] This message is a product of the NT emphasis upon the love of God, which reaches out to all of humankind, including one's enemies (Mtt. 5:44).[73] Jesus and the Apostles did not coerce those who opposed their preaching but followed the Golden Rule and waited patiently for the truth to bring conversion and change to the hearts of others.[74] Walwyn's favorite passage is Romans 14. It exhorts us to respect the conscience of others, bearing with whatever weakness we might perceive in those who see things differently.[75] This passage he inculcates over and over in his work to encourage toleration for a wide-variety of groups, including Anabaptists, Baptists, Independents, Papists, Socinians, et al.[76] All should live in peace as long as "such opinions are not destructive to human society, nor blaspheme the work of our Redemption."[77] He expresses a particular concern about the "Presbyters" renewing the same oppressive measures against other groups the bishops once leveled against them. Those who once suffered oppression should not impose a uniform version of government upon everyone else.[78]

In this scheme, freedom becomes the most essential goal of society. Everyone should be afforded liberty of conscience and the necessary space to express that liberty as long as it does not bring harm to another.[79] Freedom is extended to include areas like the press,[80] trade,[81] and a proper defense in a court of law.[82] Walwyn and the Levellers are most interested in extending the cause of freedom and justice beyond a few private matters to embrace all matters of life. The new cause that will wield the people together is no longer found in a common confession or the will of some to coerce others into submission but the love of liberty—the freedom to serve God and humankind as one deems fit in a clear and unfeigned conscience.[83] The principle of liberty is Walwyn's deconstruction of the love of God, which governs all our affairs in the public and private spheres.

> [T]he whole commandement is fulfilled in this one work LOVE; Love is the true touch-stone of all Christian performances, it instantly manifesteth how things are; so much love, so much of God. It is the surest guide in all private and publique undertakings; without a due regard to the rule of love, all things will goe wrong: observe it, & it will be like the North pole to the Marriners, to guide you to the quiet harbour of justice and peace: it is a rule easie to be understood, the meanest capacity is capable thereof, none can excuse themselves that swarve from this rule.[84]

Walwyn and the Levellers were the products of a radical political movement that started within the local churches. Freedom on the local level could not contain itself and was bound to proceed and permeate the society as a whole.[85] The grassroots of the country preceded the government in providing the major impetus for the transformation of society. The Long Parliament was much less radical in its program during the first couple years of its existence, working within a broken system, trying to restore the constitutional framework through remedial legislation, and fixing the lost balance of power. The first civil war was more about restoring ancient peerage or aristocratic authority around the Crown than the liberties, rights, and sovereignty of the people. Parliament's army was dominated by peers or sons of peers in leadership positions, and the push for radical change only came from religious zealots—the hard-core Puritan reformers and the Independents of Cromwell's army—who wanted to transform the whole country through a radical act of revolution, reforming the church, the state, and all of society.[86] Only a Puritan minister would say,

> Reformation must be Universal, . . . reform all places, all persons and callings; reform the Benches of Judgment, the inferior Magistrates, . . . Reform the Church, . . . Reform the Universities, . . . Reform the Cities, reform the Countries, reform inferiour Schools of Learning; reform the Sabbath, reform the Ordinances, the worship of God, &c.[87]

These Puritans started their revolution by inundating Parliament with demands for ecclesiastical reform, calling for the end of popery and its many accouterments within the church. Their hundreds of petitions far outnumbered any other demands about constitutional matters, which Parliament was forced to consider.[88] Eventually this call for reform became more pervasive and militant as the spirit of Independency permeated the chaplains and god-fearing men of Cromwell's army. With the political clout of an army behind them, the radicals could press their demands beyond the confines of a separatist church and extend its teaching to embrace all of society, calling for a New Jerusalem where liberty of conscience, federal government, and democratic polity reigned. According to Baxter, the army of Independents could speak of "church democracy" at one time and "state democracy" the next, using both phrases interchangeably.[89]

Political and ecclesiastical ideology was related to each other, and both sides of the struggle understood how the process worked. Walwyn saw the order of reformation starting in the church, proceeding to the ward and its officers, and then changing the Common Council and Parliament on the national level.[90] Clarendon understood that the polity of the church and state was intermingled in the country, making it difficult to create any separation between them in the mentality of the people.[91] After all, the church was the social center of their community, often serving as the school, storehouse, arsenal, fire station, and town hall. Its sermons served as the main source of political information for most people, who heard and read little else of substance throughout the week in their daily struggle to survive. Its preachers were licensed by the state, and the state used the pulpit to forward its political and ethical agenda, informing the ministers what to say and preach.[92] Of course, this process broke down when the church declared its autonomy and its structure and message began to clash with the basic designs of hierarchical government. The church was spreading a message of autonomy among the people that opposed the basic texture of the state, and the state was forced to change accordingly.

Massachusetts Bay Colony

The Puritans brought similar views of church and state to America in the early part of the seventeenth century. According to Perry Miller, Stephen Foster, and many scholars, the Puritans brought the same central vision of church and state with them when they settled in America, even if it developed in time into new constellations as an accidental product of a different set of circumstances.[93] Their views enveloped America in the centuries to come and proved to be a lasting testimony to the power and righteousness of the Levellers' cause. Of course, this process took some time and was filled with imperfections along the way, but there is no doubt that the fundamental impetus and basic outline of the American dream was conceived within the bosom of these Puritan forefathers.[94]

This dream is found at the very beginning of their experiment and embodied once again within the Reformed doctrine of covenant. Its success could be attributed to a number of factors, which come together in creating a people, but covenant theology seemed to play a most prominent role in the establishment of their political/ecclesiastical vision. This doctrine played a more decisive role than it did among the Levellers and other dispensational groups, who emphasized the NT and dismissed the idea of one, all-encompassing theme in Scripture and life. From the very outset, William Bradford and his "pilgrames" were determined to make the covenant front and center.[95] They signed a compact on the Mayflower, binding themselves into a "civil body politike," before setting foot on Plymouth Rock.[96] Upon arrival they forged churches and townships by means of the covenant, based upon the Congregationalist model, which spread throughout New England in the next few decades.[97] The first church, established in 1629 within the town of Salem, was forged upon the bonds of its own, special covenant as a testimony to its obligations before God.

> We Covenant with the Lord and one with an other; and doe bynd our selves in the presence of God, to walke together in all his waies, according as he is pleased to reveale himself unto us in his Blessed word of truth. [98]

John Cotton was considered the most eminent apologist and theologian for the Congregationalists during the first half of the seventeenth century. He was instrumental in converting many of the leading lights of the movement to the validity of the position, including the likes of John Goodwin, Thomas Goodwin, John Preston, John Davenport, and Philip Nye.[99] He brought this energy and influence with him when he left England in 1633 to set up shop in Boston, becoming the most renowned preacher and theologian in the New World and helping to insure the place of the covenant in his new surroundings. His many works display an ardent and steadfast devotion to the principles of covenant theology and Congregationalist polity, exhibiting the same basic tendencies of Robert Browne and the founders of the movement. His works exalt in the freedom of believers and autonomy of individual assemblies, while rejecting any notion of a mother church in Rome or England governing the affairs of a local church. His works include most of the basic themes that characterized the movement from its earliest days, including the Lordship of Christ, a voluntary covenant, independent rule, free elections, and local control over the membership.[100]

> The Church is a mystical body, whereof Christ is the head, the Members be Saints, called out of the world, and united together into one Congregation, by an holy covenant. . . . No church hath power of Governement over another, but each of them hath chiefe power within itselfe, and all of them equall power with another; every church hath received alike the power of binding, and loosing, opening and shutting the kingdom of heaven.[101]

Thomas Hooker wrote what is considered the best summary and defense of Congregationalist principles in the seventeenth century. He was a Puritan divine, educated at Cambridge, who came to America with Cotton on the Griffin and helped to found a colony in the Connecticut Valley a few years later. His great work was published a year after his death in 1648, and it was entitled *A Survey of the Summe of Church-Discipline*. He presents the work as a "joint concurrence" of the New England elders, expressing the consensus of their opinion on church polity and the desire of that community to provide an apologia for it, especially in light of Samuel Rutherford's challenge to their system in his *Due right of Presbyteries*. Hooker believes that toleration should rule over their differences at the present time but remains firm in the conviction of all Congregationalists concerning the rights of local assemblies and their members to "call their own officers" and the centrality of the doctrine of covenant.[102]

At the beginning, Hooker wishes to make clear that his work is based on the Word of God.[103]

> So we have ours left upon record in the holy Scriptures, unto which we must not adde, and from which we must not take any thing, Christ the King of his Church, and Master of his House, he only in reason, can make laws that are Authenticke for the government therof.[104]

Christ established his polity in the church, and he has established it for all time as the immutable rule of God.[105] No set of circumstances can intervene and compromise the essence of what Christ has established as a "fundamentall point of Religion."[106] As long as one acknowledges the primacy of his will, one can employ a variety of human means to address the concerns and details of the debate. Hooker is not adverse to employing reason throughout the work to defend what is provided in Scripture. The work supplements the exegesis of Scripture with logical argumentation and rational answers to the objections of Rutherford and others; and Ramian logic is used to outline and divide arguments into its many bifurcated categories.[107]

The first and foremost passion of the work is directed against the hierarchical system of government. This system and its many offices were created by the Antichrist to fulfill his lusts and ambitions. Christ did not ordain "Surrogates, Chancellours, Arch-deacons, Deans, Officials, Vicars-general, Abbots, Monks, Friers, Cardinals, Jesuits, etc."[108] He appointed few offices to serve a specific flock and promoted parity among the ministers of his church, rejecting those who would climb to the top of a pyramid out of worldly ambition.[109] No one has the right to add or subtract from what he has charged.[110] No classis has the power to create a pope, bishop, or any office to rule over the church at large and so abandon the orders Christ has expressed most explicitly in his Word.[111] "A Shepherd ought to have but one flock: one is as much as he can rule, one is as much as he hath authority to rule."[112]

Hooker argues that the church universal is made out of particular parts and not the other way around.[113] The church arises from a particular group of confederated saints, who are granted the power of the keys.[114] A classis and synod can provide "councell" to a particular church and even refuse it "the right hand of fellowship," but it cannot usurp the authority that

Christ has granted by issuing a binding decree or assuming the role of excommunicating individual members.[115] Even if it is wise to seek outside counsel in time of need, the church has no need of a "consociation" outside the local level to perfect its calling, and there is no admonition in Scripture to construct one.[116]

The visible church finds its constitution in the "mutuall covenanting and confoederating of the saints in the fellowship of the faith."[117] Those who are free from each other obtain "mutuall power each over [the] other . . . by their own free consent and mutuall ingagement," obliging themselves to submit to the governing principles of the fellowship.[118] But all of this must find expression through an explicit or outward form. The covenant should be provided in an explicit or written form for each assembly to read and certify.[119] Its members should be certified as "visible saints" to insure the vitality of the fellowship.[120] They are responsible for the election of officers[121] and discipline of members,[122] and their status must be certified accordingly. If they are responsible to run the church and sit in judgment of others, they must be equipped to exercise their obligations with sufficient wisdom and commitment. The membership must consist of those who have made a choice to follow Christ and join his local assembly, not those who were baptized as children or happen to live in a certain precinct.[123] Of course, the church cannot divide between the wheat and the tares, and so replace the judgment that belongs to God and God alone. Its judgment cannot discern the "thoughts and intents of the heart." It only can judge those who appear to live as saints in outward profession and conduct, making its decision with "reasonable charity," allowing for certain imperfections in itself and others, and leaving the ultimate judgment to God.[124]

In the same year of its publication, Hooker's work was embodied within the *Cambridge Platform*. The symbol presents nothing remarkable or new, especially in comparison with Hooker's more detailed account, but it still serves as "the most important monument of early New England Congregationalism" by the very fact that it represents the verdict of a synod—a most remarkable and rare occurrence for Congregationalists. Because of this, the symbol ends up acquiring unique authority among later generations of the faithful who renew their allegiance periodically to its principles.[125] A synod was possible at this time in their history because these Congregationalists represented in certain ways the established church of New England and no longer interpreted their surroundings or polity in the hostile terms of the early separatists. The platform believed that the magistrates possess every right to call a synod, even if its decisions remain subject to the authority of each congregation (XVI, 3).[126] In fact, the pretext for the synod was a call by the General Court, which was concerned with the interference of Parliament in the 1640s. The synod would end up endorsing much of what the divines determined at Westminster, except for those sections of the confession that seemed to allow for interference from outside forces into the affairs of the local assemblies.[127] Liberty remained its first and foremost concern.

The platform expresses the typical Congregationalist convictions of the day. It ascribes to Jesus Christ all power and authority over his church and believes that he has committed to the church specific instructions for its polity, which are found in his Word and partake of its perfect, complete, and eternal nature (I, 2, 3; X, 1). It denies the existence of a "universall visible church" (II, 4). The church is embodied within the local community, where all believers and officers are called to join and serve (III, 4, 5; IV, 6; IX, 6). It considers a church united together under a "visible covenant" as its very essence, whereby the members give themselves to the Lord and serve each other for the mutual edification of all involved (II, 6; IV, 3-6). The members are those who wish to join by their own voluntary consent and have passed an examination under the church's "charitable discretion," which excludes the very wicked and admits "the weakest measure of faith" (III, 1; XII, 1-3). Baptized children are subject to the same examination after the age of discretion if they wish to join in full communion with the church (XV). The platform restricts the membership to "visible saints," as those who are worthy to rule the church. They are the ones who admit and remove members when it is necessary and elect and depose officers, deferring to no higher authority (VIII, 5-7; X, 5-9). The ordinary offices of the church are limited to those established by Christ: elders (which include pastors, teachers, and administrators) and deacons (V, 3ff.).[128] A hierarchy of popes, cardinals, bishops, and other positions of authority is not a part of the Lord's instructions and incurs the same strict judgment it found in all the Congregationalists' works (VII, 6).

Of course, this doctrine was not limited in application to the affairs of the church in Puritan New England. Covenant theology extended its domain beyond the walls of the church to embrace the entire City on a Hill. It became the matrix out of which the many relations in its society were defined and determined.

> Where upon having concurrence and countenance of their deputy-governour, the worshipful John Endicott, Esq., and the approving presence of the messengers from the church of Plymouth, they set apart the sixth day of August, after their arrival,

for fasting and prayer, for the settling of a *Church State* among them, and for their making a *Confession of their Faith*, and entering into a holy *Covenant*, whereby that Church State was formed.[129]

Amongst such who by no impression of nature, no rule of providence, or appointment from God, or reason, have power each over the other, there must of necessity be a mutual ingagement, each of the other, by their free consent, before by any rule of God they have any right or power, or can exercise either, each towards the other. This appears in all covenants betwixt Prince and People, Husband and Wife, Master and Servant, and most palpable is the expression of this in all confederations and corporations; from mutual acts of consenting and ingaging each of other, there is impression of an ingagement results, as a relative bond betwixt the contractours and confederatours, wherein their *formalis ratio*, or specificall nature of the covenant lieth, in all the former instances especially that of corporations. So that however it is true, the rule bindes such to the duties of their places and relations, yet it is certain, it requires that they should first freely ingage themselves in such covenants, and then be carefull to fullfil such duties.[130]

Neither is there any colour to conceive this way of entering into Church estate by Covenant, to be the particular Paedagogy of the old Testament; it is evident by the light of nature, that All civil relations are founded in Covenant. For, to passe by naturall Relations between Parents and Children, and violent Relations between Conquerors and Captives; there is no other way whereby a people (*sui Juris*) free from naturall and compulsory engagements, can be united and combined together in one visible body to stand by mutuall Relation, fellow-members of the same body, but by mutuall Covenant; as appeareth between husband and wife in the family, Magistrates and subjects in the Common-wealth, fellow Citizens in the same Citie: and therefore in the New Testament, when a people whom the Apostles by their ministry had converted, were to be gathered . . . onely by joyning all together in one Covenant.[131]

The other kinde of Libertye I call ciuill or foederall, it may also be termed morall, in reference to the Covenant betweene God & man, in the morall Lawe, & the Politicke Couenantes & constitutions, amongst men themselues.[132]

This same deconstruction is found in the next generation of Puritan divines. Cotton Mather envisions the covenant as permeating all of society and exhorts his people to apply the covenant to all aspects of their life in church and state.

Now, In the doing of this Thing, Why should not our Churches, most explicitly Apply, the Covenant of Grace, unto all the Designs of Reformation, as well as they Apply it unto the particular Designs, of a Particular Church-state before the Lord? Our Covenant will to the most Edification, and the most Satisfaction, be Renewed, when we most of all Express the Spirit of the New Covenant in all that we do. . . . Now, if our Churches, yea, and other societies too, would thus use the Covenant of Grace, with pertinent Applications thereof, to every New Iniquity, that they Discern arising among them, how gloriously might the Spirit of Grace, then Lift up a standard against every flood of Iniquity. . . . Our Worshipful Justices are under the Oath of God, That they will dispense Justice equally and impartially in all cases, and for no cause forbear truly to do their Office. Our Grand Jury-men are Sworn by the Ever living God, That they will diligently Enquire, and true presentment make, of all things given them in Charge. . . . Our Constables are Sworn by the Ever-living God That in all that the Law has made part of their Office, thy will deal seriously and faithfully, . . .[133]

John Wise, a clergyman from Ipswich, also contains this deconstruction of the covenant in his well-known tract, *A Vindication of the Government of New-England Churches* (1717). Wise wrote the tract with the ostensible reason of defending the pure polity of Congregationalism against any semi-Presbyterian compromise, but his work displays a much larger agenda. It proceeds to base all forms of government upon "the Effect of Humane Free-Compacts"[134] and inculcates democracy as the best form of polity in church and state.

They must Interchangeably each Man Covenant to joyn in one lasting Society, that they may be capable to concert the measure of their safety, by a Publick Vote. A Vote or Decree must then nextly pass to set up some Particular speecies of Government over them. And if they are joyned in their first Compact upon absolute Terms to stand to the Decision of the first Vote concerning the Species of Government: Then all are bound by the Majority to acquiesce in that particular Form thereby settled, though their own private Opinion, incline them to forme other Model.[135]

A Democracy. This is a form of Government, which the Light of Nature does highly value, & often directs to as most agreeable to the Just and Natural Prerogatives of Humane Beings. This was of great account, in the early times of the World. And not only so, but upon the Experience of several Thousand years, after the World had been tumbled, and tost from one Species of Government to another, at a great Expence of Blood and Treasure, many of the wise Nations of the World have sheltered themselves under it again; or at least have blendished, and balanced their Government with it.[136]

That the covenant would end up defining the rest of the relationships in Puritan New England is no surprise. All that was in "the world . . . was indeed created for the sake and use of the church."[137] There was no wall to separate their lives into political and religious compartments.[138] Their church meetings and town meetings were one and the same.[139] They could not believe in democracy and federal government on Sunday and then live in a society based on a different set of principles the rest of the week.[140] They rejected the schizophrenic principles of Machiavellian government—explicitly and categorically—that would divide the leadership of the state from true Christian piety and looked up to their rulers as setting the highest examples of holy and pious living in fulfilling their office.[141] They existed as one people of God (*corpus Christianum*). They looked to themselves as the people of Israel, possessing a special role in the divine economy, complete with their own national covenant and the same curses and blessings attendant upon their faithfulness.[142] Their divines preached jeremiads, which exhorted the people to remain faithful to the covenant and the founding principles of their society, and prognosticated disaster if they refused to repent of their secular ways.[143] Their national and political lives never existed outside their faith in some nebulous world of secular autonomy, free from the will of God and the Lordship of Christ. Their religious beliefs defined their lives in a total and complete way in accordance with the divine will and demanded absolute obedience. Their belief in democratic and federal government could not remain within the confines of ecclesiastical organizations but spread in a necessary and inevitable way to encompass all associations fulfilling the perfect will of God.[144]

In the early 1630s the Bay Colony was ruled by a General Court, which consisted of a Governor, Deputy, and assistants or magistrates subject to the direct approval of the visible saints.[145] On May 8, 1632 the General Court decided that "freemen" should choose the assistants, and it would choose the Governor in turn out of the assistants every year.[146] John Winthrop, the first Governor, was elected and removed from office a number of times during his lifetime in accordance with this policy. The reason behind the annual elections involved a concern over the use (or abuse) of discretionary powers and the investiture of so much power in any one individual. When Winthrop was removed from office, he gladly stepped down and often served as the Deputy Governor or one of the assistants.[147] Of course, problems continued to plague the fledgling democracy in regard to the limits of discretionary powers (as they do all other democratic societies). Some conflict arose over Winthrop's strong belief that discretionary powers were necessary for allowing magistrates flexibility in making wise and existential decisions, with the deputies wanting more democratic and legalistic instruments to ward off the possibility of tyranny.[148] In particular, the deputies sought to take away the negative vote of the magistrates, but eventually the colony resolved the two-year dispute in March of 1644 by dividing the Court into two houses, requiring the approval of both bodies to pass a measure.[149] The Congregational model continued to exert its fundamental spirit by forcing the colony more and more into democratic reforms and autonomous rule. By the spring of 1645 the town of Hingham sent a petition to the General Court wanting more representative participation and more autonomy in governing its own civil and ecclesiastical affairs—much to the chagrin of Winthrop.[150] During the mid-seventeenth century, townships were established throughout New England where the people assembled to vote over their own affairs, making democracy a permanent aspect of its society and spreading the message to the emerging nation.[151] All of this stands as a remarkable testimony to the power of Puritan ideals that the "founders of New England [could create] most of the features of representative, balanced government in an amazingly brief interval: a theory of constitutionalism, power wielded by consent, annual elections with an expansive franchise, a bicameral legislature, local autonomies, and a Bill of Rights."[152]

In the seventeenth and eighteenth centuries, New England stood at the center of democratic, federal, and revolutionary activities within the colonies. It began to extend the message by helping to establish an experiment in Connecticut under the leadership of Thomas Hooker. This settlement was founded upon a federal and democratic philosophy of government according to its *Fundamental Order* (1639), providing more liberal standards in ecclesiastical discipline than the Bay and never making church membership a stricture upon voting or holding office in the civil realm.[153] An experiment in Rhode Island soon followed with the same basic format of Plymouth, the Bay, and Connecticut under the leadership of Roger Williams, despite his bellicose relation with the other churches in the region. Its charter advocated a "democraticall" government, based on the "free and voluntary consent of all, or the greater part of the free inhabitants."[154] The decades to come witnessed other Protestant groups who came to the middle colonies of America with a similar ideology and championed the cause of liberty. The Quakers, who grew up during the Puritan Revolution and represented certain tensions within the movement, obtained a tract of land in the Delaware Valley during the 1670s under the leadership of William Penn and brought a strong commitment to democratic and egalitarian principles—even beyond the typical Puritan standards. "Penn's Woods" was dominated by Quakers in the early decades of the settlement and later on by Scots-Irish Presbyterians, who came to the middle colonies in large numbers (up to one-third or 150,000 from Northern Ireland alone) and began to constitute a majority of the assemblies in the crucial decades of the 1770s and 1780s.[155] In fact, the Reformed faith was on the march throughout the colonies. According to Harry Stout, three out of four colonists were somehow related to the Reformed faith (mainly Congregationalists and Presbyterians) just prior at the outbreak of hostilities with England.[156] Massachusetts remained firmly within the Congregationalist fold, possibly outnumbering the rest of the denominations as much as ten-to-one,[157] but tensions over polity and politics were less evident in Reformed circles by the end of the seventeenth century.[158] According to Keith Griffin, the Presbyterians imbibed the fundamental political philosophy of the Congregationalists in the middle colonies, including its ethnocentric devotion to America as an elect nation and a special covenant people with a manifest destiny before God.[159] Even if the Presbyterians possessed more respect for authority in their polity and were less strident in their civil activity, they still found enough fervency in their ideology to favor democratic reform and justify revolution against Mother England given a sufficient set of circumstances.[160]

In New England the election sermons were filled with the virtues of limited government and the rule of law over the capricious acts of human authority from the very beginning of the experiment. As the time of the Revolution approached, the sermons became more pointed in denouncing the abuses of tyranny and contained the "footprints of the rebellion" against Parliament and the Crown.[161] Jonathan Mayhew, a Unitarian-leaning minister of Boston's West Church, afforded the most famous sermon on this provocative subject to his congregation. The sermon was first printed in1750, gained an international audience, and was acclaimed as "the morning gun of the Revolution."[162] Throughout the sermon, Mayhew advocates opposition to tyranny as a Christian duty.[163] He claims that the passages on submission in Scripture were never intended to provide "parents, masters, and husbands" with the unconditional loyalty of their subjects or require the breaking of divine commandments by those submitting to their authority.[164] These passages place limits on obedience to earthly authorities, and the same holds true for Rom. 13, the *locus classicus* on submission to the civil government. One cannot interpret this passage in a literal, absolute, or universal sense.[165] It contains a message that is limited to a certain context, in which some individuals within the church of Rome felt their status as believers exempted them from paying taxes to a pagan government. Paul wants these individuals to pay their taxes and submit unto the state no matter what form it might take within a monarchical, aristocratic, and democratic regime—as long as it works for the good of society.[166] But this act of submission is not absolute and depends upon the rulers' fulfillment of constitutional or federal conditions to work for the public welfare.[167] Paul speaks here of "good rulers," or "those who actually perform the duty of rulers, by exercising a reasonable and just authority for the good of human society."[168] It is "our duty to obey our king, merely for this reason, that he rules for the public welfare, [and] it follows, by a parity of reason, that when he turns tyrant, and makes his subjects his prey to devour and to destroy, instead of his charge to defend and cherish, we are bound to throw off our allegiance to him, and to resist, and that according to the tenor of the apostle's argument."[169] With this understanding in mind, Mayhew expresses support for the Puritan Revolution and its resistance to the tyranny of Charles I, while providing a long list of abuses to justify the demise of the king. Although he questions the justice of the execution and the "hypocrisy of those times [and] Cromwell's maleadministration during the interregnum," he also rejects all attempts by Charles II and the Episcopal clergy to turn the fallen king into a martyr by comparing him to Jesus Christ and his unjust sufferings. Charles I was an oppressor, not a saint.[170] His demise was more than justified. The Puritan Revolution served a just cause and continues to serve us today as a warning against the tyranny of all wicked magistrates in the future, but Mayhew proceeds no farther. He leaves his audience wondering whether he wants to continue the same policy against the current regime. There is no specific application drawn, although his actions will reveal a more explicit intention in the present circumstance. When the British impose the Stamp Act on the colonists in 1765, he will lead a vigorous opposition to the act and help incite riots against it in August of that year. While he died a decade before placing his official imprimatur upon the final act of defiance, he clearly helped engender a revolutionary spirit among the colonists through his words and deeds.

Congregationalism provided much of the fuel for revolutionary changes in society through its view of the church and state as institutions based on federal or covenant (*foedus*) theology. Out of the Puritan community arose a number of notable political philosophers like Thomas Hobbes and John Locke, who spoke of the government as based up on a social contract or covenant. Locke is hailed in many circles as playing a most decisive role in the formation of the new political order, but it is important to avoid exaggerating the contribution of one individual. Locke only serves as an example of what arose from a religious community, however crucial his specific contribution might be.[171] America produced its own version of "Founding Fathers" in the eighteenth century, who make an important contribution and receive much credit for doing so, but none of them can replace what is first and foremost. It is the community that provides the basic source of inspiration among the people and remains the constant force throughout the vicissitudes of political change, producing many disciples to carry on the message. It is the community that will provide the matrix out of which the many covenant-based documents emerged in the eighteenth century[172]—the Articles of Confederation, the Federalist

Papers, the Declaration of Independence, the Constitution of the United States, and the many state constitutions that were forged during the time of the Revolutionary War. All of the documents speak of federal government, and none of them are the simple product of isolated geniuses, no matter how brilliant they might be.

The Constitution of Massachusetts (1780) serves as a good case in point. It was drafted under the auspices of John Adams, one of the great "Founding Fathers" of this nation; it contains the basic elements that were later embodied in the Constitution of the United States; and its elements contain and carry on the indelible mark of the Puritan community with its emphasis upon federal government, democratic elections, and egalitarian rights—at least as they were deconstructed in the eighteenth century.[173] From the very outset, the preamble speaks of forming the body politic through the surety of a covenant.

> The body politic is formed by a voluntary association of individuals; it is a social compact by which the whole people covenants with each citizen and each citizen with the whole people that all shall be governed by certain laws for the common good. We, therefore, the people of Massachusetts, acknowledging, with grateful hearts, the goodness of the great Legislator of the universe, in affording us, in the course of His providence, an opportunity, deliberately and peaceably, without fraud, violence, or surprise of entering into an original explicit and solemn compact with each other, and of forming a new constitution of civil government for ourselves and posterity; and devoutly imploring His direction in so interesting a design, do agree upon, ordain, and establish the following declaration of rights and frame of government as the constitution of the commonwealth of Massachusetts.

The constitution then proceeds to conjoin the doctrine of covenant with a number of inalienable rights, which "all men" possess in nature as free and equal before God. These rights include the famous trilogy of "life, liberty, and property," which the government is designed to protect.[174] If the government does not protect these rights of the citizenry, the people have the right to change it.[175] The right of rebellion is conceived within the Puritan concept of covenant, which allows for rebellion against an abusive government and rejects the divine right of kings to mistreat their subjects. The constitution proceeds to develop the concept within its own revolutionary time by claiming the property rights of its people were violated and using this cause as a pretext for the War of Independence.[176] It says that the government has no right to take away the property of the people without their prior consent or implicit acceptance of a tax or a duty through their representatives in the legislature.[177] There is no taxation without representation, and the king has violated the sacred trust.

No region of the country favored the American Revolution more than New England. Its Congregationalists made up two-thirds of the total number of churches in the region and fomented much of the discontent.[178] The Congregationalists emphasized the autonomy of local congregations and translated that emphasis into creating a desire for home rule. They preached a gospel of autonomy, liberty, and independence, and rejected any interference from a consortium of pastors, an Anglican episcopate, a foreign government, or the king of England. Winthrop described his people as jealous for their liberties, not wanting any control from England, even from a parliament that arrested dominion from Charles I in1641.[179] The colony looked to the original charter as providing its government with "full and absolute power and authoritie to correct, puishe, pardon, governe, and rule" all its subjects.[180] According to the charter, the people were given "full & Ample power of choosing all Officers, that shall Commande & Rule over us: of making all Lawes & Rules of our obedience: & of a full & final determination of all Cases."[181] They owed no specific allegiance to the laws of England, even if the laws of the colony proved consonant with the "fundamental basis of [English] law" in ancient custom and "Right Reason."[182]

A firestorm erupted when Charles II ordered the Bay Colony to surrender its charter in 1683. At first, leaders like William Phips and Increase Mather rejected compromise and felt any surrender of its original charter constituted a heinous act of apostasy against the religious/political vision of their forefathers. But, after vigorous debate, they lost the struggle to retain the old charter and accepted a new one in 1692, which included provisions for a royal governor, an expanded executive, and the obligation to submit all statutes to the king in council for final approval. In turn, the colony was allowed to elect representatives in a lower house, who would elect members of the upper house, and the Congregational establishment would remain as before, with toleration extended to other Protestant groups.[183] This compromise proved tolerable for the time being in pacifying both sides, but the colonists would not tolerate their mitigated liberties for long. When George III and the British wanted to test the colonists' rights of self-taxation in the 1760s, all hell broke loose.[184] The doctrine of covenant was invoked, the long train of abuses had to come to a head, and revolution was accepted as the only recourse.

In this case, the sons of liberty and the Constitution of Massachusetts used the covenant to convict the king of violating his sacred duties, but the responsibilities were not limited to him and ran both ways in a bilateral compact. No taxation without representation reversed itself and became a justification for no representation without taxation. The reverse of the famous adage became true when the people were required to pay a poll tax or own property to receive voting privileges, which was the particular stipulation under the compact. To vote for a senator one must be a male of twenty-one years of age, who owns a freehold estate valued at sixty pounds or more.[185] To vote for a representative one must be a male of twenty-one years of age with an annual income of three pounds or an estate worth at least sixty pounds.[186] To vote for the governor or lieutenant governor one could qualify under either set of stipulations.[187] The basic principle was designed to include all those who had "a stake in society" and exclude only those who were just starting out in business, the journeymen who did not own their own tools and "the idle and profligate."[188] That the constitution fell short of modern expectations goes without saying, but it remains the only state constitution to survive from that era and it did promote the democratic and egalitarian values of the Puritan community, which will find more and more fulfillment as their domain is expanded.

Of course, there are scholars who dispute all this, dismissing the significance of Congregationalism in the development of the modern world. Typically the objections center upon the insufficiencies of the colony's experiment: the restriction of voting to church members,[189] the condemnation of pure democracy by the leadership,[190] the discretionary powers of Winthrop, the authority of the clergy,[191] the persecution of heretics like Williams, Hutchinson, Baptists, and Quakers. In this portrait, the Puritans are depicted as developing a theocratic kingdom, which meddled into the affairs of its people and imposed a narrow-minded version of orthodoxy upon them. The Puritans are remembered for depraved acts of bigotry and repression, not for any positive acts or contributions, which gave birth to a nation. If religion finds a place of honor, it is typically given to the Great Awakening and its rejection of the stifling orthodoxy and hierarchical governance of the "Old Light." The "New Light" of the Great Awakening is seen as an egalitarian, down-to-earth movement of the common people, which promoted mass meetings, individual experience, and personal decisions while challenging the institutional structure and hierarchical framework of the established church. Evangelical groups like the Baptists and Methodists arose in great number to challenge the establishment, leading to a significant drop in the size and power of state churches by the end of the eighteenth century.[192] Boston became a "Medley of Religions," and freedom now flourished.[193] But this portrait is clearly a caricature of the situation, creating a false dichotomy between the Old and New Light, especially in northern states like Massachusetts and Connecticut. While few would deny the significance of the Great Awakening in promoting democracy and liberty among the people, its importance is exaggerated by those scholars who wish to create a dark caricature of the Old Light and contrast it with the fresh beginning of the New Light. The Great Awakening was more a product of the larger tradition of Protestantism with its emphasis upon the priesthood of the believers and rejection of priestly authority than a radical new beginning. The Congregationalists already followed this fundamental program before the Awakening and even expanded it beyond the other groups of the Reformation to include democracy, egalitarianism, and liberty in their fellowship and society, even if certain events or individuals contradicted the overall doctrinal direction of the community. Perhaps the Great Awakening deserves credit for extending the program in a worthwhile direction and challenging the leadership of the church, who had grown all too comfortable with their Harvard education and position in society, but the movement of its spirit was not opposed to the democratic ideology of Congregationalism. Its people did not complain about the polity of churches in New England. They displayed no marked or increased support for the Revolution in respect to the non-revivalists.[194] They only wanted the membership to experience the same spiritual renewal.[195] In fact, many of the clergy like Jonathan Edwards became guiding lights in the revival, and those who criticized its uneducated preachers and unsound theology were expressing genuine concerns about the excesses of its passions, not rejecting all of its blessings *in toto*.[196]

The Puritan heritage will fade in the eighteenth century, but it is more from a lack of notoriety and distinction than any real dissipation in its overall substantive influence. While the Puritan heritage remains an integral part of the founding documents of the eighteenth century, its influence is not so conspicuous as it was during the beginning of the experiment. No longer does one find the biblical text and its exegesis used as a justification for the doctrines propounded. The Enlightenment brought a certain contempt for revealed religion among many of the "Founding Fathers," even though it contributed little of note or originality to the political debate—at least in regard to the essential elements of the government—and owed much of its political inspiration to specific Protestant sources. The works of the Enlightenment preferred to remain silent about these sources and attribute its findings to the self-evident power of reason or maybe the God of nature, who is known in a general way to all humankind. John Adams largely ignored religious influence in his great work, *Defence of the Constitutions of Government of the United States*, preferring to find inspiration for contemporary ideas from certain "secular" examples in classical history.[197] Thomas Jefferson went even farther and conducted a crusade to eliminate the teaching of the Bible in education, hoping to instill a curriculum that focused upon "Graecian, Roman, English, and American history," cleansed of religious reference.[198] But it is hard to believe that the essential contours of their political vision were reached in this way, outside the specific, sectarian groups that forged these same beliefs in their society. John Adams might think that his constitution is the product of enlightened thinking and provide some indications for thinking this way in the text, but it is hard to believe that his ideas are indebted to the "cultured despisers."[199] Too often the French religion became more an exercise in cynicism than faith, and much of its political capital was borrowed from outside sources, especially those in England according to Voltaire, Diderot, and scholars familiar with the era.[200] It is better to understand Adams and the rest of his colleagues as working within the specific religious tradition of their birth, which permeated the country by the time of the Revolution and included some of the great men of faith—Martin Luther, Thomas Cartwright, Jean Morély, Robert Browne, John Lilburne, and John Cotton—only to name a few.

Notes

1. The sermons were merged together during printing with a few items added and others "pared off." These two divines exerted an enormous influence over Parliament, greater than Laud according to Clarendon. Hill, *Society & Puritanism*, 77. Charles I summoned both the Short Parliament (April-May, 1640) and Long Parliament (Nov., 1640-April, 1653 or March 1660) because he needed the money to wage his Second Bishops' War against the Scots, who were resisting his attempt to impose an Episcopal polity upon them. Since the end of the thirteenth century, Parliament controlled the purse strings, and so the king could not pay his troops without their consent. Hostile relations reigned between Charles I and Parliament over this and other matters, leading to a dismissal of the latter in 1629 for eleven years. That year the Parliament defended the property rights of the people by rejecting Forced Loans, Ship Money, the imposition of tonnage, poundage, or any other charge laid on the people without their consent. R. Kirk, *America's British Culture* (New Brunswick, NJ and London: Transaction Publishers, 1994) 50; J. P. Sommerville, *Royalists & Patriots: Politics and Ideology in England 1603-1640* (London and New York: Longman, 1999) 149, 215.
2. "A Sermon Preached to the Honorable House of Commons assembled in Parliament, At their Publique Fast, Novem. 17, 1640" (London: John Legatt, 1641) 34-37, 46.
3. Ibid., 33, 48, 49.
4. Ibid., preface, 4, 24ff.
5. Ibid., 1, 10. The examples for the people to follow are drawn from the OT. The doctrine of covenant rejects a dispensational analysis that would prefer the NT to

the OT. The one eternal covenant is found in both. The Puritans related the people of God to the nation of Israel in a most direct way, more than any other wing of the Reformation.

6. Ibid., 31. He says that the concept of covenant needs expansion. There are many more covenants than the one sealed during baptism. Ibid., 40.
7. Ibid., preface, 34, 35.
8. Ibid., 7-9, 15, 16, 20, 21. The influence of Bullinger is seen in these synergistic statements.
9. W. Haller, *Liberty and Reformation*, 66, 100.
10. Ibid., 103, 349. In chapter three, illustrations of Parliament's use of covenant are provided in regard to rebellion against the state. The immediate design of the league was to extirpate the bishops and promote a uniform, Presbyterian polity with Scotland. Clarendon, *The History of the Rebellion*, 40,130, 335, 359, 468, 469; Hill, *The World Turned Upside Down*, 83; Elazar, *Covenant & Community*, 254. In the 1590s the term "covenant" was first used in a public and pervasive manner for the banding together of the kirk and people against the "popish lords." S. A. Burrell, "The Apocalyptic Vision of the Early Covenanters," *The Scottish HistoricalReview* 43 (1964): 12; C. Hill, *The English Bible and the Seventeenth-Century Revolution* (London: Allen Lane/Penguin Press, 1993) 276.
11. B. Manning, "Puritanism and Democracy, 1640-1642," in *Puritans and Revolutionaries*, D. Pennington and K. Thomas (ed.) (Oxford: Clarendon Press, 1978) 142, 147-51; Hill, *Society & Puritanism*, 503; Haller, *Liberty and Reformation*, 104, 105, 112-15, 141, 150, 192, 233, 234.
12. The Westminster Assembly convened to help settle the differences on these and other issues, but it completed its work too late to stop the prevailing anarchy. J. Morrill, *The Nature of the English Revolution* (London and New York: Longman, 1993) 18.
13. Hill, *The English Bible*, 35; S. Foster, *The Long Argument: English Puritanism and the Shaping of New England Culture, 1570-1700* (Chapel Hill, NC: The University of North Carolina, 1991) 47, 48. John Cotton did not consider his polity any different from that of Thomas Cartwright in substance. A. F. S. Pearson, *Thomas Cartwright and Elizabethan Puritanism, 1535-1603* (Gloucester, MA: P. Smith, 1966) 417.
14. J. Goodwin, *Theomachia* (London: Printed for Henry Overton, 1644) 4ff., 11, 17, 18, 21, 23, 52.
15. *Theomachia*, 29, 30, 33, 40, 42.
16. *An Apologeticall Narration* (London: Robert Dawlman, 1643) [2, 7]. The work is signed by five delegates, but Anthony Wood believes that Thomas Goodwin and Philip Nye were responsible for its production. *Athenae Oxonienses* (London, 1721) 2.738. A copy of the text is reprinted in Robert S. Paul, *An Apologeticall Narration* (Philadelphia and Boston: United Church Press, 1963).
17. Ibid., [24].
18. Ibid., [23].
19. Ibid., [5, 6]; S. C. Pearson, Jr., "Reluctant Radicals: The Independents at the Westminster Assembly," *Journal of Church and State* 11 (Aut. 1969): 474.
20. Ibid., [12-21]. The case in point is a minister who was deposed by a church but later reinstated through the work of another, when it was determined that the dismissal was done without sufficient justification.
21. Haller, *The Rise of Puritanism*, 174; Hill, *The World Turned Upside Down*, 129.
22. B. Worden, "John Milton and Oliver Cromwell," in *Soldiers, Writers, and Statesmen of the English Revolution*, I. Gentiles, J. Morrill, and B. Worden (ed.) (Cam-

bridge: Cambridge University Press, 1998) 245; E. Barker, "The Achievement of Oliver Cromwell," in *Cromwell: A Profile*, I. Roots (ed.) (New York: Hill and Wang, [1973]) 5, 6; J. C. Davis, "Cromwell's Religion," in *Oliver Cromwell and the English Revolution*, J. Morrill (ed.) (London and New York: Longman, 1990) 203, 204. The Independents failed to secure many of their demands. "In 1649-53 the Rump ruled out the separation of church and state, gave encouragement to the established ministry, left the system of tithes intact, declined to abolish the Presbyterian System, indeed came close to endorsing it." Ibid., 256, 257.

23. *The Writings and Speeches of Oliver Cromwell*, W. C. Abbott (ed.) (Cambridge, MA: Harvard University Press, 1945) 3.585, 586; J. Morrill, "Introduction," in *Oliver Cromwell and the English Revolution*, 18; Pearson, "Reluctant Radical," 479, 483, 484; Haller, *Liberty and Reformation*, 133; *The Letters and Journals of Robert Baillie, 1637-1662*, D. Laing (ed.) (Edinburgh: Bannatyne Club, 1841-42) 2.230; Yates, *The Congregationalists*, 32-34. While Cromwell's greatest and most consistent cause was religious liberty, his world had little room for "popery" and "prelacy." The Instrument of Government offered toleration to all except Catholics, and the protector and the MP's swore their allegiance to the "True, Reformed, Protestant, Christian, Religion," as it was understood in Scripture. *The Writings and Speeches*, 3.149, 4.271, 272, 565, 566; J. C. Davis, "Cromwell's Religion," 194; A. Fletcher, "Oliver Cromwell and the godly nation," in *Oliver Cromwell and the English Revolution*, 211, 217, 218. The most risky of all heresies in the seventeenth century was anti-Trinitarianism. It occasioned the last public executions for heresy in 1612. Parliament continued the death penalty for it in 1648, and the Act of Toleration excluded the heresy from its liberties in 1689. B. Worden, "John Milton and Oliver Cromwell," 247.

24. Hill, *The World Turned Upside Down*, 46, 66, 67; Haller, *Liberty and Reformation*, 129, 192; R. Baille, *Letters and Journals*, 2.153; R. Carter, *The Schismatick Stigmatized* (London: J. Okes, 1641) 7-8 (stigma 17). Cromwell caused a stir by placing men of low distinction as captains in his army. C. Hill, *God's Englishman: Oliver Cromwell and the English Revolution* (New York: The Dial Press, 1970) 66, 67. The precise nature of his religious expression has puzzled scholars. He leaves no journal, diary, or confession, beyond a cryptic account of his conversion, where he speaks like a "born-again" Christian, finding light after living in years of darkness as "the chief of sinners." His strong belief in religious liberty would align him with the Congregationalists, but whether he is serving Christ as a reformer within the church or outside as a separatist is difficult to know with any degree of certainty. Davis, "Cromwell's Religion," 183; I. Roots, *Cromwell: A Profile*, xv, xvii.

25. *The Practical Works of the Rev. Richard Baxter* (London: James Duncan, 1830) 1.52; Haller, *Liberty and Reformation*, 194, 195, 211-15. Baxter became a chaplain in the army and tried to dissuade Cromwell from his radical designs. He was unsuccessful, but out of frustration he writes one of his great works, *The Saints' Everlasting Rest*.

26. Clarendon, *The History of the Rebellion*, 838; Hill, *God's Englishman*, 51, 76, 145, 150-51, 187, 188, 195, 213, 214. Cromwell and the Puritans toyed with the idea of extending the revolution to the continent. James I had allied himself with Spain and did not support the Protestants in the Thirty Years' War. Some agents were sent to other countries during the Civil War, and Ireland was "liberated," but the revolution for the most part was confined to the homeland. Hill, *God's Englishman*, 28, 120, 155; *Puritanism and Revolution*, 132ff.; Clarendon, *The History of the Rebellion*, 348.

27. Ibid., 669; J. Sommerville, "Oliver Cromwell and English political thought," in *Oliver Cromwell and the English Revolution*, 244, 245; Morrill, *The Nature of the English Revolution*, 24; I. Roots, *Cromwell: A Profile*, xiv; Hill, *God's Englishman*, 204, 205.
28. Haller, *Liberty and Reformation*, 308. As Lord Protector Cromwell was given the power to command the army and convene the Parliament. Clarendon, *The History of the Rebellion*, 842, 843.
29. William and Youngs, *The Congregationalists*, 34; Hill, *God's Englishman*, 253.
30. Hill, *Society and Puritanism*, 506-11; *God's Englishman*, 256, 257,263; E. Barker, "The Achievement of Oliver Cromwell," 113. These comments represent the surprising results of Hill's research, the most exhaustive in the field, and overturn the typical historical and secular prejudice that would speak of the Puritans' defeat. However, scholars like Hill should not find this kind of result so shocking. Government policies have difficulty withstanding the religious affections of the people throughout history. During the 1640s the Puritans tried the same tactic with the help of Parliament, attempting to eradicate Anglicanism and eliminate its practices—the Book of Common Prayer, altar-rails, crosses, images, pictures, basins, candles, etc.—but the counties were unable or unwilling to stamp them out in general. The Restoration did not require a long transitional period to restore Anglican practices. J. Morrill, *The Nature of the English Revolution*, 149-58, 164, 165.
31. J. R. Pole, *Political Representation in England and the Origin of the American Republic* (London, Melbourne, and Toronto: Macmillan, 1966) 385, 392-94, 399; Haller, *Liberty and Reformation*, 217; Elazar, *Covenant & Commonwealth*, 262, 263; Hill, *God's Englishman*, 255. Even the royalists did not want to return to Catholicism. Henry VIII plundered the monasteries when he broke with Rome and gave the land to the "people" (i.e., the ruling class). Hill, *Puritanism and Revolution*, 32ff., 45, 46, 302.
32. D. Wooten, "The Levellers," in J. Dunn (ed.), *Democracy: The Unfinished Journey 508 BC to AD 1993* (Oxford: Oxford University Press, 1992) 71, 72; *The Writings of William Walwyn*, in J. R. McMichael and B. Taft (ed.) (Athens and London: The University of Georgia, 1989) 23, 43, 49; I. Gentiles, "London Levellers in the English Revolution: the Chidleys and their Circle," *Journal of Ecclesiastical History* 29, no. 3 (July 1978): 281, 282; J. C. Davis, "The Levellers and Christianity," in *The Politics, Religion, and The English Civil War*, B. Manning (ed.) (New York: St. Martin's Press, 1973) 224, 225; *The Leveller Tracts 1647-1623*, W. Haller and G. Davies (ed.) (New York: Columbia University Press, 1944) 3; Wooten, "The Levellers," 76. Even their opponents refer to the Leveller's religious tendencies. "Walwyns Wiles," 29. (This section uses *The Leveller Tracts* to draw its sources and works.)
33. "The Case of the Armie," 82; "Picture of the Council of State," 225; "An Agreement of the Free People of England," 326; "The Legal Fundamentall Liberties," 436. Statutes that demand church attendance, tithes, and the use of the Book of Common Prayer need to be repealed.
34. "A Declaration of Some Proceedings," 112; "The Case of the Armie," 82. Oaths must be repealed.
35. "Englands New Chains Discovered," 167.
36. "A Declaration, or, Representation," 60, 61; "The Case of the Armie," 78, 79; "An Agreement of the Free People of England," 321.
37. "A Declaration of Some Proceedings," 112; "A Declaration, or, Representation," 59; "An Agreement of the Free People of England," 322, 326. There was already

a consensus in the Long Parliament that the "commonality" should vote in "borough elections unless there was a statute to the contrary. A. Woolrych, "Putney Revisited," in *Politics and People in Revolutionary England*, C. Jones, M. Newitt, and S. Roberts (ed.) (Oxford and New York: Basil Blackwell, 1986) 110.

38. "A Declaration of Some Proceedings," 108; "Picture of the Council of State," 225; M. Goldsmith, "Levelling by Sword, Spade, and Word," in *Politics and People*, 66-69. What is intended by the "people" is sometimes difficult to discern. At the Putney debates Overton fought for the "poorest man in England" and his right to vote, but others seem to exclude paupers and wage-laborers from the franchise. The typical reason for the exclusion is economic (i.e., their status as dependents), but practical, political considerations also played a role.
39. "The Case of the Armie," 71; "A Declaration of Some Proceedings," 114.
40. "A Declaration of Some Proceedings," 109. Laws must be written in plain English, not some obscure language.
41. "An Agreement of the Free People of England," 324, 325. Self-incrimination is banned.
42. "A Declaration, or, Representation," 61; "A Declaration of Some Proceedings," 111.
43. "An Agreement of the Free People of England," 325.
44. "Englands New Chains Discovered," 161.
45. "A Declaration of Some Proceedings," 108.
46. "A Declaration of Some Proceedings," 113; "A Manifestation," 279; Goldsmith, "Levelling by Sword, Spade, and Word," 74. The Levellers point to the example of the early church in Acts 2 and 4. They deny that they would "Levell all mens estates, that we would have no distinction of Orders and Dignities among men, that we are indeed for no government. . . ." Ibid., 228. However, they do level a charge against the "Parliament-men" who serve as landlords, "customers, Excise-men, Treasurers," etc. These white-collar criminals create laws to oppress the poor out of their own vested interest. "The mournfull Cries of many thousand poor Tradesmen," 126ff. In the fall of 1648, the Levellers found it necessary to distance themselves from more zealous members of their movement like Gerrard Winstanley and the Diggers, who had communistic designs. Hill, *The World Turned Upside Down*, 31, 95, 96, 106.
47. Woolrych, "Putney Revisited," 115, 116; "Oliver Cromwell and the Rule of the Saints," in *Cromwell: A Profile*, 54. Cf. *The Writing of William Walwyn*, 49.
48. Haller, *The Rise of Puritanism*, 259.
49. Haller, *Liberty and Reformation*, 256, 293, 294.
50. "The Legall Fundamentall Liberties," 407, 408.
51. Ibid., 411-13, 433, 434; Hill, *God's Englishman*, 108, 109; *Puritanism and Revolution*, 79, 80.
52. "Picture of the Council of State," 212; "The Legall Fundamentall Liberties," 402, 403. Haller connects his conversion to the time of his suffering. *The Rise of Puritanism*, 283, 284, 287.
53. Haller, *The Rise of Puritanism*, 259, 273; Wooton, "Democracy," 75. Baptists and Quakers represent a radical expansion of certain Puritan ideals. Baptists work with the notion of "visible saints" but apply it in a more consistent manner than the Congregationalists. They simply postpone baptism to a later time when the candidates have professed and demonstrated their faith, eliminating the problem of the infamous Half-Way Covenant. Quakers extend the egalitarian and antinomian tendencies of certain Puritans groups like the Separatists and Levellers. Lilburne, Wistanley, and other dissidents practiced egalitarian gestures like using the second

person or refusing to remove the hat to superiors long before the Quakers. Gentiles, "London Levellers," 285; R. Baxter, *The Saints' Everlasting Rest* (Westwood, NJ: Fleming H. Revell, 1962) 8; Hill, *The World Turned Upside Down*, 198. Many Puritans spoke of the witness of the Spirit to all believers as the most essential means of obtaining assurance before God. The Quakers simply extend the program to include the entire life of the believer and one's relation to God. This process is most readily seen in the trials and tribulations of Anne Hutchison. She was a devout disciple of John Cotton but was banished from the Puritan community when she followed his antinomian tendencies beyond acceptable limits. She began to talk much like a Quaker, professing to experience immediate revelations from God, outside the confines of Scripture. Strehle, *The Catholic Roots of the Protestant Gospel*, 47, 48. John Winthrop thought she was one of the Grindletonians, who appeared in England during the time and emphasized the role of the Spirit more than the Word of God. Hill, *The World Turned Upside Down*, 65-67.

54. He will spend some time in Holland after 1636 as a refugee, where a number of dissident groups flourished like the Anabaptists, Baptists, and Arminians. All these groups advocated toleration and did so by emphasizing the example of the NT over the OT. "The Legall Fundamentall Liberties," 404. John Locke also will spend some time as a refugee in Holland among these groups. Afterwards he will write his famous *Letter concerning Toleration*, which defends the doctrine of toleration by advocating the supremacy of the NT over the OT.
55. "The Just Defence," 451, 452.
56. Clarendon, *The History of the Rebellion*, 849; Haller, *Liberty and Reformation*, 259, 262, 272. He speaks of reading "the Bible, the Book of Martyrs, Luthers, Calvins, Bezaes, Cartwrights, Perkins, Molins, Burtons, and Rogers works, with a multitude of other such like Books." "Legall Fundamentall Liberties," 404.
57. "The Just Defence," 452, 453; "The Legall Fundamentall Liberties," 406; "A Declaration of Some Proceedings," 107; Haller, *Liberty and Reformation*, 270, 283. Clarendon felt that Cromwell bore Lilburne's acid tongue more than "any person in authority would had ever done." *The History of the Rebellion*, 850.
58. "The Legall Fundamentall Liberties," 446, 447, 449.
59. This is the verdict of his opponents. "Walwyns Wiles," 292-93.
60. *The Writings of William Walwyn*, 20, 21; "Englands Lamentable Slaverie," 145. All references to Walwyn's writings are taken from *The Writings of William Walwyn*.
61. L. Mulligan, "The Religious Roots of William Walwyn," *The Journal of Religious History* 12 (Dec. 1982): 165, 166, 179. Mulligan finds it peculiar that any scholar would downplay Walwyn's religious commitment and treat him much like a secular humanist. Ibid., 163. See N. H. Brailsford, *The Levellers and the English Revolution,* C. Hill (ed.) (London: Cresset Press, 1961) 59; A. S. P. Woodhouse (ed.), *Puritanism and Liberty: being the Army debates (1647-9) from the Clarke manuscripts with supplementary documents* (London: Dent, 1986) 55; A. L. Morton, *The World of the Ranters: Religious Radicalism in the English Revolution* (London: Lawrence & Wishart, 1970) 145, 196.
62. H. Brooke, "The Charity of Church-Men," 337, 339 (from *Leveller Tracts*).
63. *The Writings of William Walwyn*, 2, 5.
64. "Good Counsel to All," 130.
65. "The Power of Love," 94.
66. Mulligan, "The Religious Roots," 173.
67. "A Word in Season," 207ff.; "A Parable," 259-62.
68. *The Writings of William Walwyn*, 4.

69. "A Still and Small Voice," 270-72.
70. "The Foundation of Slander Discovered," 367.
71. "Walwyn's Just Defense," 397ff.; "Walwyns Wiles," 294-98; H. Brooke, "The Charity of Church-Men," 335, 336. This last treatise is a reply by one of Walwyn's friends to the accusations in "Walwyn's Wiles." Both works are found among the *Leveller Tracts*. Walwyn reads and uses a number of books from pagans and theologians alike. He finds special attachment to Montaigne's *Essays*, quoting or alluding to it often in his works. E.g., *The Writings of William Walwyn*, 3-5; "Walwyn's Just Defense," 399. But Walwyn chastens Lilburne for relying too much on the Magna Carta during his many tribulations. Lilburne appealed to this famous charter as a classical symbol of the "rights of Englishmen." Walwyn considers the charter overrated in Lilburne's mind for several reasons. One, it only contains a paucity of rights. (It speaks of jury trials, property rights, repeal of unjust customs and fines, and "freedom of elections," which Innocent III had granted and the royals have disturbed. In its historical context, it served as a declaration of some liberties in the hope of avoiding civil war, and Lilburne looked to it as a precedent for the type of rights he wanted for himself and others in the public sphere.) Two, Parliament also appeals to it only to undermine and amend it in whatever direction suits their purpose. Three, it is better to make one's appeal to the "universall Rules of common equitie and justice," which binds "all men and all Authority," than any specific manifestation of it. "Englands Lamentable Slaverie," 146-49; "A Declaration of Some Proceedings," 109 (*Leveller Tracts*); Davis, "The Levellers and Christianity," 232, 233. It was Sir Edward Coke (1552-1634) who was most responsible for exalting Magna Carta to its inflated image. He saw it as a centerpiece of common law, which he hoped to exert against royal privileges. Hill, *The Intellectual Origins of the English Revolution*, 244-46, 258. Through the admonitions of Walwyn, Overton, and other Levellers, Lilburne came to recognize that Magna Carta was "but a beggerly thing, containing many marks of intolerable bondage." Hill, *Puritanism and Revolution*, 76. Walwyn appeals to reason at times to refute his opponents, but his reasoning is subordinate to faith (*fides quaerens intellectum*). His passion for free thought presents some problems for his opponents when he doubts what the orthodox normally accept with unquestioned piety. For example, his critics accuse him of denying the existence of hell. Brooke defends his friend saying that they have twisted his words. Walwyn remains a pious Christian and accepts the doctrine of hell based on biblical authority, but his piety does not prevent him from wondering how a little sinning could produce such a grave consequence. "Walwyns Wiles," 296, 297; "The Charity of Church-Men," 334ff.
72. He rarely refers to the OT. *The Writings of William Walwyn*, 6. Walwyn follows the dispensational understanding of dissident groups (Anabaptists, Baptists, and Arminians), with whom he has much in common. His method of interpretation emphasizes the NT over the OT and lends itself to a more tolerant position on church/state issues by following the more benign example of the NT. His method does not conjoin the testaments together under the Reformed doctrine of covenant, and this might explain why Walwyn and the Levellers do not express themselves using this powerful concept.
73. "Tolleration Justified, and Persecution Condemned," 161, 162; "A Parable," 259-261.
74. Ibid., 156, 162, 170; "Good Counsel to All," 129, 130. He also refers to the advice of Gamaliel a few times in Acts 5, interpreting it much like John Goodwin.
75. "Some Considerations," 69-72; "A New Petition of the Papists," 62; "The Compassionate Samaritane," 99; "A Helpe to the Right Understanding," 136.

76. "A New Petition of the Papists," 57ff.; "The Compassionate Samaritane," 100, 101.He rejects the practice of paying state-sponsored tithes to a particular church. He employs his dispensational analysis to prove that this practice ended with Christ. "A Whisper in the Eare of Mr. Thomas Edwards, Minister," 174.
77. "The Power of Love," 94. The states should not put to death those who deny cardinal doctrines. "Demurre to the Bill for Preventing the Growth and Spreading of Heresie," 239.
78. "Some Considerations," 68; "The Compassionate Samaritane," 105, 106; "Tolleration Justified, and Persecution Condemned," 156ff., 168.
79. "Walwyn's Just Defense," 427.
80. "The Compassionate Samaritane," 124.
81. "W Walwyn's Conceptions, For a Free Trade," 447ff. He denies the charge that he wishes to level all estates, apart from the consent of the people. The communism of the book of Acts was voluntary. "A Manifestation," 337, 338; Goldsmith, "Levelling by Sword, Spade, and Word," 70, 71. The tension between freedom and equality displays itself in a most telling way within the Leveller's desire for the free trade of capitalism and the equal results of communism.
82. "Juries Justified," passim; "The Foundation of Slander Discovered," 374, 375. Laws should be written in the plain language of the people. "A Helpe to the Right Understanding," 134. For a list of Leveller complaints and petitions, see "Gold Tried in the Fire," 283ff.
83. "Tolleration Justified, and Persecution Condemned," 169-71; "The Bloody Project," 298, 299.
84. "A Parable," 259, 260.
85. Hill, *Society & Puritanism, 226-42, 248, 249.*
86. Morrill, *The Nature of the English Revolution*, 11-14, 65, 66, 85.
87. T. Case, *Two Sermons Lately Preached at Westminster* (London: I. Raworth, 1642) 2.13, 16. Reform meant the reestablishment of the divine kingdom on earth transforming all of humankind body, soul, and spirit. According to John Knox, "a public reformation, as well in the religion as in the temporal government, were most necessary." Burrell, "The Apocalyptic Vision," 5; *John Knox's History of the Reformation in Scotland*, W. C. (ed.) (New York: Philosophical Library, 1950) 1.149.
88. Morrill, *The Nature of the English Revolution*, 75, 76.
89. Barker, "The Achievement of Cromwell," 8; Woolrych, "Oliver Cromwell and the Rule of the Saints," 52. Morrill says that "there are no historians nowadays who deny that religion was *an* important cause of the civil war," although some like Sommerville find it less important than other matters. *The Nature of the English Revolution*, 37, 38.
90. "A Whisper in the Eare of Mr. Thomas Edwards, Minister," in *The Writings of William Walwyn*, 176, 177.
91. Clarendon, *The History of the Rebellion*, 1.387; R. N. Stromberg, *Religious Liberalism in Eighteenth-Century England* (London: Oxford University Press, 1954) 124.
92. Hill, *Society & Puritanism*, 32-41, 421.
93. Foster, *The Long Argument*, xii, 153, 288. A good illustration of the influence is a comparison of the names of towns in Massachusetts and elsewhere in New England with those of East Anglia, the region with the largest concentration of Puritans. K. Phillips, *The Cousins' Wars: Religion, Politics, and the Triumph of Anglo-America* (New York: Basic Books, 1999) 20, 24, 25.

94. One imperfection is seen by most people today in the very usage of the term "forefathers."
95. These pilgrims arrived in the autumn of 1620. They were dominated by a group of separatists, who had escaped persecution by fleeing at first to Holland and then to America. They were not interested in reforming the Church of England or its state. Those who arrived with John Winthrop a decade later rejected the separatism of the early colonists and wanted to establish a Puritan commonwealth or a "City Upon a Hill." J. Winthrop, "A Modell of Christian Charity Written on Board the Arabell, On the Atlantik Ocean," in *Winthrop Papers* (Boston: The Massachusetts Historical Society, 1931) 2.295. David Fischer traces the usage of this biblical phrase to East Anglia, the center of Puritan activity in England, as describing their basic aspirations in the area. D. H. Fischer, *Albion's Seed: Four British Folkways in America* (New York and Oxford: Oxford University Press, 1989) 47.
96. "The Mayflower Compact," in W. Walker, *The Creeds and Platforms of Congregationalism* (Boston: The Pilgrim Press, 1960) 92. John Winthrop also appeals to the "Covenant" and "Commission" of God in his speech on the Arbella.
97. Bradford's colony followed the same type of democratic model in church and state as the Bay. C. Mather, *Magnalia Christi Americana* (New York: Russell & Russell, 1967) 1.111ff.; D. Hall, *The Genevan Reformation and the American Founding* (Lanham, NC: Lexington Books, 2003) 291.
98. "The Covenant of 1629," in Walker, *Creeds and Platforms*, 116. This church and the First Church of Boston elected all of its officers—teacher, pastor, elders, and deacons. Mather, *Magnalia Christi Americana*, 1.71, 72; *The Journal of John Winthrop 1630-1649*, R. S. Dunn, J. Savage, and L. Yeandle (ed.) (Cambridge, MA: The Belknap Press of Harvard University, 1996) 1.38, 39; S. Evans, *The Theme is Freedom* (Washington, D.C.: Regnery Publishing, Inc., 1996) 193. The oldest symbol of Connecticut also contains a witness to the power of the covenant. "The Winsor Creed-Covenant of 1647," in Walker, *Creeds and Platforms*, 154-56. Its church was a result of emigration from Massachusetts and developed around 1636.
99. Paul, *An Apologeticall Narration*, 83, 84.
100. J. Cotton, *The Way of the Churches of Christ* (London, 1645) 56, 61-64, 102, 103; *Of the Holinesse of Church Members* (London, 1650) 24.
101. J. Cotton, *The Doctrine of the Church* (London, 1644) 1, 12.
102. T. Hooker, *A Survey of the Summe of Church-Discipline*, reprinted from the 1648 edition by A. M. in London (New York: Arno Press, 1972) preface.
103. Ibid., 1.1, 2.
104. Ibid., 1.5.
105. Ibid., 1.56.
106. Ibid., 1.6ff.
107. Ramian charts are seen in the work at the end of the preface, 1.89, and 2.4. But the work also displays Aristotelian logic at times, using the syllogism and speaking of material and efficient causes.
108. Ibid., 1.98.
109. Ibid., preface, 1.118, 124; 4.35.
110. Ibid., 1.5; 2.4, 5.
111. Ibid., 1.99, 123.
112. Ibid., 1.110. The Apostles were given authority over all the church, but Hooker considers their office extraordinary and temporal. Ibid., 2.10, 4.35.
113. Ibid., 1.259.
114. Ibid., 1.192ff., 219; 4.19.

115. Ibid., preface, 4.1, 2, 13, 14.
116. Ibid., appendix, 49, 50.
117. Ibid., 1.46.
118. Ibid., 1.46-51.
119. Ibid., 1.48, 49. Hooker does not wish to follow some separatist groups and declare other fellowships as "no church." He prefers an explicit covenant but feels that those who do not contain one can have the same concept implicitly.
120. Ibid., 1.47.
121. Ibid., 1.66 [67]. The church also ordains its candidate, following the election. Ibid., 2.39, 40. Apparently, he is uncomfortable with the term democracy and speaks of the government at one point as a mixture of democracy (people), monarchy (Christ), and aristocracy (elders). Ibid., 1.206.
122. Ibid., 3.44, 45. Beza is cited a number of times by Hooker and always with approval. Hooker is either unaware of the controversy surrounding his name or searching for much needed authority, regardless of the clear differences between them. Hooker seems to accept Beza's contention that discipline is more the day-to-day job of the elders than the congregation. Ibid., 3.38.
123. Ibid., 1.14, 55ff., 190. Membership is limited to one specific church, although it is possible to receive a sacrament within another church. Excommunicated parents have no right to baptize their child. Ibid., 1.64; 2.65; 3.18, 24.
124. Ibid., 1.14, 15, 23, 24.
125. Walker, *Creeds and Platforms*, 171, 185; J. F. Cooper, *Tenacious for Their Liberties: The Congregationalists in Colonial Massachusetts* (New York and Oxford: Oxford University Press, 1999) 143, 144. The symbol provided a standard for generations to come, reminding them of the founding principles and guiding them away from imperfections toward the ideal, much like the famous words of the Declaration of Independence—"All men are created equal." In 1679 a synod of churches met in the Bay Colony and made the reaffirmation of the platform a sacred aspect of Congregational churches for generations to come. Mather, *Magnalia Christi Americana*, 2.237.
126. The text of the *Cambridge Platform* is found in Walker's *Creeds and Platforms*. The magistrate is placed in charge of both tables of the Mosaic Law. He can punish a corrupt or schismatic church. He can punish outward crimes such as "Idolatry, Blasphemy, Heresy, venting corrupt & pernicious opinions, that destroy the foundation, open contempt of the word preached, prophanation of the Lords day, disturbing the peaceable administration & exercise of the worship & holy things of God, & the like" (XI, 4; XVII, 6-9). But the magistrate is not to compel church-membership, participation in communion, or interfere with church-offices (XVII, 4, 5).
127. Walker, *Creeds and Platforms*, 162, 166, 171, 194-95. The role of a synod is to provide admonition and good instruction, but it should not assume the powers of the local church. The churches are exhorted to have communion with each other on an equal basis, but it is possible to shun communion with a specific church if it refuses to repent (XV, XVI).
128. The platform displays the same hesitancy toward democracy that we first observed in Morély and observed once again in Hooker. Its rhetoric prefers to speak of the government in an Aristotelian manner as mixed with elements of monarchy (Christ), democracy (visible saints), and aristocracy (elders) ruling together. It also tries to steer a middle course between Presbyterianism and Brownism. It makes some concessions to the former by allowing local elders and outside churches to "exempt" the calling of certain brethren. Mather, *Magnalia Christi Americana*, 2.248, 249, 254, 255; Foster, *The Long Argument*, 169, 170.

129. *Magnalia Christi Americana*, 1.70. Covenant renewal became an indelible mark of the early Puritan community, especially under the leadership of Increase and Cotton Mather. Ibid., 2.328, 329; Foster, *The Long Argument*, 223ff. The practice of national days of fasting and prayer became a routine aspect of Puritan culture after 1624, although Laud detested the practice and tried to suppress it during the reign of Charles I. Hill, *The English Bible*, 80, 81.
130. T. Hooker, *A Survey*, 1.69.
131. J. Cotton, *The Way of the Churches in New-England* (London: M. Simmons, 1645) 4.
132. *The Journal of John Winthrop*, 587.
133. C. Mather, *Things for a Distress'd People to think upon* (Boston: B. Green and J. Allen, 1696) 60-62.
134. J. Wise, *A Vindication of the Government of the New-England Churches* (Gainesville, Fl.: Scholars' Facsimiles & Reprints, 1958) 45, 60, 61. It was first printed in Boston, 1717.
135. Ibid., 45.
136. Ibid., 60, 61. Wise earned a reputation later on as America's first democrat, and Patriots reprinted his *Vindication* and *The Churches' Quarrell Espoused* to help incite revolution in the 1770s. J. F. Cooper, *Tenacious of Their Liberties*, 162.
137. Mather, *Magnalia Chisti Americana*, 1.28, 29.
138. The most radical Congregationalists were not Anabaptists. They separated themselves from the state out of frustration over the pace of reformation and never abandoned the desire to transform society, except in isolated times of blighted hope. Foster, *The Long Argument*, 14, 17, 50.
139. D. B. Rutman, *Winthrop's Boston* (New York: W. W. Norton, 1965) 62, 65; J. Miller, *The Rise and Fall of Democracy in Early America, 1630-1789: The Legacy of Contemporary Politics* (University Park: Penn State University Press, 1991) 27, 34. The notions of a "general parish meeting" and a "general town meeting" were synonymous in early colonial times. These notions have antecedents in East Anglia, a stronghold of Puritan sentiments in England, and were transplanted to America. D. H. Fischer, *Albion's Seed*, 196. The General Court established the New England town meeting as an institution in 1635, in order to give the freemen of every town relative autonomy in governing their own affairs and electing their own officials. T. J. Wertenbaker, *The Puritan Oligarchy: The Founding of American Civilization* (New York and London: Charles Scribner's Sons, 1947) 44, 45; Evans, *The Theme is Freedom*, 197.
140. It is difficult for secular Americans to understand how important the church was to their forefathers. Patricia Bonomi tries to illustrate this point by opening her book, *Under the Cope of Heaven*, with a view of the New York City skyline from a woodblock, dated 1771. The skyline is dominated with church buildings and spires pointing to heaven, creating a stark contrast in the mind of the reader between its view of the world and that of modern day Manhattan.
141. Mather, *Magnalia Christi Americana*, 1.70, 107ff. Of course, this merger of church and state did not mean that the two institutions served the same exact role in society. Both served a role in the overall "theocracy" (1.143), but they served in different capacities. When Nathaniel Ward tried to use secular argumentation in political and moral debate, Winthrop found this trust in human wisdom offensive. *The Journal of John Winthrop*, 359
142. Miller, *The New England Mind: The Seventeenth Century*, 475ff.; *The New England Mind: From Colony to Province*, 21ff., 482, 483; Phillips, *The Cousins' Wars*, 28; Morrill, *The Nature of the English Revolution*, 83, 84. It is the doctrine of the covenant that dictates the close relationship between the nation of Israel and the Puritan community. More than any other fellowship the Calvinists followed the example and

teaching of the OT, believing that the old and new covenants were one and the same in essence. This identification with the nation of Israel was a prevalent feature of Puritan self-understanding since the middle of the sixteenth century and drew much criticism from opponents of the movement (e.g., Richard Hooker). Hill, *The English Bible*, 266-69; K. L. Griffin, *Revolution and Religion: American Revolutionary War and the Reformed Clergy* (New York: Paragon House, 1994) 22.

143. Miller, *The New England Mind: From Colony to Province*, 29, 30, 36, 37.
144. McCoy and Baker, *Fountainhead of Federalism*, 85-88. Cotton says, "It is very suitable to Gods all-sufficient wisdome, and to the fulnes and perfection of Holy Scriptures, not only to prescribe perfect rules for the right ordering of a private mans soule to every blessednes with himself, but also for the right ordering of a mans family, yea, of the commonweath too, so farre as both of them are subordinate to spiritual ends, ... It is better that the commonwealth be fashioned to the setting forth of Gods house, which is the church: than accommodate the church frame to the civill state." *The Puritans: A Sourcebook of Their Writings*, P. Miller and T. H. Johnson (ed.) (Mineola, NY: Dover Publications, Inc., 2001) 1.209.
145. Mather, *Magnalia Christi Americana*, 266; J. R. Pole, *Political Representation in England and the Origins of the American Republic* (London, Melbourne, and Toronto: Macmillan, 1966) 34, 35; Miller, *The Rise and Fall of Democracy*, 27.
146. *The Journal of John Winthrop*, 68.
147. Mather, *Magnalia Christi Americana*, 1.123; *The Journal of John Winthrop*, 68, 116, 144, 215, 257, 292, 294, 325, 373, 507, 621, 705.
148. *The Journal of John Winthrop*, 180-183. See Ibid., 63, 77.
149. Ibid., 456, 458, 503. John Winthrop and John Cotton rejected the notion of a pure democracy and favored the negative vote.
150. Ibid., 578ff., 581, 590, 593.
151. A. de Tocqueville, *Democracy in America* (New York: Alfred A. Knopf, 1963) 1.32, 39, 40, 56, 59, 61, 81. "Massachusetts was the most assertively free of the colonies. . . . In Massachusetts and New England generally, there prevailed what Edmund Burke was to call 'the dissidence of dissent and the Protestantism of the Protestant religion.'" Kirk, *America's British Culture*, 53; C. M. Andrews, *Colonial Self-Government 1652-1689* (New York and London: Harper & Brothers Publishers, 1905) 44, 45. Popular assemblies soon developed throughout the colonies, challenging the authority of the king, governor, and council, which was elected or appointed. Ibid., 52; M. W. Jernegan, *The American Colonies 1492-1750* (New York: Longman, Green and Co., 1931) 273-77, 277.
152. Evans, *The Theme is Freedom*, 201.
153. Ibid., 194; Hall, *The Genevan Reformation and the American Founding*, 18; Foster, *The Long Argument*, 156.
154. Ibid., 195.
155. H. Miller, "The Grammar of Liberty: Presbyterians and the First American Constitution," *Journal of Presbyterian History* 54 (1976): 151-56; Hall, *The Genevan Reformation and the American Founding*, 310, 340, 342, 393, 394, 396; M. J. Westerkamp, *The Triumph of the Laity: Scots-Irish Piety and the Great Awakening*, 1625-1760 (New York and Oxford: Oxford University Press, 1988) 137, 142, 143; J. C. D. Clark, *The Language of Lib*erty, 1660-1832 (Cambridge, MA and New York: University Press, 1994) 208, 290, 291.
156. H. S. Stout, "Preaching the Insurrection," *Christian History* 15, no. 2 (1996) 17.
157. R. Brown, *Middle-Class Democracy and the Revolution in Massachusetts, 1691-1780* (Ithaca, NY: Cornell University Press, 1955) 109, 110; Evans, *The Theme is Freedom*, 200, 201.

158. The Act of Toleration brought a more ecumenical spirit among Protestant groups. Cotton Mather displays much admiration for the genuine piety of Presbyterians, Episcopalians, Anabaptists, and the Quakers (as represented by Penn, not Fox). He seems to situate himself between Presbyterians and Independents, and approves of a union that was created between the two fellowships in England through the efforts of Increase Mather. *Magnalia Christi Americana*, 1.250, 2.272, 523ff., 646-48.
159. Griffin, *Revolution and Religion*, 38, 45, 47, 48, 58, 73-75, 79. A good example is William Foster's "True Fortitude Dedicated" (Philadelphia: J. Dunlap, 1776). He speaks of the Puritan colonists and the church of America fulfilling the prophecy of Rev. 12:13, 14 through their errand in the wilderness. He believes that God intended this migration to America for the "enlargement of Christ's kingdom," all the way to the "pacific ocean" (16, 17). In the present crisis, he says a number of times that "God is on our side," assuring the soldiers that God will fight the battle for them, just like he did in OT times for the nation of Israel (15). Those who die for the cause of liberty, defending their property rights, will receive the crown of a martyr (10-12, 21).
160. Ibid., 31, 60, 69, 68-70.
161. W. P. Breed, *Prebyterians and the Revolution* (Philadelphia: Presbyterian Board of Education and Sabbath-School Work, 1876) 55-57; S. West, "On the Right to Rebel Against Governors" [Boston, 1776], in *American Political Writing during the Founding Era*, C. Hyneman and D. Lutz (ed.) (Indianapolis, IN: Liberty Press, 1883) 1.413, 414, 422, 432; Hall, *The Genevan Reformation and the American Founding*, 351ff., 356, 360-63.
162. Clark, *The Language of Liberty*, 366. This sermon had considerable influence in Europe and America. "To H. Niles" (Feb. 13, 1818), in *The Works of John Adams* (Freeport, NY: Books for Libraries Press, 1969) 10.287, 288.
163. J. Mayhew, "A Discourse concerning unlimited submission and non-resistance to higher powers; . . ." [Boston: D. Fowle, 1750], in *Sermons* (New York: Arno Press & The New York Times, 1969) iv, v.
164. Ibid., 18, 19. He makes a specific argument from the Congregational way, saying that ministers deserve our obedience only if they fulfill their duties. Ibid., 23, 24.
165. Ibid., 9, 17, 18.
166. Ibid., 14.
167. Ibid., 14, 41.
168. Ibid., 21, 22.
169. Ibid., 29.
170. Ibid., 38-44. See also Ibid., 15, 16.
171. Locke was reared in a home of deep-seated Puritan convictions. His father was a captain in a voluntary regiment of the parliamentary army. He matriculated into Oxford during the great Puritan Revolution and Cromwell's tenure as its chancellor.
172. In contrast to previous studies, recent estimates have shown no substantial decline in the American church of the eighteenth century. The number of Congregationalist churches tripled in New England from 140 to 450 by the mid-century, with Boston boasting 18 of these churches. Some 60 percent of adults attended church on a regular basis throughout the colonies. Even if many were non-communicants, they still participated in their local fellowships with zeal, serving as deacons, vestrymen, or active participants in a myriad of tasks and missions. Bonomi, *Under the Cope of Heaven*, 72, 85, 89, 90, 220.; P. U. Bonomi and P. R. Eisenstadt, "Church

Adherence in the Eighteenth-Century British American Colonies," *William and Mary Quarterly* 39 (1982): 245-86.

173. For an overview of the religious language in today's state constitutions, see T. L. Krannawitter and D. C. Palm, *A Nation under God? The ACLU and Religion in American Politics* (Lanham, MD: Rowman & Littlefield Publishers, Inc., 2005) 139-167.
174. Preamble, I, a.1, 7, 10, 13. Covenant making was a part of the early state constitutions and became an essential part of towns and cities across America. D. J. Elazar, "America and the Federalist Revolution," *This World* 10 (Wint. 1985) 67.
175. Preamble, I, a.17.
176. I, a.10.
177. I, a.23.
178. Phillips, *The Cousins' Wars*, 99, 169-72; Bonomi, *Under the Cope of Heaven*, 187, 196, 197, 209ff. There were other factors in the American Revolution, but religion played an important role. Phillips notes that High Church Anglicans were more likely to have Tory sympathies, while Congregationalists (along with Low Church Anglicans and Scots-Irish Presbyterians) constituted the hard-core of the rebellion. Ibid., 81, 92, 177-79, 193, 200. There was much uproar over the possibility of a bishop coming to America and exercising tyranny over the colonies. C. Bridenbaugh, *Mitre and Sceptre: Transatlantic Faiths, Ideas, Personalities, and Politics 1689-1775* (New York: Oxford University Press, 1962) 312, 313; Bonomi, *Under the Cope of Heaven*, 199ff., 222.
179. *The Journal of Winthrop*, 295, 296, 346.
180. *Records of the Governor and Company of Massacusetts Bay in New England, 1628-1686*, N. B. Shurtleff (ed.) (Boston: W. White, 1853-1854) 1.17.
181. *The Journal of Winthrop*, 653.
182. Ibid., 662, 665.
183. *Magnalia Christi Americana*, 1.176-80, 200-202; Foster, *The Long Argument*, 244-52.
184. Evans, *The Theme is Freedom*, 213, 214, 217.
185. II, c.1, s.2, a.1, 2. The constitution-makers of America tied the right to vote and possession of property together. E. F. Foner, *The Story of American Freedom* (New York and London: W. W. Norton & Co., 1998) 17, 18; Pole, *Political Representation*, 25. From 1776-1790, Pennsylvania was the most egalitarian of all the states, which one might expect given their heritage in Quakerism, Anabaptism, and other religious minorities. Every tax-paying free man had the right to vote. S. E. Morison, *Sources and Documents Illustrating the American Revolution 1764-1788 and the Formation of the Federal Constitution* (Oxford: At the Clarendon Press, 1962) 165. Pennsylvania had a unicameral legislature with no governor ruling over the assembly and no property qualifications for office. Virginia developed a democratic constitution in 1776, after years of oppression under the hierarchical structure of Anglican society, although it was not until the mid-nineteenth century that universal, white-male suffrage came to pass. Pole, *Political Representation*, 314, 315. Cf. The Constitution of Virginia, Bill of Rights, sec. 6.
186. II, c.1, s.3, a.4.
187. II, c.2, s.1, a.3; s.2, a.1. For holding office the property qualification was 1000 pounds for Governor, 300 pounds for Senator, and 100 pounds for a Representative.
188. Pole, *Political Representation*, 194, 205, 209, 210.
189. Cf. F. Lambert, *The Founding Fathers and the Place of Religion in America* (Princeton, NJ: Princeton University Press, 2003) 84, 85. In 1691 the original

charter of the colony was replaced, giving political rights to non-church members and toleration to all Christians except papists. Bonomi, *Under the Cope of heaven*, 61.

190. It is true that Winthrop and Cotton condemned democracy, but most of this debate is pure semantics. The term had a pejorative connotation at that time, and most preferred to speak of mixed government. One should recall that Jean Morély had similar reservations about the term. Cf. Lambert, *The Founding Fathers*, 82.

191. E.g., Darren Staloff finds the "thinking class" dominating the people and providing no real democratic forum *de facto*. *The Making of an American Thinking Class: Intellects and Intelligentsia in Puritan Massachusetts* (New York and Oxford: Oxford University Press, 1998) 6-18. James Cooper provides a most compelling refutation of this position in his *Tenacious for Their Liberties*. He examines the extant church records of Congregationalists in America up until the middle of the eighteenth century, using Harold Worthley's "Inventory of the Records of the Particular (Congregational) Churches of Massachusetts gathered 1620-1805" as a tool to track down the records. His sources range from the sermon notebook of Robert Keayne, who recorded numerous proceedings within the First Church of Boston, to the notebook of John Fiske, who served in a small frontier church in Wenham (8, 59, 65). He finds that the laity exercised significant authority from the outset of the experiment in the 1630s through making decisions, showing dissent, electing officers, admitting and dismissing members, censuring ministers, and participating in disciplinary matters (26, 27, 31-33, 37, 40-44, 59-62). Despite the attempt of some ministers to exercise more autocratic authority, the right of lay consent prevented any fundamental intrusion upon its authority and continued as an indelible mark of the fellowship throughout the period (171, 176, 177, 180). There is no evidence that Solomon Stoddard and his ministerial colleagues were able to make significant inroads and create a presbyterian polity among the local churches (158-62, 166, 167, 181). A similar attempt by Thomas Parker and James Noyes of Newbury also met with considerable lay resistance early on, even within their own church (69, 70, 73, 75, 149). At the end of the seventeenth century, Cooper and other scholars notice a laxing of rigor in discipline and admission standards, but this lack of covenantal piety in no wise diminishes the laic control of the fellowship (134-39, 208, 209). He understands Congregationalism as a "seedbed" of liberty, democracy, and mixed government that would develop into a revolution by the end of the eighteenth century (5, 217).

192. N. O. Hatch, *The Democratization of American Christianity* (New Haven, CT and London: Yale University Press, 1989) 9, 36, 37; Bonomi, *Under the Cope of Heaven,* 147, 157; Lambert, *The Founding Fathers*, 135-41, 146-48, 208; M. J. Westerkamp, *Triumph of the Laity: Scots-Irish and the Great Awakening*, 1625-1760 (New York and Oxford, Oxford University Press, 1988); S. Marini, "Religion, Politics, and Ratification," in *Religion in a Revolutionary Age*, R. Hoffman and P. J. Albert (ed.) (Charlottesville: University Press of Virginia, 1994) 190ff.; W. G. McLoughlin, "Enthusiasm for Liberty: The Great Awakening as the Key to the Revolution," in *Preachers and Politicians* (Worcester, MA: American Antiquarian Society, 1977) 47-73; H. S. Stout, *The New England Soul: Preaching and Religious Culture in Colonial New England* (New York, Oxford University Press, 1986) 210, 211.

193. W. Perry, *Historical Collections relating to the American Colonial Church* (New York: AMS Press, 1969) 3.418; Lambert, *The Founding Fathers*, 153, 154.

194. Griffin, *Revolution and Religion*, 84.

195. Cooper, *Tenacious for Their Liberties*, 204.

196. Hatch, *The Democratization of American Christianity*, 19, 20, 49. Timothy Dwight, the president of Yale, wondered how people could demand a "seven-years apprenticeship, for the purpose of making a shoe, or an axe" and "insist . . . their property shall be managed by skillful agents," while "they were satisfied to place their Religion, their souls, and their salvation, under the guidance of quackery." A Sermon at the Opening [of the Theological Institution in Andover] (Boston: Belcher & Armstrong, 1808) 8. But as "Crazy" Lorenzo Dow noted, "larnin isn't religion, and eddication don't give man the power of the Spirit. . . . St. Peter was a fisherman—do you think he ever went to Yale College?" S. G. Goodrich, *Recollections of a Lifetime* (New York and Auburn: Miller, Orton and Mulligan, 1856) 1.196, 197.
197. In the preface of the work, Adams claims that the American way of government resulted from the hard work of reason and consultation with scientific writers in the field, not "interviews with the gods" or the "inspiration of Heaven." *The Works of John Adams* (Freeport, NY: Books for Libraries, 1969) 4.292, 293, 559. He bestows much credit on a number of "secular" experiments in history, extending back to Ancient Greece and Rome, as well as his own considerable ability to analyze their strengths and weaknesses. Ibid., 4.462, 465, 466.
198. *Notes on Virginia* (1782) F 4.62; J. L. Wagoner, *Jefferson and Education* (Charlottesville, VA: Thomas Jefferson Foundation, 2004) 35. The private correspondence of Jefferson speaks in a direct and forthright manner about his dream to use public education as a means of performing a "quiet euthanasia" upon the fanatical beliefs of the church and restoring a religion of "peace, reason, and morality" in the country. "To William Short" (Oct. 31, 1819) F 12.142; R. M. Healey, *Jefferson on Religion in Public Education* (New Haven, CT and London: Yale University Press, 1962) 157, 158, 161ff., 204, 205. In October of 1776 he became a member of the committee to revise the legal code of Virginia and proposed three bills to encourage the growth of education in the Commonwealth: The Bill for the More General Diffusion of Knowledge (no. 79), The Bill for Amending the Constitution of the College of William and Mary (no. 80), and The Bill for Establishing a Public Library (no. 81). In the first bill, he wants to provide elementary education to all "free children" for three years at the public's expense, teaching them moral lessons from the history of western culture, rather than turning to the message of Scripture for answers. In his second bill, he wants to reduce Anglican control over the College of William and Mary, eliminating the school of theology, replacing the governing board, and making the administration responsible to the legislature, not the Church of England. Wagoner, *Jefferson and Education*, 33-38; R.O. Woodburn, "An Historical Investigation of the Opposition to Jefferson's Educational Proposals in the Commonwealth of Virginia" (PhD diss., The American University, Washington, D.C.) 33-38, 51, 52; Healey, *Jefferson on Religion*, 186, 187; L. W. Levy, *Jefferson & Civil Liberties: The Darker Side* (Cambridge, MA: Harvard University Press, 1963) 9-11; *A Bill for Amending the Constitution of the College of William and Mary*, B 2.539. At the University of Virginia he refuses to appoint a divinity professor and prevents ministers and religious services from obtaining access to the centers of power on campus, only agreeing after considerable pressure to make sectarian instruction available outside his famous serpentine wall for those who wanted it. "Report of the Commissioners for the University of Virginia" (Aug., 1818), in Thomas Jefferson, *Writings* (New York: The Library of America, 1984) 467; "To Dr. Thomas Cooper" (Oct. 7, 1814) L 14.200; Wagoner, *Jefferson and Education*, 139, 140; "To Doctor Thomas Cooper" (Nov. 2, 1822) L 15.405; "From the Minutes of the Board of Visitors" (Oct. 7, 1822), in *Writings*, 477, 478; L. W.

Levy, *The Establishment Clause: Religion and the First Amendment* (Chapel Hill: The University of North Carolina, 1994) 74, 75; *Jefferson & Civil Liberties*, 12.

199. Adams spent ten years as a diplomat in France, England, and Holland. He remains the quintessential Puritan in most of his attitudes, but it is clear that French culture seduces his frugality and simplicity with its luxurious life-style. He and Jefferson end up imbibing much of the French attitude toward revealed religion, but Adams never cast aspersions on Christianity, like Jefferson, Voltaire, and the other "cultured despisers." D. McCullough, *John Adams* (New York: Simon & Schuster, 2001) 113, 114, 301-306, 349; "To Thomas Jefferson" (Dec. 3, 1813) 171; "To F. A. Vanderkemp" (July 13, 1815) 193. The letters and references are found in *The Selected Writings of John and John Quincy Adams*, A. Koch and W. Peden (ed.) (New York: A. A. Knopf, 1946). See pp. xxx of this volume. His *Defence of the Constitutions of the United States of America* is filled with brilliant historical argumentation over classical models of governments, but he only considers the past through his own *Sitz im Leben*, like any other interpreter. S. Fish, *Doing What Comes Naturally* (Durham, NC and London: Duke University press, 1989). His commitment to mixed government comes from his own Puritan culture. Even his mode of argumentation remains indebted as much to faith as it does to his own rational acuity. No better illustration of this influence is found than the continuous accent upon human depravity throughout his work as providing the fundamental rationale for separating and balancing powers. Human depravity is a unique doctrine of Christian anthropology, strongly emphasized by the Reformed theology of New England and most essential in distinguishing its confession from all other religions and philosophies in the world. Christianity teaches a darker view of the human condition than other ideologies with its emphasis upon original sin, confession, and the complete dependence of its people upon divine grace. Adams argues throughout the work from this concept of human depravity, believing that no set of circumstances or values can alleviate the dark condition in which all of us are born. The selfish impulses are much stronger than any positive affection that public service might inflame toward the good of our fellow citizens. Its ambitions cannot be eradicated in this life, but only held in check by a system of government that prevents the hubris of one person or group from obtaining uncontrolled power. This argument is repeated time and again in Montesquieu, Madison, and all those who defend the need for balancing and separating powers in the modern world—an argument indebted to the dark image of the human condition in Christian anthropology. See Adams, *Works*, 4.356, 406, 407; 5.40, 49; 6.57, 61, 97, 99, 211ff.

200. *Oeuvres Complètes de Voltaire* (Paris: Garnier Frères, 1877-85) 22.99, 103, 109 [Voltaire, *Letters concerning the English Nation* (New York: Burt Franklin Reprints, 1974) 34, 41, 52, 53)]; A. J. Ayer, *Voltaire* (New York: Random House, 1986) 15, 16, 43, 49; P. Gay, *Voltaire's Politics: The Poet as a Realist* (New York: Vintage Books, 1965) 42-44, 51, 52.

3

Countervailing Government: The Separation, Balance, and Limitation of the Powers that Be

The church first developed a concept of authority in accordance with its own position in the ancient world. It lived without any designs on power and understood what was necessary to remain in good standing with Rome. Paul understood this place and exhorted the early church to live a quiet life of submission to the "powers that be" (Rom. 13:1, 1 Tim. 2:2). This simple exhortation seemed practical and necessary given the context in which it was framed, but it continued long after the initial context was gone. The exhortation of Paul became a fundamental virtue in the centuries to come as the church developed its own hierarchical view of life and structure of governance for the faithful to follow. Obedience to authority became the means of following the Lord, whose will was revealed through the developing bureaucracy. The utmost piety was embodied in the monastic ideal, which inculcated absolute submission to the abbot and all those who wielded authority. The Rule of St. Benedict exhorted the monastic community to follow the command of the abbot as if it came from the Lord, no matter how difficult or impossible the task.[1] This ideal was the standard of the day. Submission to the "powers that be" was first and foremost. The king was anointed by God. The pope was the Vicar of Christ. The priests pronounced divine absolution. The society was one body of Christ—*corpus Christianum*; the Scripture and tradition were one and the same—*semper et ubique et ab omnibus*.

But tensions developed over the course of time, and the discord became more acute when deep-seated conflicts between the scholastics of the late medieval period threatened to undermine the simple unity of earlier times. Submission was no longer the simple order of the day in the world of academic discourse, and tensions naturally arose within the church and society because of it. Theologians like John of Salisbury and Thomas Aquinas began to question the divine right of kings by authorizing the use of force to remove tyrants.[2] William Ockham rejected the papacy's claim to absolute authority in temporal and spiritual affairs, emphasizing the "rights, liberties, and possessions" of the subjects against papal incursions.[3] Machiavelli saw these and other tensions in the world as essential ingredients in the growth of a people. Dissent and rebellion were now signs of a free and healthy society.[4] While a study upon modern English society must focus upon the impact and impetus of Protestantism, it can never go along with the inflated, anti-Catholic rhetoric of the time and dismiss the debt that society owed to its past. The society that developed in the sixteenth and seventeenth centuries represented one side of a tension that was present in the medieval church and state, even if Protestantism and especially Calvinism inspired a more bellicose and pervasive attitude of rebellion among its people, leading to the modern spirit of revolution.[5]

Rebellion

The Reformation took the tensions of the late medieval period, furthered its teachings, and produced a doctrine of rebellion, which encompassed all of society. Of course, this process did not transpire over night. It was difficult to proceed from a hierarchical and submissive culture to one that emphasized the rights of its subjects and the value of their free expression. It took time to condition the people after centuries of abusive authority and indoctrination into much the opposite. The first step involved a division in the sacred unity of the church, which the Reformers found difficult to justify. They felt compelled to list the reasons why the mother church had lost its way in regard to the preaching of the Word and its sacraments and no longer deserved the allegiance of the faithful.[6] But once this schism was justified in their minds, rebellion against the powers that be and the abuses of authority became a natural part of the new world order, as long as sufficient reason or a "long train of abuses" was listed.

The transition is seen at the very beginning of the Reformation in the life of Martin Luther. He was reared in the discipline of a strict monastic order, but once he began to challenge the authority of the pope, it was difficult to halt the complete inversion of his once well-ordered life. At first he was hesitant to challenge the authority of magistrates or encourage the transformation of society as a whole. During the Peasants' War (1524-25), he rejected the use of force and revolution to bring about social change, even though he expressed sympathy for the plight of the peasants. He wrote *Against the Robbing and Murdering Hordes of Peasants*, emphasizing Paul's call to obedience in Rom. 13, and demanded the magistrates put down the rebellion if the peasants did not submit to proper authority. They had no right to rebel against unjust authority. They had no right to bear the sword.[7] But this dogmatic stance proved less than practical a few years later when he was faced with the prospects of Charles V using force to bring the land of Germany back into the fold of Catholicism. Luther's initial response was one of submission to the emperor, but Elector John and Philip of Hesse convinced him otherwise. They maintained that Charles V is subject to those who elect him and would violate the imperial constitution if he acted against the liberties of his subjects. In this circumstance, Luther reversed his course and granted an uneasy sanction to the use of armed resistance.

> Furthermore, if war breaks out—which God forbid—I will not reprove those who defend themselves against the murderous and bloodthirsty papists, nor let anyone else rebuke them as being seditious, but I will accept their action and let it pass as self-defense. I will direct them in this matter to the law and to the jurists. For in such an instance, when the murderers and bloodhounds wish to wage war and to murder, it is in truth no insurrection to rise against them and defend oneself. Not that I wish to incite or spur anyone on to such self-defense, or to justify it, for that is not my office; much less does it devolve on me to pass judgment or sentence on him.[8]

The leaders of the protesting estates took Luther's blessing and forged a league at Schmalkalden, determined to defend their faith by whatever means available. The "Protestants" were determined to serve God in their own conscience, even if it meant the use of armed force in the Schmalkald Wars, the Thirty Years' War, and the innumerable conflicts in between.[9]

The cries of liberty rang out in all Protestant lands. They were most resounding in those lands dominated by the Reformed tradition. Countries like Switzerland, France, Holland, and England became fertile ground for the dissemination of Reformed ideas, and these ideas helped further the cause of liberty. Scholars have long noted a certain relation between Calvinism and liberty, but all-too-often this relation is dismissed as a mere happenstance of history than a rigorous unfolding of a certain set of religious ideas.

> Further than this the system of Calvinism was what neither Lutheranism nor Anglicanism nor Romanism was, a republican if not a democratic system. Practically it doubtless meant the oligarchy of the preachers or the tyranny "worse than Papal" of ruling elders; certainly it did not favour individual liberty; but it was opposed in theory to secular interference, and by its own methods to monarchical power. Hence

> in spite of itself Calvinism in France, in the Netherlands and Scotland became either in the world of thought or in that of practice the basis of modern liberty. That it had of itself any such *penchant* is not the case. Illustrations of this fact may be found in Geneva under Calvin and Beza, in the Calvinistic principalities of Germany, in New England, in the very idea of the Solemn League and Covenant, and in the treatment of Episcopacy in Scotland after 1689.[10]

The relation between liberty and Calvinism is interpreted as the unwitting product of a conflict between the designs of a sectarian group and its need to resist or reform the government that is standing in the way. This interpretation contains an element of truth in its attempt to understand the historical context, but it fails to understand why this specific group and their specific ideas became so much a part of the quest for liberty.

According to Carlos Eire, part of the answer lies within the radical nature of the Reformed faith with its refusal to accept any compromise with the Catholic cultus and participate in its idolatrous rituals—unlike the Lutherans.[11] Many of its patriarchs like Zwingli and Calvin condemn any simulation in their writings and disdain the so-called "Nicomedites," who cheapen the faith in their minds by considering the outward expressions of worship a matter of indifference and participate in papal rituals.[12] True believers must shun all forms of Catholic idolatry. They must worship God in spirit and truth. They must insure the practice of true piety and devotion. Calvin even encourages a policy of emigration for those unable to escape Catholicism and maintain purity in personal devotion within their homeland.[13] He forbids the more militant measures of active iconoclasm, unless sanctioned by proper authorities within the civil government,[14] but his constraint was not heeded in all quarters and was dismissed by many of the emigrants who came to Geneva and developed a more bellicose view, probably due to their own personal plight and circumstances. The Scottish exiles, led by Charles Goodman and John Knox, experienced the bloody reign of Mary Tudor and believed it was the duty of all true believers to slay idolatrous, Catholic leaders, following the expressed command of OT Scripture. All "massmongers" commit the sin of idolatry, the worst of all transgressions, and must be punished in obedience to what God has commanded in the Word.

The Marian exiles thought of their position as a simple product of biblical exegesis and submission to the will of God. Charles Goodman served as a co-pastor with John Knox in Geneva and published an early justification of rebellion using arguments from biblical texts in his work *How Superior Powers oght to be Obeyed* (1558). The main argument was drawn from Acts 4:19, where Peter and John appear before the Sanhedrin and ask its officials whether it is right to obey their human authority rather than God. Goodman interprets the Apostles as calling for absolute obedience to God in all things. Those who follow Christ are expected to give him their undivided attention and disregard any constraint that is contrary to the will of God, even if it comes from the highest authority here on earth. Obedience to God's law means disobedience to any human law that withstands or interferes with the one and only service to the will of God.[15]

The new emphasis on Acts 4:19 meant a reassessment of the NT and its teaching upon submission. Paul's call for submission to the powers that be in Rom. 13:1 is understood as a warning to certain libertines who believe their freedom in Christ has delivered them from all obedience to earthly magistrates.[16] Peter's call for submission in 1 Pet. 2 and 3 means that Christians still owe a just obedience to masters, rulers, and husbands, even if they are "conbrous, frowarde, or . . . harde to please," but it was never intended to promote unconditional loyalty to those who are "wicked and ungodly."[17] The NT rejects blind submission or absolute obedience to earthly powers. Christians are obligated to honor those in authority only if they honor God and rule in accordance with the divine law.[18] The NT never allows any devotion to interfere with the ultimate loyalty that belongs to God and God alone. Even if Christ and the Apostles encouraged the early church in a general direction toward submission, their purpose in doing so was to keep the community focused upon the fulfillment of its Great Commission in building the church.[19] It was never their intention to dismiss the genuine rights of a people to form a nation and use the sword if necessary in building the state.

At this point Goodman is able to outline and justify his concept of the state. He merely follows the basic hermeneutical principles of the Reformed Church and its covenant by looking to the whole Scripture for answers, not just the NT. Like the Zurich theologians before him, he rejects a dispensational analysis that would limit the church to following the NT example in the slavish manner of Anabaptists and promotes the OT as a source of continued authority in matters of church and state.[20] There is one eternal message in Scripture according to the doctrine of covenant, and this doctrine makes the laws and stories of OT practice relevant to any dispensation within the overall economy of God. In particular, Goodman highlights the OT commission to root out evil through the use of the sword. The OT places an onus on all of us to use the sword and show no favoritism to anyone, including rulers who merit its wrath.[21] As long as the rulers perform their basic duties, the people must submit to them—even those who are "eville and ruoghe"—but as soon as they transgress the expressed will of God they must receive the justice prescribed in the Mosaic law. The people have a sacred duty to use the sword against rulers who openly defy the laws of God.[22] In the present case, the people are called to rebel against Mary Tudor, the wicked queen of their land.[23] She rules "contrarie to nature" as a woman;[24] she has no right to rule as a bastard or product of incest;[25] she murders the saints of God and serves the Antichrist and his religion, which constitutes her most heinous crime.[26] As a papist, she commits the sin of idolatry, the most wicked of all transgressions and the one great object of divine wrath in the OT. All "massmongers" are idolaters. They identify the Lord of all creation with creaturely elements and must be punished accordingly.[27]

This same basic analysis is found in the writings and actions of Goodman's more famous colleague, John Knox.[28] The latter gained a reputation as the most acrid and caustic of all the major Reformers in advocating the need for rebellion. He came to the Protestant faith through the ministry of George Wishart, a Reformed preacher, toward the end of 1545. He was called to the ministry at St. Andrews, but after the French seized its stronghold in 1547, he spent a couple years as a galley slave and many years after that in self-imposed exile, first in England and then Geneva. It was while in exile that he gained notoriety as a strident polemicist against Catholic rule in the homeland, inspiring many fellow exiles to return and fight for the faith. When he returned to his native land in May of 1559, the reform movement had grown into a sizable force. He became its instant leader, helping to negotiate the support of England and outlasting the challenge of the Catholic regency, which sought to depose him. He helped draft the Scotch Confession of Faith (1560) and a new constitution of the church, which contained the fundamental outline of a Presbyterian polity.

As early as 1554 his strident political position is seen in *A Godly Letter of Warning, or Admonition to the Faithful in London, New Castle, and Berwick.* In this work he conceives of himself as a prophet, giving God's final warning of doom upon the people.[29] Much of the work is based upon the severe words of admonition that Jeremiah uttered against his covenant people before their destruction at the hands of Nebuchadnezzar. Knox finds the current situation in England similar to that of Jeremiah's day and even worse in many ways.[30] He decries much the same evil, focusing upon the sin of idolatry, which he equates with participation in the Catholic mass.[31] The individual is admonished to remain aloof from those who engage in idolatrous practices. The true believer has entered a "league" with God and his people, in which no fellowship with those who practice wickedness is tolerated, no matter who they are—father, son, or king.[32] The civil magistrates are told to slay idolaters and burn their own cities (Dt. 13) if they wish to remain faithful to the sacred "league" or "covenant" with God.[33] This interpretation of Knox works within the standard Reformed doctrine of covenant, which understood the relationship with God and other human beings in terms of a bilateral arrangement based upon certain conditions.[34] This concept permeated the Scottish church and state of the time and became enshrined within the more famous pacts of the seventeenth century—the National Covenant (1638) and the Solemn League and Covenant (1643). Both were designed to ward off the threat of a one way or hierarchical structure of governance in the church and state.[35]

In 1558 Knox produced three of his most important tracts on the political situation in Britain—*The First Blast of the Trumpet Against the Monstrous Regiment of Women*, *Letter to the Regiment of Scotland*, and *Appellation to the Nobility*. These tracks continue his uncompromising position against Catholic idolatry.[36] The magistrates are given a divine admonition to establish both tables of the law. They must punish sins that are committed against the commonwealth and God.[37] They must remove the wicked priests of idolatry and instate the true preachers of the Gospel.[38] He cites many examples out of the Old Testament, including the "notable acts of Hezekiah, Jehosaphat, and Josiah [who] . . . did destroy all monuments of idolatry, did punish to death the teachers of it, and removed from office and honors such as were maintainers of those abominations."[39] He exhorts the magistrates of his day to follow this example, remove the idolatry in all its forms, and slay those who provoke the people of God to practice it.[40] In his *Apellation,* he goes even farther and includes the whole people within the charge to remove idolatry and tyranny, much like Charles Goodman, his colleague, paving the way toward the modern concept of a full-scale revolution against the government, not just an individual resistance or isolated rebellion. The people are given the same admonition as Old Testament rulers in this charge. They are all bound together by the same covenant as Israel and required to keep the Mosaic law.[41] They have no need for a specific mandate from the New Testament, since both testaments subsist under the one and eternal will of God in covenant theology. Only an Anabaptist or dispensationalist would think twice before following what God has revealed once and for all.

In these tracts, John Knox expresses a concept of the church that represents the growing consensus of the Reformed Church, far removed from any dispensational emphasis on the NT and its message of the cross. The Anabaptists are chastened for thinking of the church in NT terms, as a remnant suffering at the hands of wicked people who wield power. Knox and the Reformed Church reject this passive image by finding a sufficient justification within the doctrine of covenant to return the church to OT times and exhorting the people of God to show activism and implement its divine law and wrath. During the Puritan Revolution, divines followed this method to justify their measures and preached three-quarters of their sermons upon OT texts.[42] In America, Puritan divines of the Massachusetts Bay Colony developed an OT theology of distributive justice, believing that God visits destruction upon those who neglect the law through certain providential signs and human agency.[43] Tribulation was interpreted as a sign of divine displeasure rather than a necessary portion of those who take up their cross and follow Christ.

The OT duty is so sacred that Knox calls for an immediate revolution against Mary Tudor, "that Jezebel whom [the English] call their Queen."[44] It is "the duty of the nobility, judges, rulers, and people of England to have resisted and againststanded Mary . . . but also to have punished her to the death with all sorts of her idolatrous priests together."[45] In *The First Blast of the Trumpet*, his justification takes on a misogynist tone in the aftermath of his experience with the Catholic regency—Mary Tudor, Mary of Guise, and Mary Stuart (later on). In the absence of a Queen Elizabeth, he finds women unfit to rule a kingdom.[46] Nature and experience teaches us that they are "weak, frail, impatient, feeble, . . . variable, cruel, and lacking the spirit of counsel and regiment."[47] To promote a woman to rule above any realm is a subversion of the natural order of things and repugnant to the expressed will of God.[48] While the Scripture might allow certain exceptions, it is not appropriate for human beings to dispense with what is normative in divine law. This prerogative belongs to God alone.[49] The throne is intended for men, and the fact that a woman sits there is more a sign of divine judgment upon the people of the covenant community than a special dispensation of divine grace in their lives.[50]

Through the words and actions of Knox, advocates of rebellion became more and more emboldened throughout England and Scotland. One of the early disciples was George Buchanan, a literary scholar, who became a reformer of the church and state after his return to Scotland in 1561. He helped prepare the case against the Catholic Regent, Mary Stuart, which was presented to Elizabeth I. The case was successful and led to her imprisonment and eventual execution years later.[51] After the incident Buchanan provided a strong scholaristic argument for the measures he took against Mary in his great work, *De jure regni apud Scotos*. It was published in 1579 (Eng. 1580) more than a decade after the abdication of Mary, but its dedication shows that it was written on the occasion of her demise. The work employs a number of biblical passages, which support the new policy. These passages are conjoined with classical references to Graeco-Roman philosophers and illustrations from ancient and contemporary republics—a style indicative of the next few centuries. The work is presented in the form of a Socratic dialogue between Buchanan and Thomas Maitland, who had just returned from France (like Buchanan had done so many years ago) but its scholastic and measured tones did not mitigate its provocative message. It was confiscated and condemned by the Scottish Parliament in 1585, cited by Cromwell and the Long Parliament to justify tyrannicide, and banned after the restoration of Charles II in England, with similar steps taken in 1664 and 1668.[52]

The work found its purpose in defining the role of the ruler and justifying any actions taken to remove one who oversteps the bounds. A king is one who is subject to limitations. "A royal authority is in accordance with nature's law, while a tyrannical one is against it; a king holds power with the consent of the people, while a tyrant lacks the consent."[53] The king reigns as long as he serves the will of the people. The government finds its purpose in serving whatever the people need and will. God has called them out of nature to engage in mutual service for the common good.[54] Once united they confer authority on whomever they wish, but they never abdicate their liberties in the process.[55] The people remain the supreme power behind the laws and prescribe limits to the rule of the king through their elected representatives.[56] There is a contract between the people and their king;[57] if the king violates the sacred terms of that contract, he must abdicate his right to the throne or succumb to a violent end if more severe measures are necessary.[58] Those who cite Romans 13 and preach submission to tyranny misunderstand the circumstance, as well as the intent of Paul's words. The apostle never meant to promote a simple obeisance to the nefarious designs of demonic rule, but wanted his readers to follow all good sense when exercising their freedom in Christ. He did not want the liberty of Christians to become a pretext for disobedience or unruly behavior. The general comportment of a believer is characterized by obedience to the powers that be, even if rebellion might become necessary in extraordinary circumstances.[59]

On the continent the massacre of St. Bartholomew's Day (1572) shattered whatever illusions were left about those who wielded absolute authority. After the massacre, the French Calvinists produced a number of treatises that justified the right of the people to rebel against tyranny. The most significant were written by François Hotman, Theodore Beza, and Phillipe du Plessis-Mornay, and all three were written within a decade of the massacre.[60] No specific revolution or modern constitution followed their publication. Tyranny continued its persecution of dissidents through capricious acts of power, especially during the reign of Louis XIV.[61] But the Huguenot Church will remain to fight the battle in the centuries to come. These authors were a product of this church and represented what it will continue to produce as a community and social movement in the world to come.[62]

François Hotman published the first of the treatises in 1573. He was a French jurist, who became a Huguenot around 1548 and spent much of his career defending the cause of Calvinism against its enemies. These enemies included the Cardinal of Lorraine, the family of Guise, and all those who wanted to use their power to persecute the faith. He developed many of his views in close association with Calvin and Beza, spending a number of years in Geneva, both before and after the massacre. It was in Geneva that he published the first edition of his great work on the subject of limited government, entitled *Francogallia.*

The work refers to the office of king as limited in power and subject to the law, the people, and other branches of government. The work is filled with historical references, but it particularly points to the ancient Germanic customs of the French people (i.e., the kingdom of Francogallia) as the paradigm for this type of government.[63] The ancient Franks lived in liberty before the Romans entered and dominated the land. Their rulers were elected by the people and served for the sake of the people.[64] They chose their rulers based on merit, not heredity, and made all of them subject to specific laws.[65] If the rulers violated the trust of the people, they did not remain in office to continue the abuse of power but were subject to immediate censorship and removal.[66] This limited form of government is commended by Hotman as representing the most genuine expression of his people's spirit. It represents both the fundamental spirit of his Germanic people, as well as the universal aspirations of all humanity. Hotman proves this last point by citing a number of ancient authorities, along with an array of social experiments throughout history. He cites the authority of Plato, Aristotle, Polybius, and Cicero on limited government and commends their mixing of three forms—"the royal, the aristocratic, and the people"—to achieve this end.[67] He makes reference to other experiments like the "Ephors of Sparta" and the "Parliament of the Three Estates" as providing additional instruments to check and censor the authority of the king.[68]

These ideas found a receptive audience in Geneva, the epicenter of the Reformed world and the growing rebellion. The city attracted many prospective scholars around Europe as the center of theological education for the Reformed community. It became a favorite stomping ground for dissidents, who transformed it into a hotbed of discontent and the dissemination of that discontent throughout the Reformed world. Goodman, Knox, and Hotman published their seminal works while living as exiles in Geneva, and soon Beza would follow with a treatise of his own.[69] Calvin remained mute and passive on the subject, preferring to keep his reform within the church and away from the corrupting influence of temporal powers. Government was someone else's business. If there are responsible magistrates like ephors or tribunes, the church should let them do their duty, but God's people are placed under a different commission.[70] They must obey the powers that be. They must obey even a wicked king, respecting his "engraved," "imprinted," and "inviolable" character, or if worse comes to worse, resign themselves to the hope that God would raise up someone else to remove him.[71] The people of God are limited in their options and forbidden to take the ultimate step and revolt against the king or change the current form of government.[72] But this passive attitude of Calvin, Luther, and early Reformers soon gave way to a more militant posture among their successors. In Geneva the successor of Calvin became more strident and published *The Right of Magistrates* in 1574—a more active call to rebellion in the wake of the St. Bartholomew's massacre and the precedent for resistance set by the Lutherans at Magdeburg in 1548. The city council was hesitant to proceed in this new direction and censored the work, but Beza published it anyway, producing a Latin and French version to insure the widest possible distribution.[73] The treatise finds the political situation in France much like Hotman. It speaks of the ancient rights of the people to elect or depose the king.[74] It sees the king as a creation of the people, subject to the law of equity, which is natural and universal.[75] Any king who usurps his power or deprives the people of their liberties is illegimate.[76] The business of removing a tyrant belongs to the officers of the kingdom, who have a sworn duty to use force if necessary in preventing further wickedness.[77] The people must leave this business to others because they have made a covenant with the king to remain his loyal subjects.[78] But the treatise does not stop here and appears to proceed toward a more militant posture when considering the complexities of the current situation. What happens when the entire system of government is corrupt like it is in France? What happens when there is no meeting to elect a king and the bureaucracy is filled with graft and corruption? At this point Beza is less passive than Calvin and appears to sanction the actions of private individuals against the government. Even if this behavior is regrettable or anomalous, the people may defend legitimate institutions by resisting the king if he should commit acts of violence against the law.[79]

The most famous of the Huguenot tracts, *Vindiciae contra tyrannos* (1579), appears to draw and expand upon many of the themes found in Beza's work. Its authorship is subject to debate, but most scholars today believe that Philippe du Plessis-Mornay probably had a hand in its production.[80] Plessis-Mornay was an apologist of the Reformed faith, a chief negotiator in the Edict of Nantes (1598), and a trusted advisor of Henry of Navarre (the future Henry IV, king of France). The work follows the same *modus operandi* as Beza, using similar historical analogies out the OT, the Graeco-Roman world, and medieval times to illustrate points.[81] It expands on these illustrations and reiterates many of the themes present in Beza and earlier works, the most significant of which is the doctrine of covenant. This doctrine served as a powerful instrument to justify the revolutions to come, and the *Vindiciae* was the first major treatise to make it a centerpiece of the cause.[82] The concept was used in previous tracts and a part of the overall mentality in the Reformed world, which began to reinterpret all relations in this way, but its usage was never so pervasive or explicit in justifying rebellion until the *Vindiciae*—at least not so in print. The work served as an important part of the process in bringing the covenant to the forefront. It was reprinted in 1581 and 1589, with a partial translation into English appearing in 1588 and complete editions in 1622, 1648, 1660, and 1689. It was cited during the Puritan Revolution, burned at Oxford after the Restoration, and reprinted once the Glorious Revolution had brought about a substantive and permanent change toward limited government.[83]

The *Vindiciae* makes the Reformed doctrine of covenant the basic rationale for taking measures against the king. It follows the Reformed understanding that there is one covenant, and that covenant defines all our duties in life. The covenant began "within the narrow bounds of Judea" but now encompasses "the whole world." "There is the same covenant, the same conditions, the same punishments, . . . [the same] kings, . . . Christian princes being in the place of those of Jewry, . . . and if they fail in the accomplishing, the same God Almighty revenger of all perfidious disloyalty."[84]

The covenant is interpreted as possessing two parts, which follow the same basic line as Dudley Fenner's treatment and probably bear some relation to the work. Like Fenner, the first part involves a mutual agreement "between God, the king, and the people, that the people might be the people of God."[85] Obedience to God is considered the first and foremost requirement of the people in the covenant. They are bound to serve God as their most essential duty, and whatever allegiance they owe to other powers, including that of the king, is made secondary or subordinate to the one duty.[86] The king cannot decree what is contrary to the laws of God, and if he does, the people are under an oath to disobey him.[87] The king is a vassal of the King of kings. His reign lasts as long as he obeys the one and only Suzerain.[88] The submission of the king is extended in the second part of the covenant, which is forged "between the king and the people, that the people shall obey faithfully, and the king command justly."[89] The power of the king is based upon law and is limited to serving the people, not his own whims or licentious pleasures. The king receives his marching orders from the people. He cannot make unjust demands or impose unfair financial burdens upon them.[90] He is obligated to uphold the law and protect their possessions and estates as his sworn duty.[91] This duty is related to the law of nature, which summons the king and all of us to defend "our lives and liberties" against those who cause injury to what belongs to others.[92]

The king receives all his laws and duties from the people.[93] The king performs the duties of his office by virtue of the people. Saul, David, and the kings of Israel were elected "by the people and for the sake of the people" and reigned as long as they kept that trust.[94] The people did not abdicate their role to a dynasty or allow any specific king to rule *carte blanche*. In fact, the *Vindiciae* believes the people have a sacred duty to oppose the mischief of the king and resist his license. "It is then lawful for Israel to resist the king, who would overthrow the law of God and abolish His church; and not only so, but also they ought to know that in neglecting to perform this duty, they make themselves culpable of the same crime, and shall bear the like punishment with their king."[95] The children of Israel were punished when they failed in fulfilling this duty, leaving the transgressions of the king unchecked, and the same onus is placed on the people and their representatives today.[96] Like Beza, the *Vindiciae* assigns the primary duty of withstanding the king to the deputies and offices of the people, rather than those who act as private or individual citizens.[97] If a king should break the law and the covenant, the "whole body" may use the force of arms in deposing the king but only as "confederated and associated together" through its officers.[98] This position is stated in clear terms and reiterated throughout the work, but some equivocation is found when it considers exceptional cases. At one point, it permits a town to rebel against the sovereign if the majority of princes neglect their duty.[99] It also expresses a special concern to protect the true religion and allows the use of the sword in this special case.[100] Like Beza, the *Vindiciae* does not want to sanction a full scale revolution of the people, but it appears to provide a tacit approval for such measures in exceptional times and cases—maybe in the exceptional time of the sixteenth century and the exceptional case of France.

The *Vindiciae* provides testimony to the growing importance of the doctrine of covenant in the overall thinking of the Reformed community. The doctrine expressed the one truth about the essence of the Biblical message, and this truth resulted in a new way of looking at life for those who lived in accordance with the message. The first chapter saw the beginning of the process in the work of Robert Browne, John Milton, John Wise, and other Puritans who reinterpreted relations within the church and society through the one doctrine. They provided strong testimony to the pervasive nature of covenant theology in their community, but this process was not limited to Puritan authors. Their understanding represents a pervasive mentality within the Reformed camp and finds additional testimony among authors living in other countries. The clearest testimony is found within the work of Johannes Althusius, whose *Politica methodice digesta* (1603) represents the first major treatise to reconstruct all of society around the sacred doctrine.[101]

Althusius was a member of the Reformed community. He studied in Basel, a part of the Swiss confederation and Reformed Church, and later taught law at Herborn, which became a bastion of federal theology through its first rector, Gaspar Olevian, co-author of the Heidelberg Catechism. After the publication of *Politica*, he was invited to become syndic or chief executive of the city-state of Emden in East Friesland, a center of Reformed ideology.[102] His life was dedicated to the Reformed community, and his works reflect this devotion. Throughout the *Politica* he makes constant reference to Reformed apologists and theologians, citing them with approval and defending their specific polemical positions.[103] For example, his ecclesiology follows the basic pattern of polity found in Geneva, where the presbyters exercised discipline over the membership and nominated candidates for the ministry subject to the approval of the people. He cites Calvin's *Institutes* as a proof text and claims that his own pattern is consonant with the practice of Geneva and other Reformed churches.[104]

Of course, within this tradition there is the doctrine of covenant. The doctrine exerts a great impact upon his own ideology, especially as it is represented in his *Politica*.[105] In this work Althusius depicts all levels of society as subsisting within the bounds of a *pactum*: families, businesses, guilds, communities, provinces, and states.[106] Both private and public associations are joined by this means, and each covenant becomes a basis of forging further and more comprehensive associations until one reaches the highest level or covenant, which is the commonwealth.[107] A covenant is necessary so that specific rights and mutual responsibilities can be spelled out and the body can act as a single entity. Althusius considers politics the art of forging covenants or relating people together for the common interest. Words like *consociationes* and *symbiotici* are used throughout the work to describe this relationship.[108] He cites with approval the dictum of Aristotle that conceives of "man [as] a political animal" and chastens all those who want to deny their humanity and live in self-contented isolation. He enjoins us to "establish, cultivate, and conserve social life" for the common welfare.[109] The exhortation is offered for the benefit of all, even though it respects the freedom of individuals to desist or abandon the covenant community.[110]

The most comprehensive covenant binds together the supreme magistrate and the people. It contains mutual responsibilities, in which the king "binds himself to the body of the universal association to administer the realm or commonwealth according to laws prescribed by God, right reason, and the body of the commonwealth" and "the people in turn bind themselves in obedience and compliance to the supreme magistrate."[111] The community supplies its voluntary consent to be governed, and the king swears to uphold the law and submit to the chastisement of the people if he neglects his duty.[112] The claim to sovereignty ever remains in the hands of the people— i.e., the people as a whole "associated in one symbiotic body from many smaller associations."[113] They have ceded to the magistrate only a temporal stewardship over their rights, which cannot be "transferred" or "alienated" from them.[114] It is within this context that Althusius inculcates the natural rights tradition, which now stands together with the covenant to bolster the defense of limited government. He speaks of the common law (*lex communis*), which God has planted in nature and inscribed on tablets of stone in the Decalogue.[115] It includes the *jus naturale* that all men are created equal in nature and subject to the jurisdiction of no one unless they bind themselves one to another through a voluntary pact.[116] But even in this arrangement they never alienate their rights.[117] If the administration transgresses the law, the people are not obligated to obey the unjust demands of a wicked regime, and their representatives (ephors) can elect and create another one in its place.[118] The ephors represent the people in approving and checking whatever the king decrees.[119] If the king fails to give an account of his administration or alienates the rights of the people, he can be deposed through those who exercise authority.[120] As private individuals, the people are less than the king and should not revolt against him, except to defend their own lives;[121] but as a whole they are much greater and can use force to resist the wantonness of a tyrant, as long as they act through the structure of the covenant and the auspices of their representatives.[122]

Limited Monarchy

The paradigm for limited government was embodied for generations to come within the struggles of Charles I and Parliament. Those who spoke of a separation or balance of powers typically looked to England and its struggles in the seventeenth century as a historical precedent for their own convictions.[123] The struggle developed when Charles I grew weary of Parliament and its many grievances, and suspended its sessions for eleven years. After it reconvened, Parliament attacked the authority of the Crown, made its sessions mandatory, abolished the infamous Star Chamber, and withheld vital resources necessary for the king to conduct war—the only reason Charles had called it back into session. (Charles needed the funds to conduct his second Bishops' War—an attempt to impose the Episcopal system of governance on Scotland.) The Parliament refused to sanction the necessary taxes and so civil war ensued. In March of 1642, Parliament raised its own army,[124] defeated the king a few years later, and tried and executed him in 1649. Some decades of uncertainty followed, but after the defeat of the Stuarts, limited government became a permanent fixture in England with the ascension of William of Orange to the throne (1688).

Stephen Marshall sounded the clarion of revolution during the first months of the Long Parliament in his famous sermon, *Meroz Cursed* (Feb. 23, 1641). The sermon derived its title from the triumph song of Deborah in Judges 5:23. The town of Meroz is mentioned in that verse as a cursed place because it failed to help the Israelites gain victory over their enemies.[125] Marshall uses this verse as the basic text of his sermon and places all people under the same curse "who do not joyne their Strength and give their best assistance to the Lords people against their enemies."[126] And there is no excuse. Even "Gods meanest servants must not be afraid to oppose the Mighty."[127] At the very least, all should pray for the well-being of the church and ask for the deliverance of God's people, even if one cannot "runne, nor ride, nor write, nor fight."[128] Marshall provides at this point a long exhortation to pray as a most essential service to the cause, but he ends the sermon maintaining that some need to proceed past the passive means of prayer and consider becoming soldiers and spilling blood for the sake of the church.[129] He speaks of prayer as "the greatest help which we can give to the church of God,"[130] but he clearly envisages the church of God taking more practical and virulent measures to accomplish the goal.

The most influential pamphlet of the Civil War was Henry Parker's *Observations* (July 2, 1642).[131] It contains many of the typical themes that appear in the discussion of countervailing government in the next two centuries—covenant theology, natural rights theory, sovereignty of the people, and the separation and balance of powers—all of which are understood within a specific religious framework. The pamphlet begins with a typical Puritan discussion of the doctrine of covenant as a foundation of government. The origin of government is "nothing else amongst Christians but the Pactions and agreements of such and such politique corporations. [The] power is originally inherent in the people," who are "free and voluntary Authors" of its polity and government.[132] In this concept of government, the king is "*singulis Major*, yet he is *universis minor*" because the people are the efficient cause of his power.[133] The claim of the people is much greater than his claim upon them, making his obligations to serve them fall under a stricter scrutiny.[134] It is more important "that the king make the people happy, than the people make glorious the king,"[135] and so the oppression of a king is much worse than any treachery his subjects might commit against him.[136]

Alongside the covenant, the law of nature and the kingdom restrains the king from breaking trust with the people.[137] The royal office is fiduciary and conditional, based upon the rule of law,[138] freeing the people from capricious acts of the royal will and its arbitrary displays of power. The law reigns supreme over all decisions in the government. If the king misuses his authority by circumventing the law, it is permissible to disobey him. It is permissible in extreme cases to conduct war against his authority and armies, although attacking his person is never sanctioned.[139]

The Parliament is afforded the role of protecting the law of the land and the rights of the people against royal incursions.[140] Parker finds it unlikely that the Parliament would ever abuse the trust of the people since its power is "derivative and dependent upon publike consent."[141] The Parliament serves its purpose by representing the people, providing advice to the king, and checking aberrations in society, whether they are found in the "tyranny" of a king or the "ochlocracy" of a people.[142] Of course, the king would prefer to assert his divine rights and rule unmolested. He wants to make himself accountable to God alone and listen to the counsel of Parliament (or the People) whenever it suits his purpose.[143] But Parker distrusts the king (and all people for that matter) as filled with depravity—body, soul, and spirit. Here he invokes the anthropology of his Reformed Church, which casts suspicion upon the goodness of human nature, depicting it as filled with hubris and license through-and-through.[144] Parker finds it best to entrust the government, not to the depravity of one individual or group of individuals but a mixture of competing powers, balanced and distributed.[145] These powers would thwart the wantonness of certain special interests. They possess the duty to check the arbitrary exercise of power, whether it is seized by a king, a pope, or whoever is tempted to wield it.[146]

John Goodwin appears on the scene the same year *Observations* was published, lending a strong voice from the pulpit for the Puritan Revolution.[147] He was educated at Queen's College, Cambridge, and went to London in 1632, where he became the vicar of St. Stephen's the following year. His preaching was not confined to orthodox theological matters but integrated political and social concerns with religious principles. He was one of the first clergy to support Parliament's call to arms in 1642, even though he viewed himself as a moderate throughout much of his career.[148]

In his *Anti-Cavalierisme* (1643), he complains about the political apathy of the people. He sees more concern about accumulating and safeguarding property than protecting what is most essential to our humanity, "civil or political liberty."[149] Perhaps if his fellow citizens lived in oppressive countries like Turkey, Persia, or France they would come to appreciate the privilege of freedom and the necessity of defending it.[150] It is imperative that the people shake off this apathy and defend their liberties against those who would take them away.[151]

He calls the city of London to arms against the Cavaliers, who are spreading cruelty and bloodshed throughout the land in the name of royal and Romish oppression.[152] These warmongers want to abolish Parliament, and they must be stopped. The Parliament is the bastion of our liberties against the yoke of "popery," "prelacy," and other forms of hierarchical privilege.[153] While Goodwin still preaches submission to the king and his government,[154] he rejects the exercise of absolute authority and the temptation to abuse that authority in the present circumstance. The king has no right to sponsor injustice or take away the liberties of the people (Dan. 3, Acts 3:18, 19).[155] Disobedience is the only recourse if the king continues his policies (Acts 4:19; 5:29).[156] The call to arms is justified when the king wants to coerce others into following his unjust ways.[157] The only proviso is to spare his life and leave his person unharmed.

> [T]he unlawfull command of a King, may possibly be of that nature and condition that a Subject cannot disobey it, but by a strong hand, and taking up of Armes, though not properly or directly against the King, yet against the command of a King. In such a case, disobedience to Kings by a strong hand and with forcible resistance, is not only lawfull, but even matter of duty and obedience unto God. For instance, A Christian hath solemnly vowed & protested before God to defend the lives of his godly and faithfull Governors to the utmost of his power: or whether he hath made such a vow and Protestation or no, it is not much materiall in this respect, because he stands bound in conscience otherwise, and by the Law of God, to doe it. Now suppose such a man cannot performe this Vow, or doe that which is his duty to doe otherwise therein, but by a strong hand, and taking up Armes; in this case, if a King commands such a man not to take up Armes in relation to such a defence, it is evident that this unlawfull command of a King cannot be disobeyed, but by taking up Armes against it. There are many other cases of the same consideration and rule with this.[158]

A number of works appeared at this time hoping to limit the abuse of royal power. Along with Henry Parker and John Goodwin, there appeared a more extensive work, *A Treatise of Monarchy* (May 1643) written by Philip Hunton. He was another divine who felt it necessary to translate his theological beliefs into a political ideology. His work does not mandate a specific form of government as the exclusive teaching of Scripture[159] or attempt to overthrow the "Norman Yoke"[160] but provides a systematic way in which the power of the king may be limited. There are three methods employed to achieve this end throughout the work. One, there is the covenant. Society is created by forging a compact, which sets limits upon the king and determines the conditions of its own submission.[161] Two, there is the law. The "Lawes and Customes of the kingdome" are laid down to restrain the wantonness of a king.[162] Three, there are other powers in government. The Parliament is given special responsibilities, which are mixed with royal authority and intended to hold it in check.[163]

The concept of the three estates and the balance between them began to take a more definitive shape at this time. Hunton provides an early witness in his work to the state of the process in the middle of the seventeenth century. He argues in the typical Aristotelian manner of the time for the wisdom of mixed government. He believes that all forms of government—monarchy, aristocracy, and democracy—would deteriorate into aberrations if left to their own devices. Monarchy would become tyranny, aristocracy elitism, and democracy chaos.[164] Therefore, an ideal government involves the mixture of all three, not a simple choosing of one or another, in which each power has its own separate existence but checks the affairs of the other two to keep them from falling into evil. In this scheme the government possesses distinct and independent powers, not derived from any other branch.[165] These powers exist in their own right with their own commission but need to come together and concur in order to act on any matter. It becomes the duty of all three to check the others by exercising a veto power or denying obedience to any branch that acts out of bounds.[166]

This system seemed to create enough unanimity in the actions of government to satisfy some, but Hunton is not comfortable with it and still wants the ultimate power to reside in the monarch. In order to create a firmer union, he argues for the dominion of one branch or what he calls a "mixed Monarchy."[167] Of course, this exaltation of one branch is dangerous and could lead to dire consequences, especially when the monarch controls military operations. The possibility of creating a military dictator like Caesar is a weakness of the system, and so the community has the right to match force-with-force if problems arise.[168] However, the right of rebellion is granted only in the case of a major transgression "stricking at the very being of that Government . . . and publique liberty";[169] and even in this case one should follow the example of David, who refrained from committing a violent act against the Lord's anointed.[170] The force should be directed against his advisors and officers who led him astray, rather than the king himself.[171] Subjects remain inferior to the monarch and divest themselves of all power through the contract to strike out against the Lord's anointed and inflict physical harm.[172] Barring an act of personal vengeance, the two houses can assume the power of arms to restrain the king if he abuses his trust, and Hunton seems to believe that the present crisis justifies this extraordinary measure. He prefers to separate legislative and executive roles, but the ideal is not always easy to maintain.[173] It is difficult to withstand the evil designs of a monarch when that one branch of government contains all the muscle.[174]

In June of 1642 some of the moderates in Parliament drew up a set of proposals to limit the power of the monarch and avert a crisis. The "Nineteen Propositions" were sent to Charles in the hope of reaching a compromise and avoiding the imminent danger of civil war. Among the proposals Parliament asked for the following authority: (1) To approve members of the Privy Council, the Great Offices, and the House of Peers; (2) To educate the royal family and sanction their marriages;[175] (3) To support the cause of Protestantism at home and abroad; (4) To debate and transact the great affairs of the state; (5) To order an army for the time being. But the king was not amused by any of these proposals and dismissed them as a clandestine attempt of the subjects to become his equal. The increased power would "intoxicate persons who are not born to it," producing contempt for superiors and create a "dark equall Chaos of confusion." And so, he makes a surreptitious attempt to placate the demand for checks and balances, mentioning the three forms of government and the aberrations that ensue from just one, but he reserves all the real power to his own branch. He reserves all the might to withstand "Invasion from abroad and Insurrection at home," and the Parliament is relegated to the role of a mere advisor.[176]

The royalists produced a number of apologetic works during the era to counteract the large number of petitions and pamphlets on the other side. The most famous was Charles Dallison's *The Royalist's Defence*, published in 1648 after the defeat of the king. It was published in the hope of restoring the king to his rightful place but offered little by way of compromise. It blames the clergy for causing much of the problems through their specious use of Scripture and many preachments. It accuses the men of Westminster of usurping the justice seat and making themselves the law of the land. With the Parliament in charge, the king is removed from the process and unable to exercise restraint or cast a negative vote on Parliament's abuse of power. In this grave circumstance Dallison and the royalists think it wise to promote a sense of "joint" government in which the king retains his sovereignty, the judges declare existing law, and the Parliament creates new law in conjunction with the king.[177] They are willing to speak of a separation and balance of powers, but in spite of the rhetoric it all seems a ruse to restore real authority back to the Crown.

The treatise goes on to describe government as "Monarchicall."[178] It rejects the attempt of Parliament to usurp the place of the king and run his affairs. In ancient times no Parliament or body assembled to discuss the affairs of the state. The people were governed by a monarchy for 1200 years of recorded history before the two Houses began to emerge. There was no House of Lords or Commons until Edward I made a decision to grant the "Prelats, Peers, and Commons" a voice in raising taxes.[179] This decision did not circumvent the basic tradition of the land or provide

Parliament with a precedent to seek an inflated role. What bound them and us today is the common practice or custom passed down over centuries from "time out of mind"—a phrase Dallison repeats throughout the work.[180] Dallison and the royalists serve the customs of the land, and that custom ascribes its basic allegiance to the king. The Parliament has tried to change the ancient laws and must be seized and prosecuted for treason.[181]

The king is considered the supreme authority in the land. Dallison inculcates the oath of supremacy in a number of sections but sees no need to counterbalance the demand with a similar assurance from the king via an oath or covenant.[182] The king rules supreme. The army belongs within the domain of the king according to the custom of the land.[183] Parliament has no right to raise an army or increase taxes to pay for it without the consent of the king.[184] The king is not only the executive but the chief lawmaker of the land.[185] Both Houses possess the privilege of accepting or rejecting the legislation, but the "Law it selfe [is] His Law." The people have no right to make new laws. The king can exercise an "absolute negative voice" on whatever laws are propounded by their representatives in Parliament; And once enacted he can pardon transgressors or dispense with the law entirely if it suits his pleasure.[186]

> All *legall* proceedings [are enacted] in his name, and by His authority. The Law it selfe [is] called *His Law*; He hath usually dispensed with Acts of Parliament, at *pleasure pardoned* transgressours of the Law. To Him *appertaines* the forfeitures for *Treason*, and other offences. In a word, He is the sole *fountaine of Justice, Mercy,* and *Honour.* And with this constant practise agrees all authorities, histories, and stories: among which, that of the Oath of *Supremacy*, if there were no more, is sufficient to satisfie all the World, the words are these. I A. B. *do utterly testifie in my conscience that the Kings Highness is the onely Supreame Governour of this Realme, and of all other His Highnesse Realmes, Dominions, and Countries, as well in all Spirituall things, or causes as Temporall.*[187]

The king is given control over Parliament as the "Supreame Governour of this realme." He can summon a session of Parliament at his will and retain their services as long as he pleases.[188] The House of Lords and its peers are created by his sole authority without any consultation from the people. The House of Commons is "derived from the king too" and must act in accordance with his commission or writ, even if its members are elected by the people.[189] The Parliament possesses no right to act outside the will of the king or create a realm of authority independent of that will. This restriction is applied in a most emphatic way to the matter of setting up courts and appointing judges. The king has the sole right to appoint judges in the land. The Parliament is not fit to perform this important duty, the House of Lords is not educated in matters of law, and the House of Commons consists of uneducated wannabes elected by the uneducated masses.[190] There is only one person fit to do this job and rule over the land, and that is the king.

It is clear from this and other responses that the royalty was too obstinate for negotiations or compromise. Its intractable position led to a more decided and extreme posture on the other side. The rancor reached such a fervent pitch that the revolutionaries began to consider the ultimate solution—something that was unthinkable a few years before. Earlier treatises could justify revolt and the use of force against the abuse of royal power, but there was no thought of laying a hand upon the king himself—no matter how obstinate and unrepentant he proved to be. Now tyrannicide became a viable option, and more than just an option as events would unfold. The Puritan Revolution reached the extremity of its measure when Charles I was executed on January 30, 1649 by Cromwell and the so-called Rump Parliament. According to one source, Cromwell defended this ultimate solution as a matter of simple justice. Charles had committed a breach against the public trust and failed to defend the true religion.[191] The high court of justice accused him of committing "treasons and crimes" against the people by overthrowing their "rights and liberties" as a tyrant and waging war against them.[192]

John Milton was a secretary to the Council of State that year and provides a similar testimony in his *Tenure of Kings and Magistrates* (1649).[193] According to Milton, the obedience of Romans 13 is granted only to those rulers who obey the will of God.[194] They are the servants of God and the servants of the people according to the Scripture. The people are given the right to choose or reject their kings in Deut. 17:14, 1 Sam. 8, and many other passages in Scripture.[195] The kings are bound by the covenant and law to serve the public trust.[196] If they fail to perform their federal duties, the people have a right to depose and execute them, just as Ehud and Jehu slew the wicked kings who breached the trust of Israel in the OT.[197] Milton points to a number of examples from the Scripture, the Graeco-Roman world, and the Christian era to establish his thesis.[198] He makes special mention of recent Protestant insurrections as setting a precedent—most notably the Protestant league against Charles V and the tribulations of John Knox and the Scottish Church with Queen Mary.[199] Along with this historical evidence, a number of quotes from Protestant theologians are assembled.[200]

The position of the radicals was marked in a distinct way by a strong and increasing emphasis upon the separation and balance of powers. The doctrine came to the forefront as a result of the ongoing conflict between Charles I and Parliament in the 1640s and the need to settle the differences. The doctrine never received the vital and systematic expressions of later times, nor was it wielded together into a successful and ongoing experiment, but it did become a permanent fixture in political discussions thereafter. Its teachings were well-circulated long before Locke, Montesquieu, or the Federalist Papers put their considerable intelligence and weight of influence behind the doctrine.[201] In the 1650s the doctrine continued to develop in the work of Isaac Penington and Marchamont Nedham, both calling for a radical and systematic distinction between executive and legislative roles.[202]

That decade saw the publication of James Harrington's *The Commonwealth of Oceana* (1656), a widely-circulated and influential work on the theory of checks and balances. It became so celebrated that John Adams considered Harrington the sole author of the doctrine.

> Harrington discovered, and made out, as Toland his biographer informs us, that "empire follows the balance of property, whether lodged in one, a few, or many hands." A noble discovery, of which the honour solely belongs to him, as much as the circulation of the blood to Harvey, printing to Laurence Coster, or of guns, compasses, or optic glasses to the several authors. If this balance is not the foundation of all politics, as Toland asserts, it is of so much importance that no man can be thought a master of the subject without having well weighed it.[203]

But for all the hoopla, there is little known about Harrington beyond the barest outline. He was born on January 3, 1611, the son of Sir Sapcote Harrington. In 1629 he was a gentleman commoner at Trinity College, Oxford and later traveled to the Netherlands and Italy, where he expanded his political horizons no doubt. He accompanied Charles I to Scotland before the outbreak of the Civil War and served as a gentleman in his bedchamber in 1647 while the king was incarcerated. After the Restoration he was arrested but released a year later, suffering from physical and mental exhaustion. He apparently led a quiet life after that in Westminster, where his life came to an end on September 11, 1677.

The texture of his work is somewhat strange. It does not provide a sober, literal rendition of historical information in the typical spirit of Puritanism.[204] It creates a mixture of historical and utopian ideals more indicative of Jewish Midrashim or apocryphal literary works out of Alexandria than what a typical Puritan author would produce. It also moves in a more "secular" direction than most accounts of the time. It emphasizes historical analogies from other cultures[205] and credits its ideas to authorities less associated with religious affections. It spends less time on biblical exegesis or the deconstruction of theological concepts—at least in comparison with other Puritan accounts of the day. This "secular" approach might explain why John Adams and other sons of the Enlightenment found him more inspiring than others, but in spite of the outward façade, the religious convictions remain the same, just buried like they are today under the guise of secular authority.

His work emphasizes many of the standard Puritan doctrines—balance and separation of powers, limited government, democracy, and egalitarianism. The discussion is not remarkable in any specific way, aside from the detail of the presentation and its literary value, but it still served as a conduit of ideas and is important for that very reason. In the work Harrington presents the typical three forms of government, which need to be mixed and balanced for the health of a kingdom. This notion he attributes to Machiavelli, whom he cites throughout the work as his most important authority.[206] Along with the mixture of government, Harrington emphasizes the law as an important check upon the powers that be and cites Aristotle and Machiavelli accordingly.[207] He rejects the autocratic rule that Hobbes created in his *Leviathan* (1651) and quotes from the work of Richard Hooker and Hugo Grotius to establish the importance of the natural law in forging a society.[208] However, his view of law looks more to the free and democratic decisions of the people than any other source. "[T]he fundamental laws of Oceana, or the centre of the commonwealth, are the agrarian and the ballot"[209]—an agrarian life being most conducive to democracy.[210] The people and the senate are assigned the legislative function, while the executive branch handles the frame and course of the courts.[211] The people elect their leaders and representatives, just like they did under the Mosaic economy and the congregational polity of the NT church.[212] The power of the people is most essential to his concept of government, and Harrington spends a good deal of time discussing the equitable distribution of land to ensure that equality and democracy will flourish.[213] It is inequality in the ownership of land and its distribution that leads to chaos, not democracy.[214]

Along with Harrington, Algernon Sidney served as an important conduit of Puritan ideas in America, Britain, and elsewhere. Sidney was a cavalry officer in the parliamentary army during the Civil War, became a member of the Long Parliament in 1646, but he had difficulty with the strong measures of Cromwell and left politics for a time. Upon the Restoration of Charles II, he went into exile for twenty-seven years, at one point soliciting funds from Louis XIV to finance an uprising in England. When he finally returned in 1677, he became a member of the

Whig Party, which opposed the reigns of Charles II and his Catholic brother James. He was suspected as a co-conspirator in the Rye House Plot (1683)—an attempt to assassinate Charles and James—and was arrested and executed that year. At his trial, passages justifying rebellion and tyrannicide were read into evidence from his great work, *Discourses concerning Government*, which was written during the last two years of his life. The work was not published until fifteen years later in 1698, but its impact was enormous. Jefferson and Adams cite him prominently in their works as a champion of their cause. Jefferson considers Sidney and Locke the two leading sources for the development of popular government, political liberty, and human rights in America.[215]

The book itself is a chapter-by-chapter refutation of Robert Filmer and his radical, royalist beliefs, which are presented in his *Patriarcha* of 1680. The basic thesis of Filmer was offensive to all sons of liberty as it gave homage to a patriarchal line descending from the times of Adam, possessing a special right to rule over others.[216] That thesis incited an immediate response from Sidney and two other Whig writers during the same decade—James Tyrrell (*Patriarcha non Monarcha*, 1681) and John Lock (*Two Treatises of Government*, 1690). Sidney (and his colleagues) excoriates the notion of any family possessing a God-given, hereditary right to exercise dominion over the planet.[217] All children have inherited equal authority from Adam. No child is born superior to another. All are born equal in nature.[218]

Sidney thinks the distinctions between people arise only when society determines to come together and select its leaders. No one possesses an *a priori*, genetic right to rule over others apart from the deliberation of society and a person's gifts and merit. It is wisdom, purity, and honor that distinguish certain men above others, and society has the responsibility to select those who excel in these virtues if it wishes to act with all care and foresight. *Detur digniori*.[219] But this matter is left up to the people. God has given to human beings the right to institute and abrogate whatever government they want. There is no natural propensity that coerces the people to select one form over another. *Vox populi vox Dei*.[220] The consent of the people forges a society and confers power on whomever they wish to lead.[221] They have the right to elect leaders, impose restrictions on their powers, and depose them whenever it is necessary.[222] This right extends to the very life of the king if he should circumvent the law and become the enemy of the people.[223]

Sidney proceeds to safeguard the freedom of the people by underscoring the typical, threefold approach of the day to limit the abuse of power in government.[224] The first method is the well-established notion of separating and balancing its powers. Government must consist of a mixture of different powers constraining each other. While he extols the freedom of the people to select its leaders, he considers a government that is mixed with democratic, aristocratic, and monarchical elements to represent the wisest of all forms.[225] Every government is subject to the innate depravity of the human condition, especially when it is limited to the frailties of one man, but a mixed government is less likely to sink into utter corruption.[226] He finds the government of the Hebrews divided in this threefold manner between a judge (ruler), the Great Sanhedrin, and the general assemblies of the people. Other nations were divided in a similar manner, including those in the Graeco-Roman world, which he finds also inspiring.[227] To this method Sidney adds the Reformed doctrine of covenant as another means of limiting government. The people have entered a voluntary contract with their magistrates. The covenant spells out the specific duties for both parties, making it clear when violations occur.[228] And if this provision does not suffice, Sidney adds a third and final measure to underscore the duties of the covenant by making all of the government subject to the law. The kings of Israel and Judah all existed under the law like the rest of their brothers and sisters.[229] The kings were bound by an oath to uphold the laws of the land and were held accountable by the Sanhedrin to fulfill its demands, just like anyone else.[230] "Tis not therefore the king that makes the law but the law that makes the king."[231]

The people are given the prerogative to establish the law through their representatives in Parliament.[232] Its laws and constitution (including the *Magna Carta*) are subject to no other constraint outside the arbitrary contrivances of the people and their most free will.[233] This will is free to fashion its laws because God creates a space for his people to decide for themselves their own government, both in constructing its initial form and decreeing what is necessary in the present. Their choices are respected as free subjects, even if they are not always wise or just. They can choose any form of government, but democracy is the most "just, rational and natural" of all.[234] Sidney agrees with Grotius and those who follow the dictates of right reason (*recta ratio*) or what is natural and universal in law.[235] What is right has existed in other cultures and other times long before it was embodied in documents like *Magna Carta*.[236] Even if his accent falls upon the free decision of a covenant community, he is not such a voluntarist as to neglect the need for universal truth. He hopes in the end that the people will do what is good and just and wise.

Sidney and his work exerted a decisive influence upon the debate, but his contribution still pales in comparison to the third and final author from that decade. Of all the names associated with the Whigs and the movement toward limited government, the most outstanding and influential was John Locke. His ideas were not unique or novel in any substantive way. The community of which he remained a mere example exerted the decisive influence, and it is doubtful that America or Britain would have evolved into something much different without his specific contribution. But his exalted place remains secure. His stature and impact is unrivaled by any other author of the times, as he helped to forward and shape the debate over the government and its nature like no one else.[237]

Locke was born in Wrington, Somerset, on August 29, 1632. His father was a Puritan in his political sympathies and fought in the Civil War within the parliamentary army. In 1652 Locke matriculated into Oxford during the period of the Puritan Revolution and Cromwell's tenure as its chancellor. He grew weary of all the chaos and bloodshed of those days and welcomed the stability of the Restoration a decade later, believing that the disorder of the Revolution had brought as much evil as the previous oppression. In 1660 and 1661 he wrote a couple of treatises in which the majesty was granted "absolute and arbitrary power over all the indifferent actions of the people." Even if he shared a love for liberty, he was still tenuous in his commitment at the time to its more radical expressions and reserved some doubt about the excessive measures and impossible liberty of certain revolutionary groups.[238] Later he served as a physician on the household staff of the statesman Lord Ashley, who was raised to the peerage as First Lord Shaftesbury and became high chancellor of England. Shaftesbury was a champion of constitutional monarchy, civil liberty, supremacy of Parliament, and toleration in religion, all of which seemed agreeable to the young Locke's maturing convictions. However, the association proved dangerous when Shaftesbury fell into disfavor for his opposition to the succession of James II, a Catholic monarch, and his inability as lord president of the Privy Council to reconcile the tensions between the king and Parliament. Locke followed Shaftsbury into exile and remained for over five years in Holland until James II was overthrown. He returned in February of 1689, crossing over in the company of the princess of Orange and future Queen Mary II of England. Upon his arrival, he became the intellectual leader of the Whig party and published the *magnum opus* of Puritan political theory, *Two Treatises on Civil Government* (1690). The first treatise provides a typical, Puritan response to Filmer's patriarchal theories[239] and the second an outline of the more positive position of Locke on the nature of government. It is clearly the latter work that has proved so provocative and compelling through the years.

Locke provides in the treatise a discussion of many of the elements already embraced by his constituency. Society is forged by the same voluntary consent of its members. No one is obligated to become a part of the compact, but those who decide to join are bound to serve the will of the majority as one body politic.[240] The government itself consists of three powers that answer to what is lacking in the natural state: the need to spell out clear standards (laws), the need to settle differences (judges), and the need to exact revenge in a civil manner (executives).[241] The legislative is the supreme power of the commonwealth. It is appointed by the people and is subject to their approval or disapproval. Its main function is found in composing laws that are good and just, and these laws become the marching orders of the other two branches. If the executive and federative abuse their power, the legislative is given the authority to remove those responsible from office. But the legislative is not the sole authority. The executive and federative have their own place and value apart from the legislative. Both are needed to enact the will of the legislative because it is dangerous to combine in one branch the right to make and execute the law; and both are provided with a certain amount of latitude and discretion in fulfilling that will, even if their basic function is subject to the law. The executive serves the public by considering its interests when no legal direction is given or a rigid enforcement of the law may do more harm than good. The federative answers to the executive in its use of discretionary power, except it conducts the will of the people outside the country, whereas the executive is concerned with domestic affairs (including the judicial function). The power of war and peace, leagues and alliances, and all transactions with those outside the commonwealth falls under its domain. The executive and the federative should be united under one branch of government, but its power must remain separate from the legislative.[242]

The idea that proved most revolutionary in his account was the exaltation of the natural law to a primary place in society. Before Locke the doctrine was mentioned here and there as an ingredient of government and its law, but it was never made the central doctrine. Locke will bring it to the forefront of the discussion, making it the very basis of government and its purposes. This central role was unique within the political theories of Puritans at the time, although the concept of a universal law in nature was an integral part of his community and the Western tradition in general. The concept was so pervasive and so much a part of his culture that it is difficult to assign any specific source as responsible for his position. He mentions Richard Hooker and his *Ecclesiastical Polity* in a number of sections of his work, including those related to the natural law. He displays evidence of Samuel Pufendorf's ideas, which include the importance of the natural law in society, and refers to him with much praise in his correspondence, commending the *De officio hominis et civis* as the quintessential textbook on the subject.[243] His use of *recta ratio* reminds the reader of the metaphysical mysticism of Cicero and the Stoics,[244] and his rejection of *a priori* categories places his epistemology within the empirical tradition of Aristotle and Thomas Aquinas, as they spoke of the natural law.[245] No one source appears responsible for his total concept. It seems likely that these and other sources came together in the community of his maturation and played an integral role as a whole in his total understanding of the matter.

His *Essays* provide the foundation for his later translation of the natural law into the realm of politics. They were written in Latin when he was around thirty years of age, shortly after 1660. They were never published in his lifetime, but much of the material makes its way into his *Treatise concerning Civil Government, Second Essay*.[246] In the *Essays* Locke speaks of the mind as a *tabula rasa*. It contains no divine ideas or inner light from a heavenly reality, but possesses a capacity to transcend its sense experience and find metaphysical ideals.[247] It is a discursive faculty that can proceed from what is known to what is unknown through a "definite and fixed order of propositions."[248] It can deduce the existence of a transcendent God from a meditation upon the order and majesty of creation.[249] It can find the divine purpose in the things that surround us and instill that purpose in our lives.[250] It can transcend the created order in its form as *recta ratio* and comprehend the universal principles from which all ethical conduct is derived.[251] Of course, not all people employ their mental faculties in a proper way to discover what is necessary and essential. Most follow the traditions of their culture or pursue a life of debauchery, ignoring their duty to find and follow these laws in nature.[252] But these laws have a binding force upon all of humankind. They are discovered by right reason but dictated by God and have the onus of his will attached to them.[253] They are not the will of humankind or the practical construction of its creative powers. In fact, Locke specifically rejects the slogan, *vox populi vox Dei*, as well as any utilitarian scheme that would center ethics upon personal interest.[254] There is no law or even a basis to construct a law outside the will of God.[255] No community or democracy has the right to replace the will of God in the life of a people. No autonomous scheme of reason can fashion an ethical system or practical means of existence that is worthy of one's obedience.

Locke translates his theory of natural law into his *Treatise Concerning Civil Government, Second Essay* and makes it the foundation of the political order. The law of nature is the supreme rule of all people, whether they exist inside or outside of nature in a commonwealth.

> It is a power that hath no other end but preservation, and therefore can never have a right to destroy, enslave, or designedly to impoverish the subjects; the obligations of the law of Nature cease not in society, but only in many cases are drawn closer, and have, by human laws, known penalties annexed to them to enforce their observation. Thus the law of Nature stands as an eternal rule to all men, legislators as well as others. The rules that they make for other men's actions must, as well as their own and other man's actions, be conformable to the law of Nature—i.e., to the will of God, of which that is a declaration, and the fundamental law of Nature being the preservation of mankind, no human sanction can be good or valid against it.[256]

The law of nature involves a number of demands and rights, which God has given to all his people. The most famous of these rights include the Lockean trilogy of "life, liberty, and possession,"[257] which inspired the Declaration of Independence, the Bill of Rights, and the many state constitutions of the day. The term "life" refers to the right of the people to protect their lives and resist arbitrary acts of criminals and tyrants against oneself or others; "liberty" is the right to be free from coercive power, which would enslave one's will to that of another;[258] and "possessions" is the right to own the property over which one labors and toils.[259] These rights are universal. They belong to everyone. They are nonnegotiable. They cannot be alienated through a social contract or the will of the people. They serve the rights of every citizen, or what Americans understand as "inalienable rights" or a "bill of rights," which protect each person against the incursion of the federal government. Locke considers these rights so sacred that the government is dissolved if it dares to act against them.[260] The people should bear a "little mismanagement" and a few "slips of human frailty," but after a "long train of abuses" the government should be deposed.[261] The people have a right to resist injustice and use force against it if necessary.[262] The king has no entitlement to the throne outside the will of the people who elevated him to that office. All are created equal in nature. His temporal elevation is based upon a sacred responsibility to serve the will and the needs of the people in accordance with the laws of God in nature.[263]

Notes

1. *Rule of Saint Benedict*, F. A. Gasquet (New York: Cooper Square Publishers, Inc., 1966) chap. 5, 6 (22-26). In his great work on religious experience, William James provides the readers with a number of illustrations that exhibit Catholic piety in terms of obedience toward superiors. *The Varieties of Religious Experience* (New York: Barnes & Noble Classics, 2004) 273-77.
2. John of Salisbury, *Policraticus: Of the Frivolities of the Courtiers and the Footprints of Philosophers*, C. J. Nederman (ed. and trans.) (Cambridge: Cambridge University Press, 1990) 25; Aquinas, *Sent.*, II, d. 44, q. 2, a. 2, in *Opera Omnia* (Stuttgart-Bad Cannstatt: Frommann-Holzboog, 1980); J. N. Figgis, *Political Thought from Gerson to Grotius 1414-1625* (New York: Harper & Brothers, 1960) 7; Hall, *The Genevan Reformation and the American Founding*, 31. Evans provides some examples of resistance theories within the medieval government and the Netherlands in the sixteenth century. *The Theme is Freedom*, 170-77.
3. G. de Ockham, *Breviloquium*, 1.3.26-28; 4.10, 11; *De Imperatorum et Pontificum Potestate*, 4.7-11. Ockham's works are found in *Opera Politica*, H. S. Offler (ed.) (Manchester: Manchester University Press, 1963).
4. N. Machiavelli, *The Discourses*, B. Crick (ed.) (London: Penguin Books, 1998) 1.4, 6 (113, 115, 123, 124).
5. K. Holl, *The Cultural Significance of the Reformation*, K. and B. Hertz and J. H. Lichtblau (trans.) (Cleveland, OH and New York: Meridian Books, 1959) 65-73.
6. It was common to list "marks" of the true church (*notae verae ecclesiae*) to demonstrate that the Church of Rome was no longer a church. A typical list would include the true proclamation of the gospel and the administration of the sacraments. The Reformed often added the matter of discipline to the list. *The Augsburg Confession* [P. Schaff, *The Creeds of Christendom with a History and Critical Notes* (Grand Rapids, MI: Baker Book House, 1977)] p. 1, art. 7 (3.11, 12); D. Hollazius, *Examen Theologicum Acroamaticum* (Lipsiae: Impensis B.C. Breitkopfii et fil., 1763) 1307; P. van Mastricht, *Theoretico-Practica Theologia* (Amstelodomi, 1715) 7.1.20; M. F. Wendelin, *Collatio Doctrinae Christianae Reformatorum et Lutheranorum* (Cassel, 1660) 321; Calvin, *Institutio*, 4.1.9, 11; 2.2.
7. WA 18.357-60 (LW 46.49-53). See LW 46.5ff., 46.
8. WA 30/3, 282 (LW 47.19). See WA Br 5.660-62 (LW 49.432-35).
9. J. M. Kittelson, *Luther the Reformer: The Story of the Man and His Career* (Minneapolis, MN: Augsburg, 1986) 235-38. The Magdeburg Confession (1550) also proved a valuable source for the militants. It was drawn up by Lutheran pastors in the city to vindicate their defiance of Charles V, who allied himself with the Antichrist and no longer deserved the title of the Lord's anointed. Griffin, *Revolution and Religion*, 5, 6; E. Hildebrandt, "The Magdeburg Bekenntnis as a Possible Link between German and English Resistance Theories in the Sixteenth Century," *Archiv für Reformationsgeschichte* 71 (1981): 228-31; J. Knox, *Rebellion*, R. A. Mason (ed.) (Cambridge: Cambridge University Press, 1994) xix.
10. Figgis, *Political Thought*, 155, 156. See "Calvinismus und Demokratie im Spiegel der Forschung," *Archiv für Reformationsgeschichte* 66 (1975): 182, 183.
11. In Lutheranism the watershed event came when Luther returned from Wartburg in March of 1522 and rejected Karlstadt's iconoclastic reforms. Luther sounded much like Karlstadt before this event, but he found Karlstadt's measures of reform too extreme and he began to treat ritualism as a matter of indifference thereafter. C. M. N. Eire, *The War Against the Idols: The Reformation of Worship from Erasmus to*

Calvin (Cambridge: Cambridge University Press, 1986) 64, 67-69, 107, 270. Eire finds the issue of idolatry a "common thread" that binds the resistance theories of the Calvinists together, giving them a "distinctive shape," but he also recognizes other influences. Lutherans developed their own justification for making this step, emphasizing the cause of religious liberty and inspiring the Calvinists to act accordingly. Ibid., 284-87, 297. See fn. 28.

12. CR 6.598, 599; Eire, *The War Against the Idols*, 73, 74, 234-36, 242, 243, 246, 250, 251.
13. CR 8.419, 428, 429; Eire, *The War Against the Idols*, 260, 261.
14. CR 18.581; Eire, *The War Against the Idols*, 74, 265-70, 276, 277.
15. C. Goodman, *How Powers oght to be obeyed* (Geneva: I. Crispin, 1558) 8, 14, 15, 42, 44, 49-51. Dan. 6 is also used in illustrating the point.
16. Ibid., 107-109.
17. Ibid., 114-18. Goodman also discusses some OT examples: David's refusal to lift his hand against Saul, Jeremiah's exhortation to accept the yoke of Babylon, etc.
18. Ibid., 86, 109, 110, 139.
19. Ibid., 121-23.
20. For the position of Zwingli, Bullinger, and the Anabaptists, see Strehle, *Calvinism, Federalism, and Scholasticism*, 140-43; J. H. Yoder, *Täufertum und Reformation im Gespräch* (Zürich: EVZ-Verlag, 1968) 41, 190; J. M. Stayer, *Anabaptists and the Sword* (Lawrence, KA: Colorado Press, 1972) 120-26.
21. Ibid., 142, 180-90.
22. Ibid., 118, 119.
23. Ibid., 38, 103, 139. He commends the failed effort of Thomas Wyatt's rebellion.
24. Ibid., 34, 52-56, 96.
25. Ibid., 98.
26. Ibid., 28.
27. Ibid., 196.
28. W. Stanford Reid considers John Knox the first theologian to break with Calvin's doctrine of submission. Later monarchomachs appear to show some knowledge of his work: Hotman read *The First Blast* and rejected its misogynist beliefs; Beza prohibited its sale in Geneva; and Mornay accepted much of its doctrine, including the prohibition on female rulers. However, it seems as if Knox had some company or circle of like-minded rebels. Along with Goodman, Bishop John Ponet also composed a tract in the 1550s that advocated armed resistance against tyrants. J. Ponet, *A Shorte Treatise of Politicke Power* (Strausbourg, 1556); Griffin, *Revolution and Religion*, 6; McGiffert, "Covenant, Crown, and Commons in Elizabethan Puritanism," 167; Elazar, *Covenant & Commonwealth*, 205; W. S. Reid, "John Knox: The First of the Monarchomachs?" in *The Covenant Connection*, 120, 125, 134-37. Robert Kingdon thinks that Beza was the first of the monarchomachs and influenced Ponet, Goodman, and Knox in this direction. He refers to a small passage in Beza's *De haereticus a civili magistru puniendis* (1554) that supplies an embryonic justification for inferior officers to revolt against tyrants, even though he admits the doctrine is not sufficiently developed. Both Kingdon and Reid make strong cases for their candidate, but I think it is better to understand Beza and Knox as part of a movement and milieu that is interdependent and filled with a multitude of causes than look to one chain in a causal sequence. Even Beza's treatise looks outside of Geneva to the Lutheran resistance at Magdeburg in 1548. Magdeburg followed the example of Luther and the princes of Germany in resisting the religious tyranny of the emperor. There were many after Beza

who looked to the German resistance for their own inspiration to do likewise. R. Kingdon, "The First Expression of Theodore Beza's Political Ideas," *Archiv für Reformationsgeschichte* 45 (1955): 92-95.

29. E.g., "A Godly Letter of Warning," in *The Works of John Knox*, D. Laing (ed.) (New York: AMS Press, Inc., 1966) 3.205, 206. See M. Walzer, *The Revolution of the Saints: A Study in the Origin of Radical Politics* (Cambridge, MA: Harvard University Press, 1965) 98, 99.
30. Ibid., 188.
31. Ibid., 166, 200. The expunging of Catholic idolatry and purging of papist elements became a major impetus of his reform. *John Knox's History of the Reformation in Scotland* (New York: Philosophical Library, 1950) 1.211, 335, 336, 340; 2.71, 72, 271, 281, 283.
32. Ibid., 166, 192-94.
33. Ibid., 191-94. Of course, he shows duplicity on this point. He complains about the unjust sentences and murder of many Protestants without contemplating the horrors of his own policies. "Letters to the Regent of Scotland," 84; "An Appellation to the Nobility," 110. Both works are found in *The Political Writings of John Knox*, M. A. Breslow (ed.) (Washington: Folger Shakespeare Library, 1985).
34. Ibid., 190-91, 195; Knox, *On Rebellion*, xi, xii; R. L. Greaves, "John Knox and the Covenant Tradition," *Journal of Ecclesiastical History* 24, no. 1 (Jan. 1973): 24, 25, 32. Greaves considers John Hooper, a disciple of Bullinger, a possible source of influence on the covenant. Ibid., 31; Elazar, *Covenant & Commonwealth*, 272, 273.
35. Clarendon, *The History of the Rebellion*, 49, 359, 468, 469; Elazar, *Covenant & Commonwealth*, 277-81.
36. "Letter to the Regent of Scotland," 88, 89.
37. Ibid., 90, 91, 96-98. Knox likes to emphasize the dignity of a magistrate who fulfills an office rather than the privileges of a birthright. Walzer, *The Revolution of the Saints*, 105, 106.
38. Ibid., 118.
39. "The First Blast of the Trumpet" (*Political Writings*), 62.
40. "Apellation to the Nobility," 129, 130.
41. Ibid., 132, 133.
42. Hill, *The English Bible*, 83, 155. Out of 240 printed sermons, 181 were drawn from the OT and 59 from the NT. From Nov. 1640 to Oct. 1645, the ratio was even greater—123 to 26.
43. Mather, *Magnalia Chisti Americana*, 1.262, 263; 2.317, 335, 336, 341ff., 390, 580; *The Journal of John Winthrop*, 253-55, 340, 341. In his *History of Scotland* Knox continually speaks of God's wrath bringing down plagues upon the enemies of reform (e.g., 1.113, 275).
44. Ibid., 135; "The First Blast of the Trumpet," 75; *History of the Reformation in Scotland*, 1.111, 118. Goodman also refers to Mary Tudor as Jezebel.
45. Ibid., 134, 135.
46. "The First Blast of the Trumpet," 42-45.
47. Ibid., 43, 44. He cites the authority of Aristotle in this context.
48. Ibid., 42-48.
49. Ibid., 65, 66. Deborah, the most famous example, is said to possess prophetic or spiritual authority, but not civil or temporal authority. Ibid., 68-70.
50. Ibid., 60, 61; "The Letter to the Regent," 96.
51. Knox's "First Blast of the Trumpet" did not amuse Elizabeth and disqualified him from making a case that others could make better without all the misogynist rheto-

ric. He never renounces his opinion, but he writes a letter to Elizabeth submitting to her authority. He explains his attack on women rulers in terms of an earlier context, which was directed at others, not a personal attack on her majesty, and hopes that the reign of Elizabeth proves long and prosperous as a special dispensation in the divine plan. In this letter he is begging for a letter granting permission to visit England and also recognizes the strategic importance of the queen as an ally, who will forge a "covenant" with the nobility and the kirk, expelling the French and the papists from dominion over the land. *Knox's History of the Reformation in Scotland*, 1.285, 292, 298. The demise of Mary Stuart centered around a suspicion that she murdered her own husband on Feb 9, 1567 to marry the Earle of Bothwell only a few months later.

52. G. Buchanan, *The Art and Science of Government* (Translation of *De Jure Regni apud Scotos, Dialogus*), D. H. MacNeill (Glasgow: William MacLellan, 1964) 6, 126; G. Maddox, *Religion and the Rise of Democracy* (London and New York: Routledge, 1996) 132,133; Sommerville, *Royalists & Patriots*, 71.
53. G. Buchanan, *De Jure Regni apud Scotos, Dialogus* (Edinburg: Apud Iohannem Rosseum, 1579) 53; *The Art and Science of Government*, 58. Hereafter the Latin text is designated DJR, and the English ASG.
54. DJR 8-11; ASG 21-23. He speaks of God's law in nature, but his emphasis remains with the laws formulated by the people in society.
55. DJR 15, 16; ASG 27.
56. DJR 18-20, 32, 66, 83-87; ASG 29-31, 41, 69, 85-88.
57. DJR 96, 97; ASG 96, 97.
58. DJR 53-56; ASG 61, 62.
59. DJR 71-79; ASG 73-81.
60. Robert Kingdon and David Hall note that Peter Martyr also provides justification for rebellion when the prince does not fulfill the conditions of his "covenant" with the people. *Geneva and the Consolidation*, 219; Hall, *The Genevan Reformation and the American Founding*, 134; Vermilius, P. Martyr, *Loci Communes* (London: Kyngston, 1576) 4.20.13 (1087).
61. S. Gordon, *Controlling the State: Constitutionalism from Ancient Athens to Today* (Cambridge, MA: Harvard University Press, 1999) 127, 128.
62. The Huguenots will produce a number of articles in their journals that question the divine right of kings and advocate a limited form of government. Their time as exiles in England during the reign of Louis XIV only helped further their resolve. They will bring the example and encouragement of the Puritan Revolution back with them. J. Dedieu, *Montesquieu et la Tradition Politique Anglaise en France* (New York: Burt Franklin, 1970) 5, 6, 35, 36.
63. Historical examples became an important means of evidence in establishing the political perspective of Hotman, Beza, and the *Vindiciae*. Walzer, *The Revolution of the Saints*, 75, 76, 81. In his *Antitribonian* (1567), Hotman deplores the influence of Roman law in France and commends the Germanic customs of his ancient land as the proper basis of the society and its legal institutions. Gordon refers to his argument as "secular and historical" in nature, but it is clear that Hotman is reading his sources within an *a priori*, theological commitment. The impetus for his ideas is not coming outside the religious matrix by which he sees the world and its history. Cf. Gordon, *Controlling the State*, 122.
64. F. Hotman, *Francogallia*, R. E. Giesey (Latin text), J. H. M. Salmon (trans.) (Cambridge, MA: University Press, 1972) XIX (XV cont.) (398-401). Germanic tribes had some sense of freedom, equality, and federal government, which exceeded the Romans. When they sacked the empire, far from enslaving the Romans, they

ended up adopting their religion. However, the Germanic influences are difficult to trace in a precise way. It is clear that Hotman and many other authors of the time are forming an ideal picture of the past in order to obtain a classical source of authority, which is supposed to define the true *Geist* of the people. Elazar, *Covenant & Commonwealth*, 73-75, 125ff., 203.

65. Ibid., VII (VI cont.) (234, 235). Hotman echoes the same misogynist note as Knox. He rejects the right of women to inherit a kingdom or a fiefdom and cites a number of examples from French history to establish the thesis. Ibid., VIII (X); XIX (XX, XXVI, XXIV) (269-75, 479-95).
66. Ibid., X (XII) (286, 287).
67. Ibid., X (XII) (292-95).
68. Ibid., X (XII), XIII (X cont.), XX (XXI, XXVII, XXV) (304-307, 322, 323, 498-505).
69. Beza consulted personally with Hotman in the spring of 1573 during the writing of the treatise. Théodore de Bèze, *Du Droit des Magistrats*, R. M. Kingdon (intro., ed., et notes) (Genève: Librairie Droz, 1970) xxvii. See also fn. 28.
70. Calvin, *Inst.*, 4.20.31. Cf. Walzer, *The Revolution of the Saints*, 59.
71. Ibid., 4.20.25, 29, 30.
72. Ibid., 4.20.8, 31.
73. *Constitutionalism and Resistance in the Sixteenth Century: Three Treatises by Hotman, Beza, and Mornay*, J. H. Franklin (trans. and ed.) (New York: Pegasus, 1969) 98, 99; Hall, *The Genevan Reformation and the American Founding*, 170, 171. The French edition was the first in all likelihood, and also the most influential. The Lutheran resistance is mentioned in the subtitle. Carlos Eire thinks that Beza's treatment functions more within the Reformed impetus upon proper worship than the rationale of the Magdeburg *Bekenntnis*, which involves religious freedom and civil rights. Eire also finds some influence coming from Pierre Viret's *Remonstrances*, which emphasizes the role of the "lesser magistrates" in correcting a tyrant and the importance of obeying the First Table of the Ten Commandments. *War Against Idols*, 294-97.
74. Bèze, *Du droit des Magistrates*, 39-41; *Right of Magistrates*, in *Constitutionalism and Resistance in the Sixteenth Century*, 120, 121. Hereafter the French text is designated DDM, and the English CR. Beza speaks of a number of countries, beginning with Rome, where the people possessed power over the ruler(s). DDM 23ff.; CR 113ff.
75. DDM 9, 23, 48, 49; CR 104, 113, 126, 127.
76. DDM 11, 14; CR 105, 107.
77. DDM 19, 20; CR 44; 111, 112, 123, 124. In Huguenot theory, resistance is the right and duty of the nobles. Mere private citizens have no fundamental role in this unseemly business. Walzer, *The Revolution of the Saints*, 79, 86-88, 91.
78. DDM 15-18; CR 108-10. Gordon considers Beza's argument "secular." He admits that Beza uses numerous biblical illustrations, but this fact alone does not dissuade him. He considers the argument to be secular because it relies upon social contract theory as a basis for rebellion. In his discussion Gordon exhibits little appreciation of Reformed theology, its doctrine of covenant, and any other religious orientation that would challenge his secular *Weltanschauung*. Gordon, *Controlling the State*, 124.
79. DDM 11-13, 41; CR 121.
80. CR 138, 138; *A Defence of Liberty against Tyrants*, J. Brutus (trans.) (London: G. Bell and Sons, LTD., 1924) 57-59.
81. CR 39.

82. C. S. McCoy and J. W. Baker, *Fountainhead of Federalism: Heinrich Bullinger and the Covenant Tradition* (Louisville, KY: Westminster/John Knox Press, 1991) 47-49.
83. Maddox, *Religion and the Rise of Democracy*, 130; *A Defence of Liberty against Tyrants*, 60; Baker, "Faces of Federalism," 37.
84. *Vindiciae contra Tyrannos* (Basileae?, 1589) 30; *A Defence of Liberty against Tyrants*, 75. Hereafter the Latin text is VCT, and the English DLT.
85. VCT 24, 25; DLT 71. This phrase represents the indelible mark of Reformed influence, found in most discussions of the covenant since the days of Bullinger and Zwingli.
86. VCT 65, 66; DLT 104.
87. VCT 15, 35, 36; DLT 65, 79.
88. VCT 21-23, 40; DLT 69, 70, 83.
89. VCT 24; DLT 71.
90. VCT 156, 162; DLT 174, 178.
91. VCT 134-36; DLT 158-60.
92. VCT 178; DLT 190; Gordon, *Controlling the State*, 126; Conkin, *Self-Evident Truths*, 82-84.
93. VCT 93; DLT 126.
94. VCT 84-87, 91-94, 107-109; DLT 119-21, 124-26, 136-38.
95. VCT 55; DLT 96.
96. VCT 53-55; DLT 94-96.
97. His position relieves the individual citizen from any responsibility in punishing or resisting a wicked king. At one point he can exhort the people to accept martyrdom in dire situations if no magistrates are found to provide the necessary defense. VCT 72-75; DLT 109-11.
98. VCT 56-60, 191, 206, 207; DLT 97-99, 201, 212, 213.
99. VCT 60-62; DLT 100, 101; Eire, *The War Against the Idols*, 300.
100. VCT 78, 79; DLT 114, 115; Eire, *The War Against the Idols*, 299, 300. The *Vindiciae* believes that a neighboring nation can liberate fellow Christians from tyranny. It also sanctions the use of force in liberating those who suffer spiritual oppression from heresies like Arianism. VCT 207-226; DLT 215-29.
101. The work was enlarged in the 1610 and 1614 editions.
102. J. Althusius, *The Politics of Johannes Althusius*, F. S. Carney (trans.), C. J. Friedrich (preface) (Boston: Beacon Press, 1964) xiv-xvi; J. W. Baker, "The Covenantal Basis for the Development of Swiss Political Federalism: 1291-1848," *Publius* 23, no. 2 (Spring 1993): 33, 34; Elazar, *Covenant and Commonwealth*, 314; T. O. Hueglin, "Covenant and Federalism in the Politics of Althusius," in *The Covenant Connection*, 32, 33.
103. Zachary Ursin, John Piscator, Peter Martyr, François Hotman, Philippe du Plessis-Mornay, etc. J. Althusius, *The Politics*, 101, 141, 154; *Politica Methodice Digesta*, (Cambridge, MA: Harvard University Press, 1932) 149, 195, 256. Hereafter the English text is designated PJA, and the Latin PMD.
104. PJA 52,53; PMD 76,77. There are some differences between Geneva and him. Althusius provides for the magistrate a greater role and speaks of a hierarchical structure, where bishops and archbishops rule over a diocese. PJA 54, 55; PMD 79, 80.
105. Besides his specific background in the Reformed faith, influence is indicated by his continuous use of the covenant as a bilateral arrangement consisting of mutual responsibilities. He also cites the *Vindiciae* on a couple of questions concerning the right to disobey and resist a tyrant. This latter work shows the indelible marks

of covenant theology. Baker, "The Covenantal Basis," 38. Hueglin points out that Matthias Martini, a covenant theologian, was a contemporary of Althusius at Herborn and later taught Johannes Cocceius, the most celebrated federal theologian of the seventeenth century. Hueglin, "Covenant and Federalism," 33; M. Martini, *Synopsis s. Theologiae* (Herbornae Nassoviorum, 1603) 13ff.; *Methodus ss. Theologiae* (Herbornae Nassoviorum, 1605) 426,427.

106. PJA ix, x, 46; McCoy and Baker, *Fountainhead of Federalism*, 55-58. He adds a discussion of provinces to the 1610 edition.
107. PJA 22-28; PMD 20-32.
108. PJA xix, 12; PMD 15.
109. PJA 18, 19; PMD 18,1 9.
110. PJA 28; PMD 33.
111. PJA 116, 117; PMD 160-62.
112. PJA 35, 36; PMD 41, 42.
113. PJA 4, 5, 10, 59, 60; PMD 5, 8, 86, 87.
114. PJA 114; PMD 157. The struggles of Germany against Charles V served Althusius as an important paradigm. PJA 120-23; PMD 167, 168. He also refers to Friesland and other provinces as possessing rights against the incursions of Spain and its king. PJA 10, 11; PMD 8, 9. There is no doubt that the land of Holland will become a bastion of natural rights theory, producing some of its greatest champions (e.g., Hugo Grotius).
115. PJA 134, 135, 139; PMD 190, 191, 193. He cites Cicero on the natural law. PJA 15; PMD 16.
116. PJA 90, 91; PMD 139.
117. PJA 114; PMD 157. The sovereign exists under the *lex divina et naturalis*. PJA 66; PMD 92.
118. PJA 44, 93; PMD 59, 142, 143.
119. PJA 99, 118, 119, 195; PMD 148, 164, 404. Althusius approves of the Aristotelian notion of a government mixed with elements of democracy, aristocracy, and monarchy. PJA 197; PMD 405. As a classical scholar he is familiar with Graeco-Roman ideas and employs them throughout the work. Aristotle has particular influence on him.
120. PJA 64, 83; PMD 90, 123.
121. PJA 65; PMD 91.
122. PJA 88, 101, 104, 106, 189, 190; PMD 137, 149, 151, 152, 389, 390. He opposes William Barclay in this section. Barclay considered the king superior to the people. The notion that the people are greater as a whole than as separate individuals speaks of Aristotelian influence.
123. M. J. C. Vile, *Constitutionalism and the Separation of Powers* (Oxford: Clarendon Press, 1967) 38, 39. The most famous example is Montesquieu.
124. For the details, see Clarendon, *The History of the Rebellion*, 177-80.
125. *Meroz Cursed* (London: R. Badger, 1641) 3, 10.
126. Ibid., 9, 20.
127. Ibid., 8.
128. Ibid., 40.
129. Ibid., 53, 54.
130. Ibid., 49.
131. R. Tuck, *Natural right theories* (Cambridge: University Press, 1979) 146. Lilburne, Hobbes, and others display direct influence from his work. Parker's influence on Lilburne is seen in the latter's "Innocency and Truth Jusitified" (London, 1646). Ibid., 149; W. B. Gwyn, *The Meaning of the Separation of Powers: An Analysis*

of the Doctrine from its Origin to the Adoption of the United States Constitution (New Orleans: Tulane University, 1965) 39-41. Levellers will come to emphasize the natural rights tradition, even more than Parker. R. A. Gleissner, "The Levellers and Natural Law: The Putney Debates of 1647," *Journal of British Studies* 20, no. 1 (1980): 74-76.

132. H. Parker, *Observations upon some of his Majesties late Answers and Expressions* (July 2, 1642) 1; Haller, *Liberty and Reformation*, 73, 74. Some of the early Stuarts like John Selden and Robert Phelips saw an original contract between the king and the people, which guarantees certain privileges and liberties. Sommerville, *Royalists & Patriots*, 63.
133. Ibid., 2.
134. H. Parker, *Some Few Observations upon his Majesties late Answer to the Declaration* (May 19, 1642) 8, 9.
135. Parker, *Observations upon some of his Majesties late Answers and Expressions*, 18, 19.
136. Ibid., 19.
137. H. Parker, *Animadversion animadverted* (London, 1642), 3; Haller, *The Rise of Puritanism*, 367ff.; S. F. Wiltshire, *Greece, Rome, and the Bill of Rights* (Norman and London: University of Oklahoma Press, 1992) 59.
138. Parker, *Observations upon some of his Majesties late Answers and Expressions*, 22.
139. Ibid., 20, 42-44.
140. Ibid., 4, 5. All liberty and natural rights stand or fall with Parliament. *Some Few Observations*, 12, 13.
141. Ibid., 31; *Some Few Observations*, 12. He speaks of the composition of Parliament as equal and geometrically proportionate. *Observations upon some of his Majesties late Answers and Expressions*, 23.
142. Ibid., 5, 9, 23. Parker believes that it was the counselors of the king who led him astray. The king should follow the public advice of Parliament rather than private counselors. Ibid., 30.
143. Ibid., 46. Charles I thought of himself as responsible to God alone. He was not bound to give an account of his "Regall Actions" to anyone except God "whose immediate Lieutenant and Vicegerent Hee is." He could not be "coerced or judged by his subjects." The doctrine that the king derived his power from God alone was the fundamental teaching of the early Stuart clergy, who sought to withstand resistance theories among the Calvinists. Before the Civil War many held to what modern Catholics refer to as the "designation theory." It affirms that the authority of the king is God-given, even if the people had *designated* who would rule in an original act of democracy. Sommerville, *Royalists & Patriots*, 12, 13, 23-25, 35, 37, 108, 109, 121, 122.
144. Ibid., 39.
145. Ibid., 40-42. Of course, the basic distribution of power is between the Parliament and the Crown. He believes Rome reached the pinnacle of its greatness when it practiced "mixt government."
146. Ibid., 36.
147. Haller, *Liberty and Reformation*, 373.
148. His *Theomachia* presents a case for religious toleration among Protestant factions.
149. J. Goodwin, *Anti-Cavalierisme* (London: G. B. and R. W. for Henry Overton, 1643) 26.
150. Ibid., 23.

151. Ibid., 1, 35-37.
152. Ibid., 22, 23, 28.
153. Ibid., 28.
154. Ibid., 4. He cites 1 Pet. 2:13 and Rom. 13. He does not find one simple form of government sanctioned in Scripture. His readers are exhorted to practice submission to whatever form of government is found in the land—monarchy, aristocracy, or democracy. Once a people have chosen a specific form it is their duty to submit "so long as it continueth." Ibid., 5, 6.
155. Ibid., 12, 23. Goodwin defends the natural rights of life, liberty, and property against the Crown. Haller, *Liberty and Reformation*, 76, 77; *The Rise of Puritanism*, 371.
156. Ibid., 6, 7.
157. Ibid., 7.
158. Ibid.
159. P. Hunton, *A Treatise of Monarchy*, I. Gardner (ed.) (New York and Harrisburg, PA: Thoemmes Press, University of Durham, 2000) 12-13.
160. Some of the more radical factions like the Levellers and Diggers spoke of the "Norman Yoke." They considered the usurpation of the throne in 1066 illegal and its successors illegitimate. They thought the people had rights and lived as "free and equal citizens, governing themselves through representative institutions." The *Modus Tenendi Parliamentum* (1641) and *The Mirror of Justices* (1642) promoted the theory. But Hunton claims that William became king as the rightful successor of Edward, not as the Conqueror, and received the legitimate consent of the people. *A Treatise of Monarchy*, xx, 34, 54.
161. Hunton, *A Treatise of Monarchy*, 24, 25; Hill, *Puritanism and Revolution*, 57-60, 75.
162. Ibid., 49, 56-58. He includes the *Magna Carta* within this tradition.
163. Ibid., 48, 49. Like Hotman, Althusius, and so many others, he looks to Germanic roots to buttress his belief in liberty and limited government.
164. Ibid., 37.
165. Ibid., 40, 69. Hunton is one of the first to try and limit branches to certain functions, although his discussion displays inconsistencies. The king is seen as the executive, and the Parliament the legislative. Hunton serves as a bridge to Locke, Montesquieu, and later authors, who try to separate the function of each branch. Vile, *Constitutionalism and the Separation of Powers*, 40, 41.
166. Ibid., 43. Aristocracy is identified with the "house of Peers," and democracy within the "house of Commons." Ibid., 59ff. A judicial branch is not a part of the equation in Hunton and early theorists. Hunton subsumes it under the monarchy and rejects the notion of a judge within the government passing judgment upon the king. Ibid., 29.
167. Ibid., 37, 38, 65.
168. Ibid., 20.
169. Ibid., 30, 69.
170. Ibid., 27, 28, 43, 72. The relation between Saul and David is mentioned several times. It clearly functions as the fundamental paradigm through which his theory is developed.
171. Ibid., 70, 71.
172. Ibid., 29.
173. Ibid., 83, 91, 92, 104. He offers six suggestions in the hope of reconciling the king and the Parliament. Ibid., 103-105.

174. There are a number of works written at the time that contained the same basic themes of limited monarchy. A couple of works worth mentioning are *A Fuller Answer to a Treatise by Doctor Ferne* (London, 1642) and *A Political Catechism, or Certain Questions concerning the Government of the Land, . . .* (London, 1643). Hunton mentions the former treatise and its author, Charles Herle, along with the work of Henry Ferne. The treatise sounds much like Hunton's. It speaks of England as having a "mixt monarchy" with three "Coordinate Estates"—the king and the two houses of Parliament (3). It cites Aristotle and finds safety in the coordination of powers (19, 20). It gives Parliament real powers via a "Constitution," beyond the simple role of a mere advisor. The Parliament must consent to any law before it becomes law (4). If the king raises a hostile army, the Parliament can take up arms against it.

A *Political Catechism* also reiterates many of the same themes. It concurs with Hunton and Herle and rejects the royal claim to absolute, arbitrary authority. It provides two fundamental reasons for its position. One, the king is subject to the law and the people (2, 3). *Salus populi* is the *supreme lex* (7). Two, the government of England does not consist of one simple form but has a mixture of monarchy, aristocracy, and democracy, all of which exhibit aberrations when left to their own devices (1, 5, 6). This mixture provides the Parliament with a role beyond that of a mere advisor. It can impeach the counselors of the king and resist illegal actions (6, 7). It can raise an army against them to prevent tyranny (10, 11).

175. Charles I marriage to Henrietta Marra, a Catholic from France, was the pretext of this stipulation. The Propositions also felt that the king's children should not marry a foreigner because of this. Hill, *The English Bible*, 69ff.

176. Clarendon, *The History of the Rebellion*, 271-76. The king felt that the propositions would destroy his right to choose his own counselors and make him one of them—at best. He has no problem with expanding his branch's obligation to the law and submitting all who serve in it to an oath, but he does not wish to relinquish the power of the crown, by which his ancestors served the people. He finds the propositions a means of undermining his authority and rejects them with the simple phrase, "*Nolumus leges Angliae mutari*."

177. [C. Dallison], *The Royalist's Defence* ([London], 1648), The Epistle to the Reader, 32, 33.

178. Ibid., 70.

179. Ibid., 7, 8, 93.

180. Ibid., 94.

181. Ibid., 105 [103], 125.

182. E.g., Ibid., 17, 18.

183. Ibid., 2, 89.

184. Ibid., 36.

185. Ibid., 34.

186. Ibid., 2, 4, 7, 10, 11, 20, 28, 29, 78.

187. Ibid., 78.

188. Ibid., 23.

189. Ibid., 21, 22, 67-69.

190. Ibid., 42, 46, 48-52, 59.

191. In this passage, "the principles of de Mariana and Buchanan" are mentioned as justifying the death of a king who does not defend "the true religion." Juan de Mariana was a Catholic philosopher, who believed a private person could put the king to death for the public welfare. *De rege et regis institutione Libri III* [Aalen: Scientia Verlag, 1969 (1599)] 76; Maddox, *Religion and the Rise of Democracy*,

131-33. Sommerville sees the modern concept of resistance as more a product of Catholic political theory than what modern scholars typically admit. Catholics believed in the temporal authority of the pope, which was wielded in the Middle Ages on a number of occasions to depose or chasten non-compliant kings. Furthermore, during the time of Elizabeth, Catholic recusants justified resistance and regicide in their hope of removing the queen from power and establishing a ruler more pleasing to their vicar in Rome. However, there are several problems with his overall thesis. One, the Reformed concept of resistance finds its justification in covenant theology and natural rights theory, not the priestly power of the pope. Two, the Calvinists sought to empower the people into a revolutionary force, hoping to change all of society, not just remove a disobedient monarch through the nefarious activity of a few assassins or papal inquisitors. Three, Sommerville clearly wants to even up the calls between Catholics and Protestants, so he can promote a secular agenda and assert that the Civil War was non-religious in its fundamental impetus and nature. *Royalists & Patriots*, 181-86, 190, 213; "Oliver Cromwell and English Politcal Thought," in *Oliver Cromwell and the English Revolution*, J. Morrill (ed.) (London and New York: Longman, 1990) 236, 239; Morrill, *The Nature of the English Revolution*, 3. Cf. Walzer, *The Revolution of the Saints*, 2.

As far as an immediate cause, the Solemn League and Covenant provided some justification for the act in the mind of some. The Royalists expressed early on their concern that the king's person and authority rested upon his "preservation and defense of the true Religion" in this compact and wanted the phrase amended to exact unconditional loyalty. The more radical members of Parliament agreed with their interpretation and defended it, believing the loyalty of the people depended upon the faithfulness of the king, but not all members agreed. A number of Presbyterians felt that the prosecution of the king violated their oath of obedience as stipulated in the Solemn League. E. Vallance, *Revolutionary England and the National Covenant: State Oaths, Protestantism and the Political Nation, 1553-1682* (Woodbridge, Suffolk: The Boydell, 2005) 72, 73, 159-63. In the end, it was the army, not Parliament, who executed the king. "It is probable that no more than one in ten of all MPs and perhaps less than one in ten of all regional governors approved of the regicide." Morrill, *The Nature of the English Revolution*, 22. The Parliament was deeply divided over the issue. Hill, *The English Bible*, 329, 330.

192. Clarendon, *The History of the Rebellion*, 740, 741. William Laud, the Archbishop of Canterbury and leader of the privy council, was executed on January 10, 1645.
193. John Milton is not so important at this time, but he certainly is representative of his constituency, and his influence will grow and reach the time of Locke. Haller, *Liberty and Reformation*, 353, 354.
194. J. Milton, "The Tenure of Kings and Magistrates" [*The Works of John Milton* (New York: Columbia University Press, 1932)] 5, 16, 17.
195. Ibid., 14.
196. Ibid., 8-11.
197. Ibid., 7, 21ff.
198. Ibid., 14ff.
199. Ibid., 27-29.
200. Ibid., 46ff. Among those cited are Luther, Zwingli, Calvin, Peter Martyr, Knox, Cartwright, and Fenner.
201. Vile, *Constitutionalism and the Separation of Powers*, 38, 39, 51, 52, 58.
202. M. Needham, *From the Excellence of a Free-State* (London, 1656) 212-14; I. Penington, *The Fundamental Right, Safety, and Liberty of the People*, L. Penn

(ed.) [Los Angeles: Western Publishers, 1965 (originally published in London, 1651)] 23, 24; W. G. Gwyn, *The Meaning of the Separation of Powers: An Analysis of the Doctrine from its Origin to the Adoption of the United States Constitution* (New Orleans: Tulane University, 1965) 56, 61, 140-41. The Levellers seem most interested in egalitarian democracy and exalting the power of Parliament. Walwyn finds the notion of "three or two distinct Estates" ruling a nation an impossible idea. "The Bloody Project," 302, 303. Cf. Gwyn, *The Meaning of the Separation of Powers*, 39-41, 47, 48.

203. J. Adams, *A Defence of the Constitutions of the United States* (New York: Da Capo Press, 1971) 1.159, 160.
204. J. Harrington, *The Commonwealth of Oceana and A System of Politics*, J. G. A. Pocock (ed.) (Cambridge: Cambridge University Press, 1992) xvi, xvii.
205. E.g., Ibid., 8, 72, 73. Lacedaemon, Ancient Rome, and Venice are mentioned throughout the work as important paradigms. Of course, Israel is included within the mix. Hill finds a pervasive use of Scripture in Harrington and Hobbes—two authors who are typically treated as secularists. *The English Bible*, 20, 21. Perhaps later scholars exalt these two authors because they are perceived as moving in the right direction, away from an explicit reliance upon Scripture, but they still function within a world that exalts biblical authority.
206. Ibid., 10, 15, 16, 23-25, 38. He also extols the work of Machiavelli (and Hipprocrates) in *A System of Politics*, 293 (10.23).
207. Ibid., 8, 9.
208. Ibid., 21, 22.
209. Ibid., 100.
210. Ibid., 5. See *A System of Politics*, 288 (8.18).
211. Ibid., 38.
212. Ibid., 26, 27, 82.
213. E.g., Ibid., 101. In *A System of Politics*, he emphasizes this theme. He rejects a complete leveling of estates as a precondition for democracy, but he believes that an unfair or uneven distribution of land is dangerous to this end. Economic independence is essential to the success of democracy. Ibid., 270-72, 275, 277 (1.14; 2.6, 12-14; 4.26; 5.7). And yet, he still accepts the notion of property rights and wants to protect the gentry against the advocates of pure democracy. Hill, *Puritanism and Revolution*, 306-308; J. C. Davis, "Equality in an unequal commonwealth," in *Soldiers, Writers, and Statesmen of the English Revolution*, 230, 231.
214. Ibid., 158.
215. J. Adams, "Letter Sept. 18, 1823" [in *The Adams-Jefferson Letters*, L. J. Cappon (ed.) (New York: Simon & Schuster, 1971) 2.598; T. Jefferson, "From the Minutes of the Board of Visitor, University of Virginia" (March 4, 1825), in *Writings* (New York: The Library to America, 1984) 479; A. Sidney, *Discourses concerning Government* (Indianapolis: Liberty Classics, 1990) xv, xxi, xxvi.
216. The relationship between fathers and kings was a common aspect of Stuart literature and clearly provided inspiration for Filmer's ideas. Sommerville, *Royalists & Patriots*, 30-35.
217. Sidney, *Discourses*, 1.7, 8, 15, 18, 3.8 (24ff., 44, 45, 57, 420). Of course, Sidney is still an advocate of patriarchy according to the modern definition of this concept. He rejects female rulers, based on biblical and philosophical grounds. Ibid., 1.18 (60).
218. Ibid., 1.14, 16; 2.4, 9; 3.33 (38, 50, 93, 510). Sidney felt that the law of the primogeniture was unfair. His older brother was immoral and worthless. Ibid., xxix.

Opposition to the law of primogeniture was shared by many during the Puritan Revolution—Levellers, Fifth Monarchists, Hugh Peter, James Harrington, William Sheppard, Champianus Northtonus, Robert Wiseman, William Covell, William Sprigge, etc. D. Veall, *The Popular Movement for Law Reform in England* (Oxford: University Press, 1970) 217-19; J. Thirsk, "Younger Sons in the Seventeenth Century," History 50 (1965): 358-77; Hill, *The World Turned Upside Down*, 117, 118.

219. "Let it be given to the more worthy." Ibid., 2.1 (79ff., 86). This comment is borrowed from Aristotle, who wants the most virtuous to rule. *Politics* [*The Basic Work of Aristotle*, R. McKeon (ed.) (New York: Random House, 1941)] 1173-1173[b] (1095, 1096)
220. "The voice of the people is the voice of God." Ibid., 1.6, 18; 2.18 (20, 21, 69, 122). The formula is found in Machiavelli and has earlier antecedents. *The Discourses*, 1.58 (255). Cf. *Politics*, 1281[a]-1281[b] (1190).
221. Ibid., 2.5 (99, 105).
222. Ibid., 1.2, 6; 2.24, 31 (10, 20, 21, 225, 503, 506). Sidney makes reference to Hotman's *Francogallia* in attempting to justify his position. Ibid., 2.30 (292, 293).
223. Ibid., 2.24 (221, 222). In his exegesis of Rom. 13, he says that obedience is owed to a ruler only when the latter is endowed with virtue. Ibid., 3.10, 20 (372-74, 438).
224. Ibid., xx.
225. Ibid., 1.10 (31).
226. Ibid., 2.19 (189); Gwyn, *The Meaning of the Separation Powers*, 23. He spends a good deal of time discussing the fall of Rome into absolute monarchy.
227. Ibid., 2.16 (116, 169). His work makes an ample use of Scripture, but it combines the exegesis of the Bible with the use of reason, the wisdom of ancient philosophers like Plato and Aristotle, and a number of historical examples. It carries on the traditional belief in the Germanic roots of liberty. Ibid., 2.1; 3.28 (78, 480, 483).
228. Ibid., 3.4 (340, 341).
229. Ibid., 2.30 (287). The word "king" should be placed in quote marks. Sidney says that the title does not refer to a set office since its duties are derived from culture. John Adams also likes to make this point against his critics.
230. Ibid., 3.2, 18 (335, 336, 431).
231. Ibid., 3.14 (393).
232. Ibid., 3.13, 22 (391, 451).
233. Ibid, 3.45 (569).
234. Ibid., 2.20 (192).
235. Ibid., 2.20; 3.45 (192, 570); P. K. Conkin, *Self-Evident Truths* (Bloomington and London: Indiana University Press, 1974) 102, 103. Sidney was a close friend of Grotius and admirer of his work *De Jure Belli*. He mentions him a number of times in *The Discourses*.
236. Ibid., 2.29; 3.3 (493, 512, 513). The phrase *recta ratio* is much the same as the Stoics' notion of *logos spermatikos*. Both phrases relate reason to divinity.
237. Locke dominated political discussions of the 1760s and 1770s in America. I. Kramnick, "Republicanism Revisionism Revisited," *American Historical Review* 87 (1982): 637-39.
238. J. Locke, *Two Tracts on Government*, P. Adams (ed.) (Cambridge: University Press, 1967) 3-5, 9, 118-27, 213, 215, 218, 234, 235. Matters of indifference are not those prescribed by Scripture or mandated by God. They are left to the custom of each

community and include "Time, Place, Appearance, Posture, . . . Tempus, Locus, Habitus, Gestus, etc." Those who practice a religion other than Christianity are exempt from these stipulations, but they still must pay their taxes in support of them. Locke finds no pretext for revolution or even disobeying an unlawful edict of the magistrate in these treatises, unless it directly violates the expressed will of God. He offers no opinion about the right of the people to choose their own rulers. Ibid., 126, 168, 169, 220, 221, 231, 237-39.

239. Robert Filmer's *Patriarcha* was a favorite text of Toryism. Whigs like Sydney, Tyrrell, and Locke felt compelled to respond to it. According to Locke's version, Filmer wanted to enslave all of humankind to an absolute monarch *jure divino*. The monarch would possess an unbounded will, which represents the law to his subjects. This dominion was given to Adam in Gen. 1:28 and reiterated to Noah in Gen. 9:2. Filmer tries to use these and other verses to claim (or insinuate) that the first-born possess a special authority as the heirs of this dominion, but the position leaves him with a set of problems. Are most kings today illegitimate since only one can possess Adam's inheritance? How could we proceed and determine the rightful heir? Filmer himself seems to switch the royal seed back and forth in his own account—sometimes following the line of Moses and Joshua, then switching to David and Solomon. At this point he seems to recognize certain problems with the position and is willing to contradict himself by emphasizing the private allotment of regal authority over paternal origin. He gives all fathers absolute authority over their children to make whatever decisions they deem appropriate but remains unclear about the rational or ethical procedure by which certain children become princes and others are disinherited. Filmer's argument is dismissed by Locke as lacking biblical and historical proof and filled with contradictory assertions. Locke, *The First Treatise of Government*, in *Two Treatises of Government*, M. Goldie (ed.) (London: Everyman, 2003) passim.

240. J. Locke, *Concerning Civil Government, Second Essay*, in *Great Books of the Western World*, R. M. Hutchins (ed.) (Chicago: Encyclopaedia Britannica, Inc., 1978) 95 (46).

241. Ibid., 88, 89 (44), 123-31 (53-54).

242. Ibid., 143-68 (58-64); Vile, *Constitutionalism and the Separation of Powers*, 61, 62. His doctrine provides for a greater distinction between the branches than Harrington or Sidney. The latter two speak of separation, but the mixture remains. Conkin, *Self-Evident Truths*, 155. One of the major differences between Locke and the US Constitution concerns this matter of separation. The US Constitution provides the president with legislative powers without making the office part of the legislature. The president can veto the legislature, even though the legislature can turn around and override the veto. Cf. *Concerning Civil Government, Second Essay*, 152 (60). The US Constitution does not provide the legislature with the absolute and unlimited power of England or France. Evans, *The Theme is Freedom*, 224, 225.

243. Tuck, *Natural rights theories*, 433. Cf. P. E. Sigmund, *Natural Law in Political Thought* (Lanham, New York, and London: University Press of America, 1971) 81, 82; *John Locke: Two Treatises of Government*, P. Laslett (ed.) (Cambridge: Cambridge University Press, 1967) 22, 74, 75. Sigmund points to sections 58, 65, 74, and 105, and other sections could be listed. One should also note the pervasive influence of Grotius at the time. Tuck, *National rights theories*, 176; S. Buckle, *Natural Law and the Theory of Property: Grotius to Hume* (Oxford: Clarendon Press, 1991) 139. Locke's *Essays* were written before Pufendorf's but after Grotius' work on the subject.

244. Locke's *Essays on the Laws of Nature* (1664) abounds with parallels and references to Cicero. J. O. Hancey, "John Locke and the Law of Nature," *Political Theory* 4, no. 4 (Nov. 1976): 439.
245. He cites Aristotle on the natural law in his *Essays*.
246. J. Locke, *Essays on the Law of Nature*, W. von Leyden (ed.) (Oxford: Clarendon Press, 1958) v.
247. Ibid., 123, 136, 137, 149; Buckle, *Natural Law and the Theory of Property*, 141-43; Wiltshire, *Greece, Rome, and the Bill of Rights*, 78. There is a clear tension between his epistemology and his belief in natural law. Locke, *Two Treatises*, xxvii.
248. Ibid., 149.
249. Ibid., 153-55.
250. Ibid., 157.
251. Ibid., 111, 131, 133; Hancey, "John Locke and the Law of Nature," 441, 442.
252. Ibid., 133, 135. The discussion up to this point sounds much like Thomas Aquinas and his conception of the *tabula rasa*, the empirical basis of knowledge, the obtuse nature of most humans, divine proof, natural law, etc. *Summa Theologiae* (New York: McGraw-Hill, 1964-76) I, q. 1, a. 9; q. 2, a. 2, 3; q. 79, a. 3; q. 84, a. 3-6; q. 101, a. 1; Hancey, "John Locke and the Law of Nature," 442, 443.
253. Ibid., 11; Buckle, *Natural Law and the Theory of Property*, 126, 127, 140. The natural law is the divine law. Reason discovers it, but it is God who dictates it. More than any other scholar John Dunn has emphasized the importance of religion in Locke's political ideas. J. Dunn, *The Political Thought of John Locke* (Cambridge: Cambridge University Press, 1969) x-xii, 259, 263. The evidence seems clear enough, but it certainly does not prevent those who are committed to the wall of separation from tampering with it or ignoring it altogether. Cf. Wiltshire, *Greece, Rome, and the Bill of Rights*, 78.
254. Ibid., 161.
255. Ibid., 213; Buckle, *Natural Law and the Theory of Politics*, 146; Hancey, "John Locke and the Law of Nature," 449. Like Grotius and Pufendorf he rejects a theory of law based upon utility or private interest. He believes that an emphasis upon personal interest would cause a conflict with doing what is best for others and create friction between people. Ibid., 173, 181-83.
256. J. Locke, *Concerning Civil Government, Second Essay*, 135 (56).
257. E.g., Ibid., 6, 221, 222 (26, 75, 76).
258. Like America Locke considers freedom "the foundation of all the rest," because the one who deigns to take away freedom can take away all the rest. Ibid., 17 (29).
259. Ibid., 26 (30). Labor is valuable since it improves an object. The limits of property are set by what one can use and enjoy. Ibid., 30 (31); Buckle, *Natural Law and the Theory of Property,* 188, 189.
260. Ibid., 222 (75, 76).
261. Ibid., 225 (77).
262. Ibid., 155, 209 (60, 61, 73).
263. Ibid., 4 (25, 26).

4

Three Pillars: The Development of Natural Rights, Common Law, and Mixed Government

The modern view of government abandoned all trust in a monolithic head of state and placed countervailing forces inside and outside the administration to check and balance its power. This concept developed from a number of factors coming together in the fullness of times and creating the right conditions for its possible growth. Of course, historical factors provided a decisive context for the emergence of a new world order. They included the inglorious attempts of tyrants to reestablish authority during the Augsburg Interim of Charles V, the Massacre of St. Bartholomew's Day, the reign of Bloody Mary, and the suspension of Parliament by Charles I—all of which invited a strong reaction from the Protestant opposition. The Protestants reacted in a predictable way to the historical circumstances and searched the Scriptures to justify their discontent and revise their concept of government and its proper function. They revised their exegesis of Rom. 13 to mitigate the stricture of obedience and looked to other passages of Scripture like Acts 3-5 and Dan. 6, which appeared to sanction their belief in the authority of the believer, the duty to serve God, and the refusal to crouch before others. They developed theological doctrines out of their exegesis of Scripture, which served to create the main pillars of liberty and protect their right to serve God with a free conscience.

Among these pillars, there are four that stand out in a special way as helping the religious radicals create and justify the reconstruction of the government based on countervailing forces. The first was developed out of the doctrine of covenant, which spoke of mutual responsibilities and penalties for transgressing the will of God. The doctrine was translated from the life of the church into the realm of government and used as a means of removing a regime that failed to fulfill its federal obligations.

The second was developed out of the English concept of common law, which wove together the unwritten customs and wise decisions through the ages into an authoritative body of tradition. This common law assumed an aura of divine wisdom and righteousness in the land, exacting submission from all those in authority and withstanding any legislative fiat that established its own separate estate through the will to power. The third was developed out of the age-old doctrine of natural law, which went back to Graeco-Roman times and spoke of the universal will of God in nature. It was deconstructed in the late medieval period and early days of the Reformation to speak of the inalienable rights of citizens and the basic purpose of government in protecting those rights. The fourth was developed out of the emphasis that the Reformation placed upon the doctrine of original sin and its dark view of the human condition. The Puritans thought of the human race as fallen in Adam and inheriting an innate depravity or hubris, causing them to overstep their God-given bounds. The doctrine served as a fundamental rationale for placing restraints upon rulers to check and balance their will to power. This doctrine and the other three pillars pervaded the works of Puritans and proved their worth in producing a viable system of countervailing government. The history of the first pillar was outlined in chapter one, but the other three pillars still need a more extensive treatment to understand their importance and place within the religious/political tradition.

Common Law

The English tradition of common law has an amorphous quality attached to its understanding and history, but contains enough coherent characteristics to help provide it with meaning as a powerful metaphor. Edward Coke, its most famous exponent, saw the common law as a set of statutes, writs, and precedents, which accumulated through the years, withstood the test of time, and contain an authoritative standard of what is right and wrong in society.[1] The law establishes its claim to righteousness by seeking and preferring the collective wisdom of a nation over time to the shortsighted decisions of contemporary political insight or expediency. It prefers the ancient notion of "due process," where a jury of professionals and peers deliberate over the customs of a community, to the capricious acts of a legislative or executive branch of government at a moment in time. Its customs come from "time out of mind," which serve to invest the tradition with a sense of ancient and universal authority—eternally begotten and time-tested. According to Coke, this common law has an ancient history in England, descending from Saxon law, antedating the Norman conquest, and checking any civil law enacted by the conquest or the subsequent administrations.[2]

> The king in his own person cannot adjudge any case, . . . but this ought to be determined and adjudged in some court of justice, according to the Law and Custom of England. . . . [T]he king may sit in his Star-chamber; but this [is] to consult with the Justices, upon certain Questions proposed to them, and not in *Judicio*; So in the kings Bench he may sit, but the Court gives the Judgment. . . . [N]o man shall be put to answer without presentment before Justices, matter of record, or by due process, or by Writ Original, according to the ancient Law of the Land. . . . Then the king said, that he thought the Law was founded upon reason, and that he and others had reason, as well as the Judges: To which it was answered by me, that true it was, that God had endowed his majesty with excellent Science and great endowments of Nature; but his Majesty was not learned in the Laws of his Realm of England, and causes which concern the life, or inheritance, or goods, or fortunes of his Subjects; they are not to be decided by natural reason, but by the artificial reason and judgment of Law, which Law is an art which requires long study and experience, before that a man can attain to the cognizance of it. . . . With which the king was greatly offended, and said, that then he should be under the Law, which was Treason to affirm, as he said; To which I said, that Bracton saith, *Quod Rex non debet esse sub homine, sed* sub *Deo & Lege* [i.e., the king ought not to be under man, but under God and the law].[3]

The common law is a means of checking the power of government and repudiating the will to power in royalists like Thomas Hobbes and their concept of legal positivism that would grant the king the power to do what he wants and determine what is legal by fiat. What is right and wrong transcends the power of the king to do whatever or any branch of government to create a utilitarian policy of social expediency under a given circumstance.[4] In this, the common law contains a latent religious or metaphysical overtone—a belief in a standard of righteousness that transcends the provincial acts of a people or government in a certain time and place. By rejecting the current appetites of a society, it aspires to find what "ought" to be in our collective life or discover the divine imperative for all humankind.[5] It recognizes the law as an absolute ideal, resting within the perfect will of God and judging those who transgress the law as violating what is sacred and universal.

The exact history of the common law is somewhat obscure. Its proponents do little to resolve the problem and actually enjoy creating some mystery surrounding the origin in order to promote its ancient and universal character. Coke suggests that English law might have originated with the legendary King Brutus, when he fled Troy and arrived in England during the twelfth century B.C.E., bringing ancient Greek customs with him, but even he considers this possibility a mere speculation.[6] The real purpose of the story is to create a myth about the antiquity of the law in "time immemorial." Today more sober scholarship connects the development of common law with the policies of Henry II, who created a centralized system of justice in the twelfth century C.E. to settle the maze of local customs and overlapping jurisdictions that developed over time in Anglo-Saxon and Norman courts.[7] The new system of justice was considered equitable and exacting in its results. It discarded the barbaric practices of looking to the heavens for a sign through battles and ordeals, preferring the rational decision of twelve men, hearing witnesses and examining evidence, as a more reliable and equitable measure of truth. The new system also received a decided impetus from the church, which condemned battles and ordeals as little more than a means of tempting God to perform a miracle and refused any longer to allow clerical participation in its rituals at Lateran IV (1215).[8] During this time the *Tractatus* of Ranulf de Glanvill (1187-89) provided the first major attempt to categorize the common law into a comprehensible form,[9] but it was not until the seventeenth century that the tradition received its most lasting and celebrated treatments. Edward Coke (1552-1634) is the name most associated with the tradition in its modern expression. He brought the common law to the forefront of English society during a six-year term as chief justice of the Court of Common Pleas, where he declared in the *Boham's Case* that the common law can make an act of Parliament void and challenged the authority of the king. William Blackstone (1723-1780) provided a systematic, clear, and elegant presentation of the common law in his *Commentaries on the Laws of England* (1765-69) based upon a series of lectures delivered at Oxford University. Together they served as the great apostles of the modern doctrine, with Coke's *Institutes* and Blackstone's *Commentaries* serving as the basis of legal education for all gentlemen in England and America.[10]

No work embodied the spirit of the common law more than Samuel Rutherford's *Lex, Rex*, published during the tumultuous times of the Puritan Revolution. Rutherford was a Scotsman, born in the parish of Nisbet, Roxburghshire in 1600. He was a licensed preacher of the gospel and served for some time in the parish of Anwoth, but he was soon confined to Aberdeen after writing a book critical of Arminianism and incurring the wrath of William Laud. In 1643 he served as a commissioner to the general assembly of divines meeting at Westminster and completed *Lex, Rex* the following year during his tenure, providing a copy for all its members and preaching its radical ideas to the Long Parliament. The book was written in a polemical style, using detailed exegetical analysis of Scripture to answer Robert Bellarmine, John Maxwell, and all those royalists who espoused the divine right of kings. After the Restoration, the book was confiscated and burned throughout Britain under the order of Charles II, and the author was deprived of his office as rector of New College in St. Andrews and placed under house arrest. He was summoned to appear before the Parliament at Edinburgh and answer the charge of high treason, but he died on March 20, 1661 before he could respond to the order.[11]

In this great work, Rutherford challenges the "papists" and High Church Anglicans, who advocate the divine right of monarchical government.[12] He thinks the people have the God-given right to choose their own government and elect their own leadership to fulfill its varied roles.[13] In the OT the people created their own kings following the instructions of Moses in Deut. 17: 14, 15:

> When thou art come unto the land which the Lord thy God giveth thee, and shalt possess it, and shalt dwell therein, and shalt say, I will set a king over me, like all the nations that are about me; Thou shalt in any wise set him king over thee whom the Lord thy God shall choose: one from among thy brethren shalt thou set king over thee; thou mayest not set a stranger over thee, who is not thy brother.[14]

Rutherford reiterates these verses throughout his account, coupling them with other passages and examples from the OT, and concludes that the people are the "efficient and constituent cause" of the government and possess more "power and dignity" than the king (or the effect of their actions).[15] They are the ones who grant a king the right to rule, not nature or certain privileges descending from a birthright. There is nothing in nature that determines the rule of one man over another or ties a specific family to the crown.[16] "No man cometh out of the womb with a diadem on his head or a sceptre in his hand."[17] The king is elected by the people, and once elected his power is strictly fiduciary in nature, serving the "good, safety, peace and salvation of the people," not his own.[18] The king is elected to protect the property rights of his subjects, which are given by God in nature, and has no authority to pillage their possessions for his own purposes.[19] These and other rights are so sacred that not even the people can bestow absolute authority on the king and alienate their liberties and birthright.[20] The king fulfills his role under federal conditions of mutual responsibility, and even if there is no specific covenant or conditions stipulated in advance, he is obligated to fulfill the law as found in nature and enacted by Parliament.[21] *The king is not above the law*—a point that Rutherford emphasizes in the title of his work and throughout his argument.[22] The king might serve a "co-ordinate" function in helping establish the law of the land, but his role is merely a "derivation," subservient to the "parliaments part, *originaliter et fontaliter*."[23] The

Parliament and the Court are "above" the king, as they assign limits to his reign at the coronation and censor him in accordance with the law.[24] Even inferior judges are deputies of God, not the king, and possess the power to use the sword and make war.[25] Rutherford emphasizes all these layers of accountability to underline the lawful nature of "Protestant" government and oppose it to the arbitrary rule of tyrants, which finds its pretext in papal authority and teaching.[26] In fact, Rutherford thinks that the legal burden placed upon the king should exceed that of his common subjects in order to safeguard their freedom. He includes the following restrictions upon the king: not marrying whom he pleases, not traveling without consent, not associating with whom he wants, not following any religion (e.g., Catholicism), not corresponding with certain individuals (e.g., the pope), not educating his children as he pleases, not living where he pleases, not removing counselors and judges at will, and so forth.[27] Of course, not every transgression is so serious and sometimes the king must dispense with the law for the *salus populi*,[28] but the people have the right to rebel against a tyrant whose conduct results in the "destruction of religion, law, and common wealth," or the breaking of the royal covenant.[29] Rutherford believes that Charles I has transgressed the covenant and laws of England in the current crisis by taking up arms with papists and waging war against the Parliament and the people.[30] His actions have merited a strong reaction and deserve a severe punishment, even though Rutherford stops short of approving the execution of any tyrant, not willing to touch the person of the king through this ultimate act of defiance.[31]

Natural Rights

The natural law provides the most important aspect of the common law and the most direct testimony to a foundation rooted within religious belief and tradition. These religious roots go back to its very inception within the philosophical schools of ancient Athens. Many of their greatest philosophers possessed a vision for an ethical ideal that exists above and beyond the limited circumstances of their birth. Plato spoke of an ideal Good, which transcends the sensible and ephemeral images of this shadowy world. He believed there exists a universal standard of justice by which all particular manifestations in Athens, Thrace, and Sparta are judged. His greatest work, *The Republic*, expressed dissatisfaction with the current state of affairs and created a blueprint for an ideal social order. This vision was altered by Aristotle and other disciples, but the universal nature of ethics remained an integral aspect of their thinking.

Aristotle reduced the chasm between heaven and earth in his search for what is ultimate, but he still insisted upon a universal law in nature that binds all human beings together.[32] In fact, even the Sophists, the polemical opponents of Plato and Aristotle agreed, and provided testimony to a universal law laid down by the gods in nature. While some appeared to endorse moral relativity, others like Hippias and Antiphon went in the opposite direction and spoke of a universal law that transcends human custom.[33] This doctrine proved so popular among their students that it became a favorite legal tactic in Athens. An Athenian lawyer could contend for the right (*ius*) of his client to transgress the unjust laws of the society. Apparently, this tactic proved so popular in the fifth centaury B.C.E. that the city found it necessary to forbid any appeal to "unwritten laws" during a legal proceeding for those lawyers trying to justify illegal behavior.[34]

In Roman times, Hellenistic influences continued to permeate the Mediterranean world, and this influence stimulated many of its philosophers to adopt Greek philosophical ideals, including the natural law. The most celebrated of these philosophers was Cicero, who served as a lawyer and senator in Rome. He rejected the Epicurean emphasis on pleasure as the end of life and wanted to extol the love of virtue in private and public affairs.[35] He looked to philosophers like Plato, Aristotle, and Zeno as laying the foundation for the virtuous life through their promotion of a universal law in nature.[36] This natural law existed long before any society was forged or any specific laws were written.[37] Its virtues are subject to no human authority, whether it resides in a tyrant or the will of the majority.[38] Its origin is found within the very nature of God, the highest reason, who allows its truth to indwell each and every one of us.[39] This right reason (*recta ratio*) represents a spark of divinity within the human race, separating us from the beasts of the field and prescribing for us a higher life of moral existence.[40] Cicero brings this concept of right reason to the forefront of the discussion in the western tradition, especially through his work *de legibus*. The notion is borrowed from the cosmic speculations of Stoic philosophers, who exert their own special influence in promoting natural law.[41]

The influence of Hellenistic forces continued to exert itself as the Graeco-Roman world entered the Christian era. Its doctrine of natural law might have entered the Christian Church as early as the times of the New Testament writings. The Apostle Paul speaks of a natural law in the book of Romans, which bears some resemblance to the Hellenistic concept. This law is broadcast throughout the whole world, resonates in the hearts of all people, and serves as a means of knowing the will of God (Rom. 1:19, 20; 2:14, 15). The precise source of Paul's terse comments is difficult to identify, but it is possible that they received an initial inspiration from his upbringing in Tarsus, a center of Stoic philosophy.[42] The Hellenistic influence is problematic at this stage in the history of the church, but it is more intense and visible as the church proceeds away from its Jewish roots into the world at large. In the second century, a good example of the process is discerned in the writings of Justin Martyr. He founded a school of philosophy among the Christians in Rome and displays in his extant works a synthesis between the philosophical ideas of the day and his Christian faith.[43] As the chief apologist of the church, he uses philosophical concepts to explain and defend the faith against its many detractors. At one point he makes use of the Stoic concept of natural reason (*logos*) to explain the similarities between Christianity and Graeco-Roman philosophy. This concept he merges with the Johannine doctrine of Christ as the divine *Logos* (Jn 1:1), whose reason permeates all of humankind in Justin's deconstruction. He goes on to speak of "seeds" the *Logos spermatikos* has implanted throughout the world. This expression Justin borrows from Stoic philosophy to describe the partial knowledge of the divine will displayed in ancient Greek philosophers like Socrates and Heraclitus. These philosophers shared in a measure of divine light, although they could never participate, like Christians, in the fullness of the divine presence in Christ—body, soul, and spirit.[44]

The natural law tradition became a permanent fixture of Christian doctrine in the subsequent era. It found expression in almost all of its theologians, as they followed Justin and tried to mix the Hellenistic ideas of the day with biblical concepts from their faith. This mixture reached its zenith in the late Middle Ages, where the Schoolmen applied their considerable talents in constructing a synthesis. The most celebrated attempt was forged by Thomas Aquinas, whose account of the natural law is typical of the time and displays much of the same Stoic tendencies exhibited in Justin. In his writings, Aquinas speaks about the natural law as an eternal standard and universal witness to the truth, attested within each and every one of us through the presence of divine reason. This law serves as a basis for judging all temporal manifestations of the law found among the nations, and whatever temporal law deviates from the eternal standard is considered a "corruption of law" or "act of violence." The natural law is perfected by the divine law as revealed in Scripture but is never contradicted by what it says. It serves alongside special revelation as the eternal will of God.[45]

The Hellenistic doctrine remained a vital force in the Christian era but underwent a significant development during the twelfth and thirteenth centuries. The development is significant because it transformed the concept of natural law into a theory of natural rights, providing the foundation for its modern, political application. In this new emphasis, *ius naturale* became more a positive right that entitles each and every one to certain privileges than a law or obligation imposed from above. The *ius naturale* provided a basis of asserting one's rights against those who try to dispossess what God had given. This new direction did not appear all at once and has antecedents in the ancient world, but many scholars like Richard Tuck and Brian Tierney point to the *Decretum* and the so-called Decretalists in the twelfth and thirteenth centuries as providing an early source of inspiration for the modern idea. The *Decretum* (or *Concordantia Discordantium Canonum*) was a systematic study of canon law, published by a Bolognese monk named Gratian around 1140. It served as the basis of canon law and its study until 1918, when a new code was promulgated by the Catholic Church.[46] The *Decretum* is worth noting since it uses the *ius naturale* much like the Sophists of old as a means of questioning the arbitrary customs of the day and defending the innocence of a client before the court.

> What is natural law? The natural law is the law which is common to all nations, in so far as it comes from natural instinct, not any institution. Included in its domain are the union of a man and a woman, the inheritance of children, the education of boys, the common possession of all things, a common freedom for all, the acquisition of what is taken from the earth, sea, and sky—likewise, the restitution of money deposited with someone or entrusted to someone, and resistance of violence by force. For these and similar matters are never considered unjust but natural and fair. . . . Natural law maintains primacy [among the laws] both in time and worth, as it arises with the emergence of a rational creature. It varies not with time but remains immutable. . . . The natural laws prevail over custom and constitution [decree] in dignity. If any custom or interpretation of Scripture is adverse to natural law, it is judged to be vain and void. . . . For Augustine says, " . . . Therefore, whoever will not submit to those laws of the emperors that proceed from the truth of God will suffer a great penalty, but whoever will not submit to those laws of emperors that contradict the will of God he will receive a great reward. . . ." Therefore, decrees must be rejected, whether they come from ecclesiastical or secular authority, if they prove to contradict the natural law in essence.[47]

Hereafter the term *ius* seems to become more polysemous in nature as it slips and slides within contexts. In the hand of Decretalists, the term can alternate between different meanings, implying "law" or "right" and sometimes both, depending on the context.[48]

Among medieval scholastics the most illustrious champion of natural and human rights was William Ockham. There was no greater champion of the cause of liberty in the Middle Ages than this Franciscan theologian and philosopher. A few decades ago scholars like Michel Villey and Georges de Lagarde could exalt him as the source of subjective or individual rights in western civilization,[49] but many today consider their judgment over-exercised and situate him within a tradition that has a number of antecedents in the Middle Ages.[50] Ockham lent his considerable intellectual talents to its statement and served as a powerful force in its dissemination and justification, but he was still part of a tradition like most of us. He was born probably in Ockham, Surrey around 1285. As an Englishman, he certainly was exposed at an early age to the continuous demand for rights in his own country, which was embodied in the famous *Magna Carta* (1215). He entered the Franciscan order—an order that questioned the priorities of those who wielded worldly power—and became an avant-garde theologian at Oxford. The pope summoned him to Avignon in the autumn of 1324 to appear before a commission and answer questions concerning his heterodox opinions. During the ordeal he met with Michael de Cesena, the Franciscan general, who challenged the authority of papal opinions concerning the order and would devote most of his energies thereafter to this and other political concerns. He fled with Michael and a few renegade friars before a final word of condemnation was reached by the papal commission. Fortunately, he found a willing protector in the person of the controversial emperor, Ludwig of Bavaria, whom John XXII had excommunicated for rejecting papal supervision. Ockham lived the rest of his days under his protectorship and died in Munich at the end of the 1340s, apparently from the Black Death.

Ockham's political concerns began with a spirited campaign against the pope in his *Opus Nonagita Dierum* (or *Work of Ninety Days*), written between 1332 and 1334. It was written as a response to John XXII's decretal, *Quia Vir Reprobus*, which undermined the Franciscan vow of poverty in the eyes of Ockham and his colleagues. John XXII taught that Christ and the Apostles possessed certain material goods, contrary to Franciscan teaching. He argued that complete poverty was virtually impossible since the mere use of a commodity like food and clothing involves its consumption and implies some sense of individual ownership (*dominium*) in the one who does so.[51] This argument brought an immediate and harsh reaction from a number of Franciscans committed to a life of abject poverty. Ockham responded by calling the pope a heretic.[52] In his mind the pope had revoked previous decisions of the church and stood in opposition to the basic position of his own predecessors. In 1231 Gregory IX followed the will of St. Francis, ruling that his order should own nothing as individuals or a community but find sustenance through the use of material goods belonging to others. In 1245 Innocent IV concurred with this decision and took an additional step by placing the goods of the order into the ownership of the church, which would function as a trustee or benefactor.[53]

Ockham's understanding of property was consonant with the fundamental views of his order. He believed that one could possess a right of using consumable goods without implying actual ownership. His position is developed out of an understanding of the natural state of humankind. In the state of innocence, the Lord gave to Adam and the human race a common ownership of all things and allowed the people to use whatever they needed as a *ius naturale*. It was only because of the fall and human greed that the need to create and assign individual property rights arose.[54] But even with the advent of individual ownership, the natural right to use material goods, especially in the case of extreme necessity, remained an integral part of the divine law. It is this right, the *ius utendi*, that the Franciscans retained in their own version of extreme necessity or poverty.[55] It is this right that no one can renounce or alienate.

> For it is permissible to renounce ownership and the power of appropriating, but it is not permissible for anyone to renounce the natural right of using, because everyone has the right of using from natural law at all times, but not everyone has that right during each and every moment, only during a time of extreme necessity.[56]

Ockham proceeds in his later works to advocate the rights of the church and state against papal tyranny. He does not question the office itself or the need for the church to function as a unified body under one head, but he certainly accepts the fallible nature of those who occupy this important role.[57] They can be found in error and downright evil. They can be judged as heretics, and the church can refuse to honor them with obedience, just as Ockham and his colleagues have refused to honor the pope in Avignon.[58] In the present case, his wrath is vented against a pope who wants to exercise absolute authority, deny the liberties of the people, and persecute those who would question his right to do so.[59] The pope and his sycophants want him to possess a "fullness of power" (*plenitudo potestatis*) in temporal and spiritual matters, giving him permission to do whatever he wants in all aspects of life—at least if it does not violate natural or divine law.[60] Ockham finds this opinion "pernicious, dangerous, and heretical."[61] The pope might possess some power in both spheres, but he certainly does not possess a fullness of power.[62] If anything, he is called by the gospel to become a servant and reject the exercise of worldly dominion (Lk 22:25-27).[63] He has no right to destroy the freedom of believers and place them under a Jewish yoke. The gospel of Christ has called us to freedom. It has liberated us from the designs of human authority and slavery.[64]

Ockham reserves much of his vitriol for the papacy's abuse of temporal powers. He can understand in certain cases of necessity the pope involving himself in temporal affairs, but he finds no precedent in Scripture for an extensive involvement in worldly matters.[65] Certainly there is no precedent within the example of Christ to exercise dominion over the kingdoms of this world, and there is no mention of him granting such powers to Peter or his successors.[66] No authority is given in the Gospels or the rest of Scriptures to entangle the church in the affairs of the state. A pope has no authority to sanction a king or kingdom unless the people seek a special blessing on what remains their choice. A pope cannot intervene in the affairs of state or depose a king, unless a serious crime or attack on the faith has transpired.[67]

The present pope appears to use his authority to despoil kings of their kingdoms, grant them to his sycophants, and plunder their riches in the process.[68] The zenith of greed is reached when John XXII declares that outside his ecclesiastical domain there is no ownership of temporal things; as if no one has a right to their property except the pope![69] Against this arrogance, Ockham moves all so close to the modern concept of human and natural rights. He defends the rights of all people, including unbelievers, to enjoy the good things that God has given to them through nature and the state.[70] These rights cannot be deprived without fault or reasonable cause; and if so, one can seek redress in a court of law for the harm done.[71] Against the lusts of the pope, Ockham claims that humans are entitled to life, liberty, and possessions. Papal lusts receive no comfort from the gospel of Christ, who came to heal and restore, not pillage the world of "its rights and its possessions." No one can deprive the "rights, liberties, and possessions" of a people. It is God who has given these good things to them through nature or other civil institutions.[72]

> Therefore, a pope should appreciate the kind of power he has over others and be ready to render an account to all who demand one, just as he would provide for his faith. He must not disturb the rights (*iura*) of others . . . but conserve them. . . . Therefore, it is important that the subjects of the pope know their common rights.[73]

> The pope cannot deprive people of their rights. These rights do not come from him, but come from God, nature, or another man. For the same reason he cannot deprive the people of their liberties. They are granted to them by God and nature.[74]

> The prelates ought to strive for the affection of their subjects by securing their interest, rather than promote fear by depriving them of their rights, liberties and possessions (*iura, libertates et res*), unless the prelates back certain necessities.[75]

> As long as the faithful remain ignorant [of the extent of papal power] and the pope strives to secure his own ends, whether from the will to power, the love of material possessions, or simple ignorance, unending conflict will not cease between them, since the people have some understanding of their possessions, rights, and liberties (whether through a reason that offers itself in time of trouble or without reason they strive to preserve what is customary).[76]

The church and the papacy began to fracture from all the corruption in the next few decades. A great schism arose in 1378, where two candidates, Urban VI and Clement VII, staked their claim to the papal throne. A council met at Pisa in 1409 hoping to reconcile the church by electing Alexander V and deposing the other two. Instead, it only created more confusion with the consecration of a third pope. It took six more years before the schism was ended at the Council of Constance in 1415 and a single pope, Martin V, ruled over a unified church once again. The papal office was restored to a leading role in the church, but it lost much of its prestige by this time and never returned to its former glory, when it could "make and unmake kings."

Jean Gerson was the leader of the Conciliar Movement and the Council of Constance. In his mind, the authority of the church and its general council must stand above any future nefarious plans of a pope to usurp power. It is the church that establishes and judges the pope, not vice versa.[77] Its authority as a whole is greater than any of its parts.[78] The "fullness of power" is given to Peter and his successors, but no single individual possesses it *in toto*.[79] Authority is found as a whole in the hierarchy of the divine order, which Gerson understands much like Dionysius the Areopagite.[80] Through this collective hierarchy, Gerson tries to mediate two extreme positions in the debate: the one giving all authority and dominion to the pope and the other making him or the church a pauper.[81] The pope still exercises the fullness of power, but it must be exercised together with the church, so that it does not impinge the rights of his subjects.[82] The pope cannot usurp the rights or property of the clergy, laity, or the state.[83] God has given these rights to all in nature.[84] He has given the use of dominion of material goods to all as an equal and inalienable right (*pluribus competens ex aequo et inabdicabile*).[85]

The natural rights tradition will make its way into the modern world through a number of sources. One of the most important was the University of Salamanca in Spain, which became the theological center of Catholic Europe after the Reformation. In 1526 its principal chair of theology was awarded to Francisco de Vitoria, who served as a leading advocate of natural rights and international law in the sixteenth century. In his work *De Indis*, he championed the rights of the Indians to live a peaceful existence within their own, God-given property, over against the exploits of the Spanish government. Together with *De jure belli Hispanorum in barbaros* and *De potestate civili* this work served as a major impetus toward the development of international law in the modern world. It took the law of nature and created a "law of nations" to regulate the affairs of all governments. This emphasis upon natural rights and international law continued into the next generation with Francisco Suarez, who began his study of law at Salamanca in 1561 and served on its faculty during a part of his long and distinguished career as a professor. Among the twenty-eight volumes of his work (Paris, 1856-78) two of them proved most significant in the dissemination of his political vision: *De Bello et de Indis*, which criticized Spanish colonies in the Indies as a violation of native sovereignty, and *De Legibus* (1612), which advocated the sovereignty of the people, a theory of social contract, and the natural rights of human beings to life, liberty, and property.[86] These and other works helped to carry the natural rights tradition into the modern world and influence its most celebrated supporters. Hugo Grotius, for example, refers to Suarez and Vazquez (a follower of Vitoria and De Soto) throughout his *De Jure Belli* and clearly receives an impetus to write this *magnum opus* of international law from them. He also learns of the controversy between Ockham and John XXII through these secondary sources and arrives at a fundamental concept of property that works within this matrix.[87] He, along with Pufendorf and Locke, helped to make the theory of natural rights an integral part of government and all work within the Catholic concept of property and the human rights tradition that develop from it.

The Reformation continued the emphasis upon the natural law in the church and the Western tradition. Philip Melanchthon is credited with bringing the doctrine to the forefront of Protestant thought through his *Loci Communes* (1521), the theological textbook of the early Reformation. He speaks of a law implanted within all of us by God, providing the ground rules of basic human activity. Its message is obscure due to the effects of human depravity, but Melanchthon finds it clear enough to make three of its basic principles essential to the establishment of all societies. These principles concern the proper worship of God, the protection of one's own goods, and the sharing of possessions with one's family and community. The first principle seems clear enough without considering the many problems of its establishment, but the last two present a clear tension between them, which is not so easy to resolve. The goal of society is the sharing of all things in common (*communiter*), but the reality of human avarice does not allow Melanchthon to impose a Platonic ideal upon his republic or dispense with the need to protect the life and property of individuals from harm. Melanchthon might long for a communist ideal, but his Lutheran emphasis upon total depravity prevents him from proceeding further and considering it a viable option in a fallen world. In the meantime, some sharing is mandated to preserve the public peace, with the hope that a selfless state of perfection can be realized one day.[88]

The natural law was catapulted to the forefront of political discussions among the Protestants through the work of Hugo Grotius, a Dutch statesman, jurist, philologist, and theologian. His political career began with his appointment in 1613 to the office of city pensionary in Rotterdam. He soon became embroiled in the polemical tussles between the Remonstrants and Contra-Remonstrants, favoring the former side of the debate. He fell into disfavor after a coup d'etat by the opposition and the condemnation of the Remonstrants at the Synod of Dordrecht (1618-19). For his role in the affair he received a sentence of life imprisonment at the castle of Loevenstein but escaped a couple years later encased in a box of books, the daring design of his faithful wife. He lived the rest of his life in exile, spending the majority of his time in Paris. It was during this time that he published what is considered today the seminal work on international law, *De Jure Belli ac Pacis* (1625). This work, along with *De Jure Praedae*, helped to promote the natural law to a prominent place in political discussions.

In his great work, Grotius follows the typical Stoic deconstruction of the natural law as a product of right reason.[89] This law is a biological endowment, inscribed within the structure of our minds, and provides us with the basic ability to discern what is good and evil.[90] In fact, its judgments are so true that Grotius asserts a belief in their validity even if God did not exist.[91] Its verdicts contain an immutable and intrinsic standard of righteousness, which are so true that they judge even the conduct of God.[92] (These statements provide much fodder for secularists in their hope of freeing the natural law from its religious moorings,[93] but

Grotius has no intension of proceeding in this direction. Grotius states clearly and categorically his belief that laws have their validity only within the realm of religion.[94] His comments are intended to underscore two important theological notions. One, the law of nature answers to the way God created us to think and function. Two, the natural law is an expression of God's eternal nature, the standard of all righteousness and truth, rather than a capricious act of the divine will limited to a certain time and place.[95] Grotius falls within the intellectualist tradition of Thomas Aquinas, Francisco Suarez, and other Catholic scholars who rejected the voluntaristic views of late medieval Scholasticism.)

The natural law is employed throughout the work to bolster his attempt to create and establish laws between nations. His basic concern involves the unjust motives that cause nations to oppress one another in acts of war. He rejects the ancient notion that "might makes right."[96] He is disgruntled with the way Christian nations prosecute war and wants to develop a "just war" theory for entering a conflict and conducting the battle.[97] Much of his theory is helpful in bringing ethical concerns to this unseemly affair, but his discussion is not always satisfying and creates a considerable tension between the law of nations, the law of nature, and the Christian gospel, which is not so easy to reconcile. For example, Grotius says it is permissible according to the law of nations to slaughter with impunity all those who live in a hostile territory, including women, children, and hostages, and treat captives or slaves in any way imaginable.[98] But what is permissible according to this law may deviate from what is right in a more absolute sense.[99] Certainly, the natural law and the Christian gospel do not allow us to treat an enemy in any indiscriminate manner,[100] and so these standards end up subverting the law of nations and appear to set the necessary rules of conduct. But Grotius ends up subverting his discussion once again and creating tension between the laws of nature and Christ. Now the New Testament is said to contain "a greater degree of moral perfection" than the natural law.[101]

> Now we must see whether the law of the Gospel has more narrowly restricted freedom of action in this regard. Surely, as we have said elsewhere, it is not strange that some things which are permissible according to nature and by municipal law are forbidden by divine law, since this is most perfect and sets forth a reward greater than human nature; to obtain this reward there are justly demanded virtues which surpass the bare precepts of nature.[102]

In this dispensational scheme, the law of nature is no longer an absolute tour de force in governing the nations. A higher law can intervene. The rules of justice can be relaxed when considering weightier matters in the kingdom.[103] Christian conscience can intervene and prevent a citizen from participating in certain functions of government, which appear unseemly to the gospel, especially those invested with the power of life and death.[104] Grotius clearly has difficulty in reconciling his concept of natural law as a universal and absolute standard with what he, the Remonstrants, and other dispensational groups in Holland find supreme in the New Testament.[105] The natural law defines the rule of conduct, but not really. There always remains a higher law.

Samuel Pufendorf succeeded Grotius as champion of natural and international law in the second half of the seventeenth century. In his *Elementa Jurisprudentiae Universalis* (1660), he praised the work of Grotius and gained a general reputation as one who "bravely followed in the steps" of that great scholar.[106] He was born in Dorf-chemnitz in Saxony near Thalheim on January 8, 1632, the son of a Lutheran clergyman. He studied theology at Leipzig, a bastion of Lutheran orthodoxy, but developed a broader range of interest in the humanities and left after six years to study the likes of Descartes, Hobbes, and Grotius at the University of Jena. In 1661 he was appointed by Karl Ludway, Elector of Palatinate, to a newly created chair in natural and international law at the University of Heidelberg and featured *De Jure Belli* in his lectures. Later Charles IX offered him a post at the University of Lund in Sweden, where he remained the last twenty years of his life, first as a professor and then as a political figure. It was during this time that he published his great work on the natural law and society, *De Jure Naturae et Gentium Libri Octo* (1672), along with a compendium of it, *De Officio Hominis et Civis Juxta Legem Naturalem Libri Duo* (1673). Both works exerted a great influence across Europe and America, although most people followed the exhortation of Locke and used the smaller, more manageable edition.[107]

Pufendorf bases his concept of government upon a knowledge of human beings in nature. At first his treatment sounds much like Hobbes and the *Leviathan* (1651) with its reference to the natural state, depiction of its depravity, and emphasis upon self-preservation as a fundamental motive of humans beings.[108] But its overall understanding soon gravitates more toward the natural rights tradition of Grotius and Locke than the dark view of nature and society in Hobbes. The emphasis no longer resides with the will to power but the rights and duties of all people under the laws of God. These laws are understood much like Grotius and Locke. They are given by God in nature and subsist under that authority as the universal duty of humankind.[109] They are derived from the proper exercise of right reason and its reflection upon the common condition of humanity.[110] These laws remain in force even when it is necessary to abandon the chaotic state of nature and find security through a social contract.[111] The sovereign has the obligation to ensure the proper observance of the natural law by clarifying what is obscure, arbitrating differences, and using civil enforcement when it is necessary.[112] The rules are spelled out in written form, so that each one may understand his or her duties and rights in the clearest terms and receive an equal measure of justice. All are created equal, and all stand equal before the law.[113] The only exception results from an unfortunate consequence of the social contract. The laws of society represent what is true in nature, except in regard to the powers that be. In forging the contract, the people acquiesce to make one person or assembly above the natural state of equality and bind themselves as one body politic to the decrees enacted.[114] The very act of making the covenant elevates the sovereign above the equal standing before the law, making it next to impossible to judge whoever rules. Neither Grotius nor Pufendorf find sufficient reason within the covenant or the natural law to justify any act of insurrection against the sovereign.

> Sovereign authority, finally, has also its own particular sanctity. It is therefore morally wrong for the citizens to resist its legitimate commands. But beyond this even its severity must be patiently borne by citizens in exactly the same way as good children must bear the ill temper of their parents. And even when it has threatened them with the most atrocious injuries, individuals will protect themselves by flight or endure any injury or damage rather than draw their swords against one who remains the father of their country, however harsh he may be.[115]

The advocates of rebellion disagreed with Pufendorf and used the natural law as a means of justifying their position. The doctrine is mentioned in the first modern tracts on rebellion as seen in the works of Buchanan, Beza, Mornay, and Althusius. The latter came the closest to creating a more fully developed doctrine with talk of a general egalitarianism in nature and inalienable rights of the citizenry. Althusius lived in the neighborhood of Grotius, and it is likely that a natural rights tradition was a part of the religious/political currents of that region and community. The English also provided testimony to the doctrine in the heyday of its revolutionary period. The doctrine is mentioned during the Puritan Revolution, beginning with Henry Parker's *Observations*, and continued to play a role right up to the times of the Glorious Revolution, finding a place as well in Algernon Sidney's *Discourses concerning Government*. Sidney spoke of the natural law and equality of all in nature, although his emphasis ever remained with the free decisions of the covenant and its laws—an emphasis not much different from his predecessors. These and other scholars found a place for the doctrine in justifying their political point of view, but it was John Locke who exalted the natural law to the primary place it enjoys today in constructing social order. He might have received an impetus from Pufendorf and others to proceed in this direction, but he still deserves much credit for making the doctrine a central pillar in constructing a government and limiting its abuses.

The natural rights tradition made its way overseas and played a significant role in the formation of the United States. The tradition was entrenched within the American psyche well before hostilities broke out in the spring of 1775. Its fundamental beliefs were embraced by nearly all of the authors, pamphleteers, and orators of the time. John Locke and his concept served as the most prominent influence upon them, but many other authors proved valuable as a conduit of his ideas or the tradition in general, including Grotius, Pufendorf, Burlamaqui, Coke, Milton, Sidney, and Blackstone.[116] In one noted passage, Alexander Hamilton recommends the reading of Grotius, Pufendorf, Locke, Montesquieu, and Burlamaqui on the natural law to his opponent, a "Westchester Farmer." He rejects the basic Hobbesian notion that Government is the origin of our rights and defers our liberties to God as the supreme author of "eternal laws" and "inviolable rights."[117] Similar testimonies, arguing in the same Lockean manner, are found throughout the eighteenth century in America.[118] Nearly all the state constitutions accept this fundamental philosophy of the natural law. The preamble to the Massachusetts Constitution (1780) finds the purpose of government in the protection of natural rights, and the body of the document proceeds to enumerate a number of these inalienable rights including the famous trilogy "life, liberty, and property." The Constitution of Virginia (1776) speaks of "all men" as "equally free and independent" in nature and possessing "inherent rights," which no political compact can divest. The rights include "the enjoyment of life and liberty, with the means of acquiring and possessing property, and pursuing and obtaining happiness and safety." It proceeds to enumerate a more specific list of these rights, which clearly inspired other states to compose similar lists and served as the basis for the Bill of Rights in the Constitution of the United States.[119] The mentality for a bill of rights developed from a concern over the abuse of power and the need to secure the natural rights of its citizens.[120] Eldbridge Gerry, one of its most passionate defenders, argued that "the rights of individuals ought to be the primary object of all government, and cannot be too securely guarded by the most explicit declarations in their favor."[121] Thomas Jefferson, the most important proponent, expressed dismay when James Madison sent him an early draft of the Constitution, minus a bill of rights. He insisted that "a bill of rights is what the people are entitled to against every government on earth, general or particular, and what no just government should refuse, or rest on inferences."[122]

Jefferson ensured the preeminence of natural rights within the affections of his people by placing it front and center in his masterpiece, the Declaration of Independence. His concept is not expanded into a coherent system in this or any other work, but the basic themes and phrases are intelligible within the pervasive Lockean understanding of the times.[123] The declaration starts out,

> We hold these truths to be self-evident, that all men are created equal; that they are endowed by their Creator with certain unalienable rights; that among these are life, liberty, and the pursuit of happiness. That, to secure these rights, governments are instituted among men, deriving their just powers from the consent of the governed; that, whenever any form of government becomes destructive of these ends, it is the right of the people to alter or to abolish it, and to institute a new government, laying its foundation on such principles, and organizing its powers in such form, as to them shall seem most likely to effect their safety and happiness. Prudence, indeed, will dictate that governments long established should not be changed for light and transient causes; and, accordingly, all experience hath shown, that mankind are more disposed to suffer, while evils are sufferable, than to right themselves by abolishing the forms to which they are accustomed. But, when a long train of abuses and usurpations, pursuing invariably the same object, evinces a design to reduce them under absolute despotism, it is their right, it is their duty, to throw off such government, and to provide new guards for their future security.

Within the basic Lockean framework of the day, these words are not difficult to interpret. Jefferson is saying that government is based upon religion, not the dictates of secular society or expedient policy. The purpose of government is found in protecting the rights that God has given to all its citizens in nature.[124] These rights are inviolable and nonnegotiable considering their origin. They do not arise from culture, society, or the capricious will of a tyrant. The phrase "all men are created equal" tells King George that his elevation to the throne is a product of the social contract and subject to the will of the people. By birth no one is superior to anyone else, and the king's exalted position is subject to change.[125] The people have the right to abolish a government and create a new one, if it defies their consent, covenant, or God-given rights. This point is clear. A more precise exegesis involves the reader in a certain amount of speculation over phrases that are hackneyed or quasi-religious in texture, defying any specific limitations. In understanding the passage, it is best to adhere to the basic meaning of the phrases within the larger context or community it was intended to serve than become overly preoccupied with its unique form. This method finds the declaration consonant with the culture at large, justifying rebellion on two fundamental pillars of the day: the natural rights of the people and the Reformed doctrine of covenant.

Mixed Government

Alongside the natural law and covenant, there stood a belief in mixed government as an important countervailing force. This form of government could check its own abuses without resorting to a rebellion or full-scale revolution to change the entire political order. Like the natural law, it had antecedents in ancient Greece among the pre-Socratic philosophers and the culture at large. Anaximander makes reference to the role of opposites or a balance of antithetical forces in achieving social order.[126] The "Lycurgan" Constitution of Sparta is celebrated throughout the history of the doctrine for distributing power among contesting interests, which included two hereditary kings, a council of elders (*gerousia*), the *ephors*, and the *apella* of the people.[127]

This concept of government was brought to future generations through the work of Aristotle—the conduit of so many valuable ideas from the ancient world. He sees three basic forms of government subsisting together in a number of the cultures of his day—Cretan, Carthaginian, Spartan, etc. He considers all three elements necessary for the health of the state because each one can deteriorate into a perverse direction if left to its own devices.[128] "For tyranny is a kind of monarchy which has in view the interest of the monarch only; oligarchy has in view the interest of the wealthy; democracy, of the needy; none of them the common good of all."[129] The best solution is to mix all three elements together instead of allowing one or two to dominate as Plato did in his *Laws*.[130] This system of governance combines the wisdom of the masses with the individual talent of those who are capable of ruling through superior education and virtue.[131] It recognizes the dubious nature of individuals left to their own devices. Even philosopher-kings make evil choices that withstand their better knowledge and judgment when left to themselves.

The doctrine of mixed government was noted and appreciated by a number of authors in the Western tradition. In Graeco-Roman times, the doctrine is extolled by Cicero, Polybius, and Plutarch, all pointing to the experiment in Sparta as a powerful case in point.[132] In late medieval times, Aristotle's *Politics* is translated (ca. 1260), and a number of

Schoolmen come to appreciate the value of mixed government through this and other works, including Thomas Aquinas, Nilcolaus of Oresme, Pierre d'Ailly, Jean Gerson, and Machiavelli.[133] The most noteworthy of the list is Machiavelli, and he clearly follows the basic Aristotelian pattern in his *Discourses*. This work advocates the mixture of the three elements, the problems of their isolation, the *virtù* of individual senators, and the wisdom of the masses as a whole.[134] Machiavelli represents a standard position that developed around Venice during the Italian Renaissance. Its government was divided between the doge, Senate, and Great Council—resembling a mixture of a monarchical, aristocratic, and democratic elements in the minds of many. A number of Renaissance scholars expressed support for this type of government, and the "Venetian myth" continued to exert its influence in the centuries to come.[135]

The modern version of mixed government is entangled in a number of different influences. The ancient Greek notion plays a role, but there are other factors that lead the world in this new direction along with it. Most significant is the Protestant revolt against the authorities in the name of liberty, equality, and democracy. These ideas are indebted in a most direct way to a specific development of the Protestant faith and contain within them the recipe for countervailing government. This mentality is seen at the very beginning of the Reformation when the electors inform Luther of their constitutional duty to oppose the emperor. It continues in Geneva and the French Church, where tracts are composed advocating rebellion against the king through proper channels of authority. The zenith is reached in the struggle between Charles I and Parliament over the authority of each branch in the English system of government. This incident will serve as the main paradigm for future generations and provide the springboard upon which the greatest experiments in limited government are launched. The move is justified in the mind of Puritans through the typical staple of Protestant convictions, including a strong emphasis upon the doctrine of covenant, the rule of law, and the depravity of all human beings. Of course, other influences are joined in the mix. Among them, Aristotle appears most often in the accounts of the day with his view of the three forms of government and the necessity of combining them. His discussion provides philosophical weight to the argument and helps to crystallize their view, even if it is not the impetus of the doctrine.

The tension between Parliament and the king served as the primary impetus behind the greatest work on the subject, *l'Esprit des lois* (1748). The work was the masterpiece of Montesquieu, a French aristocrat, political philosopher, and supreme Anglophile. Montesquieu developed his system of government from an idealized version of what he witnessed in England.[136] He criticized other authors like Harrington for creating an ideal society when standing before their eyes was a perfect example of how liberty works in concrete reality.[137] Of course, his own version did much the same. The powers of the British government were more confused in reality than Montesquieu or his readers let on—the king having more legislative authority and the legislature certain judicial functions.[138] But his ideal version still found its fundamental source of inspiration within the British system. He had traveled throughout Europe, including Venice and the Dutch Republic, but found much of those cultures in decline and the political systems uninspiring. He went to England in October of 1729 and remained skeptical at first, but gradually changed in the course of his two-year visit and began to appreciate the type of liberty the country enjoyed because of its separate, yet interdependent system of government.[139] His mature position will display an affinity to Locke,[140] as well as other English authors[141] on this and other political doctrines.

The influence is displayed in the most famous section of *l'Esprit des lois*, part 2, book 11, chapter 6. Montesquieu refers to the English model and its laws throughout the section as providing the paradigm for his argument. Aristotle and other ancient authorities do not appear to exert much influence over the course of the discussion.[142] There is no mention of the Aristotelian forms of government or the inherent problem of aberrations developing when each form is left to its own devises, which is so indicative of that discussion. The fundamental concern is the same as Puritan England with its disdain for despotic rule and belief in common law. Montesquieu wants to check the license of a king to act in any capricious manner and ensure the rule of law.[143]

His view of government combines the Lockean accent upon the separation of powers with a more decided emphasis upon creating a balance between them.[144] He separates the government into three distinct branches: executive, legislative, and judicial. The executive controls the army and convokes the legislative when necessary. It has the right to veto legislation, but it contains no statutory powers to create new laws. The legislative appropriates money for the executive and its troops, enacts laws, and has the power to check the executive by impeaching its counselors. It is divided between a House of Lords and House of Commons in order to provide an additional check on its own power beyond the executive veto through this bicameral arrangement.[145] The judicial provides a role outside the system of checks and balances. It consists of *ad hoc* juries and judges appointed by the people to punish crimes and moderate differences, but it has no permanent structure or successive members of a court to usurp power.[146] The concern throughout the system is the need to check the power of the monarch. This is why the judiciary is separated from the executive branch. This is why the legislative is accorded the power to appropriate funds, disband the army, and impeach executive officers.[147] The purpose of Montesquieu's doctrine is to promote a system of checks and balances, which will limit the power of the king, much like he witnessed in England. Its importance resides more within the ability of Montesquieu to create a practical and coherent system than any radical or qualitative change in the approach.

Most scholars believe that Montesquieu exerted a considerable impact on American thought, especially concerning the separation and balance of powers,[148] but this assessment is true only so long as one recognizes the enormity of the tradition behind Montesquieu's work and the singular role he plays in a much larger picture. The basic reason why Montesquieu and others are seeing government as a conflict of opposing forces is the antecedent struggles within Britain and the social/religious movement that provided the climate for the conflict.[149] The movement and its traditions are already a vital force in America long before the publication of Montesquieu's great work. The elders of Massachusetts as early as 1644 and again in 1679 proposed a constitutional theory of mixed government, which differentiated distinctive duties or branches of government.[150] In 1717, John Wise spoke of "mixt government" as "possibly the fairest" form of governance, where each branch possessed the power to veto the actions of another.[151] In fact, the idea was so prevalent during this time that the New England clergy could thank the Almighty for the blessings of mixed government in their election sermons.[152] By the end of the eighteenth century, the doctrine had so permeated the entire country that any statement of it in federal and state constitutions must be seen and interpreted as the product of a tradition or community, not the simple result of one person's efforts. Like the Declaration of Independence, its final form did not aim at "originality of principle or sentiment, not yet copied from any particular and previous writing." It was "intended to be an expression of the American mind, . . . harmonizing sentiments of the day, whether expressed in conversation, in letters, printed essays, or in the elementary books of [persons like] Aristotle, Cicero, Locke, Sidney, etc."[153]

Of course, the pervasive influence of the community consists of many individual elements but leaves the important contribution of its outstanding individuals intact. Montesquieu served an important role as a proximate cause in relating the tradition to America and tended to shape or dominate the discussion accordingly.[154] His work and ideas are found at every level of the discussion. The main sources of reading—newspaper, journals, dailies, and weeklies—advertise *l'Esprit des lois*, especially after the publication of the first English edition (1750), and their articles make frequent reference to book XI in supporting the doctrine at hand.[155] His work and ideas become an integral part of the curricula at leading universities, beginning with the College of Philadelphia in 1756 and including such noteworthy schools as Princeton, Yale, and Brown thereafter.[156] Madison, Adams, Jefferson, Hamilton, Franklin, Wilson, and practically all the Founding Fathers display a thorough knowledge of Montesquieu and contained a typical array of his books in their libraries.[157] This knowledge is carried over into the many debates that were conducted at the time, as seen in the Constitutional Convention, the Federalist Papers, and the various state conventions. All invoked the name of Montesquieu and discussed his doctrine of mixed government repeatedly and thoroughly.[158] These and other indications are noted by the leading scholars of the field. They all point to the same unanimous conclusion that cannot help but extol the place of Montesquieu's work and ideas in the affections of the country. Paul Spurlin, the dean of these scholars, concludes:

> By the opening of the Constitutional Convention in 1787, the *Spirit of Laws* had become an "American" classic. . . . By 1787, moreover, the *Spirit of Laws*, through the popular press and pamphlet, had contributed very materially to the "harmonizing sentiments of the day." These pages prove conclusively that ideas of Montesquieu were, and long had been, "in the air." They had constituted a part of the general reading matter.[159]

The leading advocates of the day, John Adams and James Madison, both worked within the basic framework of Montesquieu's doctrine. They both shared Montesquieu's dark view of the human condition and accentuate it repeatedly in their analysis. John Adams served as the greatest apologist of mixed government and wrote an extensive treatise extolling its virtues. The title of the work was *Defence of the Constitutions of Government of the United States* (1786-87), and the first volume was made available to the Constitutional Convention. In a letter to Richard Henry Lee (1775) he explained that a "legislative, an executive and a judicial power comprehend the whole of what is meant and understood by government. It is by balancing each of these powers against the other two, that the efforts in human nature towards tyranny can alone be checked and restrained."[160] James Madison was the leading exponent of the doctrine at the Convention and within the *Federalist Papers*. Of the two patriots, it is Madison who ascribes most credit to Montesquieu for his ideas.[161] Adams refers to a number of sources (Aristotle, Cicero, Polybius, Machiavelli, Harrington, et al.) and gives special credit to Harrington as the progenitor of the modern idea.[162] He seems to belittle Montesquieu at times as a mere follower of Machiavelli, which is somewhat odd because Montesquieu's treatment is markedly different from that of Machiavelli and Adam's own position has more affinity to Montesquieu than the rest of the patriarchs he lists, including Machiavelli and Harrington.[163] Madison clearly has a better appreciation of the debt that he, Adams, and the rest of his country owe to the French baron.[164] At one point Madison refers to him as "the oracle always consulted and quoted" on the subject of checks and balances.[165]

But when all is said and done there is still something missing from both of their accounts in the etymology of the doctrine. Like so many of their successors, they display little appreciation for the spiritual matrix out of which this doctrine evolved. Both have fallen under the spell of the French Enlightenment with its contempt for the church, and both have doctored history to fit a more secular view of life.[166] Neither seems to appreciate or comprehend the spiritual impulse that Montesquieu considered so vital and clearly inspired his own analysis. Neither understands the spirit of Protestantism, which allowed its people to question authority, revolt against its abuses, and place checks and limits upon those who wielded power to prevent further abuse. Perhaps rational and practical analysis is beginning to forget the faith that inspired its mission. Maybe the mechanisms of government are beginning to technologize the world into a means without end or purpose. But no matter how distant the memory no doctrine can live without the spiritual moorings that gave it life and substance. It is the deep-seated convictions of a people that inspire whatever measures are necessary to withstand tyranny and create a new vision of the world. It is these people and their longings that created the struggle between Parliament and the king, and it is this struggle, more than any other factor, that provided a system of checks and balances in Montesquieu and those who followed him.

Notes

1. J. R. Stoner, *Common Law and Liberal Theory: Coke, Hobbes, and the Origins of American Constitutionalism* (Lawrence: University of Kansas, 1992) 13; Evans, *The Theme is Freedom*, 79.
2. Ibid., 6, 171-73. Feudalism did not reach England until the conquest of 1066. The two cultures, *Franci* (Norman) and *Anglici* (Anglo-Saxon), subsisted side-by-side for some time, but became more and more amalgamated in the twelfth century. The paucity of evidence makes it difficult to determine a priority of influence between Old English and Norman custom in the new system. R. C. van Caenegem, *The Birth of the English Common Law* (Cambridge: Cambridge University Press, 1973) 4, 5, 12, 84, 109.
3. *The Twelfth Part of the Reports of Sir Edward Coke* (London: R. and E. Atkins, 1677) 12.63, 64; Evans, *The Theme is Freedom*, 82, 83, 162.
4. Stoner, *Common Law and Liberal Theory*, 19, 69, 84, 118.
5. Laws find their ultimate justification within God. According to Einstein, "Science can only ascertain what *is*, but not what *should be*." Morals, values, and goals come outside of science and lie within the realm of religious revelation. A. Einstein, *Ideas and Opinions* (New York: The Modern Library, 1994) 33, 45, 48, 54.
6. Stoner, *Common Law and Liberal Theory*, 20.
7. Caenegem, *The Birth of the English Common Law*, 15-29, 33.
8. Ibid., 63-71, 81, 82.
9. Ibid., 1, 2, 61.
10. Stoner, *Common Law and Liberal Theory*, 13, 14, 49, 50, 162, 164; Evans, *The Theme is Freedom*, 84, 85, 208, 209.
11. S. Rutherford, *Lex, Rex or The Law and the Prince* (Harrisonburg, VA: Sprinkle Publications, 1982) xvi,-xix; Hall, *The Genevan Reformation and the American Founding*, 253.
12. Ibid., 38, 39.
13. Ibid., 6, 7, 29, 38. Rutherford prefers a limited monarchy (i.e., a government mixed with monarchical, aristocratic, and democratic elements). Ibid., 116, 192.
14. E.g., Ibid., 9, 10.
15. Ibid., 80, 81.
16. Ibid., 2, 8, 39, 40.
17. Ibid., 6.
18. Ibid., 64, 65, 69, 70.
19. Ibid., 67, 68. Common law showed much concern over property rights. Henry II was concerned about the dispossession (*disseisin*) of his subjects' property. Caenegem, *The Birth of the English Common Law*, 43-45.
20. Ibid., 46, 81, 82.
21. Ibid., 54, 59, 60, 115.
22. E.g., Ibid., 101-106.
23. Ibid., 115.
24. Ibid., 111.
25. Ibid., 88, 89.
26. Ibid., 161, 167, 168.
27. Ibid., 113.
28. Ibid., 36, 37, 58, 107, 124.
29. Ibid., 143-45.
30. Ibid., 164-66.
31. Ibid., 148, 231, 232.

32. Aristotle, *Rhetoric,* 1373ᵇ, 1376ᵇ (1370, 1377); *Nicomachean Ethics*, 1134ᵇ (1014); Sigmund, *Natural Law in Political Thought*, 9, 10. He makes reference to Sophocles' *Antigone*. The heroine is willing to die for an eternal, divine law that stands above all laws of human creation. Sophocles, *Antigone*, in *The Loeb Classic Library*, H. Lloyd-Jones (ed. and trans.) (Cambridge, MA: Harvard University, 1994) 449-70 (43-45).
33. *The First Philosophers: The Presocratics and the Sophists*, R. Waterfield (Oxford: University Press, 2000) 251, 255 (T4, T5, T6), 259, 264, 265.
34. Ibid., 252. Tierney thinks of the ancient theory of natural law as far removed from the medieval and modern concept of individual rights. This point is true in general, but the case of the Sophists shows how the theory of natural law contains an innate propensity to proceed in the modern direction. Cf. Tierney, *The Idea of Natural Rights*, 45.
35. Cicero, *De legibus*, in *The Lobe Classic Library*, C. W. Keyes (trans.) (Cambridge, MA: Harvard University Press, 1928) 1.39, 48, 49, 60.
36. Ibid., 1.35. Plato stands above all others in his affections. Ibid., 1.15; 3.1.
37. Ibid., 1.19.
38. Ibid., 1.42, 43.
39. Ibid,. 1.18-35; 2.8-10. Heraclitus paved the way for the belief in a *Logos* (reason) that fills the whole world and provides the basis of its unity. *The First Philosophers*, 32-33.
40. Ibid., 1.22-25, 32-35.
41. Sigmund, *Natural Law in Political Thought*, 21, 22; H. McCoubrey, *The Development of Naturalist Legal Theory* (London, New York, and Sydney: Croom Helm, 1987) 31; Marcus Aurelius, *The Meditations*, in *Great Books of the Western Word*, G. Long (trans.), R. M. Hutchins (ed.) (Chicago: Encyclopaedia Britanica, Inc. 1978) 2.11, 12, 4.4, 40; 7.9 53 (258, 264, 267, 280, 283); Epictetus, *The Discourses*, G. Long (trans.), 108, 114, 121. The first two books of Cicero's *De officiis* are based upon a work by Panaetus, a middle Stoic philosopher. *De legibus* also seems to display some influence from him in its emphasis upon the common capacity and universal citizenship of all humankind. Cicero, *The Republic/The Laws*, N. Rudd (trans.) (Oxford: University Press, 1998) 119 (1.61), 169, 206 (fn. 119).
42. D. Ulansey, *The Origins of Mithraic Mysteries* (Oxford: University Press, 1983) 68, 69; C. J. Roetzel, *The Letters of Paul: Conversations in Context* (Louisville, KY: Westminster/John Knox Press, 1998) 28, 29.
43. R. Seeburg, *Text-Book of the History of Doctrines*, C. E. Hay (trans.) (Grand Rapids, MI: Baker Book House, 1977) 3.13.9 (1.118).
44. Justin, *Apologia prima pro Chritstianis*, 46 (PG 6.397, 398); *Apologia secunda*, 8, 10 (PG 6.457-62); J. Daniélou, *Gospel Message and Hellenistic Culture*, J. A. Baker (ed. and trans.) (London and Philadelphia: Darton, Longman & Todd/Westminster Press, 1973) 40-43; C. Andresen, "Justin und der mittlere Platonismus," *Zeitschrift für Neutestamentliche Wissenschaft* 44 (1952/53): 170. Justin's interpretation of the Stoic terminology is colored by Platonic and Christian ideas. His overall philosophy reflects the middle Platonism of the day more than any other school of thought.
45. Aquinas, *Summa Theologiae*, I-II, q. 91, a. 1, 2; q. 93, a. 2, 3; q. 95, a. 2; q. 96, a. 6; Sigmund, *Natural Law in Political Thought*, 39, 43-45; McCoubrey, *The Development of Naturalist Legal Theory*, 49-52; Wiltshire, *Greece, Rome, and the Bill of Rights*, 36, 37.
46. Sigmund, *Natural Law in Political Thought*, 36-39; Tierney, *The Idea of Natural Rights*, 59, 62, 73-76.

47. Gratian, *Decretum*, in *Incipit concordia discordantium canonum* (Basel: Michael Wenssler, 1482) part 1, dist. 1, 5, 8, 9.
48. Marsilius von Padua, *Defensor Pacis*, R. Scholz (hrsg.) (Hannover: Hahnsche Buchhandlung, 1932) 12.12.6; 13.5, 10 (268, 279, 282); C. Summenhart, *De contractibus licitis atque illicitis* (Venice, 1580) 1.1, 1; Ockham, *Opus Nonaginta Dierum*, 91.82-87.
49. M. Villey, "La genèse du droit subjectif chez Gillaume d'Occam," *Archives de philosophie du droit* 9 (1964); G. de Lagarde, "La naissance de l'esprit laïque au déclin du moyen âge," in *Ockham: La morale et le droit*, vol. 6 (Paris, 1946) 164.
50. B. Tierney, *The Idea of Natural Rights*, 13, 14, 27-30, 105-107; J. B. Morrall, "Some Notes on a Recent Interpretation of William of Ockham's Political Philosophy," *Franciscan Studies* 9 (1949); A. S. Brett, *Liberty, Right and Nature* (Cambridge, MA: University Press, 1997) 50, 51; Tuck, *Natural rights theories*, 7, 8. A good example, cited by Tierney, is found in Hervaeus, *De Paupertate*, 235-36.
51. G. de Ockham, *Opus Nonaginta Dierum*, 2.1-79. Ockham's works are found in *Opera Politica*, H. S. Offler (ed.) (Manchester: Manchester University Press, 1963). Ockham says that Jesus and the Apostles lived a life of voluntary poverty. They renounced ownership or lordship over all temporal goods, both as individuals and as a group. This act is considered a matter of "perfection" to the Franciscans, although monastic groups are allowed to retain some possessions in common. *De Imperatorum et Pontificum Potestate*, 27; *Opus Nonaginta Dierum*, 8.27-32; 9.109; 11.95, 96, 136-59, 174, 175, 200ff.; 94.67-71.
52. Ibid., 123, 124.
53. Tierney, *The Idea of Natural Rights*, 94.
54. Ockham, *Opus Nonaginta Dierum*, 14.37-43; 88.97-100. This position is consonant with other Franciscan theologians. Alexander of Hales, *Summa Theologica* [Ad Claras Aquas (Quarrachi) prope Florentium: ex typographia Collegii S. Bonaventurae, 1924-] 4.350; Bonaventura, *Opera Omnia* [Ad Claras Aquas (Quarrachi): ex typographia Collegii S. Bonaventurae, 1882-1902] *Sent.*, II, d. 44, a. 2, q. 2, ad 4; J. Duns Scotus, *Opera Omnia* (Paris, L. Vires, 1891-95) *Sent.*, IV, d. 15, q. 2. It becomes the typical position of English scholars in the sixteenth and seventeenth centuries to believe that all things are held in common by natural law, while private property is constituted by the law of nations. J. P. Sommerville, *Royalists & Patriots: Politics and Ideology in England 1603-1640* (London and New York: Longman, 1999) 136, 137.
55. Ibid., 3.371-422, 61.34ff.; *Breviloquium de Principatu Tyrannico*, 3.8; *De Imperatorum et Pontificum Potestate*, 27.533-40.
56. Ibid., 61.140-44.
57. *De Imperatorum et Pontificum Potestate*, 12, 14.
58. Ibid., prologue, 12, 14, 17, 28; *Opus Nonaginta Dierum*, 1.54-78. *Breviloquium*, 5.14.
59. Ibid., 7.1-5; 15.30-42.
60. *Ans Princeps*, 1.8-13; 5.50-56; *Breviloquium*, 2.1.20-29.
61. Ibid., 2.104.
62. Ibid., 2, 3, 6. He thinks that the best rule of thumb is to exclude from papal power whatever is not explicitly stated in Scripture. Ibid., 6.164-73. He believes that the phrase "whatever you bind" has a number of exceptions. E.g., *Breviloquium*, 2.20, 21.
63. *De Imperatorum et Pontificum Potestate*, 7.
64. *Breviloquium*, 2.3.42-64; 2.4; *An Princeps*, 2.

65. *De Imperatorum et Pontificum Potestate*, 10
66. *Breviloquium*, 2.9; *An Princeps*, 4.40-54.
67. *Breviloquium*, 2.7; 4-6 (especially 6.2.19-24, 69-82).
68. Ibid., 2.3.59-64; *An Princeps*, 2.84-86.
69. Ibid., 3.1. In *An Princeps*, the specific controversy is whether the church is bound to contribute to Edward's just war. The pope is trying to deny royal levies on the church. Ockham sides with Edward and lists many other instances of dire need where the church is required to support the government. *An Princeps*, 1.8-13; 7.1-7; 11.1-24.
70. Ibid., 3.2, 3, 5, 6, 12; *An Princeps*, 7.
71. *Opus Nonaginta Dierum*, 61.55-64.
72. *De Imperatorum et Pontificum Potestate*, 4.7; Tierney, *The Idea of Natural Rights*, 184, 185, 190, 191.
73. *Breviloquium*, 1.3. 26-28; 4.10, 11.
74. *De Imperatorum et Pontificum Potestate*, 4.8-11.
75. Ibid., 7.157-60.
76. Ibid., 26.36-41.
77. J. Gerson, *De Potestate Ecclesiastica* [in *Oeuvres Completès*, intro., texte et notes par P. Glorieux (Paris: Desclee & Cie, 1965)] 6.216-17. The general council can question the actions of a pope and remove him under certain conditions. If the pope refuses to summons a council, the church can convoke its own and remove him. Ibid., 223, 233.
78. Ibid., 273.
79. Ibid., 222, 225.
80. Ibid., 211, 214, 219, 227, 233. He likens the church to the angelic hierarchy, which illumines what comes below. He makes reference to Dionysius in this context, especially his three-fold hierarchical structure and the three-fold ministry within the hierarchy (*purgare, illuminare et perficere*).
81. Ibid., 236-37.
82. Ibid., 228; *De Plenitudine Potestatis Ecclesiasticae*, 250-51. He makes reference to the Aristotelian concept of mixed government at one point of the discussion. Under the Mosaic economy, there were three parts to the government: Moses himself, an aristocracy of seventy-two elders, and a timocracy of the people and each tribe. *De Potestate Ecclesiastica*, 6.225.
83. Ibid., 236-240.
84. Ibid., 242.
85. Ibid,. 246. Civil dominion is not equal. It dispenses property to certain individuals for their use.
86. Cf. Tuck, *Natural rights theories*, 55, 56; Tierney, *The Idea of Natural Rights*, 256, 259-71, 301-04.
87. H. Grotius, *De iure praedae commentarius*, G. L. Williams and M. M. Zeydel (trans.) [in *Classics of International Law*, no. 22 (Buffalo, NY: Hein, 1995)] 2.226-30. On p. 227 Grotius makes reference to Vazquez's *Controversiae illustres* and papal decretals involved in the controversy. J. Kilcullen, *A Translation of William of Ockham's Work of Ninety Days* (Lewiston, Queenston, and Lampeter: The Edwin Mellen Press, 2001) 2.883-893 (Appendix 2). Grotius says that all things were held in common immediately after creation. Later, private ownership became necessary through civil agreements, but a "right of necessity" remains. In cases of emergency those in need have a right to use the property of another. H. Grotius, *De Jure Belli*, 2.2.2.1; 6.4 (1.112, 116; 2.186, 193); S. Buckle, *Natural Law and the Theory of Property: Grotius to Hume* (Oxford: Oxford University Press, 1991) 45; Kilcullen, *A Translation*, 2.913-16.

88. P. Melanchthon, *Loci Communes* (1521), in *Philippi Melanchthonis Opera, quae supersunt omnia*, in *Corpus Reformatorum*, G. C. Brettschneider und M. E. Bindseil (hrsg.) (Halis Saxonum, 1834-60) 21.116-17, 177.
89. H. Grotius, *De Jure Belli ac Pacis Libri Tres*, 1.1.10.1 (1.4, 2.38). In parenthesis there is listed the page number(s) from the first volume in *The Classics of International Law*, which contains a reproduction of the Latin edition of 1646 (Buffalo, NY: William S. Hein & Co., Inc., 1995). The second volume contains an English translation (Oxford: At the Clarendon Press, 1925). See Buckle, *Natural Law*, 8.
90. Ibid., prolegomena, 9 (1.viii, ix; 2.13).
91. Ibid., prolegomena, 11(1.ix; 2.13).
92. Ibid., 1.1.10.5 (1.4; 2.40).
93. Cf. Wiltshire, *Greece, Rome, and the Bill of Rights*, 67-69; Buckle, *Natural Law*, 24. He uses the Bible, along with Graeco-Roman sources throughout the work. He makes reference on a number of occasions to Vazquez, Suarez, the *Digest*, etc.
94. Grotius, *De Jure Belli*, 2.20.48 (1.340, 341; 2.508-10).
95. Ibid., prolegomena, 48;1.1.9.2; 10.2 (1.xvi, 3, 4; 2.26, 27, 38, 39); Buckle, *Natural Law*, 23, 24.
96. Ibid., prolegomena, 3, 17, 24 (1.vii, x, xi; 2.9, 15, 18). He finds Aristotle an ally in his struggle.
97. Ibid., prolegomena, 25, 28; 1.1.2.3 (1.xi, xii, 2; 2.18, 20, 34). There are three just reasons to engage in a war: the common defense, the recovery of property, and the execution of punishment. He also lists doubtful and unjust reasons. In cases of doubt, one should lean toward peace. War is a last resort, and peace its ultimate goal. Ibid., 2.1.2.2; 20.38; 22, 23; 23.6; 24.10; 3.25.2 (1.101; 337, 384-401, 407, 609; 2.171, 502, 546-66, 576, 577, 861). Grotius does not advocate a doctrine of rebellion against the king. One is allowed to defend oneself, but often it is better to accept martyrdom. Popular sovereignty is not a sufficient cause to justify rebellion. A free people can remove a king who violates the state in certain cases, but they cannot recover liberty through the use of force once it is abandoned. Ibid., 1.3.8.1, 4; 9.1; 10.5; 4.6.1, 3; 7.4-6; 8-14; 2.4.14.1 (1.52, 53, 56, 58, 84-87, 90, 91, 145; 2.103, 105, 111, 113, 146, 147, 150, 151, 156-59, 230).
98. Ibid., 3.4.6-16; 7.1.2; 7.2, 3 (1.458-62, 490, 491).
99. Ibid., 3.10.1.1 (1.508; 2.716).
100. Ibid., 3.7.9.2; 10.2; 11.8, 9, 15; 12.2-4; 14.2.3; 15.1.1 (1.493, 509, 510, 519, 520, 522, 533, 544, 551; 2.696, 718, 733-35, 740, 750, 762, 770).
101. Ibid., prolegomena, 48, 50 (1.xvi; 2.27).
102. Ibid., 2.20.10.1 (1.323; 2.478).
103. Ibid., 2.20.21-27 (1.330-32; 2.489-93). He believes that the act of war and capital punishment are consonant with the NT and the Sermon on the Mount. Christ did not cancel the need for punishment in his law, but he approved the policy of relaxing the severity of certain punishments in some instances. Ibid., 1.2.8, 9; 2.20.10.8; 12.3 (1.28, 29, 325-27; 2.75, 482, 484).
104. Ibid., 2.20.16 (1.328; 2.486).
105. Cf. J. Arminius, *Apologia*, in *Opera Theologica* (Prostant Francofurti: Apud Woldgangum Hoffmannum, 1635) III; S. Episcopius, *Opera Theologica* (Amstelodami: Ioann Blaev, 1665) 2.401, 402, 421, 450.
106. S. Pufendorf, *The Law of Nature and Nations*, J. Barbeyrac (ed.), B. Kennet (trans.) (London: R. Sare . . . [et al.], 1749) 68; Tuck, *Natural rights theories*, 156, 157. He follows Grotius in emphasizing just war theory. *De Officio Hominis et Civis juxta Legem Naturalem Libri Duo* (Vol. 1, a reproduction of the Latin edition of 1682, and Vol. 2, a translation by F. G. Moore), in *The Classics of International Law*,

J. B. Scott (ed.) (New York: Oxford University Press, 1927) II, 15, 16 (1.152-59; 2.136-41). Pufendorf also speaks of Hobbes' *De Cive* as a fundamentally sound work. *Elementorum Jurisprudentiae Universalis Libri Duo* (Cambridge: ex officina J. Hayes, 1672), W. Weinberg (ed.) (Oxford: Clarendon Press, 1931) 6.

107. See chap. 3, fn. 243. Cf. Buckle, *Natural Law and the Theory of Property*, 53.
108. *De Officio Hominis et Civis*, I, 3.4; II, 1.3-6 (1.18, 98-100; 2.19, 20, 89, 90).
109. Ibid., I, 3.10; 6ff. (1.22, 42ff.; 2.19, 37ff.).
110. Ibid., I, 2.16; 3.12; II, 1.8 (1.18, 23, 90; 2.16, 20, 100, 101). Pufendorf clearly rejects the Platonic concept of innate ideas.
111. Ibid., I, 3.7-9 (1.21, 22; 2.19).
112. Ibid., II, 1.9, 10; 5.7; 6.7, 14; 12. 3, 6, 7 (1.101, 102, 117, 120, 122, 140-42; 2.91, 92, 104, 107, 109, 125, 126). Like Hobbes and Locke, protection is the main reason a people forge a society.
113. Ibid., I, 7.1-3; II, 1.8 (1.47, 48, 100, 101; 2.42, 43, 90).
114. Ibid., II, 6.7, 11, 12 (1.120-22; 2.107, 108). The sovereign is given general rules to follow. Ibid., II, 7.2 (1.123; 2.110).
115. Ibid., II, 9.4 (1.130; 2.116).
116. B. F. Wright, *American Interpretations of Natural Law: A Study in the History of Political Thought* (Cambridge, MA: Harvard University Press, 1931) 7-11, 46, 47.
117. "The Farmer Refuted," in *The Works of Alexander Hamilton*, H. C. Lodge (ed.) (New York and London: G. P. Putnam's Sons, 1904) 1.61-64, 113; "The Right of the Inhabitants of Maryland" gives credit to Grotius, Pufendorf, and Locke.
118. J. Wise, *A Vindication of the Government of New England Churches* (Gainesville, FA: Scholars' Facsimiles & Reprints, 1958) 31, 36, 61; "The Right of the Inhabitants of Maryland to the Benefit of the English Laws" (Annapolis, MD: W. Parks, 1728), in *The English States in Maryland*, G. I. Sioussat (ed.) (Baltimore, MD: Johns Hopkins Press, 1903) 82-87; J. Otis, *A Vindication of the Conduct of the House of Representatives of the Province of Massachusetts-Bay* (Boston: Edges & Gill 1762) 17; *The Rights of the British Colonies asserted and proved* (Boston: Edges and Gill, 1764) 8, 9; "Benjamin Church Commemorates the Massacre, 1773" [found in H. Niles, *Principles and Acts of the Revolution in America* (New York: Grosset & Dunlap, 1965)] 39; T. Paine, *Rights of Man*, in *Complete Works of Thomas Paine* (New York: Freethought Press Assoc., 1954) 2.45ff. Of course, this list must include the many forms of teaching in the church. All denominations included an emphasis upon the natural law.
119. B. F. Wright, *American Interpretations of Natural Law* (Cambridge, MA: Harvard University Press, 1931) 147, 148. It is Virginia that takes the initiative to create a declaration or bill of rights and moves the federal government to proceed in this direction. Madison, Jefferson, Henry, and Governor Randolph supplied much of the pressure.
120. Wiltshire, *Greece, Rome, and the Bill of Rights*, 95, 96; Wright, *American Interpretations of Natural Law*, 131, 132. Of course, many argued against the need for a bill of rights using natural law theory. Ibid., 139-41.
121. *Pamphlets on the Constitution of the United States*, P. L. Ford (ed.) (New York: Da Capo Press, 1968) 13.
122. "Letter to Madison" (Dec. 20, 1787), in *The Writings of Thomas Jefferson*, P. L. Ford (ed.) (New York and London: G. P. Putnam's Sons, 1894) 4.477.
123. The final document is not the work of Jefferson *in toto*. His draft undergoes a number of alterations from Adams, Franklin, a special committee, and the Continental Congress itself.

124. There is much speculation over the substitution of the phrase "pursuit of happiness" for property in the famous trilogy. Some consider the change more a matter of style than substance. Locke, the Constitution, the State Constitutions, the Declaration of Rights in VA, etc. refer to the pursuit of happiness as the end of government and a part of the enumerated rights. They certainly do not intend to dismiss property rights from the sacred trilogy (see the Fifth and Fourteenth Amendments). Others see the substitution as more substantive. There is some evidence that Jefferson did not consider property a natural right, although he followed the Lockean concept of what constitutes the ownership of property. See Locke, *Concerning Civil Government, Second Essay,* 131 (54); Wise, *A Vindication of the Government*, 61; "Letter to Isaac McPherson" (Aug. 13, 1873), in *The Writings of Thomas Jefferson*, A. A. Lipscomb (ed.) (Washington, DC: The Thomas Jefferson Memorial Assoc., 1904) 13.333; "Letter to Charles W. Pearle" (April 17, 1813), in *The Writings of Thomas Jefferson*, 18.277; Sigmund, *Natural Law in Political Thought*, 103, 104; A. Koch, *Jefferson and Madison: The Great Collaboration* (New York: Alfred A. Knopf, 1950) 78-80.

125. This statement caused some pangs of conscience in Jefferson as a slave owner, but in the most ridiculous section of his first draft, he proceeds to blame the Crown for his own evil. "The Christian King of Great Britain" is accused of violating the "sacred rights" of human nature by enslaving Africans and preventing legislation to prohibit this commerce. The issue in the famous statement about equality is aimed at the hereditary privilege of the king, not slavery, but it takes little imagination to deconstruct it in the direction of Frederick Douglass and Abraham Lincoln and apply it to another issue. For example, John Wise takes this same notion and says that we should treat all people alike since we all come from one stock. *Vindication*, 40-45. In fact, the first draft of the declaration allows more room for this type of interpretation. It says, "[A]ll men are created equal and independent; that from that equal creation they derive in rights inherent and inalienable, among which are preservation of life, and liberty, and the pursuit of happiness." Of course, the editors change this statement enough to make one wonder about its final meaning and whose intention we are dealing with. Is it Jefferson's, the committee's, the Congress's, or the people's?

126. *The First Philosophers*, 5, 14-16; G. S. Kirk and J. E. Raven, *The Presocratic Philosophers: A Critical History with a Selection of Texts* (Cambridge: Cambridge University Press, 1963) 119

127. E. P. Panagopoulos, *Essays on the History and Meaning of Checks and Balances* (Lanham, New York, and London: University Press of America, 1985) 4-6, 16-22.

128. Aristotle, *Politics*, 10.70[b] (1167).

129. Ibid., 1279[b] (1186).

130. Ibid., 1265[b], 1266[a] (1157). Plato also recognized that aberrations can arise from different forms of government. *Republic*, in *The Collected Dialogues of Plato*, E. Hamilton and H. Cairns (ed.) (Princeton, NJ: Princeton University Press, 1978) 8.553ff. (781ff.).

131. Ibid., 1273[a], 1273[b], 1281[a], 1281[b], 1318[b] (1172, 1173, 1189-91, 1268).

132. U. Wilhelm, "Montesquieu und die Theorie der Mischverfassung: Zur Geschichte einer politischen Idee," *Saeculum* 53 (2002): 76, 77. Cicero, Polybius, and Plutarch all recognized the wisdom in the experiment and its form of government. Cicero, *De Re Publica*, in *The Loeb Classic Library*, C.W. Keyes (trans.) (Cambridge, MA: Harvard University Press, 1928) 1.43-45, 69; 2.57,58; Polybius, *The Histories*, W. R. Paton (trans.), 6.10, 11.18, 48ff.; Plutarch, *Lycurgus*, in *Lives*, B. Perrin (trans.), passim.

133. Ibid., 77-78.
134. Machiavelli, *Discourses*, 1.2, 46, 53, 57, 58 (106-11, 223-25, 238-42, 250-57). Polybius also exerts influence on his account. Panagopoulos, *Essays*, 35, 36.
135. Gordon, *Controlling the State*, 160-64. Gordon believes that Contarini's *Magistratibus* was more influential than Machiavelli's work in the history of the doctrine. Contarini helped to create the "Venetian myth," which accented its system of checks and balances. Perhaps Gordon is right, but the overall influence of either one is difficult to assess.
136. M. P. Bergman, "Montesquieu's Theory of Government and the Framing of the American Constitution," *Pepperdine Law Review* 18, no. 1 (1990): 33; Gordon, *Controlling the State*, 309.
137. Montesquieu, *De l'Esprit des lois* (Paris, Garnier Frères) II, xi, 6 (1174); *The Spirit of the Laws*, A. M. Cohler, B. C. Miller, and H. S. Stone (trans. and ed.) (Cambridge: Cambridge University Press, 1997) 174. Hereafter the French edition is EL, and the English is SL.
138. Bergman, "Montesquieu's Theory of Government," 19; J. R. Loy, *Montesquieu* (New York: Twayne Publishers, Inc., 1968) 109; Vile, *Constitutionalism and the Separation of Powers*, 92, 93; Pole, *Political Representation*, 420; G. Turbet Delof, "La Theorie de l'Equilibre des Pouvoirs avant 'De l'Esprit des Lois'," *Mondes et Cultures* 47, no. 3 (1987): 585.
139. His "Notes sur l'Angeterre" display the beginning of this change. Montesquieu, *Oeuvres Complètes* (Paris: Éditions du Seuil, 1964) 331-34. The visit causes him to reinterpret the political systems in Athens, Sparta, and Rome. He now sees these systems in terms of the separation and balance of powers. Dedieu, *Montesquieu*, 145-47, 150, 156-57.
140. Loy, *Montesquieu, 104;* Gwyn, *The Meaning of the Separation of Powers*, 108, 109; Vile, *Constitutionalism and the Separation of Powers*, 76. In his classic study, Dedieu finds some differences between the two (Locke's social contract theory and his emphasis upon popular sovereignty, Montesquieu's concrete analysis of specific experiments and mixture of the powers, etc.). See Dedieu, *Montesquieu*, 169, 170. However, the similarities seem to outweigh the differences, and Montesquieu's discussion of the separation of powers provides Dedieu with a good case in point. The influence of Locke is most apparent where Montesquieu displays a confusion of the powers. Ibid., 172-91.
141. Among them there is the English politician Viscount Bolingbroke, who made Montesquieu's acquaintance and shared a similar assessment of the English Constitution. R. Shackleton, "Montesquieu, Bolingbroke and the Separation of Powers," *French Studies* 3 (1949); Vile, *Constitutionalism and the Separation of Powers*, 79. Dedieu provides an exhaustive account of the many influences upon Montesquieu and his doctrine. The list includes the French Protestant refugees from England, the many journals and journalists of the day who praised the British way (Michel de la Roche, Armand de la Chapelle, Jean Leclerc, etc.), the author of *Lettres sur les matieres du temps* (end of the seventeenth century), and a number of other authors, especially Rabin-Thoyras, who made the parliamentary system palatable in France and mixes the three powers together in his *Histoire d'Angleterre* (1723). Dedieu, *Montesquieu*, 4-7, 12, 35-39, 41ff., 55ff., 67, 68, 76ff., 84-102; Vile, *Contitutionalism and the Separation of Powers*, 79, 80.
142. In a later section he says that Aristotle and the ancients did not understand "the distribution of the three powers in the government." EL II, xi, 9 (176); SL 168. His typical division of government consists of republics, monarchies, and despotisms. A monarchy is where the law is king (*lex rex*), and despotism is where the king

is law (*rex lex*). EL II, I, 1 (11); SL 10; Bergman, "Montesquieu's Theory," 12; Gordon, *Controlling the State*, 281, 282.

143. EL I, v, 12 (63); vi, 3(82); II, xi, 2, 3 (162); SL 58, 76, 155.

144. Conkin, *Self-Evident Truths*, 156; Gwyn, *The Meaning of the Separation of Powers*, 109.

145. EL II, xi, 6 (168-73); SL 161-65; Loy, *Montesquieu*, 105,, 106; Dedieu, *Montesquieu*, 177; Bergman, "Montesquieu's Theory," 15; Vile, *Constitutionalism and the Separation of Powers*, 94; Wilhelm; "Montesquieu und die Theorie der Mischverfassung," 84, 85; Gwyn, *The Meaning of the Separation of Powers*, 102.

146. EL I, vi; 6 (86, 87); SL 80; Bergman, "Montesquieu's Theory," 14; Gwyn, *The Meaning*, 108, 111. Before Montesquieu, it was not typical to distinguish the judicial from the executive branch. Of course, Edward Coke was a noted figure in the evolution, believing that the common law stood in judgment of the king and Parliament. In Scotland George Buchanan became an advocate for independent judges. DJR 90-93; ASG 91-93; Hill, *Intellectual Origins of the English Revolution*, 225ff., 231, 244-46. But the separation of the judicial branch was more a phenomenon of the eighteenth century. Blackstone's *Commentaries on the Laws of England* (1765-69) followed Montesquieu's concept of a separate judiciary, except in one crucial point. He thought of the court as a professional body of jurists, not a series of *ad hoc* committees appointed by the people. The colonists interpreted Montesquieu's position through Blackstone's *Commentaries*, but one must wonder how wise this reading proved to be. Is it wise to create an independent branch of government with permanent power and virtually no checks to control it? Vile, *Contitutionalism*, 102-104; Gwyn, *The Meaning*, 111; Bergman, "Montesquieu's Theory," 17. For the influence of Blackstone on the US Constitution, see R. Kirk, *American British Culture* (New Brunswick, NJ and London: Transaction Publishers, 1994) 34-40. In the US Constitution, the judicial branch received no check upon the exercise of its power outside the remote possibility of impeachment. The Supreme Court took advantage of this oversight and proceeded to usurp as much power as possible in the coming years. In *Marbury v. Madison* (1803), it accorded itself the role of reviewing the constitutionality of statutes. By the end of the nineteenth century, it began to use the "due process" clause of the Fourteenth Amendment to overturn social and economic regulations of the states (e.g., *Lochner v. New York*, 198 US 45, 1905). The US Constitution contained no check over the abuse of federal power, and the Supreme Court took advantage of the situation. D. G. LaGory, "Federalism, Separation of Powers, and Individual Liberties," *Vanderbilt Law Review 187* (40): 1357, 1358; Gordon, *Controlling the State*, 320, 321; H. Dippel, "Popular Sovereignty and the Separation of Powers in American and French Revolutionary Constitutionalism," *Amerikastudien/American Studies* 34, no. 1 (1989): 27. Thomas Jefferson is one of the few Founding Fathers who recognized the problem and feared that the notion of a separate judicial system would make that branch most powerful. Vile, *Constitutionalism and the Separation of Powers*, 165.

147. The legislative cannot remove the king because this act would dissolve the executive *in toto* and eliminate a check on its power. The separation of powers is intended to prevent the concentration of power.

> When in the same person or in the same body of the magistracy, the legislative power is united to the executive power, there is no liberty, because one would fear that the same monarch or senate might create tyranny. Nor is there liberty if the judicial power is not separated from the legislative and executive. If it was joined to the legislative, the power over the life and liberty of the citizens

would be arbitrary, because the judge would be the legislator. If it was joined with the executive power, the judge would be able to have the force of an oppressor. All would be lost if the same person or body of leaders, nobles, or people exercised all three powers [EL II, xi, 6 (164); SL 157].

148. Of course, Montesquieu's work had a profound influence in England, especially after the first edition in August of 1750. Edmund Burke based his famous defense of the British Constitution, *Reflections on the Revolution in France* (1790), upon the analysis of Montesquieu and his separation of powers. F. T. H. Fletcher, *Montesquieu and English Politics (1750-1800)* (London: Edward Arnold & Co., 1939) 11, 22, 30; L. J. Forno, "Montesquieu's Reputation in France, England, and America (1755-1800)," *Studies in Burke and His Time*, 15, no. 1 (1973): 23, 27.
149. C. C. Thach, *The Creation of the Presidency 1775-1789: A Study in Constitutional History*, in *John Hopkins University Studies in Historical and Political Science*, 40, no. 4 (Baltimore, MD: John Hopkins Press, 1922) 169, 170.
150. *Records of the governor and company of the bay in New England*, N. B. Shurtleff (ed.) (Boston: W. White, 1853) 2.92-93; *Hutchinson Papers*, in *Publications of the Prince Society* (New York: B. Franklin, 1967) 3.167-68. Vile, *Constitutionalism*, 124; P. M. Spurlin, *Montesquieu in America* (1760-1801) (Baton Rouge, LA: Louisiana State University Press, 1940) 30, 151.
151. Wise, *Vindication*, 46, 50, 151.
152. Vile, *Constitutionalism*, 125.
153. *The Writings of Thomas Jefferson*, A. A. Lipscomb (ed.) (Washington, DC: The Thomas Jefferson Memorial Assoc., 1904) 16.118, 119.
154. Bergman, "Montesquieu's Theory," 18-23; Forno, "Montesquieu's Reputation," 28; Spurlin, *Montesquieu in America*, 258-62; C. Rossiter, *The Political Thought of the American Revolution* (New York: Harcourt, Brace & World, 1953) 75; B. Bailyn, *The Ideological Origins of the American Revolution* (Cambridge, MA: Harvard University Press, 1967) 27. Of course, John Locke deserves honorable mention.
155. Spurlin, *Montesquieu in America*, 37, 40, 43, 52, 133; J. T. Adams, *Revolutionary New England 1691-1776* (Boston: Atlantic Monthly Press 1923) 288, 386-88. The American edition was published in 1772.
156. Bergman, "Montesquieu's Theory," 18.
157. Spurlin, *Montesquieu in America*, 57ff., 90, 91; J-C. Lamberti, "Montesquieu in America," *Archives Européennes de Sociologie* 32, no. 1 (1991): 200.
158. Ibid., 181-83, 188, 205ff. Panagoulos has included an extensive list of the many citations in his work. *Essays*, 255, 256 (fn. 49). Few who attended the convention opposed the separation of powers. Thomas Paine was the most famous of the Founding Fathers to oppose the notion. He wanted a single assembly with a revolving presidency. The Constitutions of Virginia and Massachusetts spoke of separation and balance of powers, inspiring other states to follow their lead. The state of Pennsylvania (and later Vermont) developed the most severe doctrine of separation. The governor and his council were made "solely executive," serving at the behest of the legislature. This experiment in unicameral government was abandoned by the state in 1790, but it lived on in the French Revolution. It was based upon the strong, egalitarian doctrine of the Quakers. Conkin, *Self-Evident Truths*, 160, 17-72; Vile, *Constitutionalism*, 136; G. S. Wood, "Democracy and the American Revolution," in *Democracy: The Unfinished Journey 508 BC to AD 1993*, J. Dunn (ed.) (Oxford: Oxford University Press, 1992) 94; Dippel, "Popular Sovereignty," 28, 29.
159. Ibid., 177.

160. "Letters to Richard Henry Lee" (Nov. 15, 1775), in *The Works of John Adams*, C. F. Adams (ed.) (New York: Freeport, 1969) 4.186.
161. *The Records of the Federal Convention of 1787* (July 17), M. Farrand (ed.) (New Haven: Yale University Press, 1911) 2.34; *The Federalist*, in *Great Books of the Western World*, R. M. Hutchins (ed.) (Chicago: Encyclopedia Britannica, Inc., 1978) no. 47 (153-54). Papers 47-51 of the *Federalist* speak of the need for a separation and balance of powers. No. 47 is the most prominent of these papers and is considered the work of Madison. Hamilton and Madison both saw dangers in pure democracy. Shay's Rebellion was used as a strong argument for withstanding the voice of the people through a system of checks and balances. Montesquieu and Madison both emphasized the doctrine of depravity in arguing for the system. This doctrine was an integral part of Madison's training at Princeton, a bastion of Reformed orthodoxy. No. 51 of the papers makes special use of the doctrine. Miller, *The Rise and Fall of Democracy*, 108, 109; Gordon, *Controlling the State*, 313; Panagopoulos, *Essays*, 170, 171; R. Wernick, "The Godfather of the American Constitution," *Smithsonian* 20, no. 6 (Sept. 1989): 194, 195; Vile, *Constitutionalism*, 78.
162. Panagopoulos, *Essays*, 127; D. McCullough, *John Adams* (New York: Simon & Schuster, 2001) 374-77.
163. Adams, *A Defence of the Constitutions*, 1.325. It is clear that Adams read Montesquieu, but he conceived of him as nothing special, or at most, one among many others. *The Works of John Adams*, C. F. Adams (ed.) (Boston: Little, Brown, and Co., 1850-56) 2.93; 6.492; Bergman, "Montesquieu's Theory," 21-23.
164. Madison received his education at Princeton, along with nine out of thirty-one college graduates at the Convention. Pres. John Witherspoon used *l'Esprit des lois* as a textbook for several years. He clearly "captured the imagination of Madison," so much so that Madison could "quote [*l'Esprit des lois*] twenty years after he had left Princeton . . . from memory without error." V. L. Collins, *President Witherspoon* (New York: Arno Press & The New York Times, 1969) 2.207; "A Letter to Jefferson" (Aug., 1793), in *Letters and Other Writings of James Madison* (Philadelphia, J. B. Lippincott & Co., 1865) 1.592; Spurlin, *Montesquieu in America*, 70, 178, 179, 190; W. S. Carpenter, *The Development of American Political Thought* (New York: Howard Fertig, 1968) 74, 75. Witherspoon provided much inspiration for the young Madison and his later emphasis upon total depravity, mixed government, and resistance theory. Witherspoon was a revolutionary and encouraged all to sign the Declaration of Independence. Hall, *The Genevan Reformation and the American Founding*, 367-71, 374, 379, 393. Hall says that the influence of Witherspoon is best exemplified by the "fact that, from his quarter-century tenure at Princeton, six of his students went on to serve in the Continental Congress; one (Madison) became president; ten held cabinet positions; twelve were governors in a day when there were far fewer governors; 30 became judges; 21 were senators; and 39 served as United States representatives, with numerous others holding state and county legislative positions." See M. L. L. Stohlman, *John Witherspoon: Parson, Politician, Patriot* (Philadelphia: Westminster, 1976) 172; W. P. Breed, *Presbyterians and the Revolution* (Philadelphia: Presbyterian Board of Education and Sabbath-School Work, 1876) 49, 60.
165. *The Federalist*, no. 47 (153).
166. For example, Adams clearly admires the British system, but his *Defence* spends its time rummaging through the annals of history going back to Homer no less to find examples of a grand secular tradition. Conkin, *Self-Evident Truths*, 152, 153.

5

The Protestant Work Ethic
The Origin of Capitalism and the Use of Money

Benjamin Franklin

Benjamin Franklin was the most distinguished representative of America ideology in the eighteenth century. His story embodied the spirit of the emerging nation with its belief in upward mobility, Yankee ingenuity, and manifest destiny. Franklin was born into a family of modest means and standing in the community—the tenth of seventeen children—but ran away at the age of seventeen to seek his fame and fortune. He landed in the city of Philadelphia almost destitute, but through hard work and determination he arose in stature and eventually became an enormous success as a printer, inventor, author, and diplomat. The story of his success became a proverb and was enshrined in his *Autobiography* for all the world to view and follow. His rags-to-riches story captured the essence of the American dream and gained an international reputation as a model worthy of emulation.[1]

At first glance, it appears that his story has little to do with the passions of religious devotion and much to do with the material or secular concerns of this world. In fact, Franklin is noted for developing a skeptical attitude toward dogmatic positions and spurning the specific orthodox tenets of his Puritan upbringing.[2] He is depicted by some authors in purely secular terms as justifying his own goals through utilitarian calculations (or more devious means) and finding his own basic inspiration within the pursuit of the almighty dollar, the acclaim of this world, and other baser instincts.[3] But his total story is much more complicated than any simple reduction to materialistic, rational, or baser concerns found within a secular purview. His life and words are driven by many currents, and prominent among them is a faith that is most devout in its basic passions. His own words provide eloquent testimony to the power of religious ideals as a motivating factor in private and public life. He continually underscores the importance of religion as providing the foundation for ethics in general.[4] While he spurns specific doctrines of the church that deify its founder or exalt its own position as unique in the world of religion, he is not against turning around and extolling the teachings of Jesus as the greatest system of ethics in history.[5] His own religious convictions seem to follow the proclivity of the intelligentsia of the day, which reduced religion to morality and rejected any specific expressions of faith as too narrow and divisive for society, but his devotion to religion as it expresses itself in a moral way of living is most pious and sincere. In fact, his values remain solidly entrenched within the fold of his Puritan background, even if they acquire at times a new rationale in his writings.[6]

He was born in Boston and reared within its Puritan heritage. His family tree joined the Protestant movement during the early days of the Reformation in England, and his father, Josiah, became a part of the more radical fringe of "Nonconformity" during the reign of Charles II.[7] Franklin points to his father's pious instructions as most instrumental to his development, especially the strong sense of values and the dedication to those principles it provided.

> My father having among his Instructions to me when a Boy, frequently repeated a Proverb of Solomon, "Seest thou a Man diligent in his Calling, he shall stand before Kings, he shall not stand before mean Men." I from thence consider'd Industry as a Means of obtaining Wealth and Distinction, which encourag'd me; tho' I did not think that I should ever literally stand before Kings, which however has since happened. –for I have stood before five, & even had the honour of sitting down with one, the King of Denmark, to Dinner.[8]

He ever remained grateful for the instruction throughout his life and inscribed on the tombstone of his parents a testimony to their "Labour and Industry," exhorting the reader to follow their example of "Diligence in thy calling," just as he had done in his own life.[9]

This work ethic was a vital part of the world in which Franklin was born. The message was heard throughout a community that instilled its values in a multitude of contacts and institutions, even if his *Autobiography* can remember or mention only a few. Among the influences, Franklin gives special credit to a couple of spiritual authors, who inculcated the work ethic throughout their writings and served as a proximate cause in conveying the message to him.

The first of the authors is John Bunyan, an English minister and author of the Puritan classic, *Pilgrim's Progress* (1678). Franklin describes himself as so "Pleas'd with the Pilgrim's Progress" that he proceeded to purchase Bunyan's *Works* and make it his first literary collection as a lad. The book served Franklin and the community as a manual for pious, practical living.[10] It depicted the Christian life as a difficult journey filled with many obstacles and hardships along the way. It disparaged any notion that reduced Christianity to a mere profession of orthodoxy and exhorted the true believer to enter and persevere in a life-long pilgrimage, the *conditio sine qua non* for entering the "Celestial City." In this way, it rejected any claim to faith without works and exemplified the Puritan concept of salvation as a practical life of piety filled with hard work and determination.

The second source of inspiration is Cotton Mather, who served as a minister, author, and apologist of Puritan ideology. Franklin particularly stresses Mather's great work on ethics, *Bonificacius*, or *Essays to Do Good* (1710), as a transitional work in his own life. "Essays to do Good . . . gave me a Turn of Thinking that had an influence on the principal future Events of My Life."[11] Franklin's very first publication paid tribute to the influence of Mather by adopting the pseudonym Mrs. Dogood as a form of parody, and his life and ideas continued to display the same appreciation.[12] Mather's work is dedicated to promoting a sense of "public spirit" among its constituency in accordance with the exhortation of Gal. 6:10: ". . . let us do good to all men."[13] Much like other Puritan works it provides strong admonitions against idleness, extravagant living, and the hoarding of wealth.[14] It exhorts the readers to fulfill the calling of God within "their daily business as a real service to the interests of piety," however mean the service might be.[15] Whole chapters are dedicated to providing specific suggestions for how to serve the Lord in certain professions. Mather encourages each individual to keep a record of his or her conduct, in order to mark the progress each one has made in living a life dedicated to moral virtue and community service.[16] He also encourages the development of societies throughout the land to supply a network of support and accountability.[17] These societies brought great social reform throughout England and other parts of the British empire.[18] They served an important role by promoting practical piety rather than deepening the divisions of the community any further through theological disputes.[19] The societies were designed to watch over the community in general and provide "methods and opportunities to do good" among the people at large—Mather's constant refrain,[20] but the impetus for his practical piety still remains within a specific theological tradition in spite of its inclusive nature. Mather develops the incentive for his work ethic out of the theological convictions of his religious community, which rejected all talk of "cheap grace" in the strongest terms and pointed to a life of piety as the mark of a true believer. The works of the law were the means of demonstrating the sincerity of faith to oneself and one's community. At the very beginning of the book, Mather clearly connects this theoretical justification with the practical admonitions in his work as the basic motivating factor behind them.[21]

> And then, secondly, though we are justified by a precious faith in the righteousness of God our Saviour, yet good works are demanded of us, to justify our faith; to demonstrate, that it is indeed that precious faith. A justifying faith is a jewel, which may be counterfeited. But now the marks of a faith, which is no counterfeit, are to be found in the good works whereto a servant of God is inclined and assisted by his faith. . . . Here the Plea must be: If our faith be not such a faith, 'tis a lifeless one, and it will not bring to life. A workless faith is a worthless faith. My friend, suppose thyself standing before the Judgment-seat of the glorious LORD. . . . "Lord, my faith was Thy work. It was a faith which disposed me to all the good works of Thy holy religion. My faith sanctified me. It carried me to Thee, O my Saviour, for grace to do the works of righteousness. It embraced that for my Lord as well as for my Saviour. It caused me with sincerity to love and keep Thy commandments; with assiduity to serve the interest of Thy Kingdom in the world." Thus you have Paul and James reconciled. Thus you have good works provided for. The aphorism of the physician, is, *Per brachium fit judicium de corde*. The doings of men are truer and surer indications, than all their sayings, of what they are within.[22]

This concept of assurance and working faith provided a strong incentive for Mather and the Puritans to develop their work ethic. The connection is readily seen in Mather's *Essay to do good*, which scholars have failed to consider in their attempt to discover the origin of the work ethic in Franklin and capitalism. Mather's book provides a definitive means of connecting the dots between Franklin and Puritan ideas. It answers the complaint of some scholars that the relationship is speculative and provides a clear historical indication of theological influence.

Franklin certainly exemplified much of what Mather and his community taught him throughout his own life and teachings. He acquired a reputation for hard work and long hours at the job, devoting himself to reading and other exercises both before and after regular work hours, spending little time with amusements, and even neglecting to attend church on Sunday so as not to waste time.[23] His many publications were devoted to the promotion of virtue and industry among the people. His newspaper was filled with moral exhortations at a time when many of the papers printed libelous stories or useless gossip leading to civil unrest.[24]

In 1732 he published the first edition of *Poor Richard's Almanack*, a popular form of literature in the colonies and his most successful publication. Besides the usual information, Franklin filled its pages "with Proverbial Sentences, chiefly such as inculcated Industry and Frugality, as the Means of procuring Wealth and thereby securing virtue."[25] This exhortation is most visible in an essay he composed for the final *Poor Richard* in 1757, which was printed numerous times thereafter as "The Way to Wealth."

> Remember, that time is money. He that can earn ten shillings a day by his labor, and goes abroad, or sits idle, one half of the day, though he spends but sixpence during his diversion or idleness, ought not to reckon that the only expense; he has really spent, or rather thrown away, five shillings besides. . . . Sloth, life rust, consumes faster than labor wears; while the used key is always bright, as Poor Richard says. But dost thou love life, then do not squander time, for that is the stuff life is made of, as Poor Richard says. . . . If time to be of all things the most precious, wasting time must be, as Poor Richard says, the greatest prodigality; since, as he elsewhere tells us, Lost time is never found again; and what we call time enough, always proves little enough. Let us then up and be doing, and doing to the purpose; so by diligence shall we do more with less perplexity. . . . Early to bed, and early to rise, makes a man healthy, wealthy, and wise, as Poor Richard says. . . . Diligence is the mother of good luck, and God gives all things to industry. Then plough deep while sluggards sleep, and you shall have corn to sell and to keep. . . . Leisure is time for doing something useful.[26]

His belief was so strong in the power of industry and frugality that it left him without much compassion on the plight for the poor. He rejected any public provision for the poor to support their laziness and even dismissed those who wanted to set a minimum wage as providing another means of encouraging idleness among them.[27]

However, the rich also incurred the wrath of Franklin for leading frivolous and unproductive lives. Franklin often refused riches in his personal life, thinking it was better to be useful than rich. He dressed plainly and drank little. He refused to spend time in "Taverns, Games, or Frolicks" or go out "a-fishing" and "shooting." He scolds those who waste money on "superfluities" or "expensive follies" such as Chinaware, Indian silks, and French pastries.[28] Money must be put to good use. It needs to be invested for the good of the community, along with one's time and energy. In fact, Franklin spent much of his time improving the quality of his community through establishing libraries, schools, postal services, fire departments, and many other utilitarian projects.[29] He refused to take out a patent on his many inventions, finding more pleasure in serving the public good than accumulating excessive wealth for himself.[30] His science was not driven by monetary or theoretical concerns but sought the simple pragmatic goal of helping humankind through "little advantages."[31] His science followed the utilitarian vision of his Puritan background, which saw unlimited development in science through the experimental method and longed to prevent disease and extend the span of human life "beyond the antediluvian standard."[32]

Franklin took his moral life in earnest. He did not accept human frailty or depravity as a sufficient excuse for his shortcomings and made a concerted effort to reach perfection, even though he confessed his many failures.[33] He composed a plan of conduct early in his career, whose four points centered around admonitions to frugality, honesty, industry, and kindness of speech.[34] He later developed a more expansive list of thirteen moral precepts, which tried to express the ethics of all sects of religion, and carried them around in a little book to chart his progress.[35] He even thought of forming a sect at one time around these moral principles and a few religious concepts, which were general in nature, but found himself too busy with more pressing concerns to lend the necessary time and effort.[36] His life was marked by the moral earnestness of Bunyan, Mather, and his Puritan background, which encouraged him to conduct a pilgrimage, chart its course, and forge a society or consistory to watch over it.[37] His life was driven by the same moral industry and conscientious devotion to the community, even if the precise nature of the service might vary with each individual calling.

Max Weber

Sociologists have taken notice of the relationship between Franklin and Puritanism ever since the days of Max Weber in the early part of the twentieth century. The moral rigor of Puritanism is seen as providing a religious foundation, from which an incipient form of capitalism in Franklin and others evolved. A number of scholars speculated over a possible relation between Protestantism and Capitalism before the time of Weber, but it was Weber's two articles on the "Protestant Ethic and the Spirit of Capitalism" (1904-1905) that brought the thesis to the forefront of academia. R. H. Tawney proceeded to popularize the theory in the English-speaking world with his publication of a series of lectures on *Religion and the Rise of Capitalism* (1926), and since then the thesis has become one of the most celebrated and controversial in all of social studies.[38] Often the thesis is juxtaposed to Karl Marx and his atheistic version of history, which centered on economic forces as paramount in the development of religious, political, and philosophical ideals. Marx reduced the doctrine of capitalism to the cynical economic interests of the bourgeoisie in their attempt to wield power over the working class.

Property rights and the meekness of Christianity are doctrines created by the bourgeoisie to insure social apathy, and Marx hoped to overturn these doctrines and create a new ideology once the proletariat seized power.[39] Weber and Tawney are seen as an alternative to Marx's atheistic agenda and his all-too-facile reduction of life to a material level. Religion is seen as an important factor in developing economic and political concerns once again.[40]

The thesis of Weber and Tawney appears to contain a modicum of good sense when one considers the cultural context of economic development. The world of Franklin was not divided as it is today into simple spiritual and secular compartments. There was "no absolute division between the inner and personal life, which is the sphere of religion, and the practical interests, the external order, the impersonal mechanism, to which, if some modern teachers may be trusted, religion is irrelevant."[41] Economic discourse was the same as moral/social discourse. Adam Smith's economic theories were developed as a professor of moral philosophy at the University of Glasgow, and Franklin conceived of his economic philosophy as a series of moral aphorisms.[42] Their community was dominated by the church and its preachers, whose words broached all aspects of life and found reverence in the culture at large since they served at the very center of society.

Any sober account of the era needs to recognize the relation between church and state, even if it is possible to exaggerate the connection. Weber and Tawney are careful in their reaction to Marx and avoid the obvious temptation of proceeding to the antithesis and exaggerating the role of the church or discounting the influence of other factors. Weber is quick to reject the idea that Puritanism simply secreted the notion of capitalism in a simple cause and effect manner. He does not want "to substitute for a one-sided 'materialistic' [interpretation] an equally one-sided 'spiritual' interpretation of civilization and history."[43] Tawney thinks its plausible to argue that religious changes were the result of a new economic spirit, but prefers to understand the relationship in terms of reciprocal causality rather than create another monolithic equation.[44] Neither one of them wants to dismiss in the name of religion any parallel developments in commerce, finance, and industry as irrelevant to the new world order. Business technologies such as credit banking, interest, double-entry bookkeeping, and joint-stock companies all played an important role. Expeditions, colonization, the expansion of trade, and manufacturing brought commerce into world markets providing a different outlook and new factors for economic development.[45] Weber acknowledges all of these factors as playing a role in the total maturation of capitalism, even if his interest is limited, much like this book, to the contribution of religion as providing a special psychological ground or *Geist* for the new system to flourish.[46]

Weber explains the relationship between religious concepts and capitalism in the following manner. He finds the impetus for the new economic philosophy within the Protestant Reformation and its emphasis upon the spirituality of each and every believer. He contrasts this emphasis with the Middle Ages, where spirituality was embodied in the hierarchy of the church or sheltered within a monastic order, far removed from the secular concerns of everyday life. At that time an ascetic life contemplated the realities of another world and exalted itself above the active life of secular business with its pursuit of the baser things of this world.[47] Weber points to a fundamental shift in paradigm that transpired during the Reformation. Luther is seen as spurning the monastic life of idle contemplation and providing a positive review of the laity's contribution to the community in everyday life. Luther's usage of *Beruf* provides Weber with an illustration of how the spiritual calling of the believers included their worldly "profession."[48] However, Weber does not credit Luther or Lutheranism with establishing a new economic order out of this one doctrine. Further religious development was needed, and Weber finds that development among the Calvinists, who receive special credit in providing the "seedbed" for the future triumph of capitalism.[49] They are given credit for adding to the doctrines of Luther a special theological construction that helped fuel the new economic philosophy and bring prosperity wherever it permeated society. Of course, this spirit permeated the Calvinists of England in a special way, and Weber cites Montesquieu's commentary on England as a proof of their success. "This is the people in the world who have best known how to take advantage of each of these three things at the same time: religion, commerce, and liberty."[50] All three seemed to go together.

Weber continues the discussion by offering an explanation as to why Calvinism became a sufficient ground for the development of capitalism. He finds the answer to his question residing in the special emphasis the Calvinists placed on works in their doctrine of assurance. Unlike Catholicism, the Reformed did not possess a sacramental means of receiving absolution or a mystical word of assurance from God in the manner of Luther and Calvin. Assurance of divine election was obtained through outward results. It was obtained through an inspection of the works wrought in the world by the believers as an outward sign of invisible grace.[51] An onus was placed on each believer to make one's election as certain as possible through worldly activity—an imperative that sounded similar in nature to the Catholic doctrine of justification and works except this time the asceticism was directed toward participation of the believer in the world rather than limited to the sacred confines of the church. Idleness became the deadliest of all sins—extravagant living a like-evil.[52]

This work ethic permeated Calvinism and the Puritan community in particular. Weber calls special attention to Richard Baxter and Benjamin Franklin as providing a good case in point.[53] He understands these men and the spirit of capitalism not in terms of materialistic or economic impulses. The pursuit of gain or *auri sacra fames* as a means of personal advantage is found in all of humanity since the beginning of time.[54] Weber finds these men and the spirit of capitalism encouraging the accumulation of profit through rational techniques in order to utilize money in a systematic way and create a greater profit. The duty that becomes so sacred in their minds is the simple turning of a profit and investing it; a duty that is much opposed to hoarding wealth or squandering it on the pleasures of this world.[55] The duty of capitalism is found in the pious admonition to invest one's time and possessions in a wise manner. Its wise counsel helped encourage the people to consider themselves stewards of God's talents and perfect rational techniques like bookkeeping and the division of labor as a means of responsible investment.[56] The people were exhorted to deduce their standing before God through rational calculation and proceeded to rationalize their sacred duty in the world at large as a means of maximizing the profit of their deeds.

Middle Ages

At the very least, the Puritans and the Reformation promoted a more active participation of its people in the world than the theology of the previous era. The Middle Ages found a higher ideal in the contemplative life of the monastery and longed for a beatific vision in the eschaton as the ultimate state. Money was a means of great temptation, and it was better to become poor by giving it to the poor than increase the prosperity of all through wise and strategic investment in the community.[57] Lanfranc considered the life of business to thrive by cheating and profiteering, comparing its lust to the struggle of wolves over carrion.[58] The Scholastics thought the life of a merchant was a dubious choice of careers since it was subject to so many temptations. Peter Lombard went so far as to exclude from the sacrament of penance those who insisted on this wicked way of making a living.[59] Most others were more compassionate in their assessment, but all of them felt that a life of trade was less than ideal and seldom free from sinful activity. The motive of a merchant was dubious because it appeared to go beyond the simple need of earning a livelihood and seek to gain an unjust profit at the expense of others.[60]

This stigma inhibited the growth of capitalism, but it was not so pervasive or powerful as to prevent certain expressions of its spirit from appearing now and again. There were any number of individuals who exemplified the spirit of capitalism in the Middle Ages despite the admonitions of the church and the need for a new religious ethos to penetrate society and create a new economic order as a whole. Adventure capitalism, where the speculator longed for some lucky windfall, existed long before the measures of capitalism accepted a more rational and systematic approach.[61] In the Renaissance there appeared a few economic dynasties such as the Medici, Fugger, and Welser families, who were highly innovative enterprisers, powerful bankers, and successful merchants. Capitalism also existed in centers of industry like Flanders and Italy—at least if "capitalism means the direction of industry by the owners of capital for their own pecuniary gain, and the social relationships which established themselves between them and the wage-earning proletariat whom they control." One can sift through the writings of the Renaissance and find certain statements in Jacob Fugger, Leon Battista Alberti, Benedetto Cotrugli, and other entrepreneurs that show a remarkable parallel to the admonitions of later capitalists.[62]

> A great merchant, then, must plan his business and apportion it in a [certain] order. And he must not keep all money together, but he should distribute it in various solid businesses. And this method, in my opinion, is very efficiently followed by the Florentines more than by any other people; this I say as a generalization, for many others also follow it.[63]

And so, the spirit of capitalism existed here and there in the Middle Ages, which afforded some help in portending the business practices of the new world, but it is not so easy to assess the precise influence in a simple cause and effect manner. One could sift through the tomes and tomes of other ages and concoct all sorts of artificial connections with capitalism, or almost any other system of thought, if given enough material to develop and contrive them. And so, whatever influence the isolated instances of the Middle Ages extended over the modern world, they were tenuous at best and still needed the advent of a more pervasive spirit in Protestantism to change the political, social, and economic landscape. In Protestantism, the people were empowered as a whole to develop a new economic order through a new sense of freedom over against the powers that be.

In England the Protestants became the "freeholders" of property with an entitlement to use their possessions, invest their resources, and reject any measures by the government to interfere in their business or pilfer their possessions by whatever means available. The Puritan Revolution swept away the monopolies and economic regulations of Stuart England, allowing free enterprise and markets to prosper.[64] Protestant freedom meant changes in society, which could never develop under the medieval synthesis, and led in due time to the development of the free enterprise system. The freedom of the people meant less constraint upon economic development and more willingness to take risks and acquire a profit for their own advantage. Montesquieu says,

> The great enterprises of merchants are always mixed with public business of necessity. But in monarchies public affairs are often more suspect for the merchants than they are in Republican states. Therefore, great enterprises are not for monarchies, but for the government of the many.
>
> Briefly, a greater certitude of one's property, which one believes to have in these states, causes all sorts of commercial endeavors to transpire; and because one believes that one's possessions are secure, one is willing to risk it to acquire more. One only takes a risk as a means to gain from it. . . .
>
> In regard to a despotic state, it is futile to discuss the issue. Here is the general rule: In a nation that is steeped in servitude, one works to preserve more than to acquire; In a free nation one works to acquire more than to preserve.[65]

Protestantism

The status of the laity arose with the advent of Protestantism. Luther rejected the monastic life of contemplation for a more active life in the community. In his teaching on the priesthood of the believers he provided a positive interpretation of the laity and their work, consecrating activity in the world as a genuine service to God and a business career as a spiritual calling.[66] This teaching resonated among all Protestants in Europe, but no one emphasized Luther's priesthood of the believers and contempt for monastic living more than the Puritans. The special calling of the laity was fundamental to their concept of Christianity as a practical, world-affirming religion.[67] William Perkins, their most distinguished theologian, wrote *A Treatise of the Vocations or Callings of Men* (1605), based on Paul's admonition in 1 Cor. 7:20 that "each one should remain in the situation that God has called him." Perkins interpreted the verse as an admonition to each and every member of the body of Christ to fulfill a special calling in the church, the family, and the community.[68]

The treatise was followed by a number of works that contained the same basic message of a calling in the world. Richard Steele provided one of the more interesting of these works with a treatise entitled *The Trades-man's Calling* (1684). It provided a "case of the conscience" for fulfilling the will of God through "some peculiar Imployment in this world."[69] The special calling was interpreted in the same casuistic manner that Perkins, Ames, and other Puritans had brought to the general call of God, established by means of the same rational calculation and attentive to every last detail of piety.

The Theology of Works

Why did the Puritans drive themselves to work so hard in the world and the community outside the church? Weber finds the answer to this intriguing question within their special doctrine of assurance and the emphasis they placed upon it. Puritans struggled in developing a satisfying doctrine within their overall theological system and exhibited a considerable amount of anxiety over their relationship with God as a consequence. Weber mentions three basic reasons behind the problem: (1) they possessed no sacramental means of assuaging their anxieties; (2) they placed a special burden on themselves to obtain certainty; and (3) they created a mystery out of the divine will through an emphasis upon the doctrine of predestination. For these reasons, assurance became a tenuous process in Reformed theology, producing only a measure of solace after a lifetime of perseverance and struggle. The only means of alleviating the anxiety was the dubious and tenuous process of searching one's deeds and seeing if they were indicative of a true Christian life and its calling. Assurance was sought through a life distinguished by good deeds, the outward sign of God's invisible grace and election. And so, the Puritans were forced to lead a life of self-examination and toil, since they possessed no cheap grace or sacramental means to find peace of mind. Weber says their doctrine of salvation emphasized good works as much as any Catholic theologian, the only difference being the direction toward which the deeds were intended.[70] This time the ascetic activity was directed outwardly to the world at large, not inwardly toward a life of solitary contemplation.[71] An honest tradesman was extolled as more fit to enter the kingdom of God than a hermit from Alexandria.

> A pious Tradesman may act Grace, as much as the greatest Rabbi. Famous is the story of Primitive Saint in Egypt, Who having for many Years retired himself from the World and chiefly imployed himself in the Acts of Mortification and Devotion; and being thereupon tempted to think himself among the holiest Men on Earth, and

long'd to know who should sit next him in Heaven, was warned to inquire for a Man in Alexandria who was holier than himself; and who should that be but, when he had found him, but a poor Cobler, that work'd hard most of the day, but was so circumspect in his Life, so just in his Dealings, so thankful with his Wife for his mean fare, and then so truly devout in the Worship of God, that the poor Hermite return'd crest-faln to his Cell, and found that the honest Tradesman was like to sit above him in Heaven. So that the Exercise of Grace should be no uncouth Business to a Christian Tradesman.[72]

A closer historical analysis seems to confirm some of Weber's theological insights. Take, for example, the relationship between assurance and the sacrament of penance. When one examines the origin of the Protestant teaching on this subject, the contrast between the Reformed concept and the original vision of Luther is most apparent. In his early writings, Luther is seen developing his concept of justification and assurance out of the sacrament of penance. Luther exhorts his followers to cease all trust in the works of penance and contrition, and simply listen to the words of assurance that the priest pronounces to each and every one in the sacrament.[73] When the priest says, "I absolve you," these words are spoken as a promise of forgiveness to each and every one from the very throne of God.[74] The priest's words are God's words, his actions God's forgiveness.[75] All that is necessary is found in the simple exhortation to trust in the words of the priest or have faith and faith alone (*sola fides*).[76] The words of the priest represent the will of God to all those who listen and believe. The penitent should not experience undue anxiety over their contrition, wondering whether this or any other condition of true penance was fulfilled on their part, because God has revealed his will concerning the forgiveness of sin to each and every individual once and for all. In this way Luther found solace for a trembling conscience and proceeded to dismiss the doubts that plagued him as a monk, blaming his former troubles on Thomistic orthodoxy and its fixation upon the human component of contrition in the sacrament.[77] He found assurance by following and extending the Scotistic tradition, which sought to minimize any human condition and promote the importance of faith in the words of the priest rather than trust in the works of penance.[78] Unfortunately, the later Calvinists lost this simple and direct means of finding assurance when they rejected the sacrament of penance and the authority of the priests. They no longer possessed a specific word from God to obtain certainty and needed to look elsewhere for a modicum of comfort. Even the sacraments of baptism and the Eucharist no longer contained a simple communication of grace, and so they struggled in finding a means of grace and assurance elsewhere, just as Weber suggests.

The search for assurance led them away from contemplating a divine word to gazing once again upon the human component in salvation. Theodore Beza and Jerome Zanchi began the process by speaking of a "practical syllogism" through which Christians could deduce their salvation from its "marks" or "signs" within them.[79] Knowing that God had promised salvation to those who exhibited certain signs Beza, Zanchi, and the Calvinists thought it possible to deduce their own rightful place in the kingdom if they could discern signs like faith, repentance, and good works in their lives. The calculation seemed all so simple, as long as it was possible to verify their own personal compliance within the minor premise of the syllogism, which demanded evidence of their own faith.

The works of Beza and Zanchi were translated into English,[80] and the Puritans above all other Reformed groups became obsessed with finding their place in the divine kingdom by means of the syllogism. The Puritans produced numerous and voluminous treatises on the subject, considering the matter of assurance the most pressing issue of the day.[81] William Perkins, their foremost theologian, considered it a sacred "dutie" to ascertain the genuine nature of a professed faith and produced a number of treatises to help the quest: "A Graine of Mustard Seede," "A Case of Conscience," "A Discourse of Conscience," and "A Treatise tending unto a Declaration, whether a man be in the Estate of Damnation or, in the Estate of Grace." Perkins exhorted his followers to descend within themselves and examine their conscience, so they might "know what they know" about the sincerity of their faith.[82] He proceeded to develop list upon list to aid in the process,[83] but all the detailed analysis only proved in the end that no simple answer was available. Even Perkins conceded that it takes a "long space" of time to find solace and there are "Many a man of humble and contrite heart" who are yet to receive consolation in the spirit.[84] This same struggle seemed to characterize his own Puritan community, as it produced tomes and tomes of analysis on the subject searching for an answer. Colleagues of Perkins like William Ames and William Fenner produced similar statements for the community,[85] and the practical syllogism or "cases of the conscience" became an indelible mark of Puritan theology, exhibiting and reinforcing the Puritan's struggle to obtain peace of mind.

Weber's analysis of the situation is correct and helpful up to this point, but he clearly goes astray when he proceeds to blame the problems of Puritanism upon their obsession with the dark mysteries of predestination. His analysis is wrong on this point for several reasons.

One, he fails to note the importance of the practical syllogism in causing the Calvinists to wrestle with their conscience and produce a scrupulous obedience. The Calvinists exchanged the original Christocentric vision of Luther and Calvin—where Christ is the object of faith, for a reflexive act of analysis upon the subject of faith, causing them to wrestle within.[86] They exchanged the benedictions of God for a narcissistic and arduous struggle, hoping to find that "mustard seed" of faith in the midst of their own total depravity.

Two, Weber misunderstands the doctrine of predestination as set forth by John Calvin and Martin Bucer and adopted by the later Calvinists. This doctrine centered upon Christ as the "mirror of predestination" (as the one who reveals the will of the Father). The doctrine found its purpose in bringing solace to the one who receives Christ, informing the believer that they were elected by the Father to persevere in the faith.[87] The will of Christ and the will of the Father, the faith of the regenerate and the decree of the Father are all one and the same. Far from containing some dark mystery, the elective purposes of God were revealed for the first time in the church through this special doctrine of eternal security or predestination. Unlike the older Augustinian concept, which distinguished believers from the elect, Calvinists equated the two groups in such a way that believers could rest assured in their perseverance, knowing for certain their ultimate status. The doctrine of election was not the source of anxiety among them. If anything their belief in eternal security—a most severe expression of predestination, where God's power is efficacious from the beginning to the end of salvation—produced at the same time the most direct means of knowing the ultimate will of the Father, and so reduced anxiety over the ultimate outcome of a present faith.[88]

Three, Weber is wrong in saying that the Puritans were obsessed with the specific subject of predestination—in spite of Calvin's severe teaching on the issue. There was a tendency in England and America to exalt the work of Calvin above all others in Reformed circles, but even Calvin did not make the doctrine the centerpiece of his theology. There was also the controversy with William Laud, the Archbishop of Canterbury, during the Puritan Revolution, but any problem with his Arminian theology was small in comparison to the struggles with his infamous career as the chief inquisitor and supporter of the hierarchical system. In New England John Winthrop successfully withstood an antinomian challenge to the synergistic tendencies of covenant theology and rejected the more consistent doctrine of predestination espoused by that group. Puritans were not as interested in theological consistency or erudite scholastic discussions as their counterparts on the continent. Their great works, *Pilgram's Progress*, *Christian Dictionary*, and *Magnalia Christi Americana*, were centered upon the exhortation to lead a godly life and emulate their forefathers, who persevered in the faith. The Puritans were far too practical in orientation to become obsessed with metaphysical speculation, let alone with one specific matter of theological concern that dominates all else. Puritans were occupied with the practical, everyday concerns of Christian living.

Beside these problems, Weber and his many followers make their most serious mistake in failing to recognize the importance of the covenant in Reformed thinking and practice. It was not the doctrine of predestination that drove the Calvinists to work hard in the world. If anything it was an opposite, synergistic tendency that drove them in this direction. This synergism was latent within their emphasis upon the practical syllogism, but it came to the forefront of their life and teaching through the influence of Heinrich Bullinger's doctrine of a bilateral covenant.[89] In adopting this teaching, the Calvinists brought in a clear synergistic tendency, which rivaled their basic belief in grace and election. The covenant minimized unconditional election and irresistible grace. It emphasized the fulfillment of certain conditions to receive God's blessings, just as Bullinger taught in his *De Testamento*, causing tension with their basic belief in grace.[90] Antinomians arose in England, where the covenant began to dominate the doctrine of grace in some quarters and accused other Puritans of forsaking all trust in Christ and returning to the Catholic doctrine of justification through works. Of course, the Puritans denied the accusation and reiterated their faith in *sola gratia*, but there was an irreconcilable tension in their theology that no amount of scholastic distinctions could resolve. Their doctrine of justification and assurance possessed clear synergistic tendencies via the covenant and left them working as hard as any Catholic to reach the heavenly rest.

Because of this and other factors, the Puritans became known as an industrious and practical people. Their faith was exhibited through its works. They gained a reputation for enforcing standards of behavior and regulating discipline both inside and outside the church, following the example of Calvin's Consistory in Geneva and Cartwright's early adaptation of this model for his "disciplinarians."[91] Practical piety, not scholastic disputes or theoretical erudition, became the focus of Puritan divines in their writings and sermons.[92] Education steered away from philosophical speculation toward vocational training and apprentice-ships, and it was limited in general to one's adolescence, especially in

America.[93] Idleness was the root of all vices, and diligence the means to prosperity.[94] The general rule of Puritan England was "to whip and punish wandering beggars" and "provide houses and convient places to set the poore to work."[95] Parliament passed an act in 1649 that established a posse to round up vagrants and offer them a choice between whipping or work. The poor were treated not as victims of unfortunate circumstances in need of compassion and help. They were victims of their own idleness.[96] Work was the fundamental virtue to instill. It took centuries before a brazen person, like Henry David Thoreau, would even dare to challenge the work ethic, complaining that its excessive demands had caused the "mass of men to lead lives of quiet desperation." He preferred to live thoughtfully with his Creator in the woods and "suck all the marrow" out of life, while a busy world passed him by. During one six-year stretch he had the audacity to work an average of six weeks per year, becoming a complete bum in the eyes of the people in Concord.[97] But his eccentric example only proved the general rule of his community, and the Puritan work ethic remained a fixture in America long after his time dominating the ethos of the people.

The Puritans included all people within their admonition to work, especially those who possessed considerable means to do otherwise. The purpose of life was found in building the community through investment of one's time, energy, and resources—not accumulating riches to squander on a worthless or frivolous life-style.[98] "[G]entility was no longer a status confidently assumed; there was the difficult matter of observing the proprieties and diligently, day after day, carrying out the correct tasks."[99] "Every man, of every degree, as well rich as poor, . . . must know that he is born for some employment to the good of his brethren, if he will acknowledge himself to be a member, and not an ulcer, in the body of mankind."[100] "A competent estate" does not excuse a gentleman from business or supply "an unlimited freedom of pursuing their pleasures at random."[101] Perkins chides the rich for spending "a greater part of their increase upon hawks, bulls, bears, dogs, or riotously misspend[ing] the same in sporting or gaming."[102] He enumerates five proper ways to use one's resources to the glory of God. They exclude a life of luxury, pomp, and excess as possessing no utilitarian value in regard to oneself or others.[103] Richard Steele also concurs with these austerities. He chastens immoderate "Gaming," "frequenting Taverns, Ale-houses, and Coffee-Houses," and "all bewitching Pleasures and Recreations" as a waste of time that could be better spent or put to good use in the productive affairs of business.[104] Of course, not all approved of the standards and some rebelled against legalistic measures and rigors of Puritanism as extreme and unnecessary. William Shakespeare displayed considerable animus toward the Puritan contempt for the arts and their ability to close down theaters. James I refused to sign the incessant stream of Sabbath bills that Parliament attempted to pass concerning sports, dancing, and plays. Charles I found it necessary to enact the "Declaration of Sports" on Oct. 18, 1633, which commended the need for mirth and exercise in building a vital nation. The majesty particularly scolded the Puritans for making recreation unlawful after worship service on Sundays, as well as the holidays.[105] But even with these counter-measures it was difficult to arrest the impact of Puritan ideas on the culture at large. Many Puritan clergy refused to read the declaration and preferred to suffer suspension than profane the Sabbath with "profane sports and pastimes."[106] The majesty had difficulty maintaining control and probably felt the sting of religious disapproval on his own frivolous and opulent lifestyle.

The Puritans rejected those who sought an abundance of riches and profit as an end in itself. Their sermons were filled with stern warnings against covetousness and the pursuit of earthly mammon. Prosperity was no sure sign of divine favor, even if its author was God and its reception a blessing on both the just and the unjust (Matt. 5:45).[107] Robert Keayne, a wealthy Boston merchant, incurred the wrath of the Puritan community in 1639 when he was convicted of selling goods at exorbitant prices and served as a grave warning against unjust profiteering the rest of his days. The Puritans tried their hand at wage and price control but knew that most merchants "sell dear" and "buy cheap," even an otherwise godly man like Robert Keayne.[108]

Weber's thesis appears to languish at this point when he contends in the face of examples like Keayne's that Puritans made the pursuit of wealth a divine calling. Maybe after the loss of spiritual moorings the earning of money became an end in itself, but the Puritan divines never sanctioned this process of secularization. Weber must hold his contention against the tide of clear and numerous exhortations to the contrary. He can only find one exhortation in Baxter and elevate it against the vast multitude of exhortations on the other side.

> If God shew you a way in which you may lawfully get more than in another way, (without wrong to your soul, or to any other), if you refuse this, and choose the less gainful way, you cross one of the ends of your Calling, and you refuse to be Gods Steward, and to accept his gifts, and use them for him when he requireth it: You may labour to be rich for God, though not for the flesh and sin.[109]

Weber is somewhat selective in his evidence, citing this one passage against a plethora of evidence on the other side, although his analysis of the profit motive is not entirely wrong. He is right when he locates the fundamental impulse of profit making outside the age-old love of money and enjoyment of its pleasures.[110] He is wrong when he limits its design to the simple motive of making a profit for its own sake[111]—at least during the early stages of Puritanism and capitalism before secularism sets it.[112] The Puritans were driven by other motives, including a social and utilitarian impulse to invest in the community and build a better tomorrow.[113] They had a futuristic vision that encompassed their society and the world as a whole.[114] They did not pick a profession for the sole sake of accumulating wealth, but were admonished by their religion to find a calling in serving others through business and becoming useful to the community.[115] If they earned money, it was not squandered on a useless life of wine, women, and song. It was invested as a faithful steward of God's talents for the sake of improving society, just like any good capitalist would do. Adam Smith employs the same basic argument in his *Wealth of Nations* when he commends investment and condemns those who use their wealth on non-productive activities and extravagant living. Money or capital is productive only if it is invested in the community.

> The Proportion between capital and revenue, therefore, seems everywhere to regulate the proportion between industry and idleness. Wherever capital predominates, industry prevails: wherever revenue, idleness. Every increase or diminution of capital, therefore, naturally tends to increase or diminish the real quantity of industry, the number of productive hands, and consequently the exchangeable value of the annual produce of the land and labour of the country, the real wealth and revenue of all its inhabitants.[116]

The Pursuit of gain became a rational enterprise in the course of time, although it is unclear exactly how religion related to the growth of the rational process. Capitalism sought to obtain profit in a rational manner through balance sheets, efficient production, large turnover, consumer prices, and the division of labor.[117] Weber considers this evolution an aspect of the *Geist* of capitalism as industry was swept into the same rational calculus that applied to salvation and its works. Even if Weber has a valid point, he displays considerable ambivalence over this aspect of capitalism and complains about the erosion of the original *Geist* through its rationalism as the system maturates. He laments the loss of the original inspiration as capitalism developed an "iron cage" of rational bureaucracies and monetary steering mechanisms. The spirit of individual freedom and creativity became reified and petrified into a mechanized system, destroying the creative impulse of its earlier days. Rationalism became reification as it expanded into a totalitarian regime and now worked at odds with the religious impulse that gave it birth.[118]

Usury

Weber's analysis fails to connect the process of rationalization with Calvinism in a coherent and definitive way. It misses an important opportunity in a number of areas, but none seems more obvious than its failure to discuss in a sufficient manner the rationalization of the monetary system through the charging of interest. No one can question the importance of finance to capitalism, and a discussion of financial techniques—like usury—would seem to go hand-in-hand with an understanding of its development. In fact, it appears that the development of capitalism took place in conjunction with the loosening of purse strings in the sixteenth century. These strides were accompanied by a new religious climate and its new outlook on the laity, which allowed for a more compassionate view of how the real world works and what is necessary to finance its operations.

Before the Reformation, the church considered the charging of interest on loans a form of exploitation. The church and its councils condemned the practice of usury as engaging in dishonest profiteering at the expense of others. The Council of Nicea (325) forbad the clergy from engaging in the practice, and subsequent councils at Carthage (345) and Aix-la-Chapelle (789) included the laity within the prohibition by threatening excommunication for those who continued to exploit others through its vices.[119] In the Middle Ages the Jews engaged in this unseemly business and suffered intense persecution at times for their participation in it. The Lateran Council (1215) found it necessary to forgive the debts of the crusaders in order to stop the bloodletting.[120] The Council of Vienne (1312) went so far as to threaten all rulers and magistrates with the power of the inquisition and the possibility of excommunication from the church if they continued to uphold usurious contracts as legal arrangements.[121] Scholastic theologians like Thomas Aquinas supported the church's position for the most part and found it "unlawful to take payment for the use of money lent."[122] But a small crack opened when Antonius of Florence and Cardinal Hostiensis suggested that the lending of money also involved the ceasing of an expected profit for the lender (*lucrum cessans*).[123] The new understanding of the arrangement seemed to entitle the lender to some interest, and many scholastics after them found this line of reasoning disturbing to the church's basic position.[124]

The Reformation did not produce a change from the medieval attitudes all at once. Luther considered the charging of interest the greatest "misfortune of the German nation," an invention of the prince of darkness, and a vice of the very lazy.[125] He listed usury as a vice of the Jewish people and suggested that they be hung as thieves or sent back to Jerusalem with a "good riddance" so they can no longer corrupt his land.[126] *Cuius regio eius religio*. Lutherans tended to agree with his position on usury for the most part, but other factions of the Reformation began to equivocate over the issue, considering it impractical or unrealistic to advocate a wholesale condemnation. Protestants tended to sympathize with the laity, and it was no surprise that the movement came to empathize with the exigencies of the calling in the world and develop a less sanctimonious attitude toward the realities of everyday life. Protestant countries showed signs of easing restrictions on the purse strings: Geneva allowed interest up to 5 percent in 1538, the Low Countries up to 12 percent in 1540, and England up to 10 percent in 1545.[127] These countries found some sanction for the practice from the church. In England, Robert Filmer composed a list of theologians who were suspected of supporting or tolerating some form of usury: "Bishop Babington, Mr. Perkins, Dr. Willet, Dr. Mayer, Mr. Brinsley, and others here at home: and abroad, Calvin, Martyr, Bucer, Billinger, Danaeus, Hemingius, Zanchius, Ursinus, Bucanus, Junius, Polanus, Molineus, Scultetus, Alstedius, Amesius, Grotius, Salmasius."[128] The authority from abroad seemed to find its center in Switzerland. Robert Fenton, an opponent of usury, depicted the Swiss theologians as the basic authority for those who sanctioned the practice in his native land. He specially singled out John Calvin as the "chief patron" of those who advocate the position and found it necessary to dispute any interpretation of him and other theologians that would sanction what the church had condemned "for the space of fifteene hundred yeeres after Christ."[129]

The clearest statement of Calvin's position is found in a letter written to a friend named Sachinus in 1545. In this letter, Calvin recognizes the difference between the demands of a modern economy and those of ancient Israel concerning usury. He recognizes that the trade of his day requires the emancipation of capital to fund its complex and wide-scale operations.[130] This letter, along with his commentaries provide a consistent defense of usury to finance commerce and trade, which its proponents were able to exploit in polemical discourse with some justification. In no uncertain terms Calvin reiterates throughout these works that the Bible does *not* condemn usury *in toto*.[131] He personally would not practice it and objects to those who make a living in this way, but he refuses to bind the conscience of those who have sufficient means and integrity in their affairs to practice what God does not condemn.[132] Calvin finds little difference between the charging of interest and the paying of rent, which all sides of the issue seem to justify.[133] He accepts the adage that money begets money and finds no particular reason to demand the lender surrender a future profit to another without just recompense. As long as both parties have sufficient means, there is no reason for the lender to surrender the use of all capital for nothing.[134] Of course, the need for interest cannot justify the exploitation of others through taking an unjust gain and so oppressing the debtor.[135] Calvin cannot justify exploitation and shows special concern in the absence of a wholesale condemnation that some will lose all "control or moderation" and forget about the Golden Rule that governs all our affairs.[136] One can charge interest as long as it does not harm another human being and serves the public good.[137] Usury is forbidden where it transgresses the law of equity and charity.[138] The Scripture permits us to exact interest of those who have means, but it forbids us to exploit the poor in this way and exhorts us to give freely and without recompense to those who have need.[139]

Protestants aligned themselves on all sides of the issue in England. Important tracts condemning the practice included Thomas Wilson's *A Discourse Upon Usury* (1572), Roger Fenton's *A Treatise of Usurie* (1611), and Robert Bolton's *A Short and Private Discourse* (1637). These tracts are worth mentioning since they probably represent the majority opinion of intelligentsia and help situate the debt in an overall context.

Wilson's discourse is written on the occasion of the Act of 1571, which overturned the absolute prohibition on usury enacted in 1552 during the reign of Edward VI. The act makes a distinction between moderate and excessive interest, setting the limit on charging interest at ten percent, but Wilson is unhappy with any compromise on this issue.[140] He wishes to answer those in favor of the statute and composes a treatise in the form of a dialogue between a lawyer, merchant, doctor, and preacher to represent all sides of the debate and provide a response. The lawyer rejects Edward VI's prohibition on usury and finds the statute that limited interest to 10 percent during the days of Henry VIII more reasonable.[141] He prefers the matter to be handled on a case-by-case basis rather than compose a sweeping verdict on one side or the other.[142] The Bible itself provides the paradigm for a sensible and moderate treatment of the subject, allowing the lending of interest to those who have means but prohibiting its use in exploiting the poor.[143] The merchant listens to the legal and biblical arguments with respect but prefers to emphasize the more practical exigencies of life over the exposition of Scripture. He finds the basic motive of trade within the desire to make a profit; otherwise a merchant would not bother to make the effort. He sees no difference between the charging of interest on a loan and basic principles of business like buying low and selling high.[144] The doctor (or civilian) joins in the conversation at this point and rejects the merchant's wholesale endorsement of business practices. At first he condemns usury in the harshest of terms, considering it worthy of death and eternal damnation,[145] but then he reverses his course by making a scholastic distinction between the payment of usury and the charging of interest. The former is condemned as receiving a mere "benefite of lendynge for time," but the latter is deemed acceptable because a loss would occur if the lender does not receive payment in due time or forfeits a future gain in the use of money.[146] Despite all the harsh words against usury, the doctor steers a moderate course in the end, allowing for the charging of interest above the principal, and defers to the wisdom of Calvin, Beza, Bucer, and Brentius on the matter.[147] The preacher (or Wilson) is not amused with this moderate position and rejects any compromise based on scholastic distinctions or worldly wisdom. All usury is evil and worthy of eternal damnation.[148] We must stick to the plain teaching of Scripture rather than trust our own wisdom.[149] The soul of England is at stake.[150] The nation may save its soul only by forsaking the idle and covetous life of usury and rediscovering the true purpose of lending as an act of charity toward the less fortunate.[151] The others, upon hearing these words, repent of their willful ignorance and agree with the preacher's message that God's word is superior to all their worldly wisdom.[152]

Robert Fenton certainly agrees with this conclusion in his discourse on usury. He expresses particular alarm over the extensive and growing nature of the practice and the government's continued toleration of what is now illegal since the thirteenth year of Elizabeth.[153] He is dismayed that a number of divines have joined the government in its policy of toleration, believing it better to accommodate human frailties than challenge this wicked practice with Scripture. These divines rely on the authority of Calvin and the Swiss theologians for support, but the actual position of the Helvetii is more ambiguous and less sympathetic to usury than its advocates suppose.[154] Fenton's own position is rather unequivocal. "All usurie properly so called, is simply unlawful."[155] It is worthy of eternal damnation.[156] The Scripture presents a consistent and unequivocal indictment of the practice, providing no special exemption for those who have means, even if its special focus is concerned with protecting the most vulnerable.[157] The money of the rich should be used in promoting trade or employing others, not taking a certain gain without risk or benefit to the community.[158]

Of course, Robert Bolton agrees with this basic position. His special concern is centered upon "some late Divines," who have found "a few supposed patrons" like "Iewell, Perkins, &tc." and are trying to overturn the age-old position of the church.[159] Bolton considers the typical verses on the subject in the Bible—"Exod.22.25. Levit. 25.35.36. Devt. 23.19. Psal. 15.5. Ezek. 18.13.17. And 22.12. Pro. 28.8. Luke 6.35"[160]—and finds all speaking with one voice against the practice. Deut. 23:19, 20 makes it abundantly clear that there are no exceptions to charging interest, whether the borrower be rich or poor.[161] The Scripture considers all usury an act of "biting" those who receive it, no matter who is the patron or what is the amount.[162] Usury turns the true spirit of lending away from charity and creates idleness and covetousness in the lender.[163] It incurs a certain gain for the lender without hazard, cost, or labor and does nothing for the community except increase the prices of its goods since the borrower must charge extra to pay the interest.[164] On these and other grounds the practice is deemed immoral, and Bolton finds no room to tolerate its ongoing desire to destroy the soul of the nation.

The other side of the debate also produced a number of outstanding representatives. William Ames and Robert Filmer serve as good examples of the other side. Ames, a disciple of Perkins, follows the moderate course of certain Calvinists by allowing for the charging of interest under certain circumstances in his influential work *de conscientia* (book 5, chpt. 44). He recognizes the generative power of money and the need to compensate those who surrender its use to another.[165] He thinks it only just to sell money for a modest gain if the borrower is relatively certain to make a profit from it.[166] Even if there is no merit in making the deal, there is nothing particularly wrong about the arrangement from the vantage point of natural reason.[167] Usury is illicit only when it seeks compensation from the poor or exacts an undue return from another human being. Usury must not hinder the true spirit of lending, which is found in works of charity toward those in need, and so undermines the Golden Rule.[168]

Filmer's treatment spends much of its time contrasting his understanding and exegesis of Scripture with that of his opponents (Fenton and Downam). He understands the OT prohibition of usury as a temporal law given to the Jews and limited to a bygone dispensation in the divine economy.[169] Even if its verses are applicable today, like his opponents want us to believe, their main concern is directed toward the treatment of the poor and has no specific application to a business arrangement between those who have means. The lending of money is an essential part of a healthy economy because the money generates wealth for those who use it and helps to create a more prosperous society as a result.[170] Fenton and Downam are simply wrong when they complain about the inflation of prices and the impoverishment of the people through the charging of interest. The commonwealth is not oppressed by the circulation of capital since the markets adjust to the real value of investment.[171] Filmer uses this line of reasoning to reject the setting of artificial ceilings on usury in favor of the market forces establishing the rate of interest.

> As for raising the market it is not caused by usury, the governors and rulers of the rates and prices of all things are the owners of money and the masters of stock, for the lenders rule the borrowers, and the richer govern the meaner. The moneyed men proportion the valuation of goods, and by practice and custom agree in a common gain to be raised by the contracts of bargaining, selling, letting and the like. For instance, the masters of money of this kingdom by their trading raise so much gains as ordinarily amounts to 20 or 30 in 100, at the year's end; which being considered by the meaner sort of people, they reckon with themselves what if they can borrow at 10 in the hundred, that then by such trading their gains may both pay the use and leave them 20 or 101 gainers: so that the borrowers do trade by buying and selling in the market at the same prices that the owners of money do, and it is the rates of the market that rules their usury, and not their usury the market. . . .
>
> But this gain they allow, so it may be conditional, if the borrower gain. And this conditional gain can only be by partnership. As for letting of money upon condition of the borrower's gain, it is a course as mischievous and impossible as the letting of land upon like condition; without experience no man can sufficiently describe it. It would make all bargains to be nothing but suits in the law, no debts should be due but upon proof and witnesses examined; nay there is no possibility of knowing men's gains or losses without racking their consciences, and opening a gap to perjury for every unthrift in his own cause.... In all letting there is a consideration had of the casualties, and because there may be a possibility of extraordinary gains, it must countervalue the extraordinary loss if any happen, both which being contingent, and seldom happening, they are set one against the other, and a middle indifferent rate between them, which doth ordinarily happen, belongs to the lender, who is not to partake in the extremes. . . . To conclude, the rule that guides the valuation in all contracts, is not what casually is or may be, but what ordinarily is like to happen.[172]

The rate of interest is set by what is likely to happen on average with the usage of the capital. This argument will lead Jansenists like Pierre Nicole and Jean Domat to develop a *laissez-faire* attitude in general, believing that self-interest (*l'amour-propre*) actually works out for the benefit of society. [173] *Cupidité* can take the place of charity in fulfilling the goals of society since it produces the same outward effect.[174] The economy works as an exchange of goods and services, which meet our needs apart from any charitable act of good and moral intention.[175] Filmer, Nicole, and

Domat are replacing the need for charitable giving with a self-interested capitalism and accomplishing the very same purpose.[176] Of course, this motivation became associated with the term capitalism in the modern world, but it was not the only possible impulse for capital investment discussed at the time. The Puritans often tried to motivate the people by appealing to an altruistic impulse to invest in the community and build a better tomorrow for future generations, accomplishing much the same purpose through a different inward intent.

Richard Baxter

Max Weber finds the essential elements of the spirit of capitalism summarized in the life and writings of Richard Baxter. No person defended the Puritan cause with more devotion during the seventeenth century, and no person embodied the Protestant work ethic with more zeal, producing almost 150 books in a lifetime of labor, many of which were massive tomes of considerable length.[177] Weber particularly points to the *Christian Directory* (1673), which consists of 1172 pages of tiny print. "His Christian Directory (1673) is the most complete compendium of Puritan ethics."[178] In this work Baxter expresses appreciation to others, like Perkins, Ames, Dickson, and Taylor, who went before him and brought the Protestant fold into practical and casuistic discussions, but he senses an insufficiency in their treatments, especially when compared with the voluminous nature of Catholic works on the subject. Baxter hopes to correct this deficit and write a *Summa Theologiae* and *Summa Moralis* all rolled into one[179]—the only difference being his rejection of speculative theology, which has little moment in the life of true believers. For Baxter, Christianity is practical. A few essential teachings are sufficient to ground the faith, but beyond the basics he finds no need to create controversy or divide the fellowship over matters that have no utilitarian value. The Christian intellectual should strive to develop a theology that is true to experience and useful to what is most essential in life, fulfilling the purpose or calling God has given to each one in the community of faith.[180]

The *Christian Directory* contains the basic themes and practical exhortations that Weber associates with the spirit of capitalism. There is the typical exhortation to redeem the time and work hard to enter the Kingdom of God for the time is short.[181] Baxter embodies this exhortation in all his works, writing with a sense of urgency, believing that death is lurking at his doorstep—each word might become his last.

> Great mercy hath trained me upon all my days, since I was nineteen years of age, in the school of affliction, to keep my sluggish soul awake in the constant expectations of my change, and to kill my pride and overvaluing of this world, and to lead all my studies to the most necessary things, and as a spur to excite my soul to seriousness, and especially to save me from the supine neglect and loss of time. Oh! What unspeakable mercy hath a life of constant but gentle chastisement proved to me! It urged me, against all dull delays, to make my calling and election sure, and to make ready my accounts, as one that must quickly give them up to God. The face of death, and nearness of eternity, did much convince me what books to read, what studies to prefer and prosecute, what company and conversation to choose. It drove me early into the vineyard of the Lord, and taught me to preach as a dying man to dying men.[182]

> To redeem time is to see that we cast none of it away in vain, but use every minute of it as a most precious thing, and spend it wholly in the way of duty. . . . The Price and Time must be redeemed with it, Above all, by our utmost Diligence. That we be still doing, and put forth all our strength, and run as for our lives, and whatever our hand shall find to do, that we do it with our might, remembering that there is no work, nor device, nor knowledge, nor wisdom in the grave whither we go, Eccl.9.10. . . . Paul preached till midnight being to depart on the morrow, Act.20.7.[183]

> I Preach'd, as never sure to preach again, and as a dying man to dying men![184]

Rest is what comes later. It is reserved as a reward for all those who lead a life of diligent service in the here and now.[185]

The worst sin is committed by those who squander the gifts of God on a life of idleness, sloth, and frivolous entertainment.[186] Dice, cards, and stage-plays are disparaged as unprofitable recreations and associated with much evil.[187] All access and self-indulgence are discouraged as ways of consuming God's resources when more profitable ventures could use the capital and spend the talents on creating a better world for the common good. The rich are the particular focus of this exhortation since they are subject to the temptations of extravagant living more than anyone else. Baxter reminds them to mortify the flesh, just like others and abstain from wasting their life on consumption, recreations, and idleness. The rich have no more liberty to indulge their lusts than the poor, and so they must make the most of the day like anyone else.[188]

The focus of life is directed toward "the service of God and the publick good."[189] One can labor for riches, but the chief end of life does not consist in accumulating more and more treasures here on earth. Baxter constantly reminds his readers that what they possess is only for "use"[190]—a use that is directed toward building what is lasting in the community—a point that Weber fails to appreciate. The goal of a Puritan does not reside in the accumulation of riches as if the mark of salvation is found in the mere act of earning money for its own sake. The purpose of life is found in the desire to invest whatever is given by God—the time, the talent, and the capital—for the betterment of all. The callings, which Baxter stresses as much as any Puritan, are driven by a single-minded concern for doing the most good for the community, rather than serving oneself in hoarding riches or becoming consumed by worldly possessions.[191] Of course, Baxter does not begrudge a businessman for "driving a [hard] bargain," as long as it is lawful and represents an "honest increase and provision."[192] He also allows for the charging of usury in trade, as long as it is grounded in the laws of justice and does not oppress the borrower or the poor, who deserve our charity.[193] But the goal of all these and other arrangements remains rooted in the obligation to serve others and build up the community in which one labors for the sake of future generations. Puritanism ever remains rooted in its utilitarian, altruistic, and teleological values. Weber's analysis of Baxter's ethical exhortations is helpful, but it fails to appreciate the fundamental orientation of the work ethic. The vision of Baxter and his people is fixated on the future and building the community in light of the dawning of God's kingdom, not making a profit for its own sake without rhyme or reason.

Weber also makes a crucial mistake when it comes to assessing the theological matrix of Baxter's ideas. He is correct in understanding the relationship between the doctrine of assurance and the impetus to work, but he is wrong when it comes to assessing the basic theological matrix from which the emphasis on works arose, assigning too much influence to the mystery of predestination. A brief inspection of Baxter's theology finds him conflicted over the doctrine of predestination and engaged in a polemical battle with those who so emphasized the doctrine as to discount all conditions for the reception of Christ's work and the need to produce and examine good works. Far from creating anxiety over divine mysteries, Baxter rejects this emphasis and points the pilgrim toward a practical and circumspect life of true Christian piety.

His basic position is seen in his very first publication, *Aphorismes of Justification* (1649). He begins the work by emphasizing the preceptive will of God as more important to our overall sanctification and edification than probing into the mysteries of the sovereign will.[194] The preceptive will spells out our responsibilities before God and the conditions necessary to receive a place in the kingdom of heaven. This will is embodied in the New Covenant, which defines the relationship between God and the believer in terms of mutual responsibilities.[195] The New Covenant stipulates the performance of conditions necessary for all to fulfill if they wish to receive the righteousness offered in Christ. One should not reduce the human element by transforming it into a testament of divine grace.[196] There are conditions of faith and obedience on our part that are necessary to fulfill in order to satisfy the demands of the covenant. Among these conditions faith serves the central role because it is the most self-effacing work of personal homage we can offer to God.[197] But its diminutive posture does not negate its efficacy as a human component in salvation, nor diminish its potency in producing as a primary cause other works of piety necessary for salvation—including repentance of sin, forgiveness of others, and acts of love. Faith alone does not justify the sinner. Faith must work through acts of love to complete the conditions Christ has presented in the gospel.[198] Even Christ himself is not divided into different functions as Lord and Savior, but exists in the entirety of his three-fold office as Prophet, Priest, and King.[199]

Baxter's position on grace never receives final clarification in his works. He often speaks of himself as situated somewhere between the theological positions of his day: Calvinism and Lutheranism, Remonstrance and Contra-Remonstrance, Antinomianism and Catholicism.[200] He shows some appreciation for the Amyraldian system at times and displays affinity to their ideas with his emphasis upon the bifurcation of the divine will, unlimited atonement, conditional covenant, and the universal offer of salvation to all upon the condition of faith. But it is difficult to describe him as part of the Amyraldian movement. Along with the universal offer of salvation, the Amyraldians speak of the unconditional decree of God, which elected a limited few to salvation and fulfills the condition of faith in the elect through irresistible grace.[201] For Amyraldians, there are two movements within the divine will: the first to save all upon the condition of faith, and the second to save a limited few since no one would believe unless God insures it. For Baxter there are two movements of the divine will, but the second remains more obscure and less potent in its desiderations.

The synergism of Baxter is best understood as a product of his emphasis upon the standard Reformed doctrine of a bilateral covenant. Unlike other theologians, Baxter makes little effort to hide the synergistic tendency of the covenant and even broaches the Catholic doctrine of justification at times in his treatment. He admits some tension between grace and works in the doctrine and tries to construct some semblance of reconciliation between them. At first he appeals, like other Reformed theologians, to the Franciscan/Nominalist solution of the Middle Ages, which emphasized the insufficient nature of our works and the mercy of God in accepting them. This solution would mitigate the value of the human component and emphasize the voluntary condescension of God to accept our works via covenant (*ex pacto*) above and beyond their actual worth.[202] Baxter compares our contribution to a mere "pepper corn," which God decides to accept as a form of payment, even if it cannot erase the enormous debt or truly earn its eternal reward.[203] Along with this argument he adds the typical Reformed emphasis upon divine grace as the only efficacious means of fulfilling the will of God. Without grace, no one can do the works of God. The conditions of the covenant are fulfilled only through the power of the Holy Spirit, who affects all things that are pleasing and acceptable to God.[204] But Baxter does not proceed as far as other Calvinists in stressing the sole efficacy of this grace. He wonders out loud whether grace is resistible or not, preferring to incur the charge of synergism than destroy the human element in the covenant.[205] Baxter ever remains committed to the covenant over against those who so stress the doctrine of predestination that they eliminate the impetus toward good works. His emphasis on good works arises from the conditional nature of the covenant, not the doctrine of predestination, and Weber is clearly wrong in this matter.

If there is any one matter that tends to define his thought, it seems to involve his obsessive concern over Antinomianism as a danger to moral living. Perhaps it is better to understand him in this negative way as an "Anti-Antinomian" than trying to establish a positive label for his ideas like Calvinist, Arminian, or anything else.[206] A prominent portion of Baxter's work is devoted to destroying this "heresy," even when it no longer existed in any appreciable form in England after the 1650s.[207] He thinks that Antinomianism is most dangerous because it destroys his central concern for Christian living by eliminating any real incentive to serve God and so encourages spiritual laziness, if not godlessness among the people. He actually displays more sympathy toward Catholics and their view of salvation in his works, because the basic concern to protect and support discipleship is more important to him than the fundamental tenets of the Protestant gospel![208]

What Baxter understands as Antinomianism grew up in England at the beginning of the seventeenth century with John Eaton and John Cotton.[209] The movement rejected the emphasis of Puritan divines like Perkins and Ames upon casuistry, self-scrutiny, and the "legal zeal for works." It preferred to exalt in the sole sufficiency of divine grace and exhort the souls of the day to turn away from the depravity of their own faith and works, look to Christ as the means of salvation, and listen to the Holy Spirit assuring their hearts before God. It preferred to glory in the righteousness of Christ and his grace than gaze upon the "menstrous cloth" of human righteousness, which leads the faithful to nothing more than a state of depression over their own shortcomings.[210] This doctrine of English Antinomians had no historical continuity with what transpired in Germany under the auspices of Johannes Agricola—at least beyond the desire of Baxter and its opponents to connect the groups under one label. Agricola wanted to disparage the preaching of the law and subsume the whole message of Christianity under the gospel. He emphasized the gospel and the ministry of the Spirit as bringing the initial repentance of conversion and directing the subsequent life of the believers apart from any appeal to the OT or its law.[211] Even Baxter does not accuse his opponents of espousing this kind of heretical teaching. When Baxter thinks of Antinomianism, his vitriol is directed toward those who overemphasize the eternal councils of God and dismiss the marks of salvation here on earth. These Antinomians are guilty of destroying the temporal nature of salvation and its conditions. They assign justification to an eternal act of God, secured by the work of Christ, and leave no place for its temporal fulfillment.[212] They make assurance a direct revelation of the Spirit without considering the outward signs or marks of grace in the inner man.[213] Baxter rejects this theocentric focus and sees assurance as the product of a lifetime of struggle and self-examination. The Christian life is hard work. Assurance is hard work. The believer is exhorted to practice diligence in examining one's faith and works and see if they measure up to the true marks of salvation.[214]

> Study also the Evidence of his Love in thy self; look over the works of his Grace in thy Soul: If thou do not find the degree which thou desirest, yet deny not that degree which thou findest; look after the sincerity more than the quantity. Remember what discoveries of thy fate thou hast made formerly in the work of self-examination; how oft God hath convinced thee of the sincerity of the heart: Remember all the former Testimonies of the Spirit; and all the sweet feelings of the Favour of God; and all the prayers that he hath heard and granted: and all the rare preservations and deliverances; and all the progress of his Spirit in his workings on thy Soul; and the disposals of Providence, conducing to thy good: The vouchsafing of means, the directing thee to them: the directing of the Ministers to meet with thy state, the restraint of those sins that thy nature was most prone to. And though one of these considered alone, may be no sure evidence of his special love, (which I expect thou shouldst try by more infallible signs) yet lay them altogether, and then think with thy self, Whether all these do not testifie the good will of the Lord concerning thy Salvation, and may not well be pleaded against thine unbelief.[215]

He encourages his readers to keep a journal of their spiritual struggles—*Relinquae Baxteriannae* representing his own attempt at developing this important genre of Puritan literature.[216]

It is here in the struggle to find assurance that Baxter and the Puritans found the incentive to work hard in the community. They struggled because they could not follow or accept the theocentric solution of Antinomianism with its focus upon the decree of the Father, the work of the Son, and the witness of the Spirit. They followed the covenant theology of Bullinger, which placed conditions upon the reception of grace. They followed the practical syllogism of Beza and Zanchi, which turned the focus of a believer toward self-knowledge and the cases of the conscience in finding that mustard seed of faith.[217] Both doctrines were anthropocentric. Both doctrines possessed synergistic tendencies and caused conflict with the basic concept of salvation through grace, but they also provided a people zealous in their service of God and country. When this zeal was combined with other teachings, it produced a religious climate that was conducive to the development of capitalism. The Reformed doctrine of assurance, work, calling, and community provided a powerful force and merged together with other factors to create a solid theological matrix for the growth of a new economic order.

Notes

1. *The Autobiography of Benjamin Franklin with Related Documents*, L. P. Masur (ed. and intro.) (Boston and New York: Bedford/St. Martin's, 2003) vii, 22, 47.
2. Ibid., 40-42, 73, 74. His religious beliefs included the existence of a God who made and governs the world, an emphasis upon ethical conduct as the most pleasing service to God, the immortality of the soul, and the Judgment Day. These principles, he says, are essential to all religions in America. Ibid., 13, 93, 94; *Benjamin Franklin Writings* (New York: The Library of America, 1987) 179, 180. He attended church on occasion and supported its ministry but wanted to hear more about virtue than specific polemical matters of theological interest. Ibid., 94; *Writings*, 426. He displayed genuine tolerance toward all sects throughout his life and writings. Ibid., 13.
3. Cf. T. Dickson and H. V. MacLachlan, "In Search of the Spirit of Capitalism: Weber's Misinterpretation of Franklin," *Sociology* 23, no. 1 (Feb. 1989): 81-89; *The Autobiography of Benjamin Franklin*, 74, 75. There are times in which utility determines what is most beneficial in his life and writings.
4. *Writings*, 149, 748, 749.
5. Ibid., 257, 1179, 1180.
6. K. J. Weintraub, "The Puritan Ethic and Benjamin Franklin," *The Journal of Religion* 56, no.3 (1976): 233, 234; *The Autobiography*, 3.
7. *The Autobiography*, 31,32; R. L. Ketcham, *Benjamin Franklin* (New York: Washington Square Press, 1966) 5; A. O. Aldridge, "The Alleged Puritanism of Benjamin Franklin," in *Reappraising Benjamin Franklin: A Bicentennial Perspective*, J. A. Leo Lemay (ed.) (Newark: University of Delaware Press, 1993) 363.
8. Ibid., 92, 93.
9. Ibid., 35.
10. Ibid., 36, 37.

11. Ibid., 37. See Ibid., 32; M. R. Breitwieser, *Cotton Mather and Benjamin Franklin* (Cambridge: Cambridge University Press, 1984) 12.
12. C. Mather, *Bonafacius: An Essay upon the Good*, D. Levin (ed. and intro.) (Cambridge: Belknop Press, 1966) viii, ix.
13. Ibid., 3-6.
14. Ibid., 9, 107-119.
15. Ibid., 32,140, 141.
16. Ibid., 32, 33.
17. Ibid., 64-68, 170.
18. Ibid., 132, 178, 179.
19. Ibid., 68, 170.
20. Ibid., 80, 81, 120, 121, 136, 137. People should ask themselves the following question: "What Good Is There to Be Done?" Ibid., 66.
21. Ibid., 29-31, 35.
22. Ibid., 29, 30.
23. *The Autobiography of Benjamin Franklin*, 39, 68, 77. Franklin was an avaricious reader. Ibid., 40. *Essays to Do Good* also contains a number of admonitions in this regard. Mather, *Bonafacius*, 39, 60, 77.
24. Ibid., 107.
25. Ibid., 4,106.
26. *The Works of Benjamin Franklin*, J. Sparks (ed.) (Boston: Tappen and Dennet, 1844) 2.87, 95-97.
27. *Benjamin Franklin's The Art of Virtue: His Formula for Successful Living*, G. L. Rogers (ed.) (Eden Prairie, MN: Acorn Publishing, 1986) 162-64; *Writings*, 625; *The Works of Benjamin Franklin*, 2.269, 370, 371; T. Mott and G. W. Zinke, "Benjamin Franklin's Economic Thought: A Twentieth Century Appraisal," in *Critical Essays on Benjamin Franklin*, M. H. Buxbaum (ed.) (Boston: G. K. Hall & Co., 1987) 114. Franklin interacted with Physiocrats and advocated along with them the importance of free trade and agriculture. He also was a personal friend of Adam Smith and influenced his *Wealth of Nations*. Ibid., 111-14.
28. *The Autobiography*, 82, 92, 93; *The Works*, 2.90; *Writings*, 1082; *The Art of Virtue*, 159. It seems as if he allowed this austerity to slip as he and his wife grew older (e.g., *The Autobiography*, 93).
29. "The Puritan Ethic and Benjamin Franklin," 236.
30. *The Autobiography*, 124.
31. Ibid., 133.
32. *Writings*, 1017, 1167; *The Autobiography*, 164.
33. *The Autobiography*, 94, 95, 101-103.
34. Ibid., 174.
35. Ibid., 95-102.
36. Ibid., 105, 106.
37. Franklin also gives credit to the Quakers for shaping his ideology. *The Autobiography*, 36. Of course, the Quakers themselves are a product of certain Puritan tendencies.
38. R. W. Green (ed.), *Protestantism and Capitalism: The Weber Thesis and Its Critics* (Boston: C. Heath and Co., 1959.) vii; M. Bergler, "Max Webers Thesen über die Entstehung des modernen westlichen Kapitalismus," *Zeitschrift für Religions-und Geistesgeschichte* 39, no. 1 (1987): 27, 28; H. Lehmann, "The Rise of Capitalism: Weber versus Sombart," in *Weber's Protestant Ethic: Origins, Ethics, and Context*, H. Lehmann and G. Roth (ed.) (Cambridge: Cambridge University Press, 1993) 197, 198; M. J. Kitch, *Capitalism and the Reformation* (New York: Barnes &

Noble, Inc., 1968) xvii, xviii. Weber's work was a response to Werner Sombart's *Der Moderne Kapitalismus* (1902).

39. K. Marx and F. Engels, *Manifesto of the Communist Party*, in *Great Books of the Western World*, M. J. Alder (ed.) (Chicago: Encyclopedia Britannica, Inc., 178) 416, 419, 424, 428; Kitch, *Capitalism and the Reformation*, 53; H. Sée, "The Contribution of the Puritans to the Evolution of Modern Capitalism," in *Protestantism and Capitalism*, 62.
40. E. Fischoff, "The History of a Controversy," in *Protestantism and Capitalism*, 109.
41. R. H. Tawney, *Religion and the Rise of Capitalism* (Gloucester, MA: Peter Smith, 1962) 20.
42. Ibid., 9, 10, 17; Kitch, *Capitalism and the Reformation*, 183.
43. M. Weber, *The Protestant Ethic and the Spirit of Capitalism*, T. Parsons (trans.) (New York: Charles Scribner's Sons, 1958) 183; Tawney, *Religion and the Rise of Capitalism*, xiv, xv; M. Lowy, "Weber against Marx? The Polemic with Historical Materialism in the Protestant Ethic," *Science & Society* 53, no. 1 (Spring 1989): 72; H. R. Trevor-Roper, "The Reformation and Economic Change," in *Capitalism and the Reformation*, 31.
44. W. S. Hudson, "Puritanism and the Spirit of Capitalism," *Church History* 18, no. 1 (March 1949): 5, 6; Kitch, *Capitalism and the Reformation*, xvii, xviii; Bergler, "Max Webers Thesen," 35, 36. Weber also speaks of a reciprocal relation at times. Lowy, "Weber against Marx?" 74.
45. Kitch, *Capitalism and the Reformation*, 56, 66, 74, 75, 201; H. M. Robertson, "A Criticism of Max Weber and his School," in *Protestantism and Capitalism*, 80, 81; W. S. Hudson, "The Weber Thesis Reexamined," *Church History* 57, supplement (1988): 57. Double-entry bookkeeping was introduced around the fourteenth century in Italy or France.
46. Weber, *The Protestant Ethic and the Spirit of Capitalism*, 1(b); "Anticritical Last Word on The Spirit of Capitalism," W. M. Davis (trans.) *American Journal of Sociology* 83, no. 5 (1978): 1113. A simple illustration from Chinese religion might help. No one believes that Chinese religion is responsible for the development of bourgeois capitalism in the modern world, but one can envision its religious principles promoting or hindering such an economic philosophy given the right set of circumstances. For example, if a society accented the Confucian concept of filial piety and venerated the ways of the ancestors, it seems unlikely that the culture would proceed toward developing an economic system like capitalism with its accent upon future betterment. Filial piety is not a sufficient ground for the culture to develop in this direction. However, if the culture chose to accent the Daoist doctrine of non-interference, a sufficient ground would exist for the development of a laissez-faire economic policy, and the free trade of capitalism might prosper under this teaching. If the conditions are right and the stars align, a society can take certain religious ideas and develop them in new and unforeseen directions.
47. Ibid., 40; M. Brocker, "Max Webers Erklärungsansatz für die Entstehung des Kapitalismus," *Zeitschrift für Geschichtswissenschaft* 43, no. 6 (1995): 501; M. Weber, *The Sociology of Religion*, E. Fischoff (trans.) (Boston: Beacon Press, 1964) 220.
48. Ibid., 79-81; Brocker, "Max Webers Erklärungsansatz," 504, 505. He sees the Augsburg Confession using *Beruf* in the same way.
49. Ibid., 43.
50. Montesquieu, *De l'Esprit des lois* (Paris: Garnier Frères) IV, XX, 7 (2.13); *The Spirit of* the *Laws*, A. M. Cohler, B. C. Miller, and H. S. Stone (trans. and ed.)

(Cambridge: Cambridge University Press, 1997) 343; Weber, *The Protestant Ethic and the Spirit of Capitalism*, 45.

51. Weber, *The Protestant Ethic and the Spirit of Capitalism*, 110, 111, 114, 117, 230-31; Brocker, "Max Webers Erklärungsansatz," 505, 506. Methodism developed a systematic "method" to find assurance. Weber, *The Protestant Ethic and the Spirit of Capitalism*, 139.
52. Ibid., 157-60, 166-69.
53. Ibid., 49-51, 156ff.; Ketcham, *Benjamin Franklin*, 63, 64.
54. Ibid., 1(e), 56-58.
55. Ibid., 2, 17, 18; Brocker, "Max Webers Erklärungsansatz," 500.
56. Ibid., 25, 64, 170; Brocker, "Max Webers Erklärungsansatz," 495. Weber provides a good example of how the process of rationalization develops on pp. 67, 68 of his work.

> What happened was, on the contrary, often no more than this: some young man from one of the putting-out families went out into the country, carefully chose weavers for his employ, greatly increased the rigour of his supervision of their work, and thus turned them from peasants into labourers. On the other hand, he would begin to change his marketing methods by so far as possible going directly to the final consumer, would take the details into his own hands, would personally solicit customers, visiting them every year, and above all would adapt the quality of the product directly to their needs and wishes. At the same time he began to introduce the principle of low prices and large turnover. There was repeated what everywhere and always is the result of such a process of rationalization: those who would not follow suit had to go out of business. The idyllic state collapsed under the pressure of a bitter competitive struggle, respectable fortunes were made, and not lent out at interest, but always reinvested in the business. The old leisurely and comfortable attitude toward life gave way to a hard frugality in which some participated and came to the top, because they did not wish to consume but to earn, while others who wished to keep on with the old ways were forced to curtail their consumption.

57. Weber, *The Sociology of Religion*, 220; Brocker, *Max Webers Erklärungsansatz*, 501; J. Viner, *Religious Thought and Economic Society* (Durham, NC: Duke University Press, 1978) 17.
58. Lanfranc, *Elucidarium*, in *Opera quae supersunt omnia*, J. A. Giles (ed.) (Oxonii: Parker, 1844) 2.18.
59. Kitch, *Capitalism and the Reformation*, 95, 96.
60. E. Schreiber, *Die volkswirtschaftlichen Anschauungen der Scolastik seit Thomas v. Aquin* (Jena: G. Fischer, 1913) 154; Gratian, *Decretum*, in *Incipit Concordia discordatium canonum* (Basel: Michael Wenssler, 1482) part 1, dist. 88, cap. 11; Viner, *Religious Thought and Economic Society*, 61.
61. M. Weber, "Anticritical Last Word," 1109; Kitch, *Capitalism and the Reformation*, xvii; G. Poggi, *Calvinism and the Capitalist Spirit: Max Weber's Protestant Ethic* (Amherst: University of Massachusetts Press, 1983) 38.
62. Tawney, *Religion and the Rise of Capitalism*, 26, 79, 84; Trevor-Roper, "The Reformation and Economic Change," 34, 35; M. H. Mackinnon, "The Longevity of the Thesis: A Critique of the Critics," in *Weber's Protestant Ethic*, 226, 227, 236.
63. B. Cotrugli, *On Commerce and the Perfect Merchant* (1458), in R. S. Lopez and I. W. Raymond, *Medieval Trade in the Mediterranean World* (New York and London: Columbia University Press, 1961) 414.
64. Evans, *The Theme is Freedom*, 295, 296; Tawney, *Religion and the Rise of Capitalism*, 187, 188, 192, 254, 258, 262; Mackinnon, "The Longevity of the Thesis," 242,

243; E. Barker, "The Achievement of Oliver Cromwell," in *Cromwell: A Profile*, I. Roots (ed.) (New York: Hill and Wang, [1973]) 6. Tawney provides on pp. 319, 320 in footnote 66 a mountain of research that deals with monopolies, exchange, speculation, and industry under the control of the Star Chamber, Privy Council, and other powers of government both before and after the Puritan Revolution.

65. Montesquieu, *De l'Esprit des lois*, IV, XX, 4 (2.11); *The Spirit of the Laws*, 340, 341. See M. Novak, *The Spirit of Democratic Capitalism* (New York: A Touchstone Book, 1982) 15-17. It is difficult to assess the data and establish the precise relation between capitalism and Calvinism throughout Europe. Calvinists in France and Holland were successful merchants, entrepreneurs, and financiers, but Scotland remained a poor country. A. Hyma, "A Case Study: Calvinism and Capitalism in the Netherlands, 1555-1700," in *Capitalism and the Reformation*, 23; Trevor-Roper, "The Reformation and Economic Change," 29-31, 33-34; W. C. Scoville, "An Alternative Hypothesis: 'Penalization' and the Huguenots," 37-39, 43. No simple relation is possible to establish, but there appears to be some truth to the stereotype that Protestant countries (especially Reformed countries) are rich and Catholic countries are poor. Viner, *Religious Thought and Economic Society*, 160, 161, 182. Weber's pupil, Martin Offenbacher, tried to establish the thesis through a statistical analysis of the Grand Duchy of Baden, pointing to the success of Protestants in education and business as opposed to Catholics. Other studies have challenged the fairness of his analysis of Baden, even the notion that there is a significant disparity in wealth and education between the groups—at least based on religious factors. K. Samuelson, *Religion and Economic Action* (Stockholm: Svenska Bokförlaget, 1961) 137-47; J. Delacroix and F. Nelson, "The Beloved Myth: Protestantism and the Rise of Industrial Capitalism in Nineteenth-Century Europe," *Social Forces* 80, no. 2 (Dec. 2001): 532-43; A. Hamilton, "Max Weber's Protestant Ethic and the Spirit of Capitalism," 152, 168.

66. WA 6.407, 408 (LW 44.127-29); Brocker, "Max Webers Erklärungsansatz," 504; K. Fullerton, "Calvinism and Capitalism: An Explanation of the Weber Thesis," in *Protestantism and Capitalism*, 9, 10; Weber, *The Protestant Ethic and the Spirit of Capitalism*, 81; Kitch, *Capitalism and the Reformation*, 3.

67. H. M. Robertson, "A Criticism of Max Weber and his School," in *Protestantism and Capitalism*, 71.

68. *The Work of William Perkins*, I. Breward (ed.) (Appleford, Abingdon, and Berkshire: The Sutton Courtenay Press, 1970) 446-49, 456. The list of those who did not possess a sufficient calling included beggars, vagabounds, monks, friars, servants, and gentlemen. M. Walzer, *The Revolution of the Saints: A Study in the Origin of Radical Politics* (Cambridge, MA: Harvard University Press, 1965) 216.

69. R. Steele, *The Trades-man's Calling* (London: J. D., 1684) 1, 2.

70. Weber, *The Protestant Ethic and the Spirit of Capitalism*, 110-14, 117, 230, 231; Mackinnon, "The Longevity of the Thesis," 250, 251; Brocker, "Max Webers Erklärungsansatz," 505, 506; Fullerton, "Calvinism and Capitalism," 13, 14; C. L. Cohen, "The Saint Zealous in Love and Labor: The Puritan Psychology of Work," *Harvard Theological Review* 76, no. 4 (1983): 458.

71. Ibid., 40; Weber, "Anticritical Last Word," 1121, 1122; R. M. Mitchell, "The Weber Thesis ...," *Fides et Historia* 4, no. 2 (1972): 57; Poggi, *Calvinism and the Capitalistic Spirit*, 60.

72. Steele, *The Trade-man's Calling*, 214, 215.

73. WA 1.30-31, 323; 4.665; 6.158, 166 (LW 39.28, 29, 40, 41); 7.374ff.; 30/2.497 (LW 40.364, 365); 40/2.449ff.; WA, TR 5, nr. 6017; *Dr. Martin Luthers kleiner und grosser Katechismus* (Berlin: Evangelischer Bücher-Verein, 1872). WA 7.119:

"Do not put confidence in your confession as a means of absolution, but in the word of Christ, 'whatever you will absolve, etc.' Put your confidence in this: If you've received absolution from the priest, believe you've been absolved and you will be truly absolved." See Strehle, *The Catholic Roots of the Protestant Gospel*, 8ff.

74. WA 2.13, 14 (LW 31.271); 30/2.411, 414; 38.243, 244 (LW 38.203-205); O. Bayer, *Promissio* (Göttigen: Vandenhoeck & Ruprecht, 1961) 194, 197.
75. WA 30/2.497, 498 (LW 40.365, 366); *Katechismus*, 17.
76. WA 2.15 (LW 31.273, 274); 7.374ff.; 30/2.412; 44.413, 414 (LW 7.154, 155).
77. Thomas Aquinas, *Summa Theologiae* (New York: McGraw-Hill, 1964-76) II-II, q. 20, a. 2; *In Quattuor libros Sententiarum* IV, d.17, q.2, a.1, 2, 5 [in *Opera Omnia* (Stuttgart-Bad Cannstatt: Frommann-Holzboog, 1980) 1.532aff., 533b, 535b]; *Canones et Decreta Dogmatica Concilii Tridentini*, session decimaquarta, cap. 4, 6 [P. Schaff, *The Creeds of Christendom* (Michigan: Baker Book House, 1977) 2.144, 152, 153, 164, 165]; Strehle, *The Catholic Roots of the Protestant Gospel*, 5-7.
78. J. Duns Scotus, *Opera Omnia* (Hildesheim: Georg Olms Verlagsbuchhandlung, 1968) 8.124, 125; 9.42, 82, 92, 300 (IV, d.1, q.6, n.10; a.14, q.2, n.13; q.4, n.3, 4, 7; d.17, q.1, n.13, 14. Gabriel Biel provides a good summation of the basic Scotist position. "One is able to know who does not place an obstacle through an intention to sin mortally and accepts the sacrament of absolution, that it confers grace *ex opera operato*, and yet does not bring any other intention except not placing an obstacle, which is the cessation from the act and purpose of sinning, as Scotus would have it in IV. He is able to know that he is not in the act of sinning and has not the purpose to sin, because the soul recognizes intuitively and evidently its own act, both in reception of the sacrament of penance and its possession of grace." *Collectorium circa quattor libros sententiorum*, W. Werbeck and V. Hofmann (ed.) (Tübingen: Mohr, 1977) II, d.27, Q (525, 526). For the position of the Scotists at the council of Trent, see *Concilium Tridentium*, Societas Goerresiana (Friburgi Brisgovia: ex aede et sumptibus Herder, 1901-30) 5.393, 404, 410, 484, 632, 633, 652, 653; 10.586, 587; 12.655, 656; Stakemeier, *Das Konzil von Trent über die Heilsgewissheit* (Heidelberg: P. M. Kerle, 1947) 100, 166, 167, 190; Strehle, *The Catholic Roots of the Protestant Gospel*, 22-25.
79. T. Bèze, *Tractiones Theologicae* (Genevae, 1582) 1.10, 15, 16, 687-90; *Quaestionum & Responsionum Christianaram libellus* (Londini, 1571); G. Zanchi, *Opera Theologica* (Genevae, 1613) 2.506; 7.230; 8.716, 717; R. T. Kendall, *Calvinism and English Calvinism to 1648* (Oxford: Oxford University Press, 1981) 32ff.
80. Perkins translates a section of Zanchi's *De Natura Dei* (*Opera Theologica*, 2.504ff.) on assurance. *The Workes* (Cambridge, 1608), 1.429ff. Two important treatises containing Beza's concept of assurance were translated into English and available to the Puritans: *Confessio de la foi* (*A briefe and pithie Summe of Christian faith*—1589) and *Quaestionum & Responsionum Christianarum libellus* (*A booke of Christian Questions and Answers*—1572).
81. Perkins, *The Workes*, 1.421; Kendall, *Calvin and English Calvinism*, 6; C. Cohen, *God's Caress* (New York and Oxford: Oxford University Press, 1986) 114. Kendall surveyed 112 treaties of 53 divines (almost every Westminister divine) and finds unequivocal testimony to the practical syllogism.
82. Perkins, *Workes*, 1.511, 529, 542.
83. Ibid., 1.80, 115, 373ff., 406, 541.
84. Ibid., 1.126-29, 367, 558. The Westminister Confession (c.18, 3) also acknowledges the difficulty in obtaining assurance. Reformed theologians on the continent expressed more doubts about the process of obtaining assurance than their Lutheran

counterpart. P. Mastricht, *Theoretico-practica theologica* (Amstelodam, 1715) 2.813b (27); F. Turrettini, *Institutio Theologica Elencticae* (Genevae, 1688) 1.4, q.14, 6; 1.15, q.17, 9, 36.

85. W. Ames, *Conscience with the Power and Cases thereof* (London, 1639); W. Fenner, *The Souls Looking-glasse . . . with a Treatise of Conscience* (Cambridge, 1640); Cohen, "The Saint Zealous in Labor and Love," 466.

86. The Calvinists speak of faith and certitude as involving a "serious exploration into oneself," a "reflexive act," in which "faith in one self is felt," or an inward knowledge of what one "feels and believes." Mastricht, *Theoretica-practica theologica*, 2.23 (830a); *Collegium Theologicum*, 1.11, 39 (291); Turrettini, *Institutio*, 1.4, q.13, 9; 25, q.17, 12; J. Heidegger, *Corpus Theologiae Christianae* (Tiguri, 1700) 1.24, 93, 109 (418b, 424a).

87. M. Butzer, *Metaphrases et enarrationes perpetuae epistarum D. Pauli Apostoli, . . .* (Argentorati: W. Rihelius, 1536) 359bff., 402-405; *Opera Latina* [*Enarratio in Evangelion Iohannis 1528, 1530, 1536* (Leiden: E. J. Brill, 1988)] 2.240, 347; J. Calvin, *Inst.*, 3.3.1-8; 24.3, 5; CO 1.74 [*Inst.* (1536)]. See *Confessio Helvetica Posterior*, c.10, 9; W. Niesel, *The Theology of Calvin*, H. Knight (trans.) (Grand Rapids, MI: Baker Book House, 1980) 171; J. Moltmann, *Prädestination und Perseveranz* (Neukirchen: Neukirchener Verlag, 1961) 47, 48.

88. Strehle, *The Catholic Roots*, 35-37, 125.

89. I did not develop this thesis from another scholar, but I have noted in the course of my study certain scholars who think that the work ethic might be a product of the covenant or preparationist theology, even if their work is sketchy on this issue and the possible connection—e.g., Sacran Bercovitch and Janice Knight. See J. Knight, *Orthodoxies in Massacutsetts: Rereading American Puritanism* (Cambridge and London: Harvard University Press, 1994) 104, 106.

Malcolm Mackinnon seems like the only sociologist of note who recognizes Weber's mistake, even if his knowledge of covenant theology and its history is limited. He recognizes that the Puritans were not so enamored with the doctrine of predestination as to exclude all else. Richard Baxter, Weber's favorite example, did not follow the doctrine so strictly—a fact that Weber himself implies in the footnotes but not the text. The lives of Baxter and the Puritans found more practical inspiration in the covenant than whiling away the hours upon idle speculation over the mysteries of predestination. Mackinnon is right on this point, and he is also right to stress the human component of the covenant as conflicting with Calvin's emphasis upon grace and election. This problem was noticed by the Antinomians and recognized by the Puritans, who attempted to resolve the tension. Even if Mackinnon possesses little understanding of its origin, he is astute enough to discern the tension the doctrine of covenant brought to Reformed theology and its emphasis upon grace.

However, he overstates an otherwise valid point by accusing the Calvinists of rejecting predestination or abandoning *sola fides* for a salvation based on works. His contention might hold true for Baxter and a few others, but generally speaking the Calvinists did not make a wholesale substitution of one for the other. It is better to understand them as living with a tension between the covenant and *sola gratia*—a tension that was difficult to resolve. Sometimes the Calvinists would emphasize divine grace as the efficacious means of producing the federal conditions, other times they would invoke a Franciscan concept of God, who accepts our works above their true value (Strehle, *The Catholic Roots*, 60, 61). But neither solution returned them to the original vision of Luther and Calvin (i.e., a salvation that depended completely upon God and found no basis in us). They never abandoned hope in finding a solution or settled on one side or the other.

Mackinnon is also wrong when he proceeds to discard the entire thesis of Weber based on a few historical and theological problems. Weber is clearly on to something. He is pointing us in the right direction. He might not understand the doctrine of covenant, but he is right to search for a connection between Puritan ethics, theology, and the economic climate of the day. Cf. M. H. Mackinnon, "Part I: Calvinism and the infallible assurance of grace: the Weber thesis reconsidered," *The British Journal of Sociology* 39, no. 2 (June 1888): 144, 156-59, 164, 171; "Part II: Weber's exploration of Capitalism," *The British Journal of Sociology* 39, no. 2 (June 1988): 178, 184-86, 191, 192; "The Longevity Thesis," 250; Brocker, "Max Webers Erklärungsansatz," 509, 510.

90. For synergistic tendencies in Bullinger's thought, see Strehle, *The Catholic Roots*, 53-58.

91. Walzer, *The Revolution of the Saints*, 30, 31, 219-21, 227. Stephen Foster points to the "orders" of Dedham in 1585 as providing an early glimpse into Puritan discipline. The orders of this town would have needed "every available institution, civil and ecclesiastical [to] have been pressed into service." Foster, *The Long Argument*, 33, 37. The Massachusetts Bay Colony used the general court, grand juries, ecclesiastical synods, and local churches to enforce their own rigorous form of discipline against "blasphemy, cursing, prophane-swearing, lying, unlawful-gaming, Sabbath-breaking, idleness, drunkedness, uncleanness, and all the enticements and nurseries of such impieties." Mather, *Magnalia Christi Americana*, 2.317-31; Foster, *The Long Argument*, 276.

92. P. Miller, *The New England Mind: From Colony to Provinces* (Cambridge, MA: Harvard University Press, 1962) 408, 418, 419.

93. A. de Tocqueville, *Democracy in America* (New York: Alfred A. Knopf, 1963) 1.52, 297, 315; 2.3.

94. M. Butzer, *De Regno Christi* [*Buceri Opera Latina* (Paris, 1955) vol. 15] 2.48-52; Steele, *The Trades-man's Calling*, 19, 22, 77-95; Walzer, *The Revolution of the Saints*, 208, 209. Bucer's work was written in England and addressed to Edward VI, his royal pupil. In the year 1551 (the year of Bucer's death) Edward enacted many of the measures Bucer proposed in his work, whether under his direct influence or not. *Melanchthon and Bucer*, W. Pauck (ed.), in *The Library of Christian Classics* (Philadelphia: The Westminister Press, 1969) 171; Hill, *Society & Puritanism*, 272; *The World Turned Upside Down*, 264. The Dutch Calvinists also gained a reputation for their industry and all-business-like approach. Walzer, *The Revolution of the Saints*, 210.

95. *Staneley's Remedy, or the Way how to reform wandering Beggars, Theeves, Highway Robbers, and Pick-pockets* (London, 1646). See S. Hartlib, *Londons Charity Inlarged* (London: M. Symmons and R. Ibbitson, 1650); J. Dod , *A plaine and familiar exposition of the Ten Commandments* (London: W. Leybourn, 1662) 259, 277, 293; R. Sanderson, *XXXV Sermons* (London: T. Hodgkin, 1681) 87-97, 197-99; Hill, *Society and Puritanism*, 284-87.

96. Tawney, *Religion and the Rise of Capitalism*, 264-66; Viner, *Religious Thought and Economic Society*, 76. Calvin, Zwingli, Bullinger, and other Swiss theologians displayed a special contempt for mendacity and idleness. Tawney, *Religion and the Rise of Capitalism*, 114.

97. H. D. Thoreau, *Walden and Civil Disobedience*, M. Meyer (intro.) (New York: Penguin Books, 1986) 23, 28, 29, 47, 50, 51, 112, 113, 378.

98. M. Butzer, *De Regno Christi*, in *Martini Buceri Opera Latina*, F. Wendel (ed.), vol. 15 (Paris: Universitaires de France, 1954-) 2.50; Hill, *The English Bible*, 159, 160.

99. Walzer, *The Revolution of the Saints*, 252.

100. J. Dod and R. Cleaver, *A plaine and familiar exposition of the eighteenth, nineteenth and twentieth chapters of the Proverbs of Solomon* (London, 1690) 11.
101. *St. Paul the Tent-Maker* (London, 1690) 10-12; Hill, *Society & Puritanism*, 136, 140.
102. Perkins, *The Workes*, 1.754. See Mather, *Magnalia Christi Americana*, 2.263.
103. Ibid., 2.128 (D).
104. Steele, *The Trades-man's Calling*, 70, 84, 85.
105. Foster, *The Long Argument*, 116; "The Declaration of Sports" (Oct. 18, 1633), in *The Constitutional Documents of the Puritan Revolution 1625-1660*, S. R. Gardiner (ed.) (Oxford: Clarendon Press, 1968) 99-101; Weber, *The Protestant Ethic and the Spirit of Capitalism*, 166, 167, 274; Steele, *The Trades-man's Calling*, 85; F. Lambert, *The Founding Fathers and the Place of Religion in America* (Princeton, NJ: Princeton University Press, 2003) 39, 40.
106. Hill, *Society & Puritanism*, 189-93, 200-01. The original Book of Sports in 1618 invited a similar reaction.
107. *The Workes*, 1.767, 768; 2.125 (B); 3.217; Steele, *The Trades-man's Calling*, 177; R. M. Mitchell, *Calvin's and the Puritan's View of the Protestant Ethic* (Washington, D.C.: University Press of America, 1979) 62ff. These exhortations continued into the early eighteenth century. Cotton Mather's *Lex mercatoria* (1705) and Solomon Stoddard's *Cases of Conscience* (1722) contain stern warnings against those who seek unjust gain in the market place. M. Valeri, "Religion and the Culture of the Market in Early New England," in *Perspectives on American Religion and Culture*, P. W. Williams (ed.) (Oxford: Blackwell Publishers, 1999) 98, 99.
108. *The Journal of John Winthrop*, 102, 306-308, 342, 345; Mather, *Magnalia Christi Americana*, 2.326; V. D. Anderson, *New England's generation: The great migration and the formation of society and culture in the seventeenth century* (Cambridge: Cambridge University Press, 1991); Tawney, *Religion and the Rise of Capitalism*, 128- 30; Lambert, *The Founding Fathers*, 81.
109. R. Baxter, *A Christian Directory: Or, A Summ of Practical Theologie* (London: Robert White, 1673) 1.450 (chap. X, part 1, par. 24).
110. Weber, *The Protestant Ethic and the Spirit of Capitalism*, 1(e), 56-58; Tawney, *Religion* and *the Rise of Capitalism*, 89. Columbus said, "[He] who possesses [gold] has all that he needs in the world." See W. Raleigh, *The English Voyages of the Sixteenth Century* (Glasgow: Jackson, Wylie & Co., 1934) 16.
111. W. S. Hudson, "Puritanism and the Spirit of Capitalism," 8-10; Mitchell, *Calvin's and the Puritan's View*, 52, 53; Walzer, *The Revolution of the Saints*, 109. Cf. Weber, *The Protestant Ethic and the Spirit of Capitalism*, 2; "Anticritical Last Word," 1124; Brocker, "Max Webers Erklärungsansatz," 500.
112. K. Fullerton, "Calvinism and Capitalism," 20; W. S. Hudson, "Puritanism and the Spirit of Capitalism," 5; Tawney, *Religion and the Rise of Capitalism*, 248, 249; W. S. Hudson, "The Weber Thesis Reexamined," 63, 67.
113. Hill, *Society & Puritanism*, 129, 130.
114. Poggi, *Calvinism and the Capitalistic Spirit*, 41; C. H. and K. George, "English Protestantism and the Capitalist Spirit," in *Capitalism and the Reformation* (New York: Barnes & Noble, Inc., 1968) 12, 13; G. A. Abraham, "Misunderstanding the Merton Thesis," *ISIS* 74 (1983): 370.
115. Steele, *The Trades-man's Calling*, 33, 38-40.
116. A. Smith, *An Inquiry into the Nature and the Cause of the Wealth of Nations* (New York: The Modern Library, 1937) 320, 321.
117. Weber, "The Author defines his purpose," in *Protestantism and Capitalism*, 2; *The Protestant Ethic and the Spirit of Capitalism*, 25, 64, 67; Brocker, "Max Webers Erklärungsansatz," 495.

118. A. Milchman, "Weber on Capitalism, Socialism and Democracy," *Socialism and Democracy* 7 (1988): 99, 103-106, 110; V. Heins, "Weber's Ethic and the Spirit of Anti-Capitalism," *Political Studies* 41 (1993): 273, 274; Brocker, "Max Webers Erklärungsansatz," 498.
119. Mitchell, *Calvin's and the Puritan's View*, 20. The Church Fathers were against the practice. T. Wilson, *A Discourse upon Usury* [1572] (New York: Augustus M. Kelley, 1963) 217ff., 280-83; R. Bolton, *A Short and Private Discourse* (London: George Miller, 1637) 2-5.
120. Wilson, *A Discourse upon Usury*, 232, 283.
121. *Corpus iuris canonici* (Lipsiae: B. Tauchnitz, 1879-81) lib. v, tit. v, cap. i, ii; tit. xix, cap. i-iii; Tawney, *Religion and the Rise of Capitalism*, 46, 47.
122. Thomas Aquinas, *Summa Theologiae*, II/2, q. 78, a. 1, 2; T. P. McLaughlin, "The Teaching of the Canonists on Usury," *Medieval Studies I* (1939), 105ff.; Viner, *Religious Thought* and *Economic Society*, 89, 90, 96.
123. Hostensius, *Commentaria super quinque libros decretalium* (Venice, 1581) 5.16 (De usuries); J. T. Noonan, *The Scholastic Analysis of Usury* (Cambridge, MA: Harvard University Press, 1957) 118; S. Antonio, *Summa Moralis* (Verona, 1740) 2.1.7, xviii (101); B. Jarrett, *S. Antonio and Mediaeval Economics* (London: Manresa Press, 1914) 65.
124. Kitch, *Capitalism and the Reformation*, 118.
125. WA 6.466 (LW 44.213).
126. WA 53.477, 478, 482, 483, 521, 524ff. (LW 47.211, 217, 218, 266, 270ff.).
127. Kitch, *Capitalism and the Reformation*, 123.
128. R. Filmer, *Quaestio Quodlibetica; or a Discourse, whether it may be lawfull to take Use for Money (1653)*, in *The Usury Debate in the Seventeenth Century: Three Arguments* (New York: Arno Press, 1972) 111. See Wilson, *A Discourse upon Usury*, 170, 351, 352. Filmer also supplies a list of those who condemn it. "Melanchthon and Chemnitz are the most noted abroad; and here at home, Dr. Downam, now bishop of Londonderry in Ireland, Dr. Fenton, and learned Dr. Andrews, late bishop of Winchester." *Quaestio Quodlibetica*, 111. See Ibid., 58, 59; Kitch, *Capitalism and the Reformation*, 124, 125, 144.
129. Ibid., 10, 11, 58-66.
130. CO 10.246; 40.430 (CC 23.226). CC stands for Calvin's *Commentaries* (Edinburgh: Calvin Translation Society). Kitch, *Capitalism and the Reformation*, 70; Tawney, *Religion and the Rise of Capitalism*, 106. While Calvin and the Calvinists followed the OT more than other theologians of the church, they did not hold to the prohibition against usury in the Mosaic economy. See Mather, *Magnalia Christi Americana*, 2.259, 260.
131. CO 10.245, 246; 40.430-32 (CC 2.226-28).
132. CO 24.682, 683 (CC 5.132).
133. CO 10.247, 248.
134. CO 24.682 (CC 5.131).
135. CO 24.680, 682, 683 (CC 5.128, 130, 132).
136. CO 31.147, 148 (CC 8.212-14); 10.249.
137. CO 31.148 (CC 8.213, 214); 10.249.
138. CO 10.247, 248.
139. CO 24.680 (CC 5.126, 127); 10.248.
140. Wilson, *A Discourse on Usury*, 159-61.
141. Ibid., 246.
142. Ibid., 233.
143. Ibid., 236, 237.

144. Ibid., 249-51.
145. Ibid., 278, 279, 285, 321-25.
146. Ibid., 314ff., 319.
147. Ibid., 342, 350-52. The preacher recognizes the tolerance of Calvin and Bucer on the subject of usury, but he says they tolerate the practice only because of the hardness of the people. Ibid., 360.
148. Ibid., 224, 229, 360. Any lending for profit is evil. He asks for capital punishment as a just reward but will settle for the confiscation of all their goods. Ibid., 182, 183, 232.
149. Ibid., 363.
150. Ibid., 366, 367. Usury creates an idle, greedy, and covetous people. Ibid., 216, 220, 221, 226, 227, 231.
151. Ibid., 189-91, 205, 206.
152. Ibid., 374-81.
153. R. Fenton, *A Treatise of Usurie* [London: Felix Kyngston, 1612], in *The Usury Debate*, 2, 72, 73, 80, 90. Fenton complains about the vacillating policies of the government on the issue.
154. Ibid., The Epistle Dedicatorie, 10, 11, 58-66, 68, 151-54. He disputes their interpretation of Calvin and other divines. Of course, he assembles his own array of scholars from the Graeco-Roman word, church history, and the Reformation to refute the practice.
155. Ibid.,Preface, 7, 8. He provides a complete definition of Usury.

    Which increase and ouerplus comming for the loane, either of money, or any thing which passeth by number, weight or measure, if it come meerely for loane, without any other valuable consideration: and merely for that loane which passeth ouer the propertie, and with the propertie the perill and adventure of the principall: and if it come for this loane, not by way of gratuitie afterward freely giuen; nor in the name of satisfaction for damage suffered by the lender without his owne act and consent; but by former couenant and voluntarie contract betwixt the borrower and the lender: and if this couenant be for lucre and gaine, cleere gaine, valuable gaine, ratable at a certaine price, either in money or money worth; then is it that vsurie whereof the question moued is now to be disfcussed (Ibid., 30).

156. Ibid., 48.
157. Ibid., 40, 41.
158. Ibid., 38, 96-98.
159. Bolton, *A Short and Private Discourse*, 1, 4, 5, 32, 33. His opponent (M. S.) cites 18 divines in favor of usury. Bolton says there are 300 divines on the other side and disputes M. S.'s interpretation of certain divines like Iewell and Perkins. Ibid., 2-5, 70-75.
160. Ibid., 1, 6.
161. Ibid., 7, 8.
162. Ibid., 35.
163. Ibid., 37-44.
164. Ibid., 14-16.
165. W. Ames, *de conscientia et ejus JURE vel Casibus* (Oxonii: G. Hall, 1659) V, c.44, ix, x (401, 402).
166. Ibid., xv, xviii (403-404).
167. Ibid., v, vi (401).
168. Ibid., xi, xii (402).
169. Filmer, *Quaestio Quodlibetica*, 112.
170. Ibid., 134.

171. Ibid., 120.
172. Ibid., 120, 130. Ames equivocates on supply and demand economic theory. On the one hand, he rejects the philosophy of buy low and sell high, believing that public estimation is an important element in deciding a commodity's price. On the other hand, he says it is proper to establish prices based on whether the buyer is seeking the seller or vice versa. Ibid., c.43, i, v, viii-ix (397-99). Steele also finds difficulty in establishing a just price. He says that the Golden Rule is the basic law, but the market price should be considered. *The Trades-man's Calling*, 108, 109.
173. Viner, *Religious Thought and Economic Society*, 135-39.
174. P. Nicole, *Essais de Morale*, L. Thirouin (ed.) (Paris: Presses Universitaires de France, 1999) 213, 384, 403, 404.
175. Ibid., 381, 401-403.
176. Ibid., 390, 391, 395, 402, 403, 408, 409. Nicole says that self-interest engages us in the same activity as charity. Self-interest makes us act in a moral and civil way for our own benefit; otherwise, society would look down upon our conduct. Domat says that self-interest promotes unity and prosperity in society. Avarice is the engine that fuels the greater part of commerce. It seems to destroy nature *prima facie*, but it actually preserves society in the end as divine providence brings the good out the bad. *Oeuvres Complètes de J. Domat* (Paris: Alex-Gobelet, Libraire: 1835) 1.25, 26; 4.96. Of course, the same argument is found in Adam Smith. He believes that the self-serving interests of supply and demand set market prices. One who works through self-interest actually works for the common good through an "invisible hand." *The Wealth of Nations*, 14, 56, 423.
177. T. Cooper, *Fear and Polemic in the Seventeenth-Century: Richard Baxter and Antinomianism* (Aldershot: Ashgate, 2001) 1, 10; N. H. Keeble, *Richard Baxter: Puritan Man of Letters* (Oxford: Clarendon Press, 1982) 18.
178. Weber, *The Protestant Ethic and the Spirit of Capitalism*, 156; R. Baxter, *The Saints' Everlasting Rest*, J. T. Wilkinson (ed.) (London: The Epworth Press, 1962) 12. The work reached twelve editions by the time of Baxter's death in 1691.
179. Tawney, *Religion and the Rise of Capitalism*, 220; Baxter, *The Saints' Everlasting Rest*, 78-80.
180. R. Baxter, *Directions for Weak, Distempered Christians*, in *The Practical Works of the Rev. Richard Baxter* (London: James Duncan, 1830) 8.337-38; *Catholic Unity* (London: R. W., 1660) 332; *Reliquiae Baxterianae*, M. Sylvester (London, 1696) 2.198; *The Saints' Everlasting Rest*, 25, 29, 72; T. R. Cooke, "Uncommon Earnestness and Earthly Toils: Moderate Puritan Richard Baxter's Devotional Writings," *Anglican and Episcopal History* 62, no. 1 (1994): 57.
181. Baxter, *A Christian Directory*, 1.58, 128, 274-93, 448.
182. Baxter, *Dying-Thoughts*, in *Practical Works*, 18. 408, 409.
183. Baxter, *A Christian Directory*, 1.275.
184. Baxter, *Poetical Fragments* (London: T. Snowden, 1681) 40.
185. This is the message of his greatest work, *Saints' Everlasting Rest* (1650). Heb. 4:9 is the key verse: "There remains a rest for the people of God."
186. Baxter, *A Christian Directory*, 1.108ff., 288, 451-60; K. Fullerton, "Calvinism and Capitalism," 16, 17.
187. Ibid., 1.65, 134, 143, 147, 461-65.
188. Ibid., 1.632.
189. Ibid., 1.448-50.
190. Ibid., 1.131; 4.147.
191. Ibid., 1.132, 133, 447-49; W. Hudson, "Puritanism and the Spirit of Capitalism," in *Protestantism and Capitalism*, 59, 60.

192. Ibid., 120, 121, 146, 147. In a later work, *The New Whole Duty of Man*, the businessman is allowed to strike a hard bargain. [R. Allestree], *The New Whole Duty of Man* ([London]: E. Wicksteed, 1744) 266, 267 (Sermon XI).
193. Ibid., 1. 125ff.; Tawney, *Religion and the Rise of Capitalism*, 221-23.
194. R. Baxter, *Aphorismes of Justification* (Hague: Abraham Brown, 1655) 4.
195. Ibid., 8.
196. Ibid., 59, 60, 70, 82, 83; *The Right Method for a Settled Peace of Conscience and Spiritual Comfort*, in *The Practical Works*, 9: 57, 58, 151; *The Saints' Everlasting Rest*, 30, 35, 37, 54, 86; H. Boersma, *A Hot Pepper Corn: Richard Baxter's Doctrine of Justification in Its Seventeenth-Century Context of Controversy* (Zoetermeer: Uitgeverij Boekencentrum, 1993) 196, 197; Baxter, *Universal Redemption of Mankind* (London, 1694) 31, 32. Baxter's understanding of Christ's death has a couple of eccentricities worth noting. One, he thinks of the death of Christ as satisfying only the violations committed under the covenant of works, but it does not atone for the non-performance of the New Covenant's conditions. Two, Christ did not satisfy the exact penalty threatened by the law. Baxter conceives of Christ's work in the manner of Anselm as an equivalent payment (*tantundem*) for our debt. Three, he mentions Grotius' *Defensio Fidei Satisfactione Christi* and follows his voluntaristic concept of God, who can "relax" the punishment exacted by the law. Baxter, *Aphorismes of Justification*, 25-28, 103-105.
197. Ibid., 84, 147, 148.
198. Ibid., 147-52, 171, 173, 186, 187, 193; *The Right Method for a Settled Peace*, 9.45, 62, 63.
199. Ibid., 163; *The Right Method for a Settled Peace*, 9.46; Boersma, *A Hot Pepper Corn*, 169.
200. *The Saints' Everlating Rest*, 78, 79; *The Right Method for a Settled Peace*, 9.xvii; T. Cooper, *Fear and Polemic*, 71, 72, 81, 82, 141-43; Boersma, *A Hot Pepper Corn*, 27, 28. His rhetoric was caustic at times and often created caricatures of opponents' more nuanced positions. Of course, he himself was too eclectic to be stereotyped in any way. He disliked unbalanced factions or revolutionary groups like the Levellers and Antinomians. His penchant was to view himself as a moderate and sensible fellow, not given over to revolutionary acts of extremism. He taught submission to the civil magistrate and national church.
201. J. Cameron, *Ta Sozomena siue opera partim ab auctor ipso edita* (Genevae: I. Chouët, 1642) 389, 529, 531, 534; *De Triplici Dei cum Homine Foedere*, II-IV, VIII, LXXXIII; M. Amyraut, *Brief Traité de la Predestination avec L'Eschantillon de la doctrine de Calvin sur les mesme suiet* (Saumur: Ches Isaac Desbordes, 1658) 66, 68, 70, 75, 76, 104; *L'Eschanillon*, 206-209; *Specimen animadversionum in exercitationes de gratia universali* (Saumur: J. Lesnier, 1648) 20 (spec.), 313-14 (gen.), 472-73. Baxter expresses appreciation for Cameron and Amyault at certain junctures, but he also denies at other times that he is a devoted disciple. Boersma, *A Hot Pepper Corn*, 26, 198-200; Keeble, *Richard Baxter*, 26, 27, 42, 194 (fn. 67, 68).
202. Baxter, *An End of Doctrinal Controversies* (London, 1691) 296, 297. Cf. Bonaventura, *Sent.*, II, d.29, a.1, q.2 [in *Opera Omnia*, 10 tomi (Ad Claras Aquas (Quaracchi): Ex typ. Collegii S. Bonaventurae), 1882-1902]; G. Biel, *Collectorium circa quattuor libros sententiarum* (Tübingen: Mohr, 1973-77) II, d.27, q.1; J. Heideggerus, *Corpus Theologicae Christianae* (Tiguri: David Gressner, 1700) I, ix, 57, 67, 68; F. Burmannus, *Synopseos Theologiae* [Trajecti ad Rhenum (Utrecht): C. J. Neonart 1672] II, ii, 20, 21; F. Turrettini, *Institutio Theologiae Elencticae* (Genevae, 1688) VIII, q.3, i, ii, xvi, xvii. Baxter shows a specific knowledge of this Franciscan/Reformed argument. *Aphorismes of Justification*, 89-91.

203. Baxter, *Aphorismes of Justification*, 83, 84, 99, 100; Boersma, *A Hot Pepper Corn*, 184, 185, 284, 289, 327.
204. Ibid., 6, 7, 49, 75.
205. Ibid., 93; Cooper, *Fear and Polemic*, 75, 76. Baxter denies he's an Arminian. He never makes a definite leap or creates sufficiently explicit statements to warrant the label, but his sympathies appear to gravitate in that direction. *Reliquiae Baxterianae*, 1.107; *Confutation of a Disseration for the Justification of Infidels* (London: R. W., 1654) 201; *Penitent Confession and his Necessary Vindication* (London, 1691) 24; M. L. Wiley, *The Subtle Knot: Creative Scepticism in the Seventeenth-Century England* (Cambridge, MA: Harvard University Press, 1952) 162, 163. Baxter thinks of common grace as a means of preparation and makes no qualitative distinction between its efficacy and that of special grace, even entertaining the possibility of non-Christians in nature finding salvation much like the Amyraldians. Boersma, *A Hot Pepper Corn*, 193, 194, 355.
206. Cooper, *Fear and Polemic*, 195; Keeble, *Richard Baxter*, 69ff. He repeats the rumor from New England that Anne Hutchinson, the infamous Antinomian, gave birth to monsters. J. Hall, *The Antinomian Controversy, 1636-38: a documentary history* (Durham, NC: Duke University Press, 1990) 280ff.; Cooper, *Fear and Polemic*, 203.
207. Ibid., 115, 135, 154, 165.
208. Baxter, *Aphorismes of Justification*, 208; *The Saints' Everlasting Rest*, 2; Cooper, *Fear and Polemic*, 2, 66, 67, 71. Cotton Mather in his *Magnalia Christi Americana* writes the same kind of hagiography about the leaders and divines of his community that Catholics write about their saints. Mather's work represents much the opposite of Luther's famous exhortation to "sin boldly."
209. William Eyre, curate of St. Thomasis, Salisbury, stated that his teaching should not be compared to the "antinomianism" of Agricola and his followers. *Vindiciae Justificationis Gratuitae* (London: J. Vousden, 1695) 28, 29. John Saltmarsh and Tobias Crisp serve as the two most prominent "antinomians" and foils in Baxter's work. Cooper, *Fear and Polemic*, 16, 22-27. Janice Knight tries to divide New England into two polemical camps: those following the preparationist side of Perkins-Ames-Winthrop and those following the antinomian side of Preston-Sibbes-Cotton. *Orthodoxies in Massacutsetts*, 4, 5, 9, 19, 29-31. She is correct in pointing out the tensions within Puritan theology and the challenge of the Antinomianism to the prevailing orthodoxy, but she is wrong in trying to divide the camps into such neat compartments. For example, Perkins can hold to the Scotist/Bezan scheme of supralapsarianism and predestination, while speaking of the relationship between God and his people in terms of a bilateral covenant. *Workes*, 1.11-16, 32, 70, 576. Perhaps the Antinomians recognize the tension more than others and try to reduce the synergistic element, but many of the Calvinists can live with arresting contradictions in their work.
210. J. Eaton, *The Honey-Combe of Free Justification by Christ alone* (Lancaster, 1642) 25, 26, 115, 206, 207, 372, 386, 468; *Abrahams Stepps by Faith* (London, 1642)] preface, 47, 135, 149, 172ff.; J. Cotton, *A Treatise of the Covenant of Grace* (London, 1671) 39-46, 49, 53, 84, 139, 149, 150, 218-20; *The New Covenant* (London, 1654) 130, 131; N. Graebner, "Protestant Dissenters: An Examination of the Seventeenth-Century Eatonists and New England Controversies in Reformation Perspectives" (PhD diss., Duke University, 1984) 164, 165, 207, 208; Hall, *The Antinomian Controversy*, 57, 58, 119.
211. J. Agricola, *In Evangelium Lucae Annotationes* (Norembergae: I. Petreium, 1525) praefatio; S. Kjeldgaard-Pedersen, *Gesetz, Evangelium and Busse* (Leiden: E. J. Brill, 1983) 94, 112, 113,133,185, 205, 223-25.

212. Baxter, *Aphorismes of Justification*, 60, 109, 114, 125, 130; *The Reduction of a Digressor* (London, 1654) 13; Boersma, *A Hot Pepper Corn*, 72, 73, 122, 123.
213. Baxter, *The Right Method for a Settled Conscience*, 9.52, 53.
214. Ibid., passim; *The Mischiefs of Self-Ignorance, and Benefits of Self-Acquaintance*, in *The Practical Work*, 16.124, 125; *The Saints' Everlasting Rest*, 108, 113, 118; Keeble, *Richard Baxter*, 133, 139; Boersma, *A Hot Pepper Corn*, 164.
215. Baxter, *The Saints' Everlasting Rest* (London, 1659) 729.
216. Keeble, *Richard Baxter*, 138-43.
217. Baxter is familiar with the practical syllogism. *The Right Method for a Settled Peace*, 9.113.

6

Manifest Destiny: The March toward the Future

There is no idea that proved more powerful in shaping the hopes and dreams of Western civilization than its belief in progress. The culture developed its policies and plans around idealistic visions and optimistic expectations of what is possible in the future. This perspective developed at first during the time of the Reformation and found its most potent representative within the Puritan community and the spirit of capitalism—a point that Weber neglects or fails to appreciate in his treatment. The Puritans reflected the spirit of capitalism not merely through hard work or worldly asceticism—the hallmarks of Weber's treatment—but also through their willingness to surrender present day security, take risks, and create something new and better in the future. They believed that change was good, the future was good, and they possessed a manifest destiny before God to bring all good things to pass. They were part of a historical process that would culminate in the dawning of the Kingdom of God. For this reason they braved tempestuous seas to settle as pioneers in a frontier wilderness filled with danger and uncertainty. They hoped to build a "City on a Hill" that would reflect the future Kingdom and prepare all of humankind for its coming.

Before the Reformation the future did not burn so bright. History was foreign to Graeco-Roman thought. Eternity was found outside of time in the form of immutable and impassible truth. Its philosophical schools tried to sell tranquility in the midst of the throes and vicissitudes of a miserable life, which no one could control (Stoics) or find meaning outside of its temporary pleasures (Epicureans). Its pessimism continued on into the Christian era with the church following the same basic understanding of time and eternity throughout much of its history. The early church and its premillennial eschatology looked for a Savior to descend from the clouds of heaven and rescue a remnant of his elect from a world that was waxing worse and worse. This interpretation prevailed among the Church Fathers until the third century when the Alexandrian school of the catechists began to discount a literal interpretation of Rev. 20 and other relevant texts, and so reject the early millennial hope. They preferred a more Hellenistic or allegorical method of interpretation, which so negated the material level that it denied the simple hope of Christ saving the world through a cataclysm. In this manner, the church began to reject the notion of a literal millennium in history and any literal hope for the world to change in a positive way or become more of what God expected, even if it took a cataclysm. Christians became pilgrims in this world, awaiting a final judgment that would separate a *civitas dei* from the *civitas terrena*. The church possessed no specific mission to reconcile the two cities or work to create a universal condition of peace on earth. This business was left to the judgment seat of Christ, who would bring all things to light and divide between the wheat and tares on that day. In the meantime, the two must grow together and evil must remain a fact of life.

Two Churches

The beginning of the Reformation saw a fundamental change in the perception of the church. The schism of those days created a rivalry between Catholics and Protestants over the true nature of the church and each one's claim to attend a fellowship that preached the Word and administered the visible means of grace in accordance with Scripture. Luther started the rancor between the fellowships by identifying the papacy and its church with the Antichrist of biblical prophecy, the very incarnation of the devil on earth. In his *Prefaces to the New Testament*, beginning in 1530, he matches historical events with prophecies in the book of Revelation and identifies the seventh angel or beast of chapter thirteen with the papacy and its attempt to wield spiritual and temporal power[1]—Hildebrand being the first pope to usurp this power in his struggles with Henry IV.[2] Thereafter, the pope and his church are portrayed in the darkest of terms, as responsible for unleashing a horrid persecution of God's people in these latter days, causing a schism between the fellowships, and creating an epic battle over the position of each church in society.

In England the reformers saw their mission in terms of destroying the kingdom of the Antichrist and establishing the Kingdom of God in its place. John Bale's *Image of Both Churches* (1541-47) depicts history as a struggle between the church of Christ and the church of the Antichrist. The Church of England was started by Joseph of Arimathea in apostolic times, but later was corrupted through the Church of Rome when Gregory I sent St. Augustine of Canterbury in 597 to the British Isles. Bale finds the current state of the church intolerable and hopes the Reformation will bring an end to the power of Rome and restore the true apostolic church once more. His basic understanding was shared by many works in the subsequent era;[3] *The Geneva Bible* (1560), John Foxe's *Actes and Monuments* (1563), and Thomas Brightman's *Apocalypsis Apocalypseos* (1616) were among the more influential. These later works tended to exalt the unique role of England in the struggle between the two realms and the reign of Elizabeth I as a turning point in its history.

John Foxe provided the most celebrated account of this conception of the church and its history. He was a friend of Bale, a fellow exile during the times of Mary Tudor, and applied his immense scholastic talents to developing the basic scheme of his friend into a fully articulated history. His work provoked considerable debate and was so popular among the people that Bishops ordered copies placed in churches throughout England, often chained to lecterns so the people would have access to its revelations. It went through no less than nine editions and several abridgments before the advent of the Puritan Revolution.[4] The work found a large audience because it dispensed with the typical hagiography of previous accounts and revealed for the first time in a "full and complete history" the atrocities of the papal church.[5] Foxe discussed in great detail how the church abandoned its original humility during the apostolic age and started to venerate the power of the world a thousand years after its inception. At the time of the first millennium, the papacy made a pact with the devil through the likes of Silvester II, Gregory VII (Hildebrand), and Innocent III. Faith and liberty waned, and corruption, bribery, graft, simony, and violence became the hallmarks of the papal church.[6] No light seemed visible during the dark ages that proceeded. The church appeared to lose its candlestick and represent much the opposite of its original mission of grace and truth. All seemed lost and would have deserved complete annihilation if not for a "rennaunt" of true believers, who still served God "within the Ark of his spirituall, and visible church," barely visible to the naked eye. Even in the midst of the dark ages, the Lord preserved a remnant of people who suffered intense persecution because of their "heresies." The persecution encompassed a multitude of true believers, who are mentioned throughout the book, and included such notable "heretics" as Berengar of Tours, Joachim, Waldenses, Albigenses, William Ockham, Dante, John Tauler, John Wyclif, Lorenzo Valla, John Hus, Jerome of Prague, and countless others.[7]

The history of England and its struggles with the papacy are given special attention by Foxe as the locus of his particular interest and focus of divine activity in these latter days. The Church of England is understood in terms of an apostolic origin, which Foxe wishes to emphasize against the claims of Catholic supremacy. To establish this point he repeats the story that Joseph of Arimathea was sent "by Phillip the Apostle, from France to Britain, about the year of our Lord 63." He admits that other testimonies cast some doubts upon the complete veracity and exact details of the story, but even so, the origin of the Anglican Church came well before the time of Augustine and cannot be accredited to the missionary activities of Rome.[8] He goes on to divide its history into a five-fold rhythm, consisting of periods that are roughly 300 years in length and terminate in a final epoch that began around 1360.[9] This last period is associated with the ministry of John Wyclif, whom God raised up to rescue the church from centuries of papal darkness.[10] The hope of renewal represents an ongoing mission of God's people in these latter days and includes the policies of magistrates as an essential part of the equation. Foxe hopes to extend the mission to all segments of society and is intrigued with the current prospects under Elizabeth as providing a real chance for reformation, especially after years of exile and martyrdom under "Bloody Mary." Elizabeth is extolled as a godly and virtuous queen, who sustained considerable persecution from her sister and refused to retaliate with the shedding of Catholic blood. Foxe hopes that Elizabeth will accept his work, just as Constantine accepted Eusebius' martyria long ago, and continue her policy of restraint in the use of the sword against the papists and other groups out of power.[11]

Brightman's commentary on Revelation also served as a prophetic justification for the future place of Britain in the grand scheme of things. It went through several English editions during the time of the Revolution and served along with Joseph Mede's later commentary as the best-known scholarly interpretations of the text.[12] Abridgments of the work were provided for popular consumption and proved invaluable in disseminating the message to a larger audience. It was typical of these shorter versions to highlight Brightman's mystical use of the seven churches in Rev. 2 and 3 as "counterpaynes" throughout history. These churches are said to represent "the universal condition of the church" as it develops at various times and places in history.[13] Laodicea, the last of these churches, receives special attention because it serves as a type of the Anglican Church, which is now vacillating in a lukewarm state between the Reformation and Rome. Brightman wants the church to become "fully Reformed" like

Philadelphia (or its present day "counterpayne" in Switzerland, France, Holland, and Scotland).[14] This reform is crucial because of England's special place in the future plans of God.[15] The last trumpet of Revelation blew at the beginning of Elizabeth's reign when she liberated the whole British Isles from the tyranny of the Antichrist. Her reign is exalted as a prototype of the eternal kingdom to come and serves as an example for us today.[16] Brightman hopes that his beloved church will continue the struggle for reform and defeat the forces of wickedness that remain in the land. He wants to end the doubt of those who vacillate between opinions and determine once and for all that "the Pope of Rome is the Antichrist," his basic purpose in writing the book.[17]

Brightman also tries to encourage reform by showing its necessary, ultimate, and imminent fulfillment in the next few years. He creates a fixed chronology and timetable of apocalyptic events to show that the time is at hand. Before 1650 his predictions call for the destruction of Rome and the conversion of the Jews to their Messiah.[18] In 1686, he expects the Antichrist to be destroyed, along with Gog and Magog (the Turks) a decade later.[19] Around the year 1696, all enemies are abolished and the Kingdom of Christ will come to earth, even though he expresses some doubt about setting an exact time for this last event.[20] Overall his chronology contains four basic periods of history—the time of John the Apostle to Constantine, the reign of Constantine to 1300, 1300 to an uncertain time in the future, and then the reign of Christ in his Kingdom, which he interprets as earthly and Jewish in nature.[21] This last period is contrasted with the final state of heavenly bliss that awaits the people of God. The final state of heaven awaits those who resisted the mark of the beast throughout history and joined the true remnant of God's people in reforming the church.

The two-church model and the need for reformation served as the basic impetus behind the Puritan's immigration to America.[22] These people certainly did not come to this country for economic, material, or secular reasons. They despised the Virginia plantation with its emphasis upon turning a profit and criticized it for neglecting weightier, spiritual considerations.[23] John Winthrop summoned his people to leave their comfortable lives behind them, suffer great hardship, and settle in an unknown wilderness—all for the sake of building the kingdom of God on earth and laying up treasures in heaven.[24] His motivation was purely religious. He wanted to preserve the church from those who wished to destroy it in England.[25] He saw what the papal church had done to other churches—the Waldenses, the Albigenses, the Huguenots, the Palatinates, and other churches in Europe that loved liberty but waited too long for reform.[26] It is better for the true church to flee into the Wilderness, following the example of the woman in Rev. 12, and find refuge for the time being than wait for the Dragon and the Antichrist to destroy it, just like they had done in the past.[27] Later on the Puritans can return and help the mother church reform her ways,[28] but safety and preservation are a priority in the present circumstance. (Winthrop clearly sees that the situation has deteriorated in England with Charles I dismissing Parliament in 1629, and his immigration will continue until Parliament and Puritan power are restored a decade later.)[29]

His immediate solution is found in the necessity of fleeing persecution and living elsewhere, but he has no desire to withdraw from the world or give up the prospect of reforming society as a whole. He understands his complete commission to include the reformation of the entire world, even if he is willing to abide by the realities of life and wait patiently for the right time. His designs while living in the wilderness include the creation of a society out of religious principles, which will shine as a beacon of light to the entire world.[30] He suffers no pangs of conscience in crowding the Native Americans, since there is plenty of space in this vast wilderness for him to build his experiment. The natives still have a natural right to use the land, even if they possess no exclusive entitlement to own it as property since they do not improve the land through their own labor or even possess a deed.[31] Moreover, the church needs the land to expand its mission, and the conversion of the natives is a part of that mission.[32] Winthrop is concerned that Catholic colonies already are winning the battle for the soul of the New World, and the true church needs to gain ground.[33]

Millenarianism

The Reformation brought the hope among many of its followers that the church and the world could change for the better, that the destruction of the Antichrist was imminent, that a godly kingdom would dawn in the near future and take the place of the forces of evil here on earth.[34] Puritans were among the people most intrigued by the prospects. They were not content with remaining in isolation and restoring a NT church or Anabaptist-type fellowship where they could enjoy personal piety separate from the world at large. They wanted to erect a kingdom of God on earth. They wanted to ameliorate all social ills. They looked for the redemption of all things and developed millennial expectations, which dreamed of a "Great Instauration" or renewal of the entire world.[35]

They thought of God as working with them, bringing about a new day, and advancing the cause of the divine Kingdom through the "progress of providence."[36] Their view of the future was bright and filled with the hope and expectation that God would fulfill what was promised of old and bring about the redemption of all things.

Early in the seventeenth century we find millenarian expectations running high among the Puritans. In September of 1645, Robert Baillie wrote home to his native Scotland and described the majority of the "divines" in the city of London as "Chiliasts."[37] In 1649, Hugo Grotius heard that England was awash with millenarian expectation and reported that some eighty tracts and treatises existed on the subject.[38] Their precise content varied, but all considered the end of the world as imminent and many followed Brightman's chronology believing the consummation would transpire in the 1690s.[39] A typical account of the times was *A Glimpse of Sion's Glory,* published in 1641. It sees the vials of the Apocalypse that were poured out upon Babylon as a contemporary event fulfilled in the destruction of Rome and its hierarchical system of government.[40] It depicts the common people as bringing this judgment to pass and preparing the way for the coming of the divine Kingdom.[41] The four kingdoms of Daniel's prophecies are giving way to a fifth kingdom, where Christ will reign with his saints on earth for a thousand years.[42] Following the prophecies in chapter 12, along with Brightman's analysis of them, the "abomination of desolation" should transpire in 1650, and all should come to a head forty-five years later in 1695 with the coming of the Kingdom of God.[43] These mysteries are being revealed to the saints of God in the latter days, just as Daniel predicted (12:4).[44]

Joseph Mede, the famous NT scholar at Cambridge, helped revive these expectations with the publication of *Clavis Apocalyptica* in 1627 (Eng. *The Key of the Revelation*—1643). William Twisse lauds the work in the preface as surpassing all others in fulfilling the prophecy of Dan. 12:4, although he expects others to exceed its insights in the years to come. Mede follows the course of the day by returning to the early church's belief in a literal millennium, but he offers some criticism of Brightman's analysis. He excludes the setting of a specific timetable from his account, and, instead of looking for a sudden cataclysm to change the course of events, he sees history ascending in an upward spiral several centuries before the Reformation and culminating in the millennium, the last epoch of world history. He interprets history in an evolutionary manner and speaks of the progressive binding of Satan and the advance of the Protestant cause. The gradual defeat of evil is symbolized in the book of Revelation by the outpouring of the seven vials of divine wrath upon the beast of Rome. The first four are interpreted in a historical manner as representing the work of the Albigensians and Waldensians, Luther and the Reformers, the anti-Catholic laws of Elizabeth, and the Thirty Years' War. The last three include the future destruction of Rome and Turkey and culminate in the final judgment of the Antichrist and his kingdom.[45]

These millenarian expectations reached a fervent pitch during the turbulent days of the Puritan Revolution. Stephen Marshall preached a sermon before the House of Commons on June 15, 1643, in which he exhorted that body of saints to fulfill the prophecy of Revelation and join Christ in ending the reign of the Antichrist.[46] Many thought the world was coming to an end and looked to Cromwell when he arose in power to fulfill the prophecy and destroy the pope, the Turks, and the forces of evil.[47] This expectation resonated in the thoughts and actions of the time and found its most zealous disciples a few years later in the men of the "Fifth Monarchy," who sought to establish the Kingdom of God through more coercive measures. This movement grew in popularity during the Rump Parliament and helped Cromwell to remove that unpopular assembly from power. Cromwell adopted much of the movement's rhetoric and theological perspective, although he found it necessary to pursue a more moderate course of order and stability as the protector.[48] Thomas Goodwin, the leader of the Independent Party, echoed the theology of those days in his *Sermon of the Fifth Monarchy* (1654). He provided their basic theological justification from Rev. 5:9, 10, which spoke of Christ exalting his people to reign on earth as a fruit of his royal office.[49] This union will find its ultimate fulfillment in a literal millennium when the saints are placed as kings over all the nations of the world.[50] In the meantime, the work of Christ and his saints is found in paving the way for the millennial kingdom by waging war against the last remnants of the Roman Empire centered in Rome and Turkey. Once these forces of evil are destroyed the saints will reign in the fifth and final kingdom of Daniel's prophecies, from which the movement derived its name.[51]

Millenarian expectations were brought to America by the Puritans and proceeded to permeate the soul of the country in the centuries to come. Tocqueville characterized the spirit of America, right from its early days, as filled with inexhaustible, futuristic energy and dedicated to a belief in its special role among the nations in bringing about a new age.[52] This spirit was a product of Puritan ideology, which thought of its people as the New Israel, chosen among the nations to lead the march of history into the millennium.[53] Even if there was some latitude in interpretation—some conceiving of the millennium as the latter-day glory of the church, while others believing in the personal reign of Christ—all tended to think that the dawning of the kingdom was imminent and the future of the world and America's place in it was bright.[54] Antebellum America was filled with an impressive array of scholars and theologians who espoused and promulgated these expectations: Michael Wigglesworth, Increase Mather, Samuel Willard, Samuel Sewall, Cotton Mather, Jonathan Edwards, Joseph Bellamy, Jonathan Mayhew, Samuel Hopkins, Joseph Priestly, Timothy Dwight, Alexander Campbell, Horace Bushnell, Josiah Strong, and so many more.[55]

Cotton Mather serves as one of the most eloquent and ardent spokesmen for the imminent, premillennial return of Christ, which, he claims, permeated the Puritan colony of his day.[56] The millenarian expectation, beginning with a couple of sermons in 1691, finds an important place in his ministry, serving as a constant source of inspiration in spurring his people on to greater things.[57] He tells them that the time is at hand, and they must prepare themselves through days of fasting and prayer.[58] He expresses some hesitation over setting an exact date, but this caveat does not prevent him from providing some indication of its immediate advent and urging the people to work hard in light of what is coming around the corner. He thinks it probable that Christ will return during his generation.[59] Godly men of old like Moses and Daniel knew they were living in a time when God would visit the people, so Mather finds no problem with discerning the signs of the times and offering his own wisdom on the subject.[60] Mather predicts that his generation will witness the destruction of Rome, the conversion of the Jews, and the coming of the divine Kingdom,[61] in which Christ will come in person and reign with his saints for a thousand years.[62] He rejects those who are "too Bold in their Suppositions,"[63] but is willing to venture a tentative calculation, assigning the year 1697 as a probable date of interest.[64] Later, when the year passes without a sign from the heavens, Mather remains undeterred and looks to other possible dates in the future such as 1716 and 1735/36.[65] The risky business of setting dates and preaching imminent expectations finds its purpose in stimulating the people to prepare and work with all diligence for the Kingdom of God, knowing that the time is short.

Early millenarian eschatology also contained elements of a progressive, American-centered spirit, which would maturate over time to encompass the nation as a whole. The best example of this optimistic eschatology is found in the writings of Jonathan Edwards, the greatest of all American-born theologians. His account is perhaps less ethnocentric than that of the nation today, but he still thinks of America as playing a vital role within the present and future plans of God.[66] Edwards understands the light of the gospel and the advancement of the arts and sciences as following the motion of the Sun in its course from east to west, like many divines during his time. The truth of God started in the east, proceeded to Continental Europe and England, and then crossed the Atlantic Ocean to America. It will continue in its procession west until it completes its course, but for now its manifest destiny is found in conquering the New World.[67] All along the way he observes progress in Christianity, theology, and general learning, and rejects in the strongest terms the notion of certain Christians, Jews, and Pagans that the world is decaying. Christianity "hath had already its different Steps, Measures and Gradations . . . [and] shall be improved by succession of Time" to a "greater Height and Perfection than it is at present."[68] Learning has accompanied the growth of Christianity and shown the same general advancement in all areas of knowledge—science, arts, humanities, and religion.[69] Edwards illustrates this progress by pointing to advances in navigation, weaponry, printing, agriculture, anatomy, astronomy, chemistry, physics, et al. He believes that science will greatly expand and improve our lives in the future as we approach the millennium;[70] and the time is close at hand. "The time is approaching when this Millennary State shall commence, when there shall be greater progress of the Gospel than ever yet hath been, when the church shall be wonderfully Advanced, and Christianity shall arrive to its Maturity and perfection."[71] He takes the biblical reference to "one thousand years" in the literal manner, although he rejects the contention of premillennialists that Christ will reign in person during this time.[72] The millennium is not a final state of absolute perfection, but it will merge the church and state into a peaceable kingdom through the work of virtuous rulers, who are devoted to the King of Kings.[73]

Perhaps no group came to symbolize the American spirit more than the Church of Jesus Christ of Latter-day Saints or the Mormons. In the course of their history, they became the most right-wing, patriotic apologists of the American way—at least when compared with the other major denominations or sects in the country.[74] Mormons came to think of America as the promised land and its Constitution a work of divine inspiration. Their own sacred text created a history of America, in which certain Hebrew families were directed by God to set sail for the New World and populate that region as if entering the Promised Land. Christ even made a personal appearance there, revealing himself to his "other sheep" after he rose from the dead. Their vision of the future understands America as the land chosen for the gathering of the Lost Tribes of Israel, the building of the New Zion, and the coming of the Millennial Kingdom. These events experienced partial fulfillment in the history of the Mormon Church, but the future contains even greater expectations and those expectations find their ultimate fulfillment within a distinctly American dream. For the Mormons, America is a special place where God manifests the truth of the gospel and fulfills the prophecies of old in the past, present, and future. These millennial expectations might sound extreme, but they are not unusual. They represent a development of an American eschatology that captivated the main line denominations and its theologians two centuries before Joseph Smith and remain a vital force in the nation today.

Modern Science

Eschatology played a significant role in developing the ideology of the modern world—at least as much as the soteriology that Weber finds so necessary to emphasize. The concept of the millennium spurred the Puritans to believe that progress was possible, that the future was filled with promise, that their energies could make a real difference in ameliorating the fallen condition of this world. The favorite verse was Dan. 12:4, which speaks of the latter days and predicts "many shall run to and fro and knowledge shall increase" (KJV). The Puritans interpreted the prophecy as finding fulfillment in their lifetime through the growth of navigation and the advance of knowledge.[75] This growth was observed and measured in a substantive way through the realm of science, helping to spur its increasing popularity in the seventeenth century. Puritans believed that the next few centuries would witness a special fulfillment of Daniel's prophecy in this area, showing advances that would match the previous millennia in chemistry, biology, physics, and other studies of nature all together.[76]

Of course, this view of Puritanism clashes with a popular notion of science that considers its objective procedures hostile to the influence of religious bias. Many people think of religion and science as opposing forces and point to the conflict between Galileo and the pope or Darwin and the Fundamentalists as a good reason why these realms must remain distinct. But science never lives in an autonomous realm, disseminating objective or dispassionate truth apart from a value system that promotes its interests and skews its results. Thomas Kuhn makes this point as well as anyone in his *Structure of the Scientific Revolution* by displaying the significant role tradition serves in producing scientific theories and interpreting experimental results. In denying scientific objectivity, he disparages any notion of linear progress in the discipline. Science makes no progress beyond the biases of a current paradigm declaring victory and mentioning history in a distorted way as if leading to its "breakthrough."[77] But even if this criticism is harsh, it is difficult to deny that science is motivated by factors other than pure, secular objectivity. It is difficult to believe that humans act without underlying motivations or gain credibility by denying their biases. Certainly, the Puritans did not find it necessary to bury religious motivation under an avalanche of "facts" with the hope of feigning credibility. Their leading scientists pursued the interests of their discipline with all the zeal and piety of a religious mission. Isaac Newton explains in his letter to Bentley that he wrote his *Prinicipia* with an "eye upon such Principles" as might prove useful for those considering a belief in God.[78] Robert Boyle exhorts his fellows of the London Society to "discover the true Nature of the Works of God [and] refer their attainments to the Glory of the Great Author of Nature, and to the Comfort of Mankind."[79]

Robert Merton, an American sociologist, finds these testimonies compelling and finds it necessary to extend the influence of Puritanism beyond Weber's interest in capitalism to the realm of science.[80] While he acknowledges the importance of other factors and actually spends more space on economic and military influences in his *Science, Technology & Society in Seventeenth Century England* (1932), the religious element is an important part of the equation and actually receives most of the press among those who analyze the work. This element is so identified with his work that the influence of Puritanism on science is known as the Merton Thesis. It seems to enjoy widespread success in the realm of sociology, with only a few disparaging voices, especially when compared to Weber's thesis, where there remains considerable diversity of opinion.[81] Merton first develops his thesis by assembling data from the *Dictionary of National Biography* and noticing a shift of interest toward science in the seventeenth century.[82] His curiosity is peaked by the data, and he naturally wants to know what provoked this new interest during the time in question. His research leads him to conclude that Puritanism served an important role in arousing scientific interest at the time. Puritans are brought forth as a decisive factor because science seems to prosper in their particular areas of influence.[83] It finds an important place in their schools[84] and receives much needed status and prestige through the Royal Society of London, which is dominated by their expertise and leadership.[85]

The Royal Society of London serves Merton and those who follow his thesis with a good case in point. The society went through various stages of development, which reached back to 1645 and the "invisible college," and continued on with the official adoption of its name and charter in 1662.[86] According to the second charter (1663), which remains in effect today, the purpose of the society is found in "promoting by the authority of experiments the sciences of natural things and of useful arts, to the glory of God the Creator, and the advantage of the human race."[87] The statement of purpose displays in graphic form the fundamental convictions of the society, and these convictions are consonant with the Puritan community and its emphasis upon utilitarian values, practical knowledge, and the glory of God as the end of life. In fact, the membership of the society was decidedly Puritan in its early days. Dorothy Stimson, the dean of Goucher College, wrote a famous article in 1935 that demonstrated this propensity to the satisfaction of many scholars. She pointed out that the "invisible college" had a clear majority of Puritans—seven out of the ten members—with only one expressing royalist sympathies. She also looked at the original membership of the Royal Society (1663), whose religious affections are known, and discovered that forty-two out of sixty-eight had clear Puritan leanings.[88] Considering the minority status of Puritans in the general population, these statistics are remarkable and betray a certain religious component in the society's understanding of science.

Following this initial result, a question immediately arises concerning the exact nature of the theological influence. The answer is not so simple this time, but a few reasons seem to suggest themselves beyond the previous emphasis upon eschatology already mentioned.

One, the climate was conducive in England for science to prosper because of the permanent changes wrought by the Revolution. There were a number of factors that helped to change the atmosphere, but none proved more crucial than the change in policy of the government that now began to encourage what it once persecuted. Other countries, like Italy produced some scientists in the past, but they did not support them like Cromwell and the Parliament and even persecuted certain of its practitioners—as in the infamous case of Galileo. Scientists in England came to the forefront in the 1640s when government policy was conducive for its growth. Bacon and his method was mentioned by Milton, Holdsworth, and a few others before this time, but it was only during the Revolution that the influence of his ideas became significant, long after his death.[89]

Two, Protestantism in general helped to facilitate the growth of science by rejecting the dependence of the church upon tradition and liberating the laity to discover the truth on their own. Thomas Sprat states this point most eloquently in his *History of the Royal-Society of London* (1667).

> From this I will farther urge, That the Church of England will not only be safe amidst the consequences of a Rational Age, but amidst all the improvements of Knowledge, and the subversions of old Opinions about Nature, and introduction of new ways of Reasoning thereon. This will be evident, when we behold the agreement that is between the present Design of the Royal Society, and that of our Church in its beginning. They both may lay equal claim to the word Reformation; the one having compass'd it in Religion, the other purposing it in Philosophy. They both have taken a like cours to bring this about; each of them passing by the corrupt Copies, and referring themselves to the perfect Originals for their instruction; the one to the Scripture, the other to the large Volume of the Creatures. They are both unjustly accus'd by their enemies of the same crimes, of having forsaken the Ancient Traditions, and ventur'd on Novelties. The both suppose alike, that their Ancestors might err; and yet retain a sufficient reverence for them. They both follow the great Praecept of the Apostle, of Trying all things.[90]

Three, Puritanism like much of science rejected speculative and impractical subjects that did not address the realities of the real world. Puritan educators developed an iconoclastic attitude toward the standard, classical education of the time and the idle speculation of scholastic metaphysics associated with it. They preferred the study of concrete matters in history and nature, which provided empirical descriptions through prose or mathematics, rather than quibbling over the analysis of words or developing flowery images and poetic phrases without concrete reference.[91] Puritans wanted a more practical, utilitarian education that would find an immediate application in serving the community. According to Baxter, "knowledge is to be valued according to its usefulness."[92] Technology served the practical needs of the community by turning stones into metal and idle land into productive farms.[93]

Four, Puritans emphasized the experimental method when it came to approaching nature.[94] Reason could not probe the mysteries of God contained in nature. If one wishes to know God, it is best to turn toward Scripture for its detail and clarity than trust in the limited powers of the human mind.

> In the general, That 'tis true indeed, that Philosophy teacheth many things which are not revealed in Scripture; for this was not intended to instruct men in the affairs of Nature, but its design is to direct mankind, and even those of the plainest understandings, in life, and manners, to propose to us the way of Happiness, and the principles that are necessary to guide us in it.[95]

> And this was not only done by Plato, who constantly anchors upon this shore; but by Aristotle, Galen, and others, who frequently introduced such causes as these: "The hairs of the eyelids are for a fence to the sight. The bones for pillars whereon to build the bodies of animals. The leaves of trees are to defend the fruit from the sun and wind. The clouds are designed for watering the earth," etc. All which are properly alleged in metaphysics, but in physics are impertinent, and as remoras to the ship, that hinder the sciences from holding on their course of improvement, and introducing a neglect of searching after physical causes.[96]

This tendency helped to free science from the need to grapple with ultimate questions about God and the meaning of life. It allowed science to reflect upon mundane questions of secondary causality or practical concern, which it could resolve with some certainty or at least make some progress through testing the answers by the experimental method. It chose to neglect the most important questions of life, leaving those matters to the "spectacles" of Scripture[97] and focus instead on an effective study of nature, which brought quantitative results to the community through this practical means of testing whatever it proposed.

Francis Bacon, the great apostle of the scientific method, served the Royal Society and the Puritan community as the guiding light of this new philosophy of nature. His writings obtained an elevated status among them as the definitive authority on the subject,[98] although he never said anything completely new or different from the typical adages found in the Puritan and scientific community of the time. In his works he speaks like any other Puritan about finding the true end of science in the "glory of the Creator and the endowment of human life." [99] He believes the knowledge of nature can increase and grow in the future, as long as it confines itself to secondary or utilitarian causes and stays within the boundaries set in Scripture (Gen. 3). He cites a number of times the prophetic words of Dan.12:4 and is enamored with the prospect of science making real progress in building the future community.[100] All of these ideas were found within the community of his day and found a ready acceptance because the community was prepared in advance to accept them.

The tone of Puritan culture was set by what was practical and necessary in shaping the future. Modern science and capitalism were a product of this mentality and serve as important symbols and reminders of the powerful impact Puritan ideas exerted on society. The influence might be less obvious or direct than the simple transition that occurred in the development of democratic and federal government out of congregational polity. This time the influence takes place in the form of an underlying psychological grid or motivation within the culture, which makes the development of capitalism and science possible.[101] But the result is just as real and palpable. A culture so oriented will tend to promote scientific adventure and forge policies that promote the spirit of capitalism through protecting private property and reducing its own size or influence on the private sector. A culture so oriented will seek to expand its kingdom and impose its own global vision of life on others, hoping to recreate the world into its image. It will promote these and other policies out of a belief in the future and its own place in fulfilling the divine mission through whatever practical means are available. It will promote a vision of the world that remains deeply entangled within its own metaphysical ideals. For no matter what the policy it will find a religious motivation invariably entangled with it, whether appearing right on the surface or existing deep within the history and psychology of a people.

Notes

1. WA, DB 7.412-17 (LW 35.405-407); WA, Tr 4.339 (nr. 4487) (LW 54.346-47); WA 50.217; 53.394; P. Althaus, *The Theology of Martin Luther*, R. C. Schultz (trans.) (Philadelphia: Fortress Press, 1975) 85, 221; B. A. Ehlers, "Luther and English Apocalypticism: The Role of Luther in Three Seventeenth-Century Commentaries on the Book of Revelation," in *Essays in History* (Richmond: The William Byrd Press, Inc., 1992) 2. In his 1522 preface, Luther dismissed the work as unintelligible and non-canonical.
2. WA, Tr., 4.339 (nr. 4487) (LW 54.346-47).
3. F. J. Levy, *Tudor Historical Thought* (San Marino, CA: Huntington Library, 1967) 91, 194; A. Zakai, *Exile and Kingdom: History and Apocalypse in the Puritan Migration to America* (Cambridge: Cambridge University Press, 1992) 26, 27, 29-31. The Geneva Bible proved an effective tool in spreading Bale's concept among the masses. It represented the type of cheap and plentiful material that the presses began to produce in the seventeenth century and the radicals used with great efficiency in disseminating their message. Foster, *The Long Argument*, 92. The Geneva Bible was offered in a cheap, pocket-size edition, which included for the first time an elaborate system of commentary in the marginal glosses, helping to make it the Bible of the people. Hill, *The English Bible*, 18; D. Daniell, *The Bible in English: Its History and Influence* (New Haven, CT and London: Yale University Press, 2003) 275, 291, 295. It proved more popular among the radicals than the AV, going through 140 editions until 1644, when government monopolies were undermined by the Puritan Revolution and the AV became cheaper and more available to the public. Daniell, *The Bible in English*, 294; Hill, *The English Bible*, 435. The first edition of the complete Bible (1560) was an anonymous work, but there is sufficient evidence that William Whittingham in collaboration with some other scholars played a primary role in its production. Some also suggest that Bale had a hand in producing the marginal notes, but many scholars reject this possibility. Ibid., 278, 279, 356, 819; Hill, *The English Bible*, 56-58, 66. The marginal notes were thought "destructive of the persons and powers of Kings" and contain the "savour of sedition" (e.g., using the term "tyrant" to describe certain OT rulers, unlike the AV). Hill, *The English Bible*, 58-60.

   The notes on the book of Revelation depict a struggle between the church of Christ and the church of the Antichrist. In the first edition, the bishops and the hierarchical church are depicted as the star falling from heaven to the earth and the locust that arise from the bottomless pit (Rev. 9:1-3, $117^{r,v}$). The pope is the Antichrist, who opens the bottomless pit in order to destroy the souls of men (Rev. 9:1, 11, 117). The first Beast of Rev. 13 refers to the Roman Empire, and the second Beast is the papal kingdom (Rev. 13-17, 118-20). The pure doctrine of the church lasted from the nativity of Christ to Pope Silvester II, who reigned at the turn of the millennium (Rev. 20:3, 121^{r}). The papal kingdom began to persecute the church at that time, but Christ will come and destroy this evil kingdom (119-21). In the 1599 edition, Franciscus Junius changed the notes in the book of Revelation and preserved only some of the original spirit or polemical edge. Gregory VII, Gregory IX, and Boniface VIII are singled out for their abuse of papal power (Rev. 9, $114^{r,v}$; Rev. 11:2, 7, 115). Rev. 13 speaks of the two phases of the Roman Empire—one civil and the other ecclesiastical. The papacy is compared to the Roman emperors as making a pretense of divinity, while containing doctrine that is false and destructive ($116^{r,v}$). Note: References for the 1560 edition are taken from *The Geneva Bible: A Facsimile of the 1560 edition* (Madison, Milwaukee, and London: The University of Wisconsin Press, 1969).

4. J. Foxe, *Foxe's Book of Martyrs*, W. B. Forbush (ed.) (New York: Holt, Rineheart, and Winston, 1963) xii, xiv; Zakai, *Exile and Kingdom*, 31; Hill, *The Intellectual Origins of the Puritan Revolution*, 178.
5. I. Foxe, *The First Volumes of Ecclesiastical history contayning the Actes and Monumentes* (London: Iohn Daye, 1570) "A Protestation to the Whole Church of England." Hereafter this work is designated FVE. Foxe mentions in "The Epistle dedicatorie" that a second, expanded edition is necessary because the papists attacked the first so viciously.
6. I. Foxe, *Actes and Monuments* (London: Iohn Dag, 1563) 7-11; FVE, "A Protestation to the Whole Church of England." Hereafter the first edition is designated AM.
7. FVE, "A Protestation to the Whole Church of England"; AM, 85. Elizabeth followed this account of history in her polemics with Rome, pointing to the ancient testimony concerning Joseph of Arimathea and the establishment of bishops and priests in England long before Augustine came from Rome. *The Letters of Queen Elizabeth I*, G. B. Harrison (ed.) (Westport, CT.: Greenwood Press, Publishers, 1981) 29, 30; F. Lambert, *The Founding Fathers and the Place of Religion in America* (Princeton, NJ: Princeton University Press, 2003) 300.
8. FVE, 145; Zakai, *Exile and Kingdom*, 34, 35.
9. The number 300 comes from multiplying the 42 months of the book of Revelation by 7 and adding the 6 years Lucinius persecuted the east and Constantine begins his ascension. FVE, 493.
10. FVE, 523; AM, 85ff.
11. FVE, "Foure Questions propounded to the Papists"; AM, "The Preface to the Quene."
12. Hill, *Change and Continuity in Seventeenth-Century England*, 269.
13. T. Brightman, *The Revelation of Saint Iohn* (Amsterdam: T. Stafford, 1644) 14. Brightman's commentary begins with an exposition of the seven churches, which serve as "counterpaynes" of the "universal condition of the church" (14). The first church of Ephesus has a "counterpayne" in the early church from the time of the Apostles to Constantine. It is commended because of its discipline of members early on, but eventually lost its first love around two hundred when it neglected this duty (14-18). The second church of Smyrna speaks of the time from Constantine to Gratian (382)—a time when Christianity itself persecuted the truth (19). The

third church of Pergamum extends from 380-1300, when the church is brought under the power of Rome and grows exceedingly dark. The popes persecuted the true church, forcing it underground, but eventually preachers arose around 1140 who challenged the evil ways of Rome (22-24). The church of Thyatira covers the time from 1300 to 1520. The papacy becomes more corrupt during the period but loses much of its power through the work of Ockham, Wyclif, Hus, Jerome, Luther, German Princes, and others who revolted against Rome (25-28). The last three churches are joined together during the same period. The "counterpayne" of Sardis is the first Reformed Church, begun by Luther. It helped revive the faith, but it did not remove all papal doctrine—consubstantiation and the ubiquity of Christ representing its most egregious errors (31-33). The antitype of the church in Philadelphia is the fully Reformed churches of Switzerland, France, Holland, and Scotland. These churches are so blessed that they will join the New Jerusalem in one covenant and society here on earth (34, 40). The final church is Laodicea. Its "counterpayne" is the Church of England, which was established some forty-two years ago during the reign of Elizabeth but has vacillated ever since, just like the church of Laodicea. It continues to vacillate between the Reformation and Rome, and finds particular temptation in the hierarchical privileges of the papacy (41ff.).

14. Ibid., 41ff.; *Reverend Mr. Brightmans Iudgement or Prophecies* (London, 1643) [1]-[4]; *Brightmans Predictions and Prophecies* (1641) 15-18.
15. Ibid., 158, 159.
16. Ibid., 41, 42 122, 123; *Reverend Mr. Brightmans Iudgement or Prophecies*, [6]; Ehlers, "Luther and English Apocalypticism," 8-10. Brightman mentions Foxe's work several times in his exposition and probably was influenced by him in this regard and others. Ibid., 126, 159, 175.
17. Ibid., 123, 135, 136, 150, 261. He sees the Beast of Rev. 13 as possessing civil and spiritual power like the Pope of Rome. The False Prophet is the Beast in his spiritual power. The mystical number is calculated from the phrase *Lateinos Latinus* (referring to a man of Rome). Cardinal Bellarmine offers an alternative explanation, which sees the Antichrist as a single person yet to come and locates his seat in Jerusalem, not Rome. Brightman offers a lengthy rebuttal of this position, as well as a defense of his own. Ibid., 179-241.
18. Ibid., 254; *Reverend Mr. Brightmans Iudgement or Prophecies*, [5]. Brightman provides a lengthy discussion of the divine judgments—the seals, trumpets, and vials—found in Rev. 6-18. These chapters refer to events transpiring after 97 A.D., the time of John's prophecy and reign of Domitian (68). The seals start with the triumph of the gospel in the second century, continue with the persecutions under Trajan, Marcus, Aurelius, Decius, Diocletian, and other emperors, include many cruelties and pestilence during the era, and end with the reign of Constantine and the council of Nicea (68-85). The trumpets include the turmoil and persecution that followed Nicea, the bishops vying for power, the corrupting influence of Arianism, Gensericus the Vandal decimating the North African church, the ascendancy of the papacy and Muhammed, the Saracenes, the Turks, and the monastic movements like the Dominicans and Franciscans after Innocent III (85ff.). The last trumpet blows in 1558 with the ascendancy of Elizabeth, whose reign serves as a type of the eternal kingdom (122, 123). The seven vials "spring out of the last trumpet" and began around 1560. They cover the evils of the papacy, the Jesuits, the Council of Trent, and look to a conversion of the Jews and a restoration of their kingdom (166ff.).
19. Ibid., 103, 104, 142; *Reverend Mr. Brightmans Iudgement or Prophecies*, [5]; *Brightmans Predictions and Prophecies*, 6. The exhortation in the abridgements is to become like Jehu and take up the sword against Rome.

20. Ibid., 103, 104, 176; *Reverend Mr. Brightmans Iudgement or Prophecies*, [6].
21. Ibid., 264ff. The Beast reigns when the heathen emperors are suppressed by Constantine. The ten horns refer to the first Christian emperors, among which Constantine is included as an unwitting defender of the Beast. This time period fulfills the prophecy of Rev. 20 concerning the binding of Satan. The "first resurrection" refers to the restoration of the gospel around 1300 through the work of men like Wyclif. Brightman seems to indicate that Christ reigns spiritually during this "millennium," although the exact length of time is uncertain. After the time of restoration and the defeat of the pope and the Turks, Christ will come to reign on earth. The prophecies of Rev. 21 and 22 refer to this state on earth, not the final, heavenly abode. Ibid., 40, 138, 275, 276, 280, 287.
22. Zakai, *Exile and Kingdom*, 118-20.
23. V. D. Anderson, *New England's generation*, 8, 11, 34-38; *Winthrop Papers* (The Massachusetts Historical Society, 1931) 2.114. Winthrop believes that God will supply their needs, but he is quick to add a proviso that mismanagement caused much of the hardship in Virginia. *Winthrop Papers*, 2.143, 144.
24. *Winthrop Papers*, 2.113.
25. Ibid., 2.111; Zakai, *Exile and Kingdom*, 138, 166, 167, 172-177. See T. Hooker, *The Dangers of Desertion*, in *Thomas Hooker: Writings in England and Holland, 1626-1633* (Cambridge, MA: Harvard University Press, 1975) 231-33, 242-45. Of course, he sees this judgment in terms of divine wrath falling upon his homeland and God providing a shelter in the wilderness from the coming storm. *Winthrop Papers*, 2.91, 92; Hill, *The English Bible*, 293, 294. But the concern over present and future persecution remained a most essential factor for the errand in the wilderness; it is prominent in the account of Winthrop and the future generations of his people. Mather, *Magnalia Christi Americana*, 1.65, 238-40.
26. Ibid., 2.112, 113, 122. Some Waldenses scattered and survived in the Alps. Ibid., 2.143.
27. Ibid., 2.125, 129, 133; Zakai, *Exile and Kingdom*, 142, 143; Anderson, *New England's generation*, 26. The second and third generation continued to use the image of the wilderness in Rev. 12. T. Shepard and J. Allin, *A Defence of the Answer* (London: R. Cotes, 1648) "The Preface"; J. Norton, *Election Sermon: Sion the Outcast Healed of Her Wounds* (1661), in *The Puritans in America: A Narrative Anthology*, A. Heimer and A. Delbanco (ed.) (Cambridge, MA: Harvard University Press, 1985) 227-28. G. H. Williams and Avihu Zakai believe that Brightman's exegesis of Revelation was the basic source of the Puritan's concept of wilderness. This image was used in the Middle Ages by other persecuted groups like the Waldenses. G. H. Williams, *Wilderness and Paradise in Christian Thought* (New York: Harper, 1962) 62; Zakai, *Exile and Kingdom*, 150, 158, 161-65, 190-206.
28. Ibid., 2.128, 133.
29. Anderson, *New England's generation*, 15-18; Zakai, *Exile and Kingdom*, 132, 133. Some 13,000 immigrants came in all.
30. Zakai, *Exile and Kingdom*, 242-45.
31. *Winthrops Papers*, 2.113, 136, 140, 141; *Journal of John Winthrop*, 283, 284. Later Locke's labor theory of property will be employed in courts against the claims of the natives. Locke specifically applied his theory to America, which he considered an unproductive wasteland without human cultivation. *Two Treatises of Government*, xlv, 129-37 (*The Second Treatise*, 28-45). At times Puritans proceeded so far in this line of argumentation that they found the purpose of nature within human exploitation. Cotton Mather refers to whaling as the good gift of God, designed to "suck the abundance of the seas." *Magnalia Christi Americana*, 1.62. Roger Williams felt differently and contested the Crown's authority to grant

land to colonists. The Indians hunted the land and at the very least deserved compensation. *The Journal of John Winthrop*, 107; Hill, *Puritanism and Revolution*, 151. After the first couple decades, Winthrop saw no particular injustice in the colonists' treatment of the Indians; either they submitted to the government, were defeated in a just war (e.g., the Pequots), or voluntarily sold their land. *Journal*, 677, 678. At the turn of the century, Cotton Mather would paint a dark portrait of the Indians as brutal "savages" in his *Magnalia Christi Americana* (1702). The Indians were possibly the descendants of the wicked Canaanites, who fled the righteous sword of Joshua (2.440, see *The Journal of John Winthrop*, 341). They worshipped many gods/demons and practiced black magic (2.426, 446) and have received for their deeds the just judgment of God, who sent his plagues among them (e.g., small pox) and greatly reduced their ranks, both before and after the Puritan immigration (1.51, 78). Even with reduced numbers, the Indians proved a greater hardship for the settlers than all the rest of the elements combined, and this is why God brought his plagues upon them to reduce their numbers for the sake of his people (1.51, 52).

32. Ibid., 2.111, 112, 122, 123, 126. England is considered too crowded.
33. Ibid., 2.111, Zakai, *Exile and Kingdom*, 138.
34. E. L. Tuveson, *Redeemer Nation: The Idea of America's Millennial Role* (Chicago and London: The University of Chicago Press, 1968) x, 19.
35. C. Webster, *The Great Instauration: Science, Medicine and Reform* (New York: Holmes & Meier Publishers, 1976) 2, 29, 30; R. A. Nisbet, *History of the Idea of Progress* (New York: Basic Books, 1980) 129; Tuveson, *Redeemer Nation*, 97, 98.
36. T. Burnet, *Treatise Concerning the State of Departed Souls* (London, 1730) 367; N. Culpeper, *Catastrophe Magnatum* (London, 1652) 72; J. Spittlehouse, *First Addresses* (1653) 5. On the continent Johannes Cocceius and his disciples helped resurrect millenarian expectations. Strehle, *Calvinism, Federalism, and Scholasticism*, 358, 359.
37. Baillie, *Letters and Journals*, 2.156; Hill, *The English Bible*, 304. John Lightfoot also contains a similar testimony. *A Sermon Preached before the Honorable House of Commons* (London, 1645) 2, 3. F. D. Dow finds millenarian expectations in seventy percent of Reformed writings between 1640 and 1653. *Radicalism in the English Revolution, 1640-1660* (Oxford: Basil Blackwell, 1985) 62.
38. H. Grotius, *Epistolae quotquot reperiri potuerunt* (Amstelodami: P. & I. Blaev, 1687) 895.
39. Hill, *Puritanism and Revolution*, 325, 329.
40. *A Glimpse of Sions Glory* (London, 1641) 1, 2.
41. Ibid., 4-7, 12, 13.
42. Ibid., 13-17. The work encourages literal interpretation of Scripture, although it qualifies its belief in the millennium as a mere "probability."
43. Ibid., 32. The year 1695 is calculated by adding 1335 (Dan. 12:12) to 360, the year of Julian's apostasy.
44. Ibid., 23ff., 31. Another good example is John Archer's *The Personall Reigne of Christ vpon Earth* (London, 1642). It follows the same basic understanding of prophecy: Scripture should be interpreted in a literal manner, four kingdoms will precede the final Kingdom of God, Christ will reign with his saints on earth, etc. The prophetic timetable includes the conversion of the Jews (1650 or 1656), the defeat of the papacy (1666), and the reign of Christ (ca. 1700).
45. J. Mede, *The Key of the Revelation*, R. More (trans.) (London: R. B., 1650); E. L. Tuveson, *Millennium and Utopia: A Study in the Background of Progress* (New York: Harper & Row, 1964) ix, 76-78; T. Olsen, *Millennialism, Utopianism, and*

Progress (Toronto: University of Toronto Press, 1982) 203; Ehlers, "Luther and English Apocalypticism," 11; M. Walzer, *The Revolution of the Saints: A Study in the Origin of Radical Politics* (Cambridge, MA.: Harvard University Press, 1965) 292. Daniel Whitby is associated with the founding of Postmillennialism. His *Paraphrase and Commentary on the New Testament* (1703) certainly provided the theory with a boost, but there were others before him like Thomas Brightman, Joseph Mede, and John Alsted who deserve mention. Tuveson, *Redeemer Nation*, 39, 40; J. Fruchtman, *The Apocalyptic Politics of Richard Price and Joseph Priestly: A Study in Late Eighteenth-century English Millennialism* (Philadelphia: The American Philosophical Society, 1983) 13, 14; R. K. Whalen, "Postmillennialism," in *Encyclopedia of Millennialism and Millennial Movements*, R. Landes (ed.) (New York and London: Routledge, 2000) 326, 327. The details of Mede's account are as follows. The seals represent the destiny of the Roman Empire, and the little book the destiny of the church (1.38; 2.1). The seals include the original victory of Christ, the persecution of emperors, and Constantine's destruction of heathendom in 311 (1.41ff.). The trumpets begin with the death of Theodosius (395) and include barbarian invasions, division of the empire into ten empires and its ruin, Islamic and Turkish exploits, and the fall of Constantinople in 1453 (1.84ff.) Mede discusses Rev. 12 and 13 at this point. Rev. 12 is fulfilled in the days of Constantine with its struggle for orthodoxy against the Arian threat and the establishment of Christian rule over the nations (2.37, 48). Rev. 13 describes the blasphemies of the Catholic Church (idolatry, transubstantiation, and the veneration of saints) as well as the two beasts (2.59, 60, 70). The first beast represents the secular Roman Empire after it was divided by the barbarians into ten kingdoms. The second beast is the bishop of Rome and his clergy. This ecclesiastical beast revives the Roman Empire, healing its mortal wound, and instructs its leaders to persecute the saints of God (2.48, 49, 62, 67). At this juncture, the vials are poured out upon the "Antichristian Beast," beginning in 1200 with the Waldenses and Albigenses (2.60-62, 92-93). The vials also include Wyclif, Huss, Luther, the Reformers, Elizabeth, the German Empire, the destruction of Rome, and the conversion of the Jews (2.114ff.). Finally, with the seventh seal, the destruction of the Beast and his followers is consummated (2.110, 120, 121).

46. S. Marshall, *The Song of Moses The Servant of God and The Song of the Lambe* (London, 1643) 21ff.; Tuveson, *Millennium and Utopia*, 87, 88.

47. Hill, *The World Turned Upside Down*, 78. Josselin notes in his diary that many expected the world to end in the mid-1650s.

48. J. F. McGregor and B. Reay, *Radical Religion in the English Revolution* (Oxford: Oxford University Press, 1984) 170, 171; R. A. Nisbet, *History of the Idea of Progress* (New York: Basic Books, Inc., 1980) 135; Tuveson, *Millennium and Utopia*, 89. No one knows how widespread the movement was in its heyday. According to Austin Woolrych, their constituents included at least eleven members of the House, the great prayer meetings at the Blackfriars (led by the millenarian gospel of Christopher Feake), several congregations in London, itinerant preachers like Vavasor Powell and Morgan Llwyd, a number of radical chaplains, and Thomas Harrison, a "redoubtable leader" of the army. They were possessed with much zeal for creating a righteous kingdom and even hoped to remodel the army into a more radical force of change. Cromwell became disillusioned with the movement for its schismatic ways and self-righteous claims to divine inspiration and started to criticize its leaders in public, beginning with his first speech to the Parliament in 1654-55. A. Woolrych, "Oliver Cromwell and the Rule of the Saints," in *Cromwell: A Profile*, I. Roots (ed.) (New York: Hill and Wang, [1973]) 57, 58, 67, 69; J. Sommerville, "Oliver Cromwell and English political thought,"

in *Oliver Cromwell and the English Revolution*, J. Morrill (ed.) (London and New York: Longman, 1990) 253.

49. T. Goodwin, *A Sermon of the Fifth Monarchy* (London, 1654) 3-5, 10.
50. Ibid., 11, 14, 15, 18, 29.
51. Ibid., 11-13, 16, 17, 21, 22. These events are depicted in Rev. 6-20.
52. A. de Tocqueville, *Democracy in America* (New York: Alfred A. Knopf, 1963) 1.296, 393, 394.
53. P. Miller, *The New England Mind: The Seventeenth Century* (Cambridge, MA: Harvard University Press, 1963) 1.475ff. This belief continued into the eighteenth and nineteenth centuries. T. Dwight, *The Conquest of Canaan* [Hartford: E. Babcock, 1785] (New York: AMS Press, 1971) 1, 253 (1.1-4; 10.501ff.); H. Melville, *White Jacket or The War in a Man-of-War*, T. Tanner (intro.) (Oxford: Oxford University Press, 1990) 152, 153 (chap. 36). See Tuveson, *Redeemer Nation*, 106, 107, 156, 157. In the middle colonies, Reformed preachers spread the same message about America and its people as an elect nation with a manifest destiny. K. L. Griffin, *Revolution and Religion: American Revolutionary War and the Reformed Clergy* (New York: Paragon House, 1994) 47, 74, 75, 79, 113.
54. Nisbet, *History of the Idea of Progress*, 195-98; Webster, *The Great Instauration*, 4,5; J. Knight, *Orthodoxies in Massachutsetts: Rereading American Puritanism* (Cambridge and London: Harvard University Press, 1994) 132; J. Hewitson, "United States, Eighteenth Century," in *Encyclopedia of Millennialism*, 417. The millenarian fever was present during the early days of the colony. Even otherwise sober scholars like John Cotton and John Davenant reflected the optimistic, millenarian spirit of the times in some of their writings. Cotton was even bold enough to suggest a date at one point, referring to the year 1655 as the beginning of a new era. J. Cotton, *An Exposition upon the Thirteenth Chapter of the Revelation* (London, 1656) 93; Knight, *Orthodoxies in Massachutsetts*, 159, 162.
55. Tuveson, *Redeemer Nation*, 53, 54; Whalen, "Postmillennialism," 326, 328; Hewitson, "United States, Eighteenth Century," 416.
56. "An Authoritative Edition of Cotton Mather's Unpublished Manuscript 'Problema Theologicum' (1703)," J. S. Mares (intro. and ed.) (M.A. Thesis: Georgia State University, 1994) 86; R. F. Lovelace, *The American Pietism of Cotton Mather* (Grand Rapids, MI: Christian University Press, 1979) 70. Mather uses a number of sources in developing his account of the end times. He points to the work of Jurieu, Alting, Witsius, and others—although his basic account, like so many others in his day, works within the matrix and spirit of Brightman's analysis. Like Brightman he refers to the seven churches of Revelation as figures of all churches; provides a similar historical interpretation of the seals, trumpets, and vials; and then attempts to establish a similar date for the coming (1696/97). C. Mather, *Things to be Looked for* (Boston: S. Green and Barth, 1691).
57. "Problema Theologicum," 64, 65.
58. C. Mather, *A Midnight Cry: an essay for our awakening out of the sinful sleep* (Boston: J. Allen, 1692) 23, 24; *Things for a Distress'd People to think upon* (Boston: B. Green and J. Allen, 1696) 9, 16, 23, 24.
59. Mather, "Problema Theologicum," 77; *Things to be Looked for*, 31; *A Midnight Cry*, 23, 24, 62-64.
60. Mather, *Things for a Distress'd people*, 33.
61. Ibid., 34. He hedges over what precise event he is predicting. At times he seems to limit the prediction to some great revival or nebulous apocalyptic event. Ibid.; *A Midnight Cry*, 63.
62. Mather, *Things to be Looked for*, 8. In "Problema Theologicum" he presents a systematic argument for premillennialism. He argues for literal hermeneutics and

cites the interpretation of the early church (Justin Martyr, Irenaeus, and Papias) as lending authority to the doctrine. "Problema Theologicum," xxiv, xxviii, 15ff., 58, 62, 53. He later abandons his belief in the national conversion of Israel, reinterpreting Rom. 11:25-27 as already fulfilled in the first century. Ibid., xiii, xvi, xix; Lovelace, *American Pietism*, 67. Cf. "Problema Theologicum," 11; *Things to be Looked for*, 8.

63. Ibid., 46, 47.
64. Mather, *A Midnight Cry*, 30-32, 63; "Problema Theologicum," 52-54, 87, 88; *Things for a Distress'd people*, 35; *Things to be Looked for*, 28-30. He derives the date in several ways: adding the "half a time" of Daniel (180 years) to the beginning of the Reformation (1517), adding 397 (Rev. 9:15) to the beginning of Turkish hostilities (1300), adding 2300 to the beginning of the Babylonian Captivity, adding 1260 (the reign of the Antichrist) to the beginning of its reign (440/50), etc. In his *Magnalia Christi Americana* (1702), he still stands by the imminency of his expectation in the year 1696 (653).
65. K. Silverman, *The Life and Times of Cotton Mather* (New York: Harper & Row, Publishers, 1984) 303; Lovelace, *American Pietism*, 65, 66; Mather, *Things to be Looked for*, 28; "Problema Theologicum," 87, 88. The year 1716 is derived by adding 1260 to 456 (the destruction of Rome). The year 1736 is derived by counting 6000 years from the beginning of the world, following the chronology of the Samaritan Pentateuch.
66. Nisbet, *The History of Progress*, 195, 196. Whether a theologian was pre- or postmillennial in their eschatology (and often there existed much confusion and mixture in individual authors) all tended to participate in the basic optimism that Edwards represents. S. Bercovitch, *The American Jeremiad* (Madison: The University of Wisconsin, 1978) 94-100. Janice Knight disagrees with this analysis. She tries to distinguish the more tribal, ethnocentric position of the "orthodox" colonists from the minority position of antinomians and postmillennialists like Edwards, who developed a more optimistic and global perspective. *Orthodoxies in Massachutsetts*, 166, 167, 199ff., 266, 267. However, this simple distinction often breaks down in the work of Edwards and others. For example, Edwards becomes as ethnocentric as the later Mormons when he considers the possibility that the Ten Lost Tribes of Israel made their way to America. He thought that America would lead the great renewal and help usher in the millennium. *The Works of Jonathan Edwards*, P. Miller, J. E. Smith, and H. S. Stout (eds.) 4.353-58; J. Edwards, *Polypoikilos Sophia. A Compleat History Or Survey Of all the Dispensations and Methods of Religion* (London, 1699) 695. Hereafter the work is designated PS.
67. PS, 689-91. Christopher Hill finds this westward movement in Herbert, Sibbes, Ward, Vaughan, Trapp, Winstanley, and Twisse. According to Twisse, "many divines saw a westward movement, and he himself wondered whether New England might not become the New Jerusalem." *The English Bible*, 139, 140. In *A History of the Work of Redemption*, Edwards divides world history into four great periods, which are marked by the work of Christ (and the destruction of Jerusalem in 70), the rise of the Holy Roman Empire with Constantine, the destruction of the Antichrist, and the second coming of Christ. *Works*, 9.351; G. Marsden, *Jonathan Edwards: A Life* (New Haven, CT & London: Yale University Press, 2003) 196, 198. Apparently, in his notebooks on the "History of Redemption" he planned on creating a seven-fold rhythm of history. *Works*, 9.61-72, 546-47; Marsden, *Jonathan Edwards*, 483, 485.
68. PS, 610, 612, 642. George Hakewill (1578-1649) was a significant figure in combating the theory of cosmic decay. Hill, *Intellectual Origins of the Puritan Revolution*, 224.

69. PS, 614, 615, 621, 634, 637.
70. PS, 744.
71. PS, 672.
72. PS, 665-72. He is familiar with the work of Joseph Mede and Thomas Brightman and refers to them at several points, although not always in agreement. PS, 655, 668-71.
73. PS, 724, 725, 731-35. He interprets the lion lying down with the lamb in a literal manner.
74. R. L. Moore, *Religious Outsiders and the Making of Americans* (New York and Oxford: Oxford University Press, 1986) 26.
75. Webster, *The Great Instauration*, 9ff. The progress in knowledge included all areas of life. R. Boyle, *The Works of the Honourable Robert Boyle* [London, 1772] (Bristol: Thoemmes Press, 1999) 4.16-18; W. Whiston, *A New Theory of the Earth* [1696] (London, 1725) 62, 81.
76. J. Emerson, *Lectures on the Millennium* (Boston: S. T. Armstrong, 1818) 76, 95, 276.
77. T. S. Kuhn, *The Structure of the Scientific Revolution* (Chicago: University of Chicago Press, 1970) 2, 7, 34, 137, 138, 166, 167; J. Mali, "Science, Tradition, and the Science of Tradition," *Science in Context* 3, no. 1 (Spring 1989): 143-45; I. B. Cohen, "Introduction: The Impact of the Merton Thesis," in *Puritanism and the Rise of Modern Science: The Merton Thesis*, I. B. Cohen (ed.) (New Brunswick, NJ and London: Rutgers University Press, 1990) 43, 51.
78. "Newton to Bentley" (Dec. 10, 1692), in *The Correspondence of Isaac Newton*, H. W. Turnball (ed.) (Cambridge: Cambridge University Press, 1961) 3.233. It is most likely that Newton was reared with Puritan convictions, even though he conformed to the restored Episcopal Church for the sake of his career and rejected the doctrine of the Trinity very early in his life. He was a strong opponent of the papacy, which he identified with the Antichrist, and was captivated by the apocalyptic expectations of the day. His theological manuscripts are as massive as his work in mathematics and science. Hill, *Change and Continuity in Seventeenth-Century England* (Cambridge, MA: Harvard University Press, 1975) 260, 261, 266, 271.
79. G. Burnet, *A Sermon Preached at the Funeral of the Honourable Robert Boyle* (London, 1692); F. Bacon, *Advancement of Learning and Novum Organum* (New York: P. F. Collier & Son, 1900) 23.
80. D. Struik, "Further Thoughts on Merton in Context," *Science in Context* 3, no. 1 (1989): 231.
81. R. K. Merton, *Science, Technology & Society in Seventeenth Century England* (New York: Howard Fertig, 1970) xii; I. B. Cohen (ed.), *Puritanism and the Rise of Modern Science*, xi, xii; T. K. Rabb, "Puritanism and the Rise of Experimental Science in England," in *Puritanism and the Rise of Modern Science*, 210.
82. Ibid., 32, 35. *The Dictionary of National Biography* (London: Smith, Elder, & Co., 1885) contains 29,120 biographical notes that provide some indication of the occupation, except in 120 cases.
83. Ibid., 122.
84. Ibid., 17-19, 118, 119, 122, 123, 128, 134, 135.
85. Ibid., 112-14.
86. Cf. Webster, *The Great Instauration*, 54-56, 61, 88. It was not the prestigious universities that gave birth to the new science but a tiny, insignificant, blue-collar institution in London by the name of Gresham College. Its professors were sympathetic to the populist religious uprising among the Puritans, while the universities were dominated by Anglicans and Royalists. Its administrators were

merchants by profession in accordance with the wishes of the founder, Thomas Gresham (1518-79), who spent his career as a merchant and financier. Its origins were humble, but all seemed to work out in the grand scheme of things, because the triumph of science was a victory of the common merchant and artisan over the social elite. In its early days science spoke the everyday, practical language of "traders, merchants, seamen, carpenters, surveyors of lands, or the like." Gresham College accommodated this language and study long before more prestigious universities recognized its importance. *Peter of Langtoft's Chronicle*, T. Hearne (ed.) (Oxford, 1725) cxlvii (Appendix); Hill, *The Intellectual Origins of the English Revolution*, 34-64, 128; *Change and Continuity in the Seventeenth-Century*, 127-29. Cf. N. Tyacke, "Science and Religion at Oxford before the Civil War," in *Puritanism and Revolutionaries*, 80, 81, 92, 93.

87. *The Record of the Royal Society of London for the Promotion of Natural Knowledge* (London: Morrison & Gibb LTD., 1940) 237 (251).
88. D. Stimson, "Puritanism and the New Philosophy in Seventeenth-Century England," in *Puritanism and the Rise of Modern Science*; Cohen, "Introduction," 14; R. Hookyas, "Science and Reformation," in *Puritanism and the Rise of Modern Science*, 189. Webster finds the precise makeup of the society more difficult to assess, although he agrees that "[c]omitted Puritans and Parliamentarians were . . . the dominant element in the scientific community, and they were responsible for the great bulk of the scientific publications." Webster, *The Great Instauration*, 93-95, 178, 491, 496, 497, 504.
89. Hill, *Intellectual Origins of the English Revolution*, 19ff., 81-83, 96. In this work, Hill asserts that Puritanism is the most important factor, but he also wishes to speak of others. A good example he uses is Walter Ralegh, a patron of science who was connected to navigation and exploration. Ralegh's *History of the World* was a very popular book with Cromwell and the Puritans and underwent a number of editions and abridgements. Ibid., 145, 146, 203, 204, 209-11.
90. T. Sprat, *The History of the Royal Society of London* [1667], J. I. Cope and H. W. Jones (ed.) (St. Louis: Washington University Studies, 1959) 370, 371.
91. F. Bacon, *Advancement of Learning*, 14-18; Nisbet, *History of the Idea of Progress*, 17-19; Webster, *The Great Instauration*, 189, 190, 199, 200; Miller, *The New England Mind: The Seventeenth Century*, 270, 271, 299ff., 332, 333, 327, 328, 349.
92. Baxter, *Christian Directory*, 1.13.
93. Webster, *The Great Instauration*, 50, 328.
94. R. F. Jones, "The Advancement of Learning and Piety," in *Puritanism and the Rise of Modern Science*, 164, 165.
95. J. Glanvill, *Philosophia Pia (1671)*, in *Collected Works of Joseph Glanvill*, B. Fabian (ed.) (Hildesheim and New York: George Olms Verlag, 1970) 5.119. See Sprat, *The History of the Royal Society*, 353-59.
96. Bacon, *Advancement of Learning*, 97. See Ibid., 5, 137.
97. Calvin uses this metaphor to describe how the Scripture clarifies our bleary-eyed view of God in nature. *Inst.*, 1.6.1-4; 14.1. For Calvin and Luther philosophy had no ability to find God apart from revelation. This position stood in contradistinction to the basic Thomistic/Aristotelian tradition of finding God through philosophical means.
98. Hill, *The Intellectual Origins of the English Revolution*, 111, 115-18; R. F. Jones, "The Advancement of Learning," 164ff.; Rabb, "Puritanism and the Rise of Experimental Science," 211; Webster, *The Great Instauration*, 24, 514. Bacon is not original in his thinking. Others made similar comments before him. Hill, *The Intellectual Origins of the English Revolution*, 85ff.

99. Bacon, *Advancement of Learning*, 23. See Cohen, "Introduction," 69; Webster, *The Great Instauration*, 56, 99.
100. Bacon, *Advancement of Learning*, passim; Webster, *The Great Instauration*, 22-24.
101. Of course, the term "science" is subject to the same language-game as the term "capitalism" or any other word. In this context science is associated with technology, the experimental method, and practical results, although the term is not always used this way. Sometimes it is used of concepts like Darwinism and Superstring Theory, where laboratory experiments and practical results are minimal.

7

The Noble Lie: The Growth of Toleration, Pluralism, and Separation

Christianity came to emphasize the knowledge of God and the world more than any other religious movement. This emphasis started at the beginning of the movement with a new concept of God, which rejected the typical stress of the time upon a unique, isolated, and transcendent deity. Christianity depicted its God as possessing the self-awareness of an inner-Trinitarian life and the capability of communicating that self-knowledge or revelation to humankind (Jn 17). God was related as the subject, object, and seal of revelation from all eternity and able to send that revelation to those who existed in space and time. Through the revelation of Christ and the seal of the Holy Spirit, all of humankind could participate in the knowledge that God alone possessed within the divine nature from all eternity (Jn 1:1, 14).[1] Christians claimed to possess this same knowledge and know God in a direct relationship, while other religions limited themselves to mystical contemplations (Hinduism and Buddhism) or following the will of God contained within a law (Judaism and Islam) without the intimate knowledge of God or the why and wherefore behind the law. Christians became theologians, who spent their time talking about God in a discursive and analytic manner. Their fellowships developed confessions, which contained detailed accounts of what was necessary to know about God and the works of creation, providence, and salvation. The churches established most of the great universities in the West, where knowledge continued to abound in all aspects of life, far surpassing the total contributions of all other religions within the global community.

The pursuit of divine knowledge brought many secondary blessings to the West in the form of advancement and prosperity, but it also brought along with these blessings a number of pitfalls, including the temptation toward pride and intolerance. The pursuit of knowledge contained the temptation to judge others who were less than orthodox in their understanding of things, and the history of Western civilization provided many examples of this intolerance in the life of the church. Theodosius I (347-395) was the first ruler of the Holy Roman Empire to use coercive measures in establishing a uniform faith in his subjects. Augustine confirmed this policy by advocating coercive measures in his own battle with the Donatists, thereby lending his much-needed authority to the practice for the medieval church. The eleventh century brought the beginning of large-scale persecutions and the pervasive use of capital punishment in dealing with heretics when fourteen of these infidels were burned at Orléans in 1022. Thereafter, the papacy used the power of the Inquisition to quell the growing rebellion of Albigensians, Waldensians, Lollards, and all other heretics who challenged the authority of Rome.[2]

By the end of the Middle Ages, the church seemed to represent much the opposite of its original vision in the life of Jesus and his disciples. Fortunately, by the dawning of the sixteenth century, many challenged what the church had become since the days of Theodosius and called the people to turn once again to the sources of faith (*ad fontes*) for religious inspiration. Christianity as a founded religion always possessed the means of checking its intolerance through the example of Christ and could not continue to live in open defiance of its basic paradigm. There might be some justification for the continued practice in the OT, but certainly the NT contained no precedent for the continued use of the sword in persecuting those of a different ideology and appeared to command much the opposite. Those who defended coercion considered the Mosaic law and the kings of Israel as providing a precedent for their conduct, but the advocates of toleration will win the day by discounting the value of a bygone dispensation and accentuating the fullness of divine revelation in Christ. The dispensationalists will accentuate the NT over the OT, and so accentuate the need for toleration. This approach is followed by many sectarian groups (Anabaptists, Arminians, Baptists, and Levellers) and many of the early champions of toleration (Sebastian Castellio, Desiderius Erasmus, Roger Williams, and John Locke). It is even followed by those who rejected the basic dogma of the church—all still admiring the simple, moral teachings of the carpenter from Nazareth (Diderot, Voltaire, and Thomas Jefferson). All these advocates of toleration found the NT and its nonviolent approach in spreading the gospel the basic paradigm for the relationship between church and state.[3]

Ambiguity

While the emphasis upon the NT is crucial, the precise history of toleration is not so simple to trace beyond a few generalizations about the basic trend and the theological viewpoint. There is no simple way to identify people or groups as good guys and bad guys without a certain amount of equivocation. Because of this problem, many scholars prefer to speak of the "rise of toleration" in the modern world, displaying a slow, uncertain, and arduous process of many ups and downs, rather than credit a certain patriarchal lineage, moving upward and onward in a teleological development.[4] For example, the general trend finds more Protestants than Catholics leading the way, but even this simple stereotype is fraught with many exceptions on all sides and a lack of perfection in any one person or group. Often Catholics gain a reputation for bigotry from Protestant sources, but there are many great champions of the cause among them. Cary Nederman has found the spirit of toleration already existing among a number of medieval theologians like Ramon Lull, John of Salisburg, Marsilius of Padua, and Nicholas of Cusa who dreamed of a new world of inter-faith dialogue and diversity.[5] Joseph Lecler, the Jesuit scholar, has displayed the many Catholic contributions to the cause of liberty in his work on toleration during the times of the Reformation.[6] No greater proponent of toleration can be found than Desiderius Erasmus, the prince of all humanists, who inspired both Catholics and Protestants in this regard and so many other areas. He preferred the example of Christ to the Turkish sword, rejected its use in punishing heretics, and considered Christianity more in terms of a sanctified life than a dogmatic confession.[7] There were even Catholic countries like Poland and France that outpaced Protestant lands in the degree of toleration shown to religious minorities—at least during certain times of their history.[8]

The ambiguity of the story continues when one considers the lead actors on the Protestant stage. Reformers like Luther and Calvin emphasized the spiritual nature of the Kingdom of God and helped to foster a more general spirit of toleration than the Catholic Church, but practical concerns and circumstances often dictated a compromise with the basic ideology. When Luther was one of the persecuted, he pleaded his cause in a treatise *On Secular Authority*, stating in no uncertain terms that civil authorities have no power over the souls of their subjects.[9] They should not use any force in punishing a heretic or converting anyone to a different religion.[10] The sword does not belong to the Kingdom of Christ.[11] While Christians may serve in government and punish the wicked for crimes against humanity, the spiritual and temporal kingdoms must ever remain distinct from each other—a position that Luther continued to hold throughout his lifetime as the most basal thought on the subject.[12] Luther ever remained a religious animal and considered civil magistrates "the biggest fools and worst scoundrels."[13] He rejected Muntzer's, Zwingli's, and Hutten's call to arms, even if their cause of democracy, egalitarianism, and nationalism found some basis for sympathy in his writings.[14] Luther wanted to separate church and state in order to purify the church from corruption—the corruption of temporal powers, which so blemished the papacy and the church within the medieval synthesis. However, once his reformational activities took hold, he felt threatened by Catholic forces undermining his efforts and would not permit the work to crumble while holding to an impossible dream. In this context, he began to advocate the practical policy of *cuius regio, eius religio* (whose region, his religion) in 1525. "A secular ruler should see to it that his subjects are not led into disunity by rival preachers causing schisms and disturbances, but in any one place there should only be one kind of preaching."[15] This policy came to fruition at Augsburg in 1555, where the principalities of Germany were sectioned off between Catholic and Protestant churches. Under this arrangement, each religion tried to gain the upper hand in the state, and it took the Thirty Years' War to end much of the haggling.[16]

These and other challenges also faced the Reformation in Switzerland and John Calvin's attempt to remain within a similar concept of church/state relations. In his *Institutes of the Christian Faith*, he condemns the worldly power of the pope and his church in the Middle Ages, its "battles, bloodshed, slaughter of armies, sacking of some cities, destruction of others, massacres of nations, and devastations of kingdoms—solely to seize other men's dominions."[17] The church does not possess the authority to compel, force, or punish anyone in the name of Christ. It possesses no right to bear the sword. The spiritual and civil kingdoms must be kept "completely distinct," otherwise the church will become corrupted with "worldly power."[18] This distinction seems clear and absolute and provides a general outline of what sounds ideal, but there are certain practical concerns that cause Calvin to amend the basic policy to insure the success of his reformation when all things are considered. Much like Luther, the civil government is needed to protect the position of the church and prevent "sacrilege against God's name, blasphemies against his truth, and other public offenses against religion from arising and spreading among the people."[19] This amended policy will lead to the most infamous episode in the career of the great reformer—the burning of Michael Servetus, the anti-Trinitarian heretic and blasphemer, at the stake. Calvin justifies his decision in the *Defense of the Christian Faith* (1554) by insisting on the need to maintain public order and using the extreme measure of death against the worst sort of blasphemers. The decision of Calvin seems harsh to modern sensibilities, but there were few to disagree with him at the time. Luther proposed a similar measure against the Jews of his land, because they blasphemed the name of Christ, spitting at the utterance of his name, calling him a liar and his mother a whore. [20] The action of Calvin found approval among the Protestant cantons of Switzerland, Lutherans in Germany, and even some of the greatest spokesmen for toleration in England like John Jewel and John Owen. [21] Calvin will gain an infamous reputation in later centuries for this one act, but the burning of a blasphemer like Servetus was consonant with the spirit of the times and almost trifling compared to the thousands of heretics burned by Catholic Inquisitors. [22]

Dispensationalists and Dissidents

There were dissenting voices, who wished to push the cause of liberty much farther than Luther or Calvin were willing to proceed. One of the earliest was Sebastian Castellio, a professor from Basel and unrelenting critic of Calvin. Early in his career he left Geneva, feeling disgusted with the way Calvin ruled the city like an autocrat and theological bully.[23] After the execution of Servetus, he went ballistic and wrote a number of tracts condemning Calvin for conspiring with papists in the unseemly affair and forsaking the principles of the Reformation by committing this atrocity. [24] In his most celebrated and influential work, *Concerning Heretics* (1554), he puts forth the example of Christ as his main source of inspiration and claims that Calvin has transformed the savior of humanity into Moloch. [25] He also cites the parable of the wheat and tares, where Christ commanded us to let the tares grow together with the wheat, lest we uproot what God has planted. [26] Human beings are much too obtuse in their understanding of human nature and God's will to judge one another, let alone to label as heretics those who appear to seek the truth in matters that remain hidden. Speculative matters like the doctrine of the Trinity and predestination remain unclear and unrelated to the fundamental articles of the faith, necessary for the salvation of the soul. Who are we to judge fellow believers about matters that seem so obscure and remain hidden within the depths of God and the parables of the divine word?[27] Besides, history is replete with many instances where the church condemned as heretics those who spoke the truth of God. This meant that the true people of God are downtrodden in this world and suffer at the hands of the powers that be. It is only those who seek power and dominion that coerce, compel, and persecute others to follow their will—not the true remnant of God's elected people.[28] The Scripture limits the discipline of the church to the power of excommunication, and the civil magistrate has no right to meddle in its affairs or exercise spiritual dominion whatsoever.[29]

Sectarian groups were most significant in spreading the message of Castellio and others to the masses. Castellio's work found a receptive audience in a number of countries, especially in the Low Countries, [30] where the people were prepared through years of persecution and the work of scholars like Erasmus to accept the radical message. But even the impact of Castellio, Erasmus, Koonhert, and other scholars pales in comparison to the power of religious communities that were able to reach the people, institutionalize doctrine, procreate disciples, and disseminate the message in society generation after generation. The liberty and toleration that became so much a part of the Netherlands owes its greatest debt, not so much to a few, isolated scholars in academic situations, but to the many sectarian groups that suffered and died for the cause in spreading the word. Among these groups, the Anabaptists and Arminians stand out for special mention in leading their society as a whole toward a more tolerant posture.

The term Anabaptist was used of many different groups in the Reformation, but the particular strain that became most identified with the movement and emerged over time has its origins in Switzerland (Conrad Grebel), Southern Germany (Balthasar Hubmaier), and the Netherlands (Menno Simons). [31] These Anabaptists came to represent the most radical expression of the basic Protestant desire to follow the Scripture and separate the church from the state. They were a dispensational group, holding to the priority of the NT over the OT, and sought to follow that text with the radical and absolute devotion of literal obedience. They rejected infant baptism because the practice was based on an analogy with OT circumcision and not specifically taught or found in the NT. They refused to take an oath, based on Jesus' literal words in the Sermon on the Mount to refrain from such practices (Mtt. 5:33-37). They wanted to establish a NT church, which shared its resources (Acts 2:44, 45; 4:32), excommunicated the immoral (Mtt. 18:15-17, 1 Cor. 5), refused the sword (Mtt. 5:39), and suffered for the Kingdom of God (2 Tim. 3:12). [32] In the Schleitheim Confession (1527) of Michael Sattler, they went so far in following Christ and separating themselves from the state that they opposed all participation in it as "outside the perfection of Christ"—a position that did not endear them to the magistrates of Christian nations.[33] If there was a political message, it consisted only in the simple exhortation for the magistrates to renounce the use of the sword in pursuing heresy, leaving some of them to dream of a pluralistic society, where Jews, Turks, pagans, and all sorts of Christians could live together in peace despite all their differences.[34]

Their greatest testimony was sealed in what they called the "Baptism of Blood." They wanted to suffer like the early church as a faithful remnant in a world shrouded in darkness. They possessed little hope of changing the lot of Christians in the world or recreating the state into a more Christ-like image,[35] but because of their faithful witness society as a whole grew weary of shedding innocent blood and stopped persecuting them and others in the seventeenth century.[36] At this time, the Anabaptists produced a memorial of the suffering, entitled *The Bloody Theater* or *Martyrs Mirror*,[37] which provided a testimony to the lasting impact of their martyrs in the Netherlands, much like the *martyria* of John Foxe in England. (Menno Simmons himself was converted through the pangs of conscience he suffered upon watching the martyrdom of some three hundred Anabaptists at the Old Cloister near Bolsward in 1535.)[38] Like Foxe's work, *The Bloody Theater* divides its history between two separate churches, the one serving the truth of God and the other subservient to the wiles of the devil.[39] The true church is depicted as a visible remnant, existing through all the ages of biblical and ecclesiastical history and possessing a fundamental understanding of baptism and other doctrines, which the Anabaptists of the day hold in a more perfected form.[40] At times the people of God are few in number and insufficient in understanding, but they still hold to the same essential teaching of the faith.[41] Included within the remnant are OT saints, a number of Church Fathers, and certain medieval sects like the Donatists, Berengarians, Waldenses, Albigenses, and Lollards.[42] This church was "born to suffer . . . from the beginning and all through, even as gold in the furnace that her purity might become more manifest."[43] The church of the Antichrist is marked by its lust for blood in persecuting the remnant of God and murdering all the so-called "heretics."[44] This persecution never accomplished its intended results in converting anyone or destroying the many sectarian groups, because faith is the gift of God. The church is admonished to follow Christ and renounce the use of the sword as a tool of the devil. No one should compel the conscience of another. All should allow the Spirit to move and convict what comes from the heart. Even the king should allow his people to choose a faith of their own free will in accordance with each individual conscience.[45]

The Arminians were another dispensational group, who aided the Anabaptists in their fight for toleration in the Low Countries. They challenged the Calvinists' belief in the perspicuity of revelation and pleaded for more latitude when determining doctrinal issues. The Calvinists saw the revelation of God in a simple manner, as embodied within one basic covenant, which was clearly understood throughout all the dispensations of biblical history by those who heard the divine word. Because the message of the Old and New Testament was essentially the same, the old applied to the new and the new to the old in a more direct way than was typical of Christian exegesis. The saints of old knew the message of the gospel in clear detail, including the doctrine of divine incarnation and vicarious atonement, and the saints of the new economy can find in the Mosaic Law and the prophets many teachings directly applicable to the life of the church. The merger of the biblical message allowed the Calvinists to translate the example of the Jewish theocracy almost directly into the present time and so merge the church and state together. In fact, the beginning of covenant theology in Zurich finds Zwingli on the battlefield fighting Catholic cantons, slaying dispensational heretics, and attempting to establish a *corpus Christianum*. This approach tended to follow Calvinism wherever it was planted. Hugo Grotius complained that those who followed the teachings of Calvinism "bring tumult wherever they prevail,"[46] and his fellow Arminians proceeded to challenge the intolerance, questioning the Calvinistic concept of covenant, which caused much of the problem. James Arminius thought it debatable that the OT saints possessed a clear knowledge of the covenant of grace.[47] Simon Episcopius contrasted the merciless and austere demands of the OT law with the New Covenant of divine grace in Christ. He thought maybe it was possible to interpret the promises of the OT in hindsight as a shadow of the eternal blessings in Christ, but it is difficult to believe that the average OT believer saw much more in these promises than temporal and earthly blessings.[48] The Calvinists simply overestimated the insight of others, as well as their own. They overestimated their own insights in the present debate over divine sovereignty by displaying too much arrogance about their knowledge of divine secrets. Arminians felt that theological questions like the relationship between divine grace and human freedom are subject to honest debate, and it is simply wrong to bind the faithful to a creed of the church or a synod appointed by the magistrate. Each believer should be free to develop his or her own interpretation on speculative matters. There might be some "Fundamental Articles of the Faith," which all Christians should believe, but these articles are few and far between. All believers are capable of judging what is necessary and determining doctrinal matters without the aid of synods, creeds, or inquisitions.[49] The civil and ecclesiastical authorities should refrain from persecuting heretics or inflicting corporeal punishment in matters of conscience, which remain the private concern of each believer before God.[50]

In the year after the death of Arminius, under the direction of Janus Utyenbogaert, forty-six Arminian ministers assembled together at Goulda to sign the *Remonstrantia*, remonstrating five offensive doctrinal points of the Calvinistic opposition and framing five positive doctrinal points of their own. The memorial was submitted to John van Olden Barneveldt, Advocate-General of Holland and Friesland, with the hope of securing toleration for their opinions from the states of Holland.[51] In March of 1611, a group of Calvinist ministers followed suit by preparing their own memorial, the so-called Contra-Remonstrance, and submitted it to the states of Holland. While the Arminians pleaded for toleration in areas of doctrinal difference, the Calvinists wanted the issues in the articles decided through an examination of Scripture.[52] At first, the states ruled in favor of peace through the efforts of Barneveldt, Hoogerbeets, and Grotius, but when Prince Maurice of Nassau, the Stadtholder and military leader of the Republic, arose in power, he cast these political rivals in prison and allied himself with the Calvinists.[53] Through these and other political intrigues an international synod convened at Dordrecht in 1618, consisting of some 150 delegates, in order to render its judgment upon the *Remonstrantia*.[54] The Arminians protested against the very nature of the proceedings, calling for toleration and considering the synod a kangaroo court of their former enemies.[55] Episcopius led the appeal and proposed in an oration before the synod that mutual toleration should reign in disputed areas of doctrine, citing a number of examples where this policy prevailed in other states and countries—but all to no avail.[56] Within a year, all Arminian meetings were forbidden under law, and two hundred Arminian leaders were deprived of their ecclesiastical and academic offices; many of them decided to flee the country.[57] Some of the foreign delegates thought the penalties were too harsh, causing Walter Balcanqual to exclaim that never in the history of the church had "so many articles" been proposed "under the penalty of excommunication."[58] Nevertheless, the concerns were soon abated when Maurice died in 1625 and toleration became more and more normative under his successor and brother, Frederick Henry.[59] The Netherlands became a place of refuge for persecuted minorities and served as a beacon of toleration in continental Europe and across the channel in England, where its impact was felt the strongest through bustling trade, the exchange of refugees, and the ascension of William of Orange to the throne.[60]

Religious dissidents also comprised a disproportionate number of those who argued for religious toleration in England. Many of them were found in sectarian groups like the Brownists and Barrowists—those disenchanted with the state and wanting the space to worship in their own voluntary community, free from persecution.[61] Others were attached to dispensational groups like the Levellers, Baptists, and Anabaptists, who wanted to follow the NT message of love and freedom of conscience, preferring the way of martyrdom to coercing others into following a certain prescribed path.[62] The Puritan Revolution brought many of these groups, along with their issue of toleration to the forefront in society. The year 1644 saw the production of some of the great classics on the subject: William Walwyn's *The Compassionate Samaritane*, Roger Williams' *The Bloudy Tenent*, Henry Robinson's *Liberty of Conscience*, and John Milton's *Areopagitica*. In the Whithall debates of 1648, religious radicals advocated complete freedom of conscience and rejected any role of the magistrate in punishing heretical or blasphemous opinions. The Puritan Revolution witnessed the rise of groups who entertained profane, skeptical, and anti-Christian positions (like the Ranters) yet were accorded a modicum of toleration far beyond previous expectations.[63]

Cromwell belonged to this new spirit of toleration among the dissidents. He was willing to extend toleration to every community in England, even if some of his enthusiasm was tempered by the politics of the time. (He was unable to disestablish the Church of England or end the practice of tithing.) He tolerated Anglicans and Catholics, as long as they did not participate in royalist plots to overturn the regime. He rejected the persecution of Quakers, as long as they did not disrupt peaceful assemblies with uncivilized behavior. He welcomed the Jews back into the country after decades of banishment, hoping to utilize their considerable capital and expertise in trade to enhance his own country's wealth. Even if there were laws against denying the Christian faith, Cromwell showed little interest in pursuing these and other matters against Jews, Ranters, Socinians, skeptics, and other unorthodox groups who suddenly arose in number and visibility at the time. He liked the vague language of the *Instrument of Government* (1653), which upheld the Christian religion as the public profession of the kingdom but contained little detail for those who preferred a more specific agenda. Of course, this broad interpretation did not appeal to many Puritans who wanted to cleanse the church and state from religious impurity—the very reason they sought political power in the first place. At times, Cromwell's fight for religious liberty was curtailed by Parliament, whose Presbyterian faction wanted a uniform faith and sought to exclude Romanism, Anglicanism, and sectarianism from the overall definition of the National Church.[64] Nevertheless, there was a marked increase in tolerance during his tenure and a positive step toward a fuller liberty in the future.

Anti-Catholicism

The freedom of religious conscience received its first lasting symbol in England a few decades later with the Act of Toleration (1689) under William and Mary. Penal sanctions against Protestant dissenters were lifted in the course of time, and freedom of worship was granted to nonconformist congregations, even if the full participation of civil rights was reserved for those who followed more mainstream beliefs. The Church of England remained established by law. It received the tithes of the citizens, and its parishioners were accorded the privileges associated with membership in the state religion. The Test Act (1673) remained in force, which barred from office Catholics, non-Trinitarians, and all those who refused the very taking of an oath as a matter of conscience. The spread of Catholicism and the danger of its polity was the basic concern of Puritans. Initially, William wanted to grant Catholics the freedom of worship, but he eventually acquiesced to the demands of Parliament and the interests of an anti-Catholic unity. Catholicism remained a prohibited religion, and even William came to recognize the danger of allowing Catholics into the public domain.[65]

Problems developed in England for the Catholic faith at the beginning of the Reformation when Henry VIII, in a series of three acts, made himself "the only supreme head on earth of the Church of England" and demanded a loyalty oath from his subjects, forswearing any other foreign authority. The nation seemed to accept the new arrangement passively and meekly, but pious Catholics could not obey two masters and preferred the sentence of death to forswearing the Vicar of Christ, as happened in the famous case of Sir Thomas More.[66] Catholics would receive a measure of revenge when Mary Tudor ascended to the throne in a bloody fury, murdering three hundred Protestants for heresy and sending hundreds more into exile during her short, four-year reign of terror.[67] But the lesson England drew would lead to the exclusion of Catholics from public office and the determination of the country to remain solidly within the Protestant fold.

Elizabeth, the Protestant sister of Mary, was the next daughter of Henry to ascend to the throne, and she was determined at the beginning of her tenure to steer a different course than her sister and tolerate all Christians—except the most seditious and rebellious on either side of the spectrum. The first twelve years of her reign fulfilled much of these good intentions and were relatively peaceful with Catholics receiving a measure of toleration in accordance with their own traditions.[68] However, two ill-conceived threats caused the situation to worsen for the Catholic minority, forcing Elizabeth to change her benevolent policy: one, Pope Pius V issued a bull (*Regnans in Excelsis*, 1570) excommunicating Elizabeth and releasing the faithful from submission to their queen[69]; and two, the government perceived a growing threat from Jesuits, foreign activists, and other militants, stirring up the Catholic population in the hope of restoring the country to the faith and overturning the government.[70] Elizabeth reacted harshly to the threat by executing a total of 189 Catholics during the last three decades of her reign—all for the ostensible crime of treason. Only six individuals were executed for the explicit reason of blasphemy or heresy during this time, and only two in the subsequent reign of James I.[71]

Protestants found it difficult to trust Catholics in any position of authority or accord them the same kind of religious liberties enjoyed by others considering the possible negative impact upon their own civil rights. The people of the sixteenth and seventeenth centuries lived in one universe, outside the modern concept of church/state separation, and were unable or unwilling to circumscribe religious ideals within a limited sphere of devotion. To the Protestants of Elizabethan England, Catholicism stood for the suppression of individual rights, authoritarian rule, and a hierarchical form of government both inside and outside the church.[72] Protestants and Catholics had no religious or secular interest in creating a dichotomy between the polity of the church and the polity of the civil government, but it was this peculiar dichotomy that the Protestant majority demanded of Catholics if they wanted to participate in their world as full citizens. Of course, this process was not easy to institute after years of conditioning in much the opposite. It took some time for Catholics to change their view of civil government as they became related to the world around them and even longer for Protestant countries to trust that the Catholic citizens had made a sufficient distinction between the policies of the Roman hierarchy and the liberties of a

Republican government. The Church of Rome proved so obstinate in the process that it continued to oppose political and religious liberalism right up until Vatican II.[73] It is no wonder that some of the great defenders of liberty and democracy felt compelled to limit their ideological zeal out of pragmatic necessity when it came to endorsing the full acceptance of Catholics into positions of authority.

A good example of the problem is John Locke's "Letter Concerning Toleration." The work is enshrined by secular intelligentsia into their hall of fame as the first important statement of toleration in the modern world, much for the same reason that Hobbes and Rousseau are exalted for the social contract theory; its arguments are perceived as less religious and more philosophical in nature.[74] This secular bias prevents these scholars from recognizing two fundamental facts about the work: one, it is far from the first work to emphasize toleration and probably not very important in the overall history of the doctrine, and two, it is more Protestant and anti-Catholic than those who like to exalt its philosophical orientation care to admit. The letter was composed in the fall of 1685 during Locke's exile in Holland, where he befriended the many sectarian groups of the country, including French Protestants who sought refuge in Holland just before and after the revocation of the Edict of Nantes that year.[75] Among his friends were included Phillip Limborch, the leading Arminian theologian, to whom he dedicates the letter and Bejamin Furly, a freethinking English Quaker, whose house he shared for two years while residing in Rotterdam. His personal library contained a collection of books by dissident Protestants like Castellio, Grotius, Episcopius, Milton, and Penn on toleration, along with other sons of liberty like Koonhert, Spinoza, Bayle, and a number of Socinian authors.[76] While his overall style of argumentation reflects the more secular orientation of the Enlightenment, he remains deeply indebted to the basic religious viewpoint of a Protestant dissident at important junctures in the overall argument. Like a Congregationist, he defines the church as a "free and voluntary society" of believers, who are "join[ed] together of their own accord in order to the public worshipping of God in such a manner as they judge acceptable to Him."[77] Like a dispensationalist, he rejects the direct application of the Mosaic Law to the practice of the church, whether it is found in the moral, judicial, or ceremonial aspects of that law. Christ prescribed "no such thing under the Gospel as a Christian Commonwealth" or the "absolute theocracy" of OT law.[78] These concepts he borrows from dissident groups and uses them throughout the discussion as a basis for creating his theory of toleration.

This same religious matrix also informs his equivocal attitude toward granting Catholics toleration and citizenship within society, much to the chagrin of secularists who never seem to grasp the relationship between religion and politics. He expresses a broad range of toleration toward "Lutherans, Calvinists, Remonstrants, and other sects," whose doctrinal differences are insignificant to society and left to the personal convictions of each individual. But Catholicism is treated as an altogether different religion, because it is based upon the imposition of papal authority and ecclesiastical tradition.[79] In his "Critical Notes" of 1681, the best he can do is offer a "regulated toleration" to the Catholic citizenry, believing that the religion possesses "an unalterable designe to destroy us."[80]

These reservations came to the forefront during the reigns of Charles II, who wanted to grant more toleration to Catholics, and James II, who actually converted to the religion and produced a son ready to continue the tradition. Both of these monarchs tried to grant more toleration to dissidents with the prospect of assuaging the fears of a royalist/Catholic tyranny, but they never succeeded in their efforts because of the religious and political concerns of Parliament. James II turned to find new support and ally himself with dissidents, offering them even more concessions in exchange for their loyalty, but when this tactic failed, he made a crucial error by attempting to bypass the Parliament and impose toleration by fiat, a maneuver that only deepened the suspicions of all Protestants in the country about his ultimate intensions. Eventually he was forced from the throne in 1688 when William of Orange invaded England and established a limited constitutional monarchy, much to the delight of the Protestant majority, including the many sectarian groups, John Locke, and his famous party of Whigs.[81]

Anti-Catholic sentiment was transported to the New World by the many Protestant groups who first populated the land from England. The Quakers stand out among these emigrants in a special way as the most persecuted group in England and the most vociferous defenders of freedom in America, and yet they had little sympathy for the plight of Catholics in their society.[82] William Penn, the leader of the "Holy Experiment," called for all Protestants to unite and protect their common civil interests against "the designs of Rome."[83] The difference between Protestantism and Catholicism consists of more than just a simple quibble over the points of doctrine in the church. It is an important civil matter effecting the future of the colonies.[84] His solution was the enactment of an oath, making all crypto-papists forswear allegiance to Rome and denounce the Catholic religion and its doctrines as idolatrous.[85] In Connecticut and

Massachusetts, similar oaths were exacted for those who held office and were not revoked until 1818 and 1833 in these colonies respectively.[86]

Even without these oaths, Catholics still remained under an onus to separate their political ideology from the teachings of the church. The nineteenth and twentieth century witnessed a more subtle form of discrimination, in which Protestants invoked church/state separation to eliminate Catholics from public office and protect the quasi-Protestant domain over public education. To participate in the public domain, Catholics were forced to embrace secularity (e.g., John Kennedy) or confirm a secular purpose for dollars provided by the state (e.g., *Everson v. the Board of Education*). Fewer and fewer Americans wanted to accept the more overt forms of discrimination in the past or identify with the redneck tactics of marginal groups like the Ku Klux Klan. A more subtle approach was needed to suit the times, but the new tactic soon backfired. The doctrine of church/state separation soon turned upon the Protestant majority and became a means of eliminating religion in general. The dichotomy separating Catholics from their religion soon transmuted into a general policy, separating all religious ideals from the government. Secularity was demanded of all citizens, Catholics and Protestants alike, if they wanted to participate in the ever-expanding domain of the government. No longer was the Protestant heritage honored for its important role in shaping the country but forgotten and even dismissed as a source of bigotry and intolerance from the past.[87]

The Noble Lie

The Massachusetts Bay Colony has obtained the most infamous reputation through the years as the leading sponsor of bigotry and religious intolerance among the early colonies. This reputation is somewhat unfair considering the oppressive nature of more hierarchical cultures like Virginia and the overall commitment to democratic and egalitarian ideals in the colony, which brought liberation in the course of years to the rest of America.[88] The overall direction of their ideology provided a positive foundation for the future, but in spite of the many contributions, there were forces at work that led the colony into the opposite direction from what their basic orientation would dictate. In all too many instances they acted with the intolerance of the era in which they lived. They followed the Lutheran principle of *cuius regio, eius religio*, as well as the Anglican policy of imposing religious uniformity upon the citizenry. They remained steadfast to the Reformed doctrine of covenant, which found in the Jewish commonwealth of the OT a model for the relationship between church and state. According to John Winthrop, the Bay Colony was based upon a federal system, which one could join or not of their own free will, but once within its jurisdiction those inside the system must respect the basic rules of the *corpus Christianum*.[89] Those who showed open contempt for the magistrate and the teaching office of the church, like Roger Williams and Anne Hutchinson in the 1640s, were banished from the colony unless they repented of their sins. Those who brought outside teachings to the colony, like Quakers and Baptists in the 1650s, were treated in a similar fashion and sometimes hung for their missionary zeal.[90] At one point in the year 1637 Winthrop and the General Court became so provincial and isolated within their own world that they decided to ban further immigration from those who seemed theologically suspect.[91] It was not until the Act of Toleration (1689) and their new charter (1691) that the colony became more inclusive concerning conflicting ideologies, and its leading theologians, Increase and Cotton Mather, advocated the virtues of religious liberty.[92]

The most celebrated dissident of the early colony was Roger Williams. He drove the principles of congregationalism and separatism to extreme lengths, hoping to create a fellowship of true believers, untainted by any association with unregenerate members, problematic churches, and governmental power. His concept of separation had more affinity with the Congregationalists who settled in Plymouth than Boston, but even their rigor proved insufficient for his high-minded standards. Some historians have identified him as a Baptist in his theological and political ideals, although he was so much a separatist and seeker that no specific sect seemed to please his demands for purity.[93] Whatever the specific affiliation, his sanctimony became a public spectacle, and the General Court felt obligated to banish him to the woods in January of 1636 for causing divisiveness in the colony and expressing contempt toward its civil and ecclesiastical officials.[94] John Cotton, the great theologian of the day, wrote a letter to him during his exile justifying the sentence of the court and trying his best to exact some form of repentance from him. He told Williams that his "corrupt doctrines" had caused a "disturbance both of civil and holy peace" and exhorted him to steer a more moderate course in the future.[95] The early church accepted in their fellowship those who were weak in faith and incomplete in their confession of sin. It tried to steer a moderate course between the demands of repentance and the necessity of forgiveness.[96] But none of these exhortations prevailed upon Williams' extreme concept of a sanctified fellowship. Eventually he chose to develop his own "livelie experiment" in Rhode Island, which made great strides in civil liberty even if it was filled with the same sort of civil strife and human depravity he hoped to leave behind in Boston.[97]

The great work of Williams upon the subject of separation and toleration is *The Bloudy Tenet* (1644). It enjoyed a wide circulation in England, where it was first published, and later became a classic in America after the times of toleration dawned and identified with its message.[98] His arguments are filled with the exegesis of Scripture throughout the work.[99] He argues much like a dispensationalist in promoting the message of the NT as the most direct and literal model for Christians to follow in the present age. The civil law of the Mosaic economy does not bind the governments of today. Its nation and leaders serve the present dispensation only as a shadow of the spiritual kingdom to come, not a literal pattern to compete with the higher revelation of Christ.[100] Even the prophets, when they utter words of condemnation and slay the enemies of Yahweh, provide merely an image of the true spiritual battle in Christ; otherwise, their literal words and deeds would contradict the clear message of NT forgiveness and mercy.[101] Christ abolished the national state of Israel and the persecution of religious infidels in his coming.[102] He commanded his disciples to leave the wheat and tares alone (Mtt. 13:30,38); he told them to leave those who are blind to their own devices (Mtt. 15:14); he reproved those who wish to devour their enemies with fire (Lk 9:54,55); and he exhorted all of us to bless our enemies and do good in return for evil (Mtt. 8:44).[103] Even the OT prophets foretold of a time when the Messiah would "beat their swords into Mattocks," and "then shall none hurt nor harm in all the mountain of my holiness" (Isa. 2:4; 9:9).[104]

These verses lead Williams to divorce the religion of the church from the power of the state and erect a wall between them. The civil government has no authority in spiritual matters whatsoever.[105] Constantine's attempt to unify the Holy Roman Empire under a single concept of God brought more harm to the cross of Christ than the sum total of all the persecutions surrounding Nero, Domitian, and the Roman Colosseum.[106] The magistrate is not the custodian of the first table of the Mosaic Law.[107] The church can judge the magistrate in spiritual cases and the magistrate the churches in civil cases, but neither can exercise authority in the other's realm.[108] These two authorities must remain completely distinct. The citizens of the church and state possess two different sets of loyalties—the same dualistic loyalties that Baptists embraced at the time and continued to promote thereafter.[109]

In his response to Cotton's letter, Williams will fortify his dual citizenship by building a "wall of separation" between church and state, and so protect these two realms from influencing each other. His wall represents a consistent development of the basic spirit of the Reformation, which wanted to protect the church from the corrupting influences of temporal powers. The wall is erected for the church's sake to preserve its spiritual message, uncorrupted by the desire for greatness and the will to power in the state.[110] However, Williams does not wish to proceed too far in this direction and deny in concert with Anabaptist doctrine the legitimate role of Christians in government. Instead, he prefers to create a noble lie by permitting his people to dwell in two worlds and pretending the one hand does not know what the other is doing. Of course, the magistrate and radical Reformers never thought of the government as free from the onus of the divine will, but in order to create the dichotomy Williams is forced to envision the state as a godless institution, separate from the religion, ethics, and social norms of the church. A magistrate might arise from any religious background and serve the commonwealth just as well.

> And I ask, whether or no such as may hold forth other worships or religions, Jews, Turks, or anti-Christians, may not be peaceful and quiet subjects, loving and helpful neighbors, fair and just dealers, true and loyal to the civil government? It is clear they may, from all reason and experience in many flourishing cities and kingdoms of the world, and so offend not against the civil state and peace . . . These I observe to prove, that a subject, a magistrate, may be a good subject, a good magistrate, in respect of civil or moral goodness, which thousands want; and where it is, it is commendable and beautiful, though godliness, which is infinitely more beautiful, be wanting, and which is only proper to the Christian state, the commonweal of Israel, the true church, the holy nation. (Eph. 2; 1 Pet. 2) . . . I dare not assent to that assertion, "That even original sin remotely hurts the civil state." It is true some do, as inclinations to murder, theft, whoredom, slander, disobedience to parents, and magistrates; but blindness of mind, hardness of heart, inclination to choose or worship this or that God, this or that Christ, beside the true, these hurt not remotely the civil state, as not concerning it, but the spiritual.[111]

When taken literally, these comments of Williams seem to suggest that religious ideology is unrelated to political agendas. As a metaphor, these words find a semblance of value with its heart-felt desire to encourage purity in the church and promote toleration in society, but a problem arises when they are taken so literally and used to discount the clear differences between religious groups and people over political matters. However noble his motive might be in fostering a spirit of toleration, the religious groups who came to this country deconstructed the message of the Scripture and developed distinctive and specific political agendas, which patently contradict each other. Democracy and egalitarianism certainly did not arise in the south where the Anglican Church supplied much of the spiritual inspiration and produced a hierarchical society. It was not the southern aristocracy or Virginia plantation owners who supplied the original and fundamental impetus toward democracy in America.[112] It was not as if democracy developed in the consciousness of people regardless of the religious milieu.

In the south, the major impetus came from dissident groups who immigrated from the north in the eighteenth century and challenged the old patriarchal order and gentry-dominated churches. It was the Baptists in particular who took the lead and challenged the gentry order, rejecting sumptuary laws, addressing everyone as "brother" and "sister," and bringing Puritan republicanism with them as they settled in the region.[113]

According to Jefferson, "two thirds of the people had become dissenters at the commencement of the present revolution,"[114] and the Baptists became the most potent members of the dissenting groups in challenging the oppressive climate of the state. No one knows their precise numbers, but they were a sizable and vocal minority by the time of the Revolutionary War and served as an impetus toward this radical change. A large number of Virginians joined sectarian groups like the Baptists, Presbyterians, and Methodists, beginning in the 1740s, as a result of the missionary zeal of the Great Awakening. These evangelical groups brought with them a tremendous appeal to the common folks, who suffered under years of Anglican-dominated oppression and naturally preferred to hear the good news of freedom and equality. Baptists and Methodists made particular inroads into the Black population, who suffered the most anguish under the established order, as the dissidents combined their message of freedom and equality with a strident denunciation of slavery. Through their efforts the old vestry system of Virginia died out and the Anglican Church dwindled in size and lost considerable power after the Revolutionary War. Today it exists with flagging numbers, less than one-tenth the size of the Baptist faithful in the state.[115]

Of course, all this history was soon forgotten as the power of the Enlightenment began to usurp the role of any church in the founding of the country and exalt the personal contributions of its own disciples. The new "Founding Fathers" are selected from those who point to the power of reason or secular sources in establishing the nation. Thomas Jefferson is selected and creates his own version of history, exalting the place of the Enlightenment and creating a negative stereotype of the church and its involvement in politics.[116] In his mind it is necessary to erect a wall that prevents ecclesiastical dogma and zealotry from corrupting the people for the sake of the state, and he promotes a government policy to exclude Christian symbols, devotion, and teachings from the public domain.[117] Through this way and means he expresses a genuine desire to promote toleration and religious freedom in society, but he also hopes to diminish the role of the church in the affections of the people and replace it with a religion more conducive to his own version of spirituality—a motive that is not surprising for a son of the Enlightenment or even an Anglican who possesses no other experience within the church universal.[118] However, what is surprising about the wall is not that a man like Jefferson would espouse it, but how readily Williams and the Baptists adopted it without considering the consequences for the church and its place in society. They wanted to promote the noble lie in society for the sake of giving and receiving toleration, but the price they paid was high in diminishing their own vital role in establishing the country and submitting to the designs of Jefferson—designs that included a "quiet euthanasia" for the church in public education and a wall separating it from the power structures of government.[119]

The Baptists were strong advocates of both toleration and separation from the very beginning of their existence. As dispensationalists, they were more consistent with the voluntary nature of the church and more tolerant of other faiths than most Congregationalists, who still possessed within covenant theology the countervailing tendency to seek a theocratic kingdom.[120] Both John Smyth and Thomas Helwys, the founders of the movement, denied the right of a magistrate to "meddle with religion, or matters of conscience, to force and compel men to this or that form of religion or doctrine: but to leave the Christian religion free to every man's conscience, and to handle only civil transgressions, injuries and wrongs of man against man."[121] The magistrate has no power to "make laws and ordinances [for] his subjects" or set "spiritual lords over them" because "men's religion to God is between God and themselves. The king shall not answer for it."[122] This position became one of the few consistent doctrines of a fellowship, which often took pride in its non-dogmatic posture and the individual freedom of each member. This doctrine of freedom was disseminated wherever the Baptists landed. In America, the Baptists took the lead in disestablishing the Episcopal Church in the south and the Congregational Church in the north by overturning the long-established practice of public support for the clergy.[123] The Baptists gained a great victory in this context and took great pride in their special role of bequeathing the separation of church and state to the entire nation.

> On and on was the struggle waged by our Baptist fathers for religious liberty in Virginia, in the Carolinas, in Georgia, in Rhode Island, and Massachusetts, and Connecticut, and elsewhere, with one unyielding contention for unrestricted religious liberty for all men, and with never one wavering note. They dared to be odd, to stand alone, to refuse to conform, though it cost them suffering and even life itself. They dared to defy traditions and customs, and deliberately chose the way of non-conformity, even though in many a case it meant persecutions and punishments. They pleaded and suffered, they offered their protests and remonstrances and memorials; and, thank God, mighty statesmen were won to their contention, Washington and Jefferson and Madison and Patrick Henry, and many others, until at last it was written into our country's Constitution that church and state must in this land be forever separate and free, that neither must ever trespass upon the distinctive functions of the other. It was pre-eminently a Baptist achievement.[124]

> So far as the Baptists were concerned, the Established Church from 1768 to 1774 had taught "instructions which being taught returned to plague" her successor, the Protestant Episcopal Church, from 1784 to 1802. During all those years, the Baptists followed with passionate eagerness the ideal of religious freedom to its logical consequence of absolute separation of Church and State. In the process they had a large share, and for the result they deserve immense credit.[125]

Among the early leaders of the movement, no one stood greater than John Leland, the self-educated preacher from the farm lands of New England and political patron of Thomas Jefferson. He spent much of his time traveling as an itinerant preacher in the north and south, hoping to secure religious freedom for all dissidents and end the religious establishments in the Commonwealth of Virginia, Connecticut, and Massachusetts.[126] In his works, he argues that "a man has a civil right to believe that which is erroneous, and do that which is morally wrong."[127] This liberty is not a "favor granted" by the capricious will of a civil government but a "right inherent," which no one can alienate or withdraw.[128] To guarantee this liberty he finds it necessary to denounce whatever establishments remain standing within the many states and all practices associated with them: paid clergy, military chaplains, Sabbatarian laws, religious tests for office, et al.[129]

This position is indebted in a most direct way to his dispensational understanding of the Scripture and the place of the church in society. Leland extols the example of the NT church as represented in the first three centuries of its existence, before it was corrupted by Constantine and the "shocking monster of a Christian Nation" was established.[130] His concept of the church rejects any place for the nation of Israel as a model worthy of respect and emulation in the present age.[131] The church does not derive its laws from the "Mosaic constitution."[132] Leland prefers to think of the church in NT terms as a voluntary fellowship, subsisting as a remnant in society, rather than a social force working in the culture at large for the common good of all humankind.[133] He transforms religion into a private matter between the individual and God, following the voluntary nature of church membership.[134] Religion possesses no message whatsoever for the state to follow.

> Is uniformity of sentiments, in matter of religion, essential to the happiness of civil government? Not at all. Government has no more to do with the religious opinions of men, than it has with the principles of mathematics. Let every man speak freely without fear, maintain the principles that he believes, worship according to his own faith, either one God, three Gods, no God, of twenty Gods; and let government protect him in doing so.[135]

The Christian religion has never brought any benefit to society during its history of involvement with temporal powers.

> But still a question arises, whether Christianity, as a national characteristic, or political institute, has ever been of any advantage to the nations and governments on earth, in their collective capacities? Was Rome more virtuous or prosperous after Christianity was established there, than it was when Paganism was their religion? Are the papal kingdoms, now subject to the see of Rome, governed by the Christian princes, and directed by the successor of Peter, more honest, peaceable, chaste, brave in war, or renowned for just maxims of jurisprudence, than they were under Pagan rulers?
>
> Can Christian nations produce greater geniuses than Greece and Athens—more superb cities that Babylon and Nineveh—or more flourishing commerce than Tyrus? Was there ever a more unjust and cruel conquest than that of Spain over South America? Or when was there ever a confederation of Goths, Vandals and Moors, more unreasonable, mischievous and disasterous, than the crusades, etc., etc.
>
> If simply Christianity is all innocent and interesting, and yet the most horrid evils have existed, and do still exist, in Christian kingdoms and states, the cause should be sought for, and shunned.[136]

The position of Leland and the Baptists is motivated by a heart-felt devotion for the church and its purity, along with a genuine love for the rights of all human beings. Their position made important strides in rejecting any *a priori* commitment to a sect, ideology, or confession in the government. Any sect or person could participate in the civil government through the elective process, and no specific group would receive lasting favor in the contest for the affections of the people from an exclusionary policy. However, their position contained a clear problem when it tried to preclude religious affections *a posteriori* from the people in selecting a person to represent them or determining a specific form of government. Regardless of what Baptists say, religious affections seem to play a role in their lives during this stage of the process.[137] Each voter, candidate, and platform are informed by their own interpretation and application of an overall ideology—an ideology that is entangled with religion in most every way—historically, philosophically, and theologically. Disestablishing churches and eliminating tests for office certainly helped in freeing the process for all to participate, but someone's ideology must prevail once a candidate is selected or a specific course of action is chosen. One might add a special exhortation to reduce the size of government and so maximize the freedom of the citizens to lead their own lives, but some values are still necessary for a government to inculcate in determining a course of action, even if the government is limited in scope. Even the Baptists notion of church/state separation is informed by their ecclesiology, leaving an arresting contradiction in the very statement of the position!

But outside of these and other theoretical concerns, the Baptists' doctrine of separation seemed to align itself with those who wished to denigrate revealed religion and reduce its principles to impractical orthodoxies, which divided denominations from each other. Religion was assigned by these partisans to the realm of mystical doctrines like transubstantiation or forensic justification or whatever remained outside the corporate life of the nation. Religion became much too holy for the real world and was given a special warning to stay within its own separate sphere of existence. This attitude seemed to permeate the Republican party during the times of Jefferson, who saw within the political opposition a dangerous mixing of religion and politics. During Jefferson's campaign for the presidency in 1800, Republicans denounced all preachers who questioned Jefferson's piety and hoped to promote a general policy that would exclude the preaching of politics from the pulpit.[138] Tunis Wortman said that no one should prophane "heavenly doctrines [with] party purposes."[139] Jesus "dreaded the pollution of his celestial system, . . . carefully abstaining from all activity in political affairs, . . . exclusively confining himself to the duties of his station, . . . [and] disavowing all concerns with the affairs of the state."[140] Ministers who engage in political affairs only become "poisoned and perverted" by temporal concerns.[141] In this context, the Republicans joined the Baptists in calling for the complete separation of church and state, but were their motives entirely the same? Were the Republicans interested in the welfare of the church, or were they developing a ruse to empower themselves and marginate their enemies? Did the Republicans really care about the purity of the church or want to promote their own will to power? Perhaps the Republican sermons about separation would sound more sincere coming from Anabaptists, who actually lived a life of purity and separated themselves from worldly power, than those who denounced their own participation in this tainted realm. As it is, the sermons sound hollow and hypocritical, filled with patronizing rhetoric and questionable logic, meant to promote their own place and status at the expense of the church. It is even possible to hear within their words considerable contempt for the church in general and a desire to destroy it in accordance with the admonitions of Voltaire, the patron saint of the "cultured despisers."[142]

Notes

1. K. Barth, *Church Dogmatics* (Edinburgh: T&T Clark, 1975) I/1.291, 296, 297, 309-11.
2. P. Zagorin, *How the Idea of Religious Toleration Came to the West* (Princeton, NJ and Oxford: Princeton University Press, 2003) 1, 23-32; J. Coffey, *Persecution and Toleration in Protestant England, 1558-1689* (Harlow: Pearson Education, 2000) 22, 23.
3. Coffey, *Persecution and Toleration*, 8, 31, 32, 44, 58ff., 62, 63, 211, 212, 289; A. R. Murphy, *Conscience and Community* (University Park: The Pennsylvania State University Press, 2001) 59, 104. The arguments in favor of toleration are filled with biblical and religious references. Next to the example of Christ, the parable of the wheat and tares served as an important biblical reference for the advocates of toleration. Some scholars today try to emphasize the secular line of argumentation and ignore the many biblical and theological justifications, but their analysis speaks more of a commitment to the dogma of the church/state separation than fair and sober scholarship. W. K. Jordan's *The Development of Religious Toleration in England* (4 vols.) displays this prejudice on a massive scale, even if his work remains a valuable resource. Biblical arguments were simply a part of normal discourse in the era, and the teachings of Jesus were first and foremost. Even the most vicious opponents of Christianity displayed a deep-felt reverence for his teachings. Voltaire finds the Bible to be a mingle-mangle of juvenile, superstitious, and fanatical stories, but he displays great admiration for the historical Jesus as a teacher of liberal toleration. *Oeuvres Complètes de Voltaire* (Paris: Garnier Frères, 1877-85) 20.186, 187, 517-23 [*Works of Voltaire* (Paris: E. R. DuMont, 1901) 14.102, 104, 108, 146-48], 24.439ff., 449-51; A. J. Ayer, *Voltaire* (New York: Random House, 1986) 70, 71, 97, 132; Zagorin, *Religious Toleration*, 297. Jefferson finds the teachings of Jesus "the most perfect and sublime that has ever been taught by man," "more pure than those of the most correct philosophers." Jesus reforms the religion of his day by opposing the monstrous view of a "cruel, vindictive, capricious and unjust" God, which the Jewish people inherited from Moses and their forefathers. He rejects the ethnocentric nature of the religion and the anti-social attitudes toward other nations as the "chosen people" of God, extending his gospel of "universal philanthropy" to all humankind, "gathering all into one family, under the bonds of love, charity, [and] peace." "To Benjamin Rush" (April 21, 1803) F 9.462; "To William Canby" (Sept. 18, 1813) L 13.377, 378; "To Joseph Priestly" (April 9, 1803) F 9.458, 459; "To Edward Dowse, Esq." L 10.376, 377; "To Doctor Benjamin Rush" (April 21, 1803) L 10.382-85; "To William Short" (Aug., 1820) L 15.260; H. W. Foote, *The Religion of Thomas Jefferson* (Boston: Beacon Press, 1960) 45, 54ff. Both Voltaire and Jefferson think the

church transformed the historical Jesus into the Son of God through interpolating "Platonising" elements into his life when they composed the canonical Gospels. *Oeuvres Complètes de Voltaire*, 20.523 [*Works of Voltaire*, 14.108], 24.451; Ayer, *Voltaire*, 132; Zagorin, *Religious Toleration*, 297; Jefferson, "To John Adams" (Oct. 13, 1813) L 13.390; "To John Adams" (July 15, 1814) F 11.397, 398; "To Charles Thomson" (Jan. 19, 1816) F 11.498, 499; "To F. A. van der Kemp" (April 25, 1816) L 15.2, 3; R. M. Healey, *Jefferson on Religion in Public Education* (New Haven, CT and London: Yale University Press, 1962) 118.

4. Coffey, *Persecution and Toleration*, 208, 218; Murphy, *Conscience and Community*, 15, Zagorin, *Religious Toleration*, 299. Many scholars today try to differentiate the concept of religious liberty from toleration. Religious liberty is more positive and expansive and includes the notion of disestablishment. For example, the Act of Toleration (1689) developed a policy of living together in mutual toleration, while denying dissident groups a full share of the government and continuing the practice of tithing to the Church of England. As T. S. Eliot once said, "The Christian does not want to be tolerated." M. Cranston, "John Locke and the Case for Toleration," in *John Locke: A Letter Concerning Toleration in Focus*, J. Horton and S. Mendus (ed.) (Routledge: London and New York, 1991) 78; R. Murphy, *Conscience and Community*, x, xi, 15.
5. C. J. Nederman, *Worlds of Difference: European Discourses of Toleration c. 1110- c. 1550* (University Park: The Pennsylvania State Press, 2000).
6. J. Lecler, *Toleration and the Reformation*, T. L. Westow (trans.), 2 vols. (New York: Association Press, 1960); Coffey, *Persecution and Toleration*, 4, 40.
7. "Erasmus to Leo X" (May 21, 1515), in *Opus Epistolarum Des. Erasmi Roterodami*, P. S. Allen (ed.) (New York: Oxford University Press, 1992), 2.85; "A Letter to Carondelet" (Jan. 5, 1523), in *Opus Epistolarum*, 5.177-178. Cf. WA 18.625-27 (LW 33.51-53); J. M. Stayer, *Anabaptists and the Sword* (Lawrence, Kansas: Coronado Press, 1972) 53; Lecler, *Toleration and Reformation*, 1.114-29.
8. Poland had a history of sheltering heretical sects like the Waldensians, Fraticelli, and Flagellants. The country extended toleration to Catholics, Protestants, and even dissident groups like anti-Trinitarians beginning with the reign of Sigismund II in 1548 and ending with the death of Sigismund III in 1632, when Catholic uniformity was imposed once again. Lecler, *Toleration an Reformation*, 1. 386-422. Ibid., 2.486: "In Poland the tolerance which, in fact, had already been extended to the churches and sects under Sigismund II, was legally recognized by the Confederation of Warsaw in 1573. From that date onwards till the death of Sigismund III in 1632, Poland was looked on in Europe as the 'refuge of heretics'. The Anabaptist and anti-Triniarian sects which were persecuted found their peace and even set up scholastic centres, such as the Socinian school at Rakow."
9. WA 11.246, 247 (LW 45. 83, 84); Stayer, *Anabaptists and the Sword*, 40; Lecler, *Toleration and the Reformation*, 1.154, 155; Coffey, *Persecution and Toleration*, 51; Zagorin, *Religious Toleration*, 74.
10. WA 11.249, 264, 268, 269 (LW 45.88, 108, 114, 115).
11. WA 11.252, 253, 269 (LW 45.93, 115).
12. WA 11.248, 249, 251-55, 257, 258, 260 (LW 45.86, 87, 90-96, 100, 103).
13. WA 11.267, 268 (LW 45.113).
14. H. A. Oberman, *Luther: Man between God and the Devil*, E. Walliser-Schwarzbart (trans.) (New Haven, CT and London: Yale University Press, 1989) 47-49; Stayer, *Anabaptists and the Sword*, 75, 76.
15. WA Br 4. 28 (no. 978) [Lutheran Kurfürst Johann, Feb. 9, 1526]; Lecler, *Toleration and the Reformation*, 1.156, 157.

16. Lecler, *Toleration and the Reformation*, 1.146, 258, 259, 287; Zagorin, *Religious Toleration*, 10.
17. *Inst.* 4.11.14 (CO 2.902, 903).
18. *Inst.* 4.11.11-14; 20.1-3, 9 (CO 2.899-903, 1092-1094, 1099); Lecler, *Toleration and the Reformation*, 1.322.
19. *Inst.* 4.20.3 (CO 2.1094).
20. Of all the contradictions in Luther's career, perhaps the most infamous is found in his treatise *On the Jews and their Lies* (1544), where he calls for the expulsion of the Jews from Germany. He justifies this extreme measure by listing a number of their sins, although the blasphemy of the name of Jesus Christ appears to constitute the most heinous and inexcusable evil in his eyes. He suggests some other measures, including the seizure of their sacred books, the burning of their houses, schools, and synagogues, the confiscation of their usury, and the murder of Rabbis, unless they repent or leave the land. WA 53.450, 461, 462, 513-529, 535, 538 (LW 47.178, 191, 192, 256-76, 284, 288); Oberman, *Luther*, 290. Cf. WA Tr. 5.166, 167 (no. 5462) (LW 54.426). Fortunately, no magistrate acted on these suggestions, and the work was condemned by the theological community, including Melanchthon, Osiander, Bullinger, and the churches of Zurich.
21. Coffey, *Persecution and Toleration*, 24-26, 42; Lecler, *Toleration and the Reformation*, 1. 328-31, 490, 491.
22. "Baron Albrect von Haller to Voltaire" (April 11, 1759), in *Les Oeuvres Complètes de Voltaire* (Oxfordshire: The Voltaire Foundation, 1971) 104.118; G Adams, "Myths and Misconceptions: The Philosophe View of the Huguenots in the Age of Louis XIV," *Historical Reflections* I, no. 1 (1974): 69.
23. Lecler, *Toleration and the Reformation*, 1.337, 338; Zagorin, *Religious Toleration*, 99, 116, 116, 140. There were a number of doctrinal issues between them. Castellio will question the orthodox doctrine of the Trinity later in his career.
24. Zagorin, *Religious Toleration*, 97.
25. S. Castellio, *Concerning Heretics*, R. Bainton (trans.) (New York: Octagon Books, Inc., 1965) 125 (9, 10), 133 (26, 27), 213 (119). The pages shown in parenthesis are from the Latin text, *De Haerecticis an sint persequendi* (Genève: Librairie E. Droz, 1954). The English translation contains a translation of the French edition's "Dedication to William Hesse" (pp. 136-41) and Castellio's *Reply to Calvin's Book* (pp. 265ff.).
26. Ibid., 242 (158).
27. Ibid., 122 (5), 139, 218 (127, 128), 267; Lecler, *Toleration and the Reformation*, 1. 352. He includes a special plea for the Anabaptists. Those who believe in adult baptism should not suffer condemnation. Ibid., 123 (10, 11), 218 (127, 128), 275.
28. Ibid., 127, 128 (15-17), 222, 223 (133, 134), 242, 243 (158, 159), 251, 252 (171). He finds it ironic that Calvin would allow the publication of the Qur'an, as well as a host of other "pernicious books," while censoring the works of Christians. He wonders why Christians can suffer Jews and Turks more than their own fellow believers. Ibid., 215 (123), 269. He also tries to distinguish heretics from blasphemers. The former are not guilty of rejecting faith in God or reviling the Christian religion. There is no precedent for punishing them under the law. Ibid., 267, 283, 284; Zagorin, *Religious Toleration*, 118-21.
29. Ibid., 137, 220 (131).
30. Zagorin, *Religious Toleration*, 142, 143.
31. The famous article about Anabaptist origins is "From Monogenesis to Polygenesis: The Historical Discussion of Anabaptist Origins" by James Stayer, Werner

Packull, and Klaus Depperman, MQR 49 (April 1975): 83-121. James Stayer's *Anabaptists and the Sword* creates a more complicated picture of the Anabaptists' relation to the sword than our brief synopsis can offer.

32. *Anabaptism in Outline: Selected Primary Sources*, W. Klaasen (ed.) (Scotsdale: Gerald Press, 1981) 23, 85ff., 102ff., 108, 109, 140, 232ff., 265-67, 282, 302.
33. *The Legacy of Michael Sattler*, J. H. Yoder (trans. and ed.) (Scottsdale, PA.: Herald Press, 1973) 37-40 (art. 4, 6).
34. *Anabaptism in Outline*, 290-92.
35. *The Bloody Theater or Martyrs Mirror of the Defenseless Christians, . . . From the Time of Christ to the Year A. D. 1660*, T. J. van Braght (compiler) and J. F. Sohm (trans.) (Scottsdale, PA: Herald Press, 1950) 7, 8, 337.
36. Ibid., 8, 1101.
37. The book is written in stages. The old book (*Martyrs Mirror*) is a compilation of different authors, beginning in 1562 and going through a number of editions. Van Braght places this material in the second part of his edition (pp. 413-1100). The older work covers the history from 1524-1614, and van Braght extends the account up till 1660, making reference to Foxe's work and several other sources to fill out the detail. *The Bloody Theater or Martyrs Mirror*, 15, 19, 334, 341ff., 413. Throughout the book, two basic sections divide the discussion: one that speaks of baptism and its history and the other that relates the history of the martyrs.
38. W. R. Estep, *The Anabaptist Story* (Grand Rapids, MI: William B. Eerdmans Publishing Co., 1975) 116-18.
39. *The Bloody Theater or Martyrs Mirror*, 21.
40. Ibid., 12, 13, 17, 24, 63. The third century saw the introduction of infant baptism. In the sixth century, the darkness of the papacy shrouded the church. Ibid., 118, 202.
41. Ibid., 19, 202.
42. Ibid., 153, 208, 271, 301, 334. He divides the true Albigenses, who rejected violence, from the magistrates and citizens in the area. Ibid., 300, 301.
43. Ibid., 12.
44. Ibid., 358.
45. Ibid., 359, 1099.
46. H. Grotius, *Animadversiones in Animadversiones Andrea Riveti*, in *Opera Omnia Theologica* (Londini: Prostant venalia apud Mosem Pitt, 1697) 3. 649.
47. J. Arminius, *Apologia*, in *Opera Theologica* (Francofurti: Apud G. Anglum, 1631) III, X, XI (109-11, 118-22). Arminius thinks that a general knowledge of divine mercy is sufficient for salvation and even muses over the possibility that the Holy Spirit could affect divine grace apart from any message at all. Ibid., XVIII (127, 128).
48. S. Episcopius, *Opera Theologica* (Amstelodami, 1665) 2.401-403, 420, 421, 450.
49. J. Arminius, *Disputationes Publicae & Privatae*, in *Opera Theologica*, 324, 325; *Articuli Nonnulli Diligenti Examine Perpendendi*, in *Opera Theologica*, 775 (iii); S. Episcopius, *Opera Theologica* (London, 1678) II, 2 (26-29); P. Limborch, *A Compleat System, or Body of Divinity*, W. Jones (trans.) (London, 1702) 37-39, 911, 970ff., 999, 1005. Limborch likes to point out that words such as "Trinity, person, Homo-ousion, Merit, Satisfaction," etc. are not found in Scripture and unnecessary for salvation. Ibid., 100.
50. Limborch, *A Compleat System*, 983ff.; J. Arminius, *Apologia*, XXXI (XI) (143-45); H. Grotius, *De Jure Belli ac Pacis Libri Tres*, 2.20.48-50 (1.344-47; 2.516-21) (see chap. 4, fn. 89). F. Laplanche, *Orthodoxie et Prédication: L'Oeuvre d'Amyraut et la Querelle de la grace universelle* (Paris: Presses Universitaires de France, 1965)

30; F. Calder, *Memoirs of Simon Episcopius* (New York: T. Mason and G. Lane, 1837) 104, 105; D. Nobbs, *Theocracy and Toleration: A Study of the Disputes in Dutch Calvinism from 1600 to 1650* (Cambridge: Cambridge University Press, 1938) 93, 94, 97, 98, 102-104, 252, 262, 268. Grotius accepts punishment for blasphemers (atheists and deists) and evil acts in the name of religion (e.g., human sacrifice). *De Jure Belli ac Paci*, 2.20.46, 47 (1.342-44; 2.513-16).

51. G. Brandt, *History of the Reformation in the Low-Countries* (London: T. Wood, 1722) 2. 74-77; W. R. Godfrey, "Tensions within International Calvinism: The Debate on the Atonement at the Synod of the Dort" (PhD diss., Stanford University, 1974) 45; A. W. Harrison, *The Beginnings of Arminianism* (London: University of London Press, 1926) 45.
52. P. Y. De Jong, *Crisis in the Reformed Church* (Grand Rapids, MI: Reformed Fellowship, 1968) 33ff., 211ff.; Calder, *Memoirs*, 110, 111; G. Brandt, *History of the Reformation in the Low-Countries*, M. de la Roche (Abridged) (London: R. Knaplock and W. and J. Innys, 1725) 317, 318; Harrison, *Arminianism*, 159.
53. Brandt, *Reformation* (1725) 1.285, 327-29, 343, 369, 379, 385, 387, 390, 391, 540, 541; P. Bayle, *The Dictionary of Mr. Peter Bayle* (London, 1734-38) 2.793; Nobbs, *Theocracy and Toleration*, xi (intro.); Calder, *Memoirs*, 108, 112, 209, 212, 241, 323-25; Harrison, *Arminianism*, 160-62, 226-40, 270, 281-90. Maurice's rationalization was that the Remonstrants presented an imminent threat of civil war and a synod was needed to restore unity. Even so, some provinces still protested the convoking of the synod.
54. *Acta Synodi Nationalis* (Dordrecht: Isaac Ioannid Canin, 1620) 1.8ff.; Brandt, *Reformation* (1725), 2.394-98, 400, 442, 443, 470, 503, 504; De Jong, *Reformed Churches*, 215-20; Harrison, *Arminianism*, 290, 303, 378, 379. The Synod held 154 sessions from Nov. 13, 1618 to May 9, 1619. The selection of delegates and officers was strictly partisan. Johannes Bogerman, a strong Contra-Remonstrant, was elected president and Festus Hommius, a leader of the Contra-Remonstrants at The Hague in 1611, was first secretary. Seventy-nine of the delegates were Dutch and favored the Calvinist side of the debate. The foreign delegates were less bigoted in general, often speak of the impropriety of the proceedings, and refused to be concerned with the judgment of the Remonstrants.
55. Ibid., 1.67ff.; J. Hales, *Golden Remains of the ever Memorable Mr. John Hales* (London: C. Pawlet, 1711) 408, 412-14, 416; Calder, *Memoirs*, 269ff.
56. Ibid, 1.218-24, 395-400; Brandt, *Reformation* (1725), 1.103ff., 197ff., 357. Episcopius cited examples of more amiable policies: the decree of Holland and West Friesland, the policies of the States-General, the toleration of Calvinists toward Lutherans, who held essentially the same points as the Remonstrants, the tolerance of the province of Utrecht, where the Remonstrants constituted a majority, the freedom of opinion at universities, the conduct of Beza, the advice of James I, and the practices of France and Germany.
57. Ibid., 1.323; Calder, *Memoirs*, 320.
58. Hales, *Golden Remains*, 526.
59. P. Schaff, *The Creeds of Christendom* (Grand Rapids, MI: Baker Book House, 1977) 1.515. For more specific information concerning the state of the Remonstrants after the Synod of Dort, see Brandt, *Reformation* (1725), 2.539-759; Harrison, *Arminianism*, 283-401.
60. Zagorin, *Religious Toleration*, 178, 179; W. K. Jordan, *The Development of Religious Toleration in England* (Gloucester, MA: Peter Smith, 1965) 2.348, 349.
61. Coffey, *Persecution and Toleration*, 211; Murphy, *Conscience and Community*, 12, 13, 64; Zagorin, *Religious Toleration*, xii. John Goodman's *Theomachia*

(1644) and *An Apologeticall Narration* (1643) are a couple of examples of treatises that are sympathetic to congregationalism and promote toleration. See pp. 42, 43; Zagorin, *Religious Toleration*, 194, 210ff.; Jordan, *The Development of Religious Toleration*, 2.460, 461. Jordan recognizes that the emphasis upon local, voluntary organizations among the Congregationalists leads to toleration, even if other concerns might prevent the fulfillment of this tendency in some of them. Lecler disagrees. He thinks that England is the worst of all the countries divided by the Reformation as far as toleration is concerned. He says the separatists are no more tolerant than the Puritans. While they believe in a voluntary church, the separatists still maintain the right of the magistrate to punish "false religion." Lecler, *Toleration and the Reformation*, 394, 493; Jordan, *The Development of Religious Toleration*, 2.217, 218. See Murphy, *Conscience and Community*, 87, 88. Both Browne and Barrow grew weary of waiting for the government to reform the church and began to envision the church and state as possessing two different missions. Harrison and other Congregationalists (e.g., the Massachusetts Bay Colony) thought the magistrate should help inculcate the true religion. See p. 6; Jordan, *The Development of Religious Toleration*, 1.265-69, 277ff., 294.

62. See pp. 46ff.; Jordan, *The Development of Religious Toleration*, 176, 177, 184; Zagorin, *Religious Toleration*, 227-34. The Levellers will expand the list of tolerated groups to include Catholics, Jews, Separatists, Socinians, the Family of Love, etc.

63. Hill, *The English Bible*, 229ff., 232, 233; Coffey, *Persecution and Toleration*, 47, 145; J. Holland, porter, *The Smoke of the bottomlesse pit* (London, 1651) 1-6; T. Edwards, *The First and Second of Gangraena* (London: T. M. and E. M., 1646) 1.5. Holland rejects the use of "carnal weapons" to punish the blasphemers and calls for toleration. He composes a list of blasphemous teachings that circulate among the Ranters: personal identification with God, belief in reincarnation, holiness in the Spirit (as opposed to the letter), promiscuous sexual relations, and rejection of the Scripture, incarnation, virgin birth, vicarious atonement, and Judgment Day. They consider the Bible a "bundle of contradictions," the "greatest curse" upon humankind, and "the cause of all blood, that hath been shed in the world." There would be "no peace in the world, till all the Bibles in the world were burned."

64. C. Hill, *God's Englishman: Oliver Cromwell and the English Revolution* (New York: The Dial Press, 1970) 118, 187, 195, 204, 205, 213, 214; Jordan, *The Development of Religious Toleration*, 3.145-47, 169, 170, 177, 183, 185, 190, 195, 207, 214, 218, 248, 249, 462; 4.139; Murphy, *Conscience and Community*, 32, 119. Jordan prefers to distinguish the Puritans from sectarian groups. Of course, if one follows Jordan's definition and limits Puritans to those who rejected separation and tried to purify the state, then one must find the group intolerant *de facto*. Cf. Jordan, *The Development of Religious Toleration*, 1.239ff.; 2.199, 210, 315, 316, 320ff.

65. S. C. Pearson, "Reluctant Radicals: The Independents at the Westminster Assembly," *Journal of Church and State* 11 (Aut. 1969): 484; Murphy, *Conscience and Community*, 158-62; Zagorin, *Religious Toleration*, 267.

66. H. Gee and W. J. Hardy, *Documents Illustrative of English Church History*, reprinted by Kraus Reprint Corp. (New York, 1966) (London: Macmillan and Co., 1910) 243-51; Lecler, *Toleration and the Reformation*, 2.333, 334.

67. Coffey, *Persecution and Toleration*, 80.

68. "A Declaration of the Queen's Proceedings since her Reigne," in *A Collection of State Papers*, W. Cecill and S. Haynes (London: William Bowyer, 1740-49) 592, 593 (From the Year 1542 to 1570); Jordan, *Development of Religious Toleration*, 1.86, 114, 120-29.

69. *Excommunicatio Elisabeth reginiae Anglia eiusque adhaerentium* [S. Pius V, 1566-1572]. *In Ecclesia et Status*, I. B. Lo Grasso (ed.) (Roma: apud Aedes Pontif. Universitatis Gregorianae, 1952) 254-57; Lecler, *Toleration and the Reformation*, 2.358, 376-78; Coffey, *Persecution and Toleration*, 1.85, 86, 90.
70. *State Trials* (Hatfield Mss.) 2.222; Lecler, *Toleration and the Reformation*, 1.112, 113, 116, 118.
71. Lecler, *Toleration and the Reformation*, 1.84, 85, 88; Coffey, *Persecution and Toleration*, 26, 80, 90, 100-102, 106; Zagorin, *Religious Toleration*, 189. There were a total of 314 Catholic martyrs in England between 1535 and 1680 according to G. F. Nuttall's "The English Martyrs 1535-1680: a statistical review," *Journal of Ecclesiastical History* 22, no. 3 (July 1971): 191-97. Lecler tries to even up the calls between Mary and Elizabeth in accordance with his overall thesis that Protestants are just as wretched as Catholics. Some of his work helps correct the exaggerations of Protestant accounts, but the overall motive of Mary and Elizabeth seems different *prima facia*. Mary is an activist from the beginning of her reign, seeking out heretics and burning them at the stake, while Elizabeth's measures are reluctant and defensive, hanging those whom she truly thought posed a threat to the regime. Of course, Protestants also posed a threat to Mary's autocratic government, but it is difficult to find sympathy for her tyrannical ways and measures. Coffey, *Persecution and Toleration*, 2.408, 409, 492, 493. James I also tried to tolerate non-subversive Catholics and was true to his intention for the most part, but Jesuits tried his patience when they returned the favor with an assassination attempt in 1605.
72. K. Phillips, *The Cousins' Wars: Religion, Politics, and the Triumph of Anglo-America* (New York: Basic Books, 1999) 12, 52, 53. Even many of the most tolerant Protestants, including Richard Hooker, Ussher, Selden, Robinson, Erbery, Milton, and Locke could not extend their irenic disposition to Catholics. Roger Williams and William Walwyn were notable exceptions to this rule. Hill, *The English Bible*, 296, 297.
73. *Documents of Vatican II*, A. P. Flannery (ed.) (Grand Rapids: William B. Eerdmans Publishing Co., 1975) 64.75 (982, 983); Zagorin, *Religious Toleration*, 305, 309, 310. As late as the turn of the last century, American Catholics lost considerable ground in their quest for full citizenship when Pope Leo XIII issued his strictures against "Americanism" in 1899, leaving his flock stranded between loyalty to Rome and the desire to become integrated into the mainstream of American life. R. L. Moore, *Religious Outsiders and the Making of Americans*, 49, 57, 60.
74. *Difference & Dissent*, C. J. Nederman and J. C. Lauren (ed.) (Lanham: Rowman & Littlefield Publishers, Inc., 1996) 7; J. Waldron, "Locke: Toleration and Rationality of Persecution," in *John Locke: A Letter*, 99, 100; S. Mendus, "Locke: Toleration, Morality and Rationality," in *John Locke: A Letter*, 147, 148.
75. *John Locke: A Letter*, 1; Coffey, *Persecution and Toleration*, 48. The letter was written in Latin several years before it was published in 1689 with an English and Latin edition. Locke's basic view of toleration is seen already in a letter he wrote to S. H. around 1659. J. W. Gough, "The Development of Locke's Belief in Toleration," in *John Locke: A Letter*, 59. His early tracts express some hesitancy about the chaos and impossible liberty that the Puritan Revolution brought to England. *The Two Tracts of Government* (1660-61) and *An Essay Concerning Toleration* defend the right of the magistrate to determine matters of indifference ("meats and habits," "places and times," etc.) for the sake of public peace. J. Locke, *Two Treatises of Government*, M. Goldie (ed.) (London and Vermont: Everyman, 2003) 121, 123, 127, 213, 215, (189), 218 (190, 191); Gough, "The Development of

Locke's Belief," 64, 67ff., 71; P. T. Kelly, "Authority, Conscience and Religious Toleration," in *John Locke: A Letter*, 129.

76. *John Locke: A Letter*, 5; Gough, "The Development of Locke's Belief," 73; Zagorin, *Religious Toleration*, 255, 258-60. Lord Shaftesbury also should be mentioned as an important influence. He advocated toleration for all Protestants against the majority in Parliament. M. Cranston, "John Locke and the Case for Toleration," 79.

77. *A Letter Concerning Toleration*, in *Great Books of the Western World*, R. M. Hutchins (ed.) (Chicago: Encyclopaedia Britannica, Inc., 1978) 4; Gough, "The Development of Locke's Belief," 65, 66.

78. Ibid., 14.

79. Ibid., 9, 21, 22; Coffey, *Persecution and Toleration*, 187; *Locke: A Letter*, 2; Gough, "The Development of Locke's Belief," 59, 60; Cranston, "John Locke and the Case for Toleration," 84, 85; Zagorin, *Religious Toleration*, 150, 264. Even in the emerging Dutch Republic, where all sects were tolerated, Catholicism remained under suspicion and censorship. Philip II, ruler of Spain, and his persecution of the Low Countries left a bitter taste for Catholicism within the mouths of the people. Brandt, *Reformation* (1725), 1.92, 116, 117; Calder, *Memoirs*, 14, 15.
Locke is not so concerned about the many doctrinal differences between Catholicism and Protestantism. He cares little about one's belief in purgatory or transubstantiation. What matters is whether your religion has an adverse effect on government policy. His own personal beliefs center on a basic confession of Jesus as the Messiah and Savior of the world through his death, burial, and resurrection. He avoids specific matters of dogma, which divide the faithful, and finds true Christianity within a plurality of churches. Gough, "The Development," 67, 68; P. Nicholson, "John Locke's Later Letters on Toleration," in *John Locke: A Letter*, 177-80; B. A. McGraw, *Rediscovering America's Sacred Ground: Public Religion and Pursuit of the Good in a Pluralistic America* (Albany: State University of New York Press, 2003) 57-59.

80. MS Locke c34.7-11 (in Locke Room, Bodlein Library, Oxford), as cited by J. Marshall, *John Locke: Resistance, Religion, and Responsibility* (Cambridge: Cambridge University Press, 1994) 110.

81. "Declaration of Indulgence" [April 4, 1687], in *The Stuart Constitution 1603-1699*, J. P. Kenyon (ed.) (Cambridge: Cambridge University Press, 1966) 410-13 (115); Murphy, *Conscience and Community*, 127, 135, 140; S. Gordon, *Controlling the State: Constitutionalism from Ancient Athens to Today* (Cambridge, MA: Harvard University Press, 1999) 255, 266, 267; J. Dedieu, *Montesquieu et la Tradition Politique Anglaise en France* (New York: Burt Franklin, 1970) 36, 72; Coffey, *Persecution and Toleration*, 184, 188, 190.

82. "The Great Case of Liberty of Conscience," in *The Select Works of William Penn* (New York: Kraus Reprint Co., 1971) 2.132-36, 141, 142; Jordan, *The Development of Religious Toleration*, 244, 246; Coffey, *Persecution and Toleration*, 170, 178. All Protestants in the middle colonies were fundamentally anti-Catholic, fearing what papal intrusions might mean for their liberty. K. L. Griffin, *Revolution and Religion: American Revolutionary War and the Reformed Clergy* (New York: Paragon House, 1994) 45.

83. "One Project for the good of England," in *The Select Works of William Penn*, 3.191-93.

84. Ibid., 3.197; "The Great Case of Liberty of Conscience," 2.133.

85. Ibid., 202.

86. In Maryland, the Baltimores were hounded by anti-Catholic sentiment in their attempt to establish the colony even though they defended religious toleration

more than most Protestants. In April of 1649 the Maryland Assembly passed an "Act of Toleration," which provided toleration for all Trinitarians and prohibited "reprouchfull words or speeches" against the Virgin Mary, but this semblance of toleration did not last long. Charles Carroll, a signer of the Declaration of Independence, could not run for office in the state because of his Catholic faith. Even without an establishment, a Protestant majority can enact laws and elect officials who favor their position in society. P. U. Bonomi, *Under the Cope of Heaven*, 22, 23; J. Butler, *Becoming America: The Revolution before 1776* (Cambridge, MA: Harvard University Press, 2000) 189; N. Trott, *The Laws of the British Plantations in America* (London, 1721) 231-43; C. Zollman, *American Church Law* (St. Paul, MN: West Publishing Co., 1933) 2-6. "In New Hampshire, the requirement that one had to be Protestant to serve was continued until 1877. In New Jersey, Roman Catholics were not permitted to hold office until 1844. In Maryland, the stipulation that one had to be a Christian lasted until 1826. As late as 1835, one had to be a Protestant to take office in North Carolina; until 1868, the requirement was that one had to be a Christian; thereafter that one had to profess a belief in God." Evans, *The Theme is Freedom*, 278.

87. P. Hamburger, *Separation of Church and State* (Cambridge, MA: Harvard University Press, 2002) 191, 192, 213, 219-23, 228, 229, 279, 283, 284, 391ff. The Blaine Amendment of 1876 is a good example of Protestant bigotry undermining its own civil liberties. In December of 1875 President U. S. Grant went to Congress and urged them to pass a new constitutional amendment that would make "Church and State for ever separate and distinct." His proposal showed a special interest in requiring states to provide funds for secular education and prevent religious schools from sharing any of these recourses. A week later James G. Blaine, who was a congressman from Maine and presidential hopeful within the Republican party, offered a less secular version of the amendment that focused upon the desire to prevent sectarian schools from receiving public funds. The major motivation behind the amendment and the later versions in the House and Senate was to pacify the Protestant majority in the country for the upcoming election who feared the growing threat of Catholic immigration and wanted to keep public money out of the hands of parochial schools. The majority of Americans also wanted to preserve the quasi-Protestant character of the public school system with its emphasis on Bible reading, hymns, and democratic/capitalistic views, and so Blaine and most of Congress wanted to please the voters. However, the amendment failed to receive the necessary two-thirds majority by a couple of votes in the senate, after the House had passed it by an overwhelming majority of 180 to 7. W. M. McAfee, "The Historical Context of the Failed Federal Blaine Amendment of 1876," *First Amendment Law Review* [electronic text] 2 (2003): 1-22; T. E. Buckley, "A Mandate for the Anti-Catholicism: The Blaine Amendment," *America: The National Catholic Weekly* 191, no. 8 (Sept. 27, 2004); Hamburger, *Separation of Church and State*, 323-27, 334. Thereafter, most states will adopt constitutional provisions prohibiting state funding for sectarian schools, but the attempt by the Protestant majority to prevent parochial schools from receiving tax dollars soon became a double-edged sword. In the course of time this sword was wielded to prevent public funding of any sectarian school and eliminate the customary Bible reading and hymn singing in the public schools that catered to Protestant religious sensibilities.

88. Cotton Mather thought their infamous reputation was unfair, but even the Congregationalists who still lived in England complained about the intolerant policies of the Bay, believing that these policies made their own lot more difficult when

asking for toleration from others. *Magnalia Christi Americana*, 2.535, 536; *The Journal of John Winthrop*, 611. Mather clearly lived in more tolerant times than Winthrop; Winthrop banished Anabaptists, whereas Mather considered them true and pious Christians. Ibid., 1.250.

89. J. Winthrop, "A Declaration in Defense of an Order of Court made in May, 1637," in *Winthrop Papers*, 3.423; Murphy, *Conscience and Community*, 44, 45; E. Greene, *Religion and the State: The Making and Testing of an American Tradition* (New York: New York University Press, 1941) 39.
90. *The Journal of John Winthrop*, 158, 240, 241; Mather, *Magnalia Christi Americana*, 2.497, 509, 510; P. Miller, *The New England Mind: From Colony to Province* (Cambridge, MA: Harvard University Press, 1962) 9, 357; D. Staloff, *The Making of an American Thinking Class: Intellects and Intelligentsia in Puritan Massachusetts* (New York and Oxford: Oxford University Press, 1998) 38, 39; L. A. Breen, *Transgressing the Bounds: Subversive Enterprises among the Elite in Massachusetts, 1630-1692* (New York and Oxford: Oxford University Press, 2001) 213; Green, *Religion and the State*, 42; Murphy, *Conscience and Community,* 56. According to John Norton, the Quakers were treated with a modicum of respect and toleration as long as they held their heresies in private and did not disturb the public peace. *The Heart of N-England rent at the Blasphemies of The Present Generation* (Cambridge, MA: S. Green, 1659) 53, 54, 57. Quakers were subject to persecution for several reasons: they were false prophets who claimed to possess divine light, undermining the special revelation of God in Scripture; they disrupted meetings and caused public disturbances as a tactic for raising consciousness; and they displayed an egalitarian contempt for authority. On October 27, 1659, after milder means proved fruitless, four Quakers were ordered to be hanged for their vile behavior. Bonomi, *Under the Cope of Heaven*, 27, 28; R. P. Hallowell, *The Quaker Invasion of Massachusetts* (Boston, 1887) 138, Appendix. Later on Cotton Mather expresses some reservations about the hangings, but he feels the Quakers provoked their own execution by returning after their banishment and causing further public disturbances and spectacles. He distinguishes this old-style Quakerism of George Fox from the doctrine and behavior of the Quakers in Pennsylvania. *Magnalia Christi Americana*, 2.523-26; Hill, *The English Bible*, 40. The Quakers embraced principles of peace after 1660.
91. Breen, *Transgressing the Bounds*, 68.
92. Miller, *The New England Mind*, 166, 167, 218, 374, 375.
93. *The Correspondence of Roger Williams*, G. W. LaFantasie and B. F. Swan (ed.) (Hanover, NH and London: Brown University/University Press of New England, 1988) 1.36, 37; 2.12-14; Haller, *Liberty and Reformation*, 153; Hamburger, *Separation of Church and State*, 39, 40, 44; T. G. Sanders, *Protestant Concepts of Church and State* (New York: Holt, Rinehart and Wilson, 1964) 179.
94. Ibid., 1.20, 21; Murphy, *Conscience and Community*, 64; Hamburger, *Separation of Church and State*, 41.
95. Ibid., 1.33, 34. Williams probably started corresponding with Cotton in the summer of 1635. The letter in question comes from the first weeks of Williams' exile from the colony in the dead of winter. The letter makes its way into print some time later, maybe through the auspices of Williams himself. Ibid., 1.31, 32.
96. Ibid., 36, 38, 41, 42.
97. Green, *Religion and State*, 49ff.; Murphy, *Conscience and Community*, 67-69. Theodore Dwight Bozeman speaks of the chronic problem of civil disorder that early Rhode Island faced from political and religious radicals. "Religious Liberty and the Problem of Order in Early Rhode Island," *The New England Quarterly* 45 (March 1972): 44ff., 56ff. Later on Noah Webster claimed that Rhode Island

became in the course of years an irreligious and licentious place because of Williams' disdain for the clergy. Webster argued against a policy of church/state separation that would exclude the good influence of the clergy and Christianity upon society. N. Webster, *A Collection of Essays and Fugitiv Writings* (1790) (Delmar, NY: Scholars' Fascimiles & Reprints, 1977) 336, 346, 347, 363, 364.

98. Jordan, *The Development of Religious Toleration*, 3.472; Haller, *Liberty and Reformation*, 125ff.; Zagorin, *Religious Toleration*, 200. The second edition changes the spelling to "Tenent."
99. E.g., R. Williams, *The Bloudy Tenent of Persecution for Cause of Conscience*, R. Groves, (ed.) (Macon, GA: Mercer University Press, 2001) 55ff.
100. Ibid., 3, 128, 214, 215, 225; Lecler, *Toleration and the Reformation*, 2.469, 471; Murphy, *Conscience and Communtiy*, 99.
101. Ibid., 66, 67.
102. Ibid., 110.
103. Ibid., 11ff., 76, 77. The most revered of these texts is the parable of the wheat and tares in Mtt. 13. The field is interpreted in the parable as the world or civil state, not the church. The tares are idolaters, false worshippers, anti-Christians, etc., who must remain unmolested in the world as long as no civil laws are broken. Ibid., 62, 68, 69.
104. Ibid., 12.
105. Disturbances within the church do not affect the civil peace. Ibid., 40.
106. *Bloudy Tenent*, 112.
107. Ibid., 140; *The Journal of John Winthrop*, 50, 149, 150; N. Riemer, "Religious Liberty and Creative Breakthrough: The Contributions of Roger Williams and James Madison," in *Religion in American Politics*, C. W. Dunn (ed.) (Washington, D.C.: CQ Press, 1989) 16; Hamburger, *Separation of Church and State*, 41, 42. The methods of ecclesiastical punishment involve excommunication, not beheading, hanging, or burning. *Bloudy Tenent*, 51. He rejects for a number of reasons Augustine's argument that spiritual death is worse than capital punishment. Ibid., 126.
108. Ibid., 69ff., 86, 142, 143.
109. Ibid., 83; Riemer, "Religious Liberty and Creative Breakthroughs," 18; Jordan, *The Development of Religious Toleration*, 3.484.
110. R. Williams, *Mr. Cottons Letter Lately Printed, Examined and Answered* (London, 1644) 45; Hamburger, *Separation of Church and State*, 43-45, 51, 52, 59.
111. *Bloudy Tenent*, 83, 153, 239. See Jordan, *The Development of Religious Toleration*, 3.484-87.
112. D. H. Fischer, *Albion's Seed: Four British Folkways in America* (New York and Oxford: Oxford University Press, 1989) 220ff., 234, 235, 278-80, 298-300, 314, 315, 358, 384, 399, 408ff.; R. Isaac, *The Transformation of Virginia* 1740-1790 (Chapel Hill: The University of North Carolina Press, 1999) 61, 65, 133. The Anglican Church was dominated by the vestry system in the absence of an episcopalian hierarchy. The vestries were groups of gentlemen—usually white men of privilege and wealth—who levied taxes for the needs of the church, administered a welfare system, conducted discipline, and hired and fired the clergy. Over the course of time, vestries were controlled by the Randolphs, Byrds, Lees, and other families of privilege who basically filled their own vacancies and elected themselves to the offices. After 1680, the Church of England became more concerned about the Anglicans of Virginia and wanted to bring them under the control of the bishop of London, eventually sending a commissionary or lesser church official, James G. Blair, to watch over the flock. D. L. Holmes, "The Anglican Tradition in Colonial

Virginia," in *Perspectives on American Religion and Culture*, P. W. Williams (ed.) (Oxford: Blackwell Publishers, 1999) 70; Bonomi, *Under the Cope of Heaven*, 41-43; Lambert, *The Founding Fathers*, 54, 55, 65.

113. D. Thomas, *The Virginia Baptist*, in *Early American Imprints* (no. 13651) (Baltimore: Enoch Story, 1774) 17, 19, 20, 31, 54-59; *Virginia Gazette*: "To the Country Gentleman" (May 30, 1771), "The Country Gentleman's Answer" (July 4, 1771), "The Country Farmer to the Publick" (Dec. 19, 1771), in the John D. Rockefeller, Jr. Library (Colonial Williamsburg); Isaac, *The Transformation of Virginia*, 146ff., 157, 164, 171-73, 193, 194.

114. *The Works of Thomas Jefferson*, P. L. Ford (ed.) (New York and London: G. P. Putnam's Sons, 1904) 4.75.

115. Holmes, "The Anglican Tradition," 72; N. O. Hatch, *The Democratization of American Christianity* (New Haven, CT and London: Yale University Press, 1989) 102, 103; Bonomi, *Under the Cope of Heaven*, 181, 182; Lambert, *The Founding Fathers*, 150, 151, 226.

116. Like all sons of the Enlightenment, Jefferson develops a secular view of history, which finds its cultural roots in the Graeco-Roman world and eliminates the positive influence of the Judeo-Christian tradition. He often depicts religious groups as creating schisms among the human race and spilling "oceans of human blood" over the pettiest doctrinal concerns. The Puritans are considered the most intolerant of all religious sects because of their early persecution of Quakers and Baptists. Jefferson believes that democratic ideals first arose in the south, not in the north, where the Puritan forefathers left a legacy of bigotry that continues to the present time. *Notes on Virginia* (1782) F 4.62, 74, 75; "To Rev. Thomas Whittemore" (June 5, 822) L 15.373, 374; "To James Fishback" (Sept. 27, 1809) L 12.315, 316 (along with Jefferson's missing composition draft); *Autobiography* (1743-1790) F 1.156; "To Marquis de Lafyette" (May 14, 1817) F 12.62; "To John Adams" (May 5, 1817) L 15. 108, 109; Wagoner, *Jefferson and Education*, 35.

117. This concept of church/state separation finds its most famous expression in a letter to the Danbury Baptist Association of Connecticut, dated January 1, 1802. He interprets the First Amendment in a broad manner as prohibiting the federal government from enacting anything of a religious nature like a national day of prayer and "building a wall of separation between church & state." "To Mssrs. Nehemiah Dodge and Others, a Committee of the Danbury Baptist association in the State of Connecticut" (Jan. 1, 1802), in *Writings*, 510; "To the Attorney General (Levi Lincoln)" (Jan. 1, 1802) L 10.305; D. Dreisbach, *Thomas Jefferson and the Wall of Separation between Church and* State (New York and London: New York University Press, 2002) 17, 41ff., 46, 48, 56, 185; Hamburger, *Separation of Church and State*, 159-62.

118. At the University of Virginia Jefferson refused to appoint a divinity professor or teach "theology, apologetics, and Scripture" against the customary practice of the time. Instead, he commissioned the professor of ethics to teach "the proofs of the being of a God, the creator, preserver, and the supreme ruler of the universe, the author of all the relations of morality and the laws and obligations those infer"—all the religion he deemed necessary to believe. "Report of the Commissioners for the University of Virginia" (Aug. 4, 1818), in *Writings*, 467; "To Dr. Cooper" (Oct. 7, 1814) L 14.200; "To Doctor Cooper" (Nov. 2, 1822) 15.405; "From the Minutes of the Board of Visitors" (Oct. 7, 1822), in *Writings*, 477, 478; Wagoner, *Jefferson and Education*, 139, 140; Healey, *Jefferson on Religio*n, 170-72, 216ff.; Levy, *The Establishment Clause*, 74, 75; *Jefferson & Civil Liberties*, 12.

119. "To William Short" (Oct. 31, 1819) F 12.142; Healey, *Jefferson on Religion*, 157, 158, 161ff., 204, 205. Cf. Jordan, *The Development of Religious Toleration*, 3.505, 506. Jordan canonizes Williams for his "individualistic genius," "prescience," and "a kind of divination," which paved the way toward modern secularity. This critique of Williams is indicative of Jordan's exaltation of secularity and its contributions to civil liberties.
120. Ibid., 2.258, 259.
121. *The Confession of Fayth Published in Certayn Conclusions by the Remaynders of Mr. Smithes Company* (art. 265). See Jordan, *Development of Religious Toleration*, 2.264 for details about this work.
122. T. Helwys, *A Short Declaration of the Mystery of Iniquity* (1611/1612), R. Groves (ed.) (Macon, GA: Mercer University Press, 1998) 53; Jordan, *The Development of Religious Toleration*, 269-75I.
123. I. Backus, "An Appeal to the Public for Religious Liberty" [Boston, 1773], in *Political Sermons of the American Founding Era 1730-1805* (Indianapolis, IN: Liberty Press, 1991) 340, 341; Hamburger, *Separation of Church and State*, 10-12, 90-92. Isaac Backus led the charge in Massachusetts against its establishment. Baptists gained specific exemption from the tithe in 1734, although "the Congregational stalwarts threw sand in the machinery of reform when they could," making it an ongoing battle. Bonomi, *Under the Cope of Heaven*, 65; S. S. Reed, *Church and State in Massachusetts, 1691-1740* (Urbana: The University of Illinois, 1914) 103-41, 164, 185; W. G. McLoughlin, *New England Dissent, 1630-1833: The Baptists and the Separation of Church and State* (Cambridge, MA.: Harvard University Press, 1971) I, part 2; Lambert, *The Founding Fathers*, 223-25.
124. G. W. Truett, *The Inspiration of Ideals*, P. W. James (ed.) (Grand Rapids, MI: Wm. B. Eerdmans, 1950) 100, 101.
125. W. T. Thom, *The Struggle for Religious Freedom in Virginia*, in *John Hopkins University Studies in Historical and Political Science*, H. B. Adams (ed.) (Baltimore: John Hopkins Press, 1900) 91.
126. *The Writings of John Leland*, L. F. Greene (ed.) (New York: Arno Press and The New York Times, 1969) 35; D. Dreisbach, *Thomas Jefferson and the Wall of Separation*, 13. Tax support was an embarrassing necessity in the eyes of Puritan divines, who preferred to receive their sustenance from the voluntary contributions of the church. *The Journal of John Winthrop*, 491ff.; Mather, *Magnalia Christi Americana*, 2.288, 423; Foster, *The Long Argument*, 192, 193.
127. Ibid., 476, 477.
128. *The Writings of John Leland*, 39.
129. Ibid., 118, 119, 122, 182, 354, 441, 446, 564. He rejects the idea that ministers of the gospel cannot run for public office.
130. Ibid., 181.
131. Ibid., 118.
132. Ibid., 216, 217.
133. Ibid., 107, 108, 118.
134. Ibid., 181. Theology has little effect on the practical/ethical lives of the people inside or outside the church. Ibid., 111.
135. Ibid., 184. It is rational, not religious arguments that win debates. Ibid., 185.
136. Ibid., 475. Leland has little understanding of history. He thinks of the religious community in Massachusetts as contributing little more than bigotry to America. Ibid., 220.
137. Hamburger finds more equivocation upon this issue within Baptist circles than our analysis. For example, he points to the Baptist testimony concerning the religious

foundations of society. *Separation of Church and State*, 58, 59, 63, 68, 70, 72, 77, 177. However, similar remarks are found in most champions of the wall, including Jefferson. This equivocation presents an interesting case study in deconstruction, showing how authors often contradict themselves, making it difficult for the reader to discover one simple intent or meaning within their writings. This problem of interpretation is found in all writings, especially those dealing with this particular issue, but the many contradictions can never discount the fundamental penchant to separate the two realms in Jefferson, Leland, and the Baptists.

138. T. Wortman, "A Solemn Address to Christians and Patriots" [New York, 1800], in *Political Sermons of the American Founding Era 1730-1805*, E. Sandoz (ed.) (Indianapolis, IN: Liberty Press, 1991) 1481, 1483, 1494.
139. Ibid., 1481.
140. Ibid., 1485.
141. Ibid.
142. The spirit of the Enlightenment centered much of its devotion upon the life and teachings of this one man. His life and work seemed to embody all that was fashionable among the social elite of the day—the cynicism, the satire, and the wit—the love of toleration and the hatred of the church. His influence upon the French Revolution and its Civil Constitution of the Clergy (1790) was immortalized when his body was exhumed and enshrined as the first and foremost deity in the *Panthéon* of leading Enlightenment figures. The apotheosis was accompanied with a cavalcade of "military and civil organizations carrying banners and flags, a model of the Bastille, busts of Rousseau and Mirabeau, a statue of Voltaire surrounded by pyramids bearing the titles of his works, and a golden casket containing the seventy volumes of the edition published by Beaumarchais at Kehl." M-M. H. Barr, *Voltaire in America 1744-1800* (Baltimore: The John Hopkins Press, 1941) 55; R. O. Rockwood, "The Legend of Voltaire and the Cult of the Revolution, 1791," in *Ideas in History*, R. Herr and H. T. Parker (ed.) (Durham, NC: Duke University Press, 1965) 111, 113; Ayer, *Voltaire*, 171, 172; D. Mornet, *Les Origines intellectuelles de la Révolution Française 1715-1787* (Paris: Librairie A. Colin, 1967) 225, 226; Gay, *Voltaire's Politics*, 243, 310, 334, 335. Voltaire sees the history of Christianity as filled with little more than "fraud," "errors," and "disgusting stupidity," and so "every sensible man . . . must hold the Christian sect in horror." In his *Sermon des Cinquante* (1762) he declares war upon *l'infâme*. He wishes to "terminate and destroy the idol from top to bottom." This solution is summarized in his famous cry *écrazer l'infâme* (crush the filth), which he incessantly repeats throughout his later works. The self-professed man of tolerance is now willing to have certain enlightened despots develop a final solution and destroy the infamous religion as a necessary step in creating a better world. *Oeuvres de Voltaire*, 20.517ff., 521 [*Works*, 14.100ff., 104], 24.252; 26.298; Gay, *Voltaire's Politics*, 89, 170, 225, 226, 236, 239, 244-46, 252, 271, 272; Ayer, *Voltaire*, 27, 99; C. Gliozzo, "The Philosophes and Religion" *Church History* 40, no. 3 (1971): 275 (fn. 12).

Conclusion

The Bible was a central part of society in the sixteenth and seventeenth centuries. The Bible was cited as an ultimate authority in astronomy, medicine, farming, geology, history, politics, economics, and all aspects of the human enterprise.[1] While a multitude of factors contributed to the shaping of Western civilization, the Bible, as interpreted by the people, contained a special place, invariably and inseparably entangled within the multifaceted nature of causality that formed the modern world. Its influence was especially noteworthy within Protestant communities, where the laity used its sole authority to challenge the catechism with their own independent access to knowledge and truth. Through the power of the press, the Protestants gained access to the Scripture and were able to use its authority to undermine or question those in power.[2]

The Bible provided the Western world with much inspiration in developing its modern republics of "liberty and justice for all." William Walwyn, the leading intellectual of the Levellers, rejected a Machiavellian view of the world where evil was an inevitable part of our corporate life and the government was severed from the moral goodness of the Christian gospel. He saw no reason why the love of Jesus Christ could not permeate all of life. His favorite passage was Romans 14, where Paul admonished the church to bear the conscience of others and refrain from passing judgment on those who serve God through their own expression of faith. After all, Paul was the Apostle of liberty in the NT. He rejected oppressive, legalistic standards and exhorted the faithful to serve God through the power of the Spirit and the gift of faith. He said, "It is for freedom that Christ has set us free. Do not be burdened again by a yoke of bondage" (Gal. 5:1). This message of freedom found a willing audience with Walwyn, Levellers, and other Protestants who wanted to recast their society into its image. Their return to the NT meant the rejection of coercive measures to bind the conscience of others in the church and state. It also meant a return to the example of Jesus, who played a prominent role in this discussion, inspiring the humanists, reformers, Levellers, and all those who advocated toleration, whether Christian or not. Jesus clearly rejected the use of the sword in spreading his gospel, telling Pilate that his "kingdom was not of this world" and admonishing his disciples to turn the other cheek and suffer injustice without retribution. Sons of the Reformation and the Enlightenment looked to the words of Jesus alike and used them to promote toleration toward the religious, philosophical, and political ideology of all humankind. Jesus' parable of the wheat and tares became a special *locus classicus* in exhorting all of us to let God judge the souls of others in these matters of opinion.

The Bible continued to provide inspiration in developing other areas of modern government. Sometimes it was used to promote much the opposite of toleration in society, as in the case of the Reformed use of the OT.[3] During the sixteenth and seventeenth centuries, the Reformed developed their doctrine of covenant out of the many covenants in the Hebrew Scriptures and forged a federal system of governance, which held magistrates accountable to the rule law. The Reformed went so far in their teaching as to encourage a radical notion for the time—the doctrine of open rebellion against a wicked ruler, based on their allegiance to the covenant as the foundation of society. Their doctrine of the covenant made the bellicose nature of the OT more applicable to the people of God than the typical interpretation of the church. It integrated all the dispensations of Scripture into a unified message and allowed the Reformed to cite many examples out of the OT to sanction the use of the sword against wickedness. It changed the people of God from the NT image of a remnant, suffering in this world and submitting to the authority of godless rule (Rom. 13), into a nation with constitutional rights, privileges, and responsibilities. The Reformed found some justification for rebellion in the NT, especially in the example of Peter and John (Acts 4:19), but they needed the OT to justify a doctrine of revolution and the establishment of a righteous kingdom through more coercive means.

The Bible provided a most direct and important influence upon Western civilization through its doctrine of egalitarianism. The NT was written during cosmopolitan times, in which the process of hellenization helped to foster an interchange between cultures and the spirit of universalism. Stoics considered themselves citizens of the world and valued each and every individual as a vital part of society in the grand scheme of things. Gnostics tried to create a syncretistic system of truth, merging the best of all religious and philosophical ideas into a grand cosmic order. These philosophies and so many others helped to shape the spirit of universalism in the world to come, but none of them proved more efficacious in purveying this spirit than the church of Jesus Christ. Its power remained long after the death of the Graeco-Roman world and its many philosophies, permeating Western culture for centuries to come and dominating all of its communities with the witness of local churches.

The egalitarian spirit of Christianity was first formulated in reaction to an aberrant form of Judaism, which grew up after the Babylonian captivity in the sixth century B.C.E. The Jews were sent into captivity at that time as punishment for their many sins against the Lord. The prophets of the OT considered the Jewish people responsible for their own fall from divine favor (Ezek. 18), but it was clear to them that the influence of foreigners in the Holy Land and the region also helped to corrupt their ways through idolatrous and immoral practices. The answer to the Jewish woes after the captivity came in the form of severe measures to restrict contact with corrupting influences. It came in the form of complete separation from alien elements, so that their presence might no longer serve as a source of temptation. For example, Ezra and Nehemiah demanded upon their return to the land that Jewish men divorce their foreign wives immediately and send them away along with their children (Ezra 10, Neh. 10). This spirit of separation became an integral part of religious commitment and was embodied in the religious leaders of the subsequent era as a sign of self-righteousness. The Pharisees or "separate ones" took pride in building a "fence" around the law and themselves in order to reduce the possibility of temptation. They separated themselves not only from gentiles but even from their own people, the so-called *am ha-aretz* (the people of the land), because these people did not concern themselves with tithing what they bought or sold and neglected the labyrinth of traditional purity laws, making their own persons and meals filled with contamination.[4] The Pharisees took special pride in the purity of their own stock and status in the world, believing that people inherited the kingdom of God as a special birthright, and hoped to keep themselves pure by remaining aloof from those of inferior birth and unclean behavior.

It was in this context that Christianity and its spirit of egalitarianism was born. Much of it was aimed against the Pharisees as a rebuke against their extreme measures and practices of segregation.[5] Much of what Jesus did and said in his ministry was specifically designed to annoy their religious sensibilities. To aggravate the Pharisees, Jesus chose as his disciples the *am har-aretz*—uneducated, blue-collar workers from the region of Galilee, not Rabbinic students from Jerusalem. He defended his disciples when they failed to follow the purification ceremonies of punctilious Pharisaic devotion and flaunted his own liberty by breaking their strict observance of the Sabbath. He sat down with tax-gatherers and sinners to drink wine in their unclean dwellings. He conversed with Samaritans, Canaanites, and Romans, whom he declared as having greater faith than most of the Jews of his day. He declared that God was turning now to the gentiles to welcome them into the kingdom. His Apostles were commissioned to "go and preach the gospel to all nations." Paul, his greatest Apostle, became a missionary to the gentiles and preached as the very essence of the gospel that the gentiles were fellow-heirs, members, and partakers of the gospel, together with the Jews (Eph. 3:5, 6; Gal. 2). This gospel integrated the whole human race into its message as the essence of the message. Paul said, "There is neither Jew nor Greek, slave nor free, male nor female. You are all one in Christ Jesus" (Gal.3:28).

This gospel took some time to resonate throughout the church and society in the centuries to come. The church fell under the influence of Graeco-Roman society as it moved away from Palestinian soil and began to imitate its social structure in the next few centuries. As it moved into the Middle Ages, the church developed a hierarchical view of government, making the laity dependent upon the sacramental power of priests and creating layers of authority that reached all the way to the pope in Rome. This concept of ecclesiastical authority dominated the church until Martin Luther challenged the priority of the papal office at Leipzig in 1519 and proclaimed the priesthood of believers. This doctrine considered the laity just as capable of exerting the same spiritual authority as the clergy. A few decades later, the Huguenots and the Congregationalists extended Luther's doctrine by emphasizing the authority and autonomy of each believer before God, rejecting the hierarchical structure of the Catholic Church, and developing a democratic form of polity. They both claimed that democracy was the original polity of the NT church before it was corrupted by the hubris of popes, bishops, and priests. Robert Browne and Robert Harrison rejected ecclesiastical hierarchy in the strongest of terms and felt that living in direct communion with Christ and under his authority in a democratic polity was the true mark of the church, not a secondary matter of limited concern. This spirit of democracy spread throughout the Western world and became a vital force outside the confines of the church. Judaism itself became one of the great champions of democracy in modern society after so many centuries of experiencing injustice and oppression—often at the hands of Christians. Their strong belief in egalitarianism helped to insure the empowerment of other oppressed groups but also incurred the wrath of the chancellor of Germany, who blamed them for leveling society in Vienna and destroying his superior German race and culture.[6] The Jewish people suffered horrible injustice once again but this time in order to forward the cause of democracy and equality in a fallen world, which continued to favor the likeness of its own kind and distrust any differences in others.

Of course, the Bible did not teach democracy or any of these other political doctrines in any literal or clear sense. Its message never existed *in abstracto* apart from the interpretation of communities providing it with concrete form. Even Christianity itself never existed *in abstracto* apart from those who took the words of the Bible and translated them into specific doctrines, formulated creeds, and created individual denominations of faith. Political ideas were often the product of theological constructions, which involved the church in the process of interpreting passages, formulating a unified doctrine through reason, and applying the formula to other aspects of life. The doctrine of covenant was formulated at first in Zurich as an attempt to wield the message of Scripture together into a simple, theological construct, and then deconstructed by the Puritans and applied to the realm of government as well as the rest of society. The doctrine of countervailing government involved a process of reinterpreting concepts from the ancient world like natural law and mixed government and combining them with Christian elements to develop a new theory of natural rights and the separation and balance of powers. Here the process of interpretation showed its syncretistic nature by combining elements from inside and outside the faith and changing both the church and the state in the process. Often the construction of political concepts involved many ideas and forces coming together and changing each other, even if the separate influences are difficult to discern and untangle. Sometimes the influence of the Bible and Christianity subsisted well below the surface and provided a mentality or matrix by which certain ideas could flourish or become entangled with religious motivation. The development of capitalism found a fertile ground within the Puritan worldview in developing its specific economic outlook, although it was never a simple matter of translating the Bible or Puritan culture and developing an economic philosophy. At the foundation of capitalism the spirit of Puritanism is discerned in a number of its ideas, which included the importance of hard work, the religious nature of business, the acceptance of usury, the vision of the future, and the investment of capital in the community. These ideas and others like them helped to forge the ideology of the modern world, even if they subsisted underneath the surface and were pushed ever farther down by the power the Enlightenment and its secular culture. These ideas were never the literal product of a simple and direct exegesis of Scripture and easy to dismiss by those who possessed a secular agenda, but all of them contained vital elements necessary to the development of modern political and economic ideals. Typically they started within the church as a deconstruction of the text of Scripture, developed into theological doctrines, and then found application to the society at large where the political world was transformed by the doctrines of the church.

The reason that the church and its ideology were so significant in the process relates to its position in the center of society during the formative years. The church became an important mechanism for the dissemination of democracy, federalism, tolerance, and other modern ideals because of its position in local communities and its ability to develop disciples generation after generation with a set message. Sometimes the message was found in accentuating the NT over the OT as in the case of dispensational groups like the Anabaptist, Baptists, Arminians, and Levellers. These groups stood at the forefront of the debate over toleration in their society and transformed the world around them into a more Christ-like image by pointing to the example of the NT. Other times the message was found in the opposite tendency by merging the two testaments together into one covenant as in the case of the Reformed Church and its doctrine of federalism. The Congregationalists deconstructed this message, applied it to the church and the society around them, and changed the political landscape wherever they landed or arose in power. These communities of faith were more significant than the Bible itself or individual theologians because they transformed their message into the concrete form of a mass movement that stood at the center of society. Their church meetings were town meetings. Their church polity became the polity of the state. Their doctrines changed the ideology of their communities, who heard the message week in and week out, within assemblies, both inside and outside of a church that had no walls.

The place of the church was marginated beginning in the eighteenth century by forces that blamed its dogmatism for all the evils and strife in society. Sometimes the religious community itself joined the fray and performed an act of self-flagellation by making disparaging remarks about its own history. Baptists, who were among the greatest missionaries of freedom and democracy in the Western world, denied that religious ideology was related to politics in any positive way and blamed the church for much of the turmoil and conflict in America and Europe over the last millennium. They created this noble lie in order to end the special privileges of certain denominations and promote toleration between religious groups, but they paid a heavy price by denying their own important role in promoting the cause of liberty. They also joined anti-Semitic and anti-Christian forces that wanted to reduce the role of revealed religion in society and promote a culture of abstract religious expression and toleration by eliminating the Judeo-Christian tradition. Voltaire blamed all the social ills of Europe on the church and exhorted his benevolent despots to "crush the filth." Jefferson wanted to perform a "quiet euthanasia" on the tradition through the public school system and erected a "wall of separation between church and state" to prevent the pervasive influence of the church from corrupting the government. Both of them practiced the worst sort of revisionist history to justify their program, promoting secular and pagan prototypes of old, exalting their own intellectual prowess in nature, denying the considerable influence of Puritanism on their own political thought, and denigrating the church as the fundamental sponsor of evil in society. This version of history became a mainstay in the secular community and a fundamental justification for excluding the church from the increasing powers and privileges of the government, as seen in the watershed case of *Everson v. the Board of Education* (1947). The position gained ground for a few decades in the Court and public opinion, but many began to question its excessive nature after the 1960s. Today many see the relationship between church and state in terms that are more complex. They believe in the separation of church and state, but also consider religion as an indelible aspect of culture and a foundation of national values and principles. In *Lemon v. Kurtzman* (1971) the Court replaced the "wall" of separation with a "line," which is "blurred, indistinct, and variable," recognizing how difficult it is to divide what remains entangled in culture within the life of a people as a nation.

Notes

1. C. Hill, *The English Bible and the Seventeenth-Century Revolution* (London: Allen Lane/Penguin Press, 1993) 7, 26-31. Hill speaks of the importance of Scripture in the seventeenth century throughout his work, but as a Marxist he undermines its value in the end and treats it as mere window dressing, masking the real force or "locomotive" behind the emergence of the modern world—i.e., tensions within society. Ibid., 415. Hill displays little appreciation for the doctrinal positions of the church and their power to transform society. He also limits himself by trying to explain reality through an underlying mono-causal force, where one billiard ball strikes the next in a chain of events. Life is too systematic and multi-causal for this type of analysis to ring true.
2. Ibid., 15-18.
3. Jordon, *The Development of Religious Toleration*, 3.276.
4. *Demai* 2.2, 3.2, *Hagigah* 1.8, *Kiddusin* 4.1, 2, *Abodah Zarah* 2.1, 3, 6, 7, *Nezikin* 3.8, *Oholoth* 18.7, 9, 10 [H. Danby, *The Mishnah* (London: Oxford University

Press, 1974) 20-22, 214, 327, 437ff., 452, 466, 675-76, 726]. Another good example of the relationship between purity laws, hierarchy, and segregation is the caste system of Hinduism. A Brahmin must maintain separation from Sûdras and the unrighteous to avoid contamination. The lowest or "unclean" castes engage in degrading occupations, which make them unclean according to the law codes. In sections of India, the "untouchables" must announce their presence or move out of the way to allow the "twice-born" to pass without contracting defilement. "If a Brahmin neared, the untouchables had to get off the road into a field. Should they approach the Brahmin too closely, the latter bathed, renewed his sacred cord, and underwent other purification." D. S. Noss, *A History of the World's Religions* (Upper Saddle River, NJ: Prentice Hall, 2003) 145, 146; *The Laws of Manu*, G. Bühler (trans.) (Dehli: Motilal Banarsidass, 1975) 138 (4.60, 61).

5. Even if the gospel found fertile ground in the Hellenistic world for its dissemination, Jesus' egalitarianism is best explained within its natural setting as a reaction to Pharisaic Judaism. Palestinian Jews reacted strongly against Hellenism after the atrocities of Antiochus IV and the Maccabean revolt in the 160s B.C.E. Jews began to name their children after patriarchs in the OT, as was the case with Jesus and his family: Joseph, Mary (Miriam), Jesus (Joshua), James (Jacob), Joses (Joseph), Simon (Simeon), and Jude (Judah). After the Maccabean revolt, the Jews were in a constant state of revolt against Hellenism. They spoke mainly in Aramaic, not Greek. Josephus relates several instances where the Romans needed to converse with the Jews in Aramaic, and, of course, Jesus himself spoke Aramaic in the Gospel of Mark. It is unlikely that Greek thinking was a strong influence in developing his ideas. J. P. Meier, *A Marginal Jew: Rethinking the Historical Jesus* (New York: Doubleday, 1991) 1.205-208, 259-61.

6. A. Hitler, *Mein Kampf*, R. Manheim (trans.) (Boston and New York: Houghton Mifflin Co., 1999) 15, 52ff., 60, 61, 65, 123, 449, 639.

Index